NASPO

National Association of State Procurement Officials

STATE AND LOCAL GOVERNMENT PROCUREMENT:
A Practical Guide

Third Edition

Published by:

The National Association of State Procurement Officials
110 West Vine Street, Suite 600
Lexington, Kentucky 40507

(859) 514-9159   FAX (859) 514-9166
https://www.NASPO.org

Copyright © 2019 National Association of State Procurement Officials

ISBN-13: 978-1-60427-163-8

Printed and bound in the U.S.A. Printed on acid-free paper.

10 9 8 7 6 5 4 3 2 1

Library of Congress Cataloging-in-Publication Data

Names: National Association of State Procurement Officials (U.S.), issuer.
Title: State and local government procurement : practical guide / by NASPO.
Description: Third Edition. | Plantation, FL : J. Ross Publishing, [2019] |
　Revised edition of State and local government procurement, 2015. |
　Includes bibliographical references and index.
Identifiers: LCCN 2019005007 (print) | LCCN 2019013252 (ebook) | ISBN
　9781604278088 (e-book) | ISBN 9781604271638 (hardcover : alk. paper)
Subjects:　LCSH: Government purchasing--United States--States.
Classification: LCC JK1683 (ebook) | LCC JK1683 .S698 2019 (print) | DDC
　352.5/32130973--dc23
LC record available at https://lccn.loc.gov/2019005007

Copyright © 2019

The National Association of State Procurement Officials
110 West Vine Street, Suite 600
Lexington, Kentucky 40507

(859) 514-9159　　FAX (859) 514-9166　　https://www.NASPO.org

FOREWORD

The National Association of State Procurement Officials is proud to make the *State and Local Government Procurement: A Practical Guide, 3rd Edition*, available to government professionals, students, suppliers, educators, and others interested in learning about public procurement. Whether you are a seasoned procurement professional or new to the field, this guide should provide you a valuable reference tool in your efforts. This edition of NASPO's flagship guide features many changes, improvements, and additional content.

On behalf of the NASPO Board of Directors and members, I would like to thank the Practical Guide Steering Committee, the Professional Development Committee, and their chair, Deb Damore, for enthusiastically taking on the extensive task of updating this important resource. In addition, NASPO truly appreciates the work of all the members and other professionals who thoroughly reviewed this guide and made recommendations to the Work Group. Finally, I would like to thank all of the NASPO staff for working together with us to see the project through.

Lisa Eason
Deputy Commissioner of the State Purchasing Division, State of Georgia
2019 President, National Association of State Procurement Officials

ACKNOWLEDGMENTS

The process of revising and publishing this book has been a truly collaborative effort. This endeavor could never have been achieved without the dedication of our volunteers and staff.

A Steering Committee was developed to provide leadership and guidance throughout the development process. This group was involved in reviewing the previous edition of the text and offering recommendations on improvements. Their knowledge and expertise helped shape the focus of the text. Many of them also served as contributors and leads on chapter revisions. I would like to thank each of you for your commitment to this effort. The list of Steering Committee Members is included below:

John Adler, NASPO Life Member
Ron Bell, NASPO Life Member
Valerie Bollinger, State Purchasing Manager, State of Idaho
Symone Bounds, Director of Marketing, Travel and Card Programs, State of Mississippi
Deb Damore, Director of Purchasing and Contracting, State of Vermont
David Gragan, NASPO Life Member
Norma Hall, NASPO Honorary Member
Peter Korolyk, Deputy Director, State of Delaware
William McAvoy, Deputy Assistant Secretary for Supplier Diversity, State of Massachusetts
Margaret McConnell, NASPO Life Member
Sara Redford, Director of State Bureau Procurement, State of Wisconsin
Kathy Reilly, Deputy Assistant Secretary, Commonwealth of Massachusetts
Jason Soza, Chief Procurement Officer, State of Alaska
Christine Weber, State of Colorado
Mike Wenzel, NASPO Honorary Member

I would also like to thank the following individuals for their contributions, advice, and knowledge sharing, who without which this publication wouldn't be the show piece that it is:

David Borsykowsky, State of Vermont
Don Casella, State of Connecticut
Holly Elwood, Senior Advisor, EPA (Environmentally Preferable Purchasing Program)
Betsy Hayes, State of Minnesota
Justin Kaufman, State of Minnesota
Bruce Krug, State of Delaware
Jenna Larkin, EPA (Environmentally Preferable Purchasing Program)
Anne P. McConnell, PhD
Jonathan Rifkin, Director of Strategic Partnerships, Green Electronics Council
Tammy Rimes, Executive Director, National Cooperative Procurement Partners
Delbert Singleton, State of South Carolina
Thomas Vergis, State of Oklahoma
Julia Wolfe, State of Massachusetts
Christine Warnock, State of Washington

ACKNOWLEDGEMENTS

This guide would not be possible without the dedication and hard work of the NASPO Staff. They served in various roles throughout the process, providing expertise and support to help shape the guide.

Matthew Oyer, Director of Learning Solutions
Jordan Henson, Instructional Design Project Manager
Mariam Alabdali, Learning and Development Coordinator
Megan Smyth, Director of Research & Innovation
Elena Moreland, Senior Project Manager
Kevin Minor, Research Coordinator

Finally, I want to thank Margaret McConnell, NASPO Life Member, who served as our primary editor and writer for this project. She has been an editor and steward of this text since its first edition. Her efforts were essential to the success of this project. On behalf of the NASPO Board of Directors and Staff, I would like to express my sincerest gratitude for all her efforts.

Sincerely,

Dianne Lancaster, MBA, JD, CPPO
Chief Learning Officer, National Association of State Procurement Officials

CONTENTS

Chapter 1: INTRODUCTION — 1
    Edition Highlights — 1
    History and Organization of this Text — 1
    Changes in State and Local Public Procurement — 3
    Some Critical Issues — 4
    The Model Procurement Code for State and Local Governments — 5
    New to This Edition of the *Practical Guide* — 5
    Conclusion — 6
    Endnotes — 6

Chapter 2: PROCUREMENT LEADERSHIP, ORGANIZATION, AND VALUE — 7
    Recommended Best Practices — 7
    The Case for a Single Procurement Administrator at an Executive Level — 8
    Staffing for Strategic Procurement Services — 10
    Drafting a Comprehensive Procurement Law — 11
    Procurement Rules/Regulations — 13
    Creating Tools for Public Employees and Suppliers — 14
    Responsibilities of the Central Procurement Office — 16
    A Few Words on Performance Metrics — 17
    The Value of Procurement — 17
    Conclusion — 19
    Endnotes — 19

Chapter 3: THE IMPORTANCE OF COMPETITION — 21
    Recommended Best Practices — 21
    Why Competition Matters — 22
    Defining *Adequate Competition* — 23
    Procurement Practices That Encourage Competition — 23
    Practices and Laws That Restrain Competition — 25
    Combating Anticompetitive Practices — 28
    Detecting Antitrust Violations in Procurements — 30
    Cooperation with Enforcement Authorities — 31
    Federal and State Antitrust Laws — 32
    Business Practices That Unreasonably Restrain Trade — 38
    State Antitrust Laws — 39
    Procurement Case Law — 41
    Immunities, Exemptions, Exceptions, and Defenses To Antitrust Laws — 42
    Conclusion — 45
    Endnotes — 46

Chapter 4: STRATEGIES AND PLANS — 47
    Recommended Best Practices — 47
    Planning with Users and User Agencies — 48
    Procurement Office Planning — 49
    Research and Other Pre-Solicitation Groundwork — 50

CONTENTS

Devising Procurement Strategies	52
Planning for Negotiations	63
Managing Risks	66
Conclusion	68
Endnotes	68

Chapter 5: NON-CONSTRUCTION SPECIFICATIONS AND SCOPES OF WORK — 71

Recommended Best Practices	71
Objectives of the Procurement and the Specifications	73
Management of Specifications	74
Types of Specifications	75
Samples and Technical Data	79
Standardization of Specifications	80
Procedures for Developing Specifications	81
A Word About Specification Requirements When Using Federal Funds	84
Conclusion	85
Endnotes	85

Chapter 6: SUSTAINABLE PROCUREMENT CONSIDERATIONS AND STRATEGIES — 87

Recommended Best Practices	87
Overview of Sustainable Procurement	88
Public Policy Reasons for the Procurement of Sustainable Commodities and Services	90
Creating a Sustainable Procurement Program	90
Drafting a Policy for a Sustainable Procurement Program	92
Implementing a Sustainable Procurement Program	94
Using Credible Standards, Third-Party Certifications, and Ecolabels	98
Measuring and Marketing Effectiveness	100
Benefits Calculators	101
Maintaining Your Sustainable Procurement Program	101
Conclusion	102
Endnotes	102

Chapter 7: COMPETITION: SOLICITATIONS AND METHODS — 105

Recommended Best Practices	105
Terminology and Overview	106
eProcurement Systems	107
Overview of Formal Competition Source Selection Methods	107
Competitive Sealed Bidding	108
Competitive Sealed Proposals	112
Multi-Step Bidding	118
Reverse Auctions	119
Small Purchases	120
Bidder and Offeror Conferences	121
Notifying Suppliers	122
Affirmative Responsibility Criteria	124
Other Types of Source Selection Methods	124
Conclusion	126
Endnotes	126

Chapter 8: NONCOMPETITIVE AND LIMITED COMPETITION PROCUREMENTS — 127

Recommended Best Practices	127
Authority and Central Oversight	128

A Word About Competitive Requirements When Using Federal Funds	128
Investigation and Preservation of Records	129
Types of Noncompetitive or Limited Competition Procurements	129
Conclusion	135
Endnotes	135

Chapter 9: BID AND PROPOSAL EVALUATION AND AWARD — 137

Recommended Best Practices	137
Evaluations and Awards	138
Evaluation of Bids and Proposals Generally	139
Evaluation of Bids	141
Evaluation of Proposals	144
The Negotiation Process	148
Price and Cost Analysis	150
Multiple Source Awards	150
Evaluations Using eProcurement Systems	151
Conclusion	151
Endnotes	151

Chapter 10: CONTRACTING FOR SERVICES — 153

Recommended Best Practices	153
Definition of Terms	155
Preparation of Service Descriptions and Statements of Work	156
Measuring and Paying for Performance	158
Alternative Delivery of Governmental Services	161
A Look at Human Services Contracting	165
Conclusion	166
Endnotes	166

Chapter 11: PROCUREMENT OF CONSTRUCTION AND RELATED SERVICES — 167

Recommended Best Practices	167
Definition of *Construction*	168
Authority to Conduct Construction Procurements	168
Selecting the Appropriate Construction Project Delivery Method	169
Short-Term Project Delivery Methods	169
A Snapshot of the Risks and Benefits of Short-Term Project Delivery Methods	172
Source Selection Methods for Architects and Engineers	175
Selection Methods for Project Delivery Methods	176
Sources of Contract Forms	176
Types of Contracts	177
Bonding Requirements	177
Contract Administration	177
A Word About Environmentally Friendly Construction	178
Conclusion	178
Endnotes	179

Chapter 12: COOPERATIVE PURCHASING — 181

Recommended Best Practices	181
Definitions and Overview	182
Legal Authority for Cooperative Purchasing	183
An Overview of Cooperative Purchasing Alliances and Trends	185
Best Practices for Initiating a Cooperative Purchase	188

CONTENTS

Costs of Administration	190
Benefits and Challenges of Cooperative Purchasing	190
Federal Government Cooperative Purchasing Issues	192
Conclusion	194
Endnotes	194

Chapter 13: **QUALITY ASSURANCE**	**197**
Recommended Best Practices	197
Definitions and Overview	198
Quality in the Crossfire	199
Authority to Establish Quality Assurance Programs	200
Quality Assurance Programs	200
A Word about Article 2 of the Uniform Commercial Code	203
Non-UCC Warranties	205
Other Ways of Supporting Quality Assurance	205
Conclusion	207
Endnotes	207

Chapter 14: **CONTRACT MANAGEMENT AND CONTRACT ADMINISTRATION**	**209**
Recommended Best Practices	209
Definition Of Terms	210
Overview of Contract Management	211
Contract Administration Plans	214
Steps in Contract Administration	214
Conclusion	218
Endnotes	218

Chapter 15: **PROCUREMENT PROGRAM INTEGRITY AND CREDIBILITY**	**221**
Recommended Best Practices	221
Openness and Maintenance of Records	222
Ensuring Integrity within Government	222
Ensuring Supplier Integrity	226
Organizational Conflicts of Interest	228
Laws Addressing Unethical Behavior	228
Conclusion	230
Endnotes	230

Chapter 16: **SURPLUS PROPERTY MANAGEMENT**	**231**
Recommended Best Practices	231
Definitions of Key Terms	232
Authority Over Surplus Property	232
The Disposition Process	232
Allocation of Sales Proceeds	235
Federal Surplus Property	235
Conclusion	236
Endnotes	236

Chapter 17: **PROTESTS, DISPUTES, AND CLAIMS**	**237**
Recommended Best Practices	237
Overview	238
Value and Risks of Administrative Procedures	240
Preventing or Defusing Disputes	241

Tips Relating to Bid Protests and Protest Responses	242
A Model for Administrative Processes	244
Details About Administrative Processes	244
Judicial Remedies for Disappointed Bidders	245
Disputes and Claims	246
Conclusion	246
Endnotes	246

Chapter 18: EMERGENCY PREPAREDNESS — 249
Recommended Best Practices	249
Federal Law and Directives	250
Procurement in the Emergency Management Process	252
Conclusion	256
Endnotes	256

Chapter 19: ePROCUREMENT — 257
Recommended Best Practices	257
The Before eProcurement Experience	258
eProcurement Benefits and Savings	259
Existing eProcurement Solutions in State Central Procurement Offices	260
Essential Elements of Order-To-Pay eProcurement Solutions	261
Some Development and Implementation Challenges	263
Enterprise Resource Planning Solutions and eProcurement	267
Conclusion	269
Endnotes	269

Chapter 20: PROCUREMENT OF INFORMATION TECHNOLOGY — 271
Recommended Best Practices	271
Calls for and Collaboration on Reform	272
Foundational Planning	273
Establishing a Governance Plan	277
Preparing Project Plans	278
Managing Risks	279
Sourcing and Procurement Issues	281
IT Procurement Negotiations	283
Alternatives to Buying IT Hardware and Software	287
Contract Terms and Conditions	292
Contract Management	294
Quality Assurance	295
Conclusion	296
Endnotes	296

Chapter 21: PROFESSIONAL DEVELOPMENT — 299
Recommended Best Practices	299
The Case for Public Procurement as a Profession	300
Professional Certification	300
Sources of Procurement Education	305
Effective Negotiation Teams	306
Conclusion	308
Endnotes	308

CONTENTS

Chapter 22: **EMERGING ISSUES IN STATE AND LOCAL PROCUREMENT**	**311**
Recommended Best Practices	311
Recognizing Emerging Issues	312
Resources for State and Local Procurement Offices	314
Conclusion	315
Endnotes	315
Appendix A: **RESOURCES**	**317**
Appendix B: **CHECKLIST FOR ESSENTIAL STATUTORY OR ORDINANCE COVERAGE**	**321**
Appendix C: **SAMPLE CHECKLIST FOR CONTRACTOR SECURITY AND HOSTING STANDARDS AND PRACTICES**	**323**
Appendix D: **NASPO-NASCIO RECOMMENDATIONS FOR IT PROCUREMENT**	**339**
INDEX	**341**

CHAPTER 1: INTRODUCTION

This 3rd Edition of *State & Local Government: A Practical Guide* (hereafter referred to as this *Practical Guide*) identifies the current and rapidly changing forces that are encountered by state or local government procurement officers and suggests ways in which they may be addressed. The text also describes the principles and practices that are at the heart of a procurement system that must remain both flexible and accountable.

A combination of the factors that are discussed in the pages of this *Practical Guide* indicates that the challenges that public procurement officers are facing are rapidly evolving. State and local central procurement offices are obliged to find creative and innovative ways to adapt to new situations while still upholding traditional legal and ethical standards. Because of this, it is essential to recognize that a central procurement office cannot provide the effective leadership that is required in order to meet today's complex procurement needs if it is located several tiers below the public entity's highest executive level.

EDITION HIGHLIGHTS

There are several differences between this edition and the 2015 edition. They include:

- Issues such as the procurement of information technology (IT), sustainability principles in procurement, and the use of eProcurement systems have been updated. Additionally, the narratives relating to the *bones* of the state and local government procurement process—such as procurement planning, source selection methods, evaluation of bids and proposals, quality assurance, and contract management—have been significantly expanded upon.
- Each chapter of this *Practical Guide,* except for this one, includes a comprehensive list of recommended best practices that are pertinent to that chapter's topic. Lists of recommended topics for statutory and regulatory coverage have been eliminated in favor of the more practical *best practices* lists.
- A comprehensive list of the resources that were used in the text of this *Practical Guide* is noted for each chapter through endnotes citing those resources.
- There is a significant increase in cross-referencing within each chapter to demonstrate the interrelationships among all of the subject matters that they address.
- Many of the changes in this edition are aimed at providing foundational definitions and explanatory overviews to benefit those readers who have no knowledge of state and local government procurement.

Terminology has been made consistent throughout this *Practical Guide*, and a guide to that terminology is provided at the end of this chapter.

HISTORY AND ORGANIZATION OF THIS TEXT

Although the National Association of State Procurement Officials (NASPO) was founded in the 1940s, it did not achieve its long-held goal of publishing a text on the public procurement profession at the state and local government level until the 1970s, when the Law Enforcement Assistance Administration of the United States Department of Justice provided funding for a study of state and local procurement. As a

CHAPTER 1: **INTRODUCTION**

result, NASPO, through its then-parent organization the Council of State Governments, published *State and Local Government Purchasing* in 1975.

The book became a companion to NASPO's survey of state purchasing practices, which the organization began conducting in 1949. The second survey was entitled *Purchasing by the States II* and was published in 1954–55. The third version came ten years later. Subsequent broader surveys became part of each edition of the original book. NASPO separated the text and the survey in 1997. NASPO now provides the most recent survey results to everyone through the website.[1]

NASPO published a completely updated and restructured edition of this *Practical Guide* called the *First Edition* in 2008. This 3rd Edition is the second update since then.

When studying this text, the reader should keep in mind that state and local governments are not carbon copies of each other. Every procurement program has its own strengths and weaknesses that are attributable to governing law, operating rules/regulations, quality of management, political tradition, and availability of resources. This *Practical Guide* is a roadmap with effective procurement as the destination rather than a detailed blueprint that limits ingenuity and innovation.

Scope of the Text

The word *procurement* as used in this text means the *cradle to grave* of purchasing—from when the need to buy a certain commodity, construction, or service is first identified to the time for a commodity to be disposed of at the end of its useful life or when a service or construction project is concluded. Each chapter of this *Practical Guide* covers the role that the public procurement officer should play at each point of that process.

Given the increasing reliance on IT, Chapter 19 (*eProcurement*) and Chapter 20 (*Procurement of Information Technology*) have gained in importance in this edition.

New challenges and increasing complexity in procurement mean that public procurement officers need specialized training and education. The availability of college courses and majors, in-house training and online programs, and the creation of certifications and other credentials for public procurement officers reinforces the view that persons who possess such education and credentials are truly members of a specific profession. Chapter 21 (*Professional Development*) addresses this very current topic.

Organization of this Text

This *Practical Guide* is divided into 22 chapters—each addressing a component of, or issues pertaining to, the state and local government procurement process.

Guiding Principles of Procurement

This *Practical Guide* seeks to paint a clear picture of the principles of public procurement: competition, impartiality, openness, effective use of public funds, and innovation and flexibility. Those fundamentals call for a public procurement program in which: public business is open to competition; suppliers are treated fairly; contracts are administered impartially; value, quality, and economy are basic and equally important aims; public procurement officers are innovative to meet needs; and the process is open to public scrutiny.

Successful outcomes depend on the effective implementation of those principles. An ideal procurement program derives from a comprehensive law that is accompanied by an easy-to-use set of rules/regulations and guidelines. Effective implementation requires sufficient resources—an adequate budget, competent personnel, and resourceful management—situated at a high level within the public entity's organizational structure, along with positive executive and legislative government support.

Some fundamental guiding principles of a good public procurement program are:

- Assurance of consistency of procedures and decision making
- Assurance of consistency of goals, objectives, and policies
- Measurement of the performance of the procurement system in light of its goals and objectives
- Recognition of procurement as a profession
- Recognition that procurement is a strategic function in government
- Centralized leadership of all aspects of the procurement process
- Recognition that procurement begins with coordinated planning with contracting user agencies
- Assurance of the day-to-day adherence to the principles of public procurement, including a balance between accountability, innovation, and flexibility
- Timing to meet user agency requirements and to benefit from advantageous markets and technologies
- Maintenance of an environment of openness and fairness
- Balance between the need for fiscal accountability, the needs of user agencies, and opportunities for suppliers
- Effective leadership through close working relationships and effective communication with users and user agencies

CHANGES IN STATE AND LOCAL PUBLIC PROCUREMENT

Although there have been a number of changes in the role of the state and local public procurement officers over the last decades, it is also noteworthy that some of the same issues that existed in the past still exist today.

A Look Back

As the procurement process became more complex, the role of the public procurement officer began to evolve into a more strategic one. The procurement officer moved to the center of the web of relationships among key contractors, government administration, and user agencies. He or she was expected to provide expertise to user agencies as they determined their needs, to conduct a process to select a contractor in a manner that generally satisfied both the user agency and competing suppliers, and to manage the resulting contract strictly, but congenially.

As the technology developed that made it possible to automate the procurement system, expectations were raised that faster service was achievable. The public procurement officer was expected to be a leader in the charge to streamline the procurement process. Demands for change occurred at the same time that government's reliance on purchased services and commodities increased, the services and commodities sought were less routine, and the role that public procurement played within the executive branch became more strategic to the success of essential government programs.

A Look Ahead

The public procurement officer is still responsible for the accountability of the procurement process, while the competing and complex demands of user agencies dictate that the officer be a flexible and creative problem solver, exercising whatever latitude the procurement laws permit. Caution and the temptation to implement all possible safeguards must be balanced with a more user-friendly process that is flexible and cuts through red tape.

CHAPTER 1: **INTRODUCTION**

The push to exercise that latitude more freely is complicated by the fact that state and local government procurements often receive intensive scrutiny. The public procurement officer and the process become lightning rods for criticism when the media, the legislature, and even the user agency assume that something went awry.

That criticism often demonstrates a lack of understanding of the procurement process. For instance, the media may denounce a failure to award to the low bidder, even though it may be that the public procurement officer used the competitive sealed proposal process authorized by law, permitting award based on multiple factors rather than price alone.

The failure of some executive government officials to recognize that sound public procurement requires strong leadership is an impediment to the future development and maintenance of a sound, modern procurement system, which in turn, mandates placement of a central procurement authority at an executive level within the governmental structure. Public procurement officers cannot be key players in the planning, acquisition, and management of strategic services, construction, and commodities if executive government officials view procurement as a clerical function with commensurately low pay and minimal authorization and training.

NASPO and its members are eager to be agents of change. They urge all those who participate in the state and local procurement process, particularly government executives, to ensure that public procurement officers are provided with the support and resources that are necessary to make those changes.

SOME CRITICAL ISSUES

Some of the most critical issues that challenge procurement professionals now (and most likely in the future, also) are addressed in the various chapters of this *Practical Guide*. A brief scan of the chapter titles and subheadings will offer the reader a summary of these issues. The following topics are especially challenging.

Procurement Leadership

A central procurement officer cannot offer expertise at the critical decision-making point without being a part of executive-level decisions. The reader will find the case for this primarily in Chapter 2 (*Procurement Leadership, Organization, and Value*), but it is also a theme in many other chapters, such as Chapter 4 (*Strategies and Plans*).

Procurement as a Profession

NASPO continues to work directly with colleges and universities to develop a public procurement curriculum at those institutions. NASPO also continues to be a partner with the National Institute of Governmental Purchasing (NIGP): The Institute for Public Procurement on the Universal Public Procurement Certification Council to advocate for the certification of all public procurement officers at the state and local government level. Chapter 21 (*Professional Development*) provides a narrative on this important issue.

Technology

Technology projects and their procurement are a major focus of resources, and will be so in the future, and eProcurement will continue to grow in importance going forward. Chapter 19 (*eProcurement*) and Chapter 20 (*Procurement of Information Technology*) discuss in more detail the latest thinking on those issues.

Value of Procurement

Today, procurement has become a critical function within the public entity with the potential of contributing as much as, or more than, other governmental functions to the efficient and effective operation of that public entity. For instance, the genesis of eProcurement systems regarding the significant savings in time

CHAPTER 1: **INTRODUCTION**

and money that they have achieved is an effort that is being led by central procurement offices throughout the country.

Without the oversight of central procurement offices, the integrity of the procurement process can break down with potentially embarrassing or even legal consequences for public leaders.

THE MODEL PROCUREMENT CODE FOR STATE AND LOCAL GOVERNMENTS

It is important to address a noteworthy event in the history of state and local public procurement—the publication in 1979 of the American Bar Association Model Procurement Code for State and Local Governments (hereafter referred to as the Model Procurement Code).[2]

The American Bar Association revised the Model Procurement Code and its regulations for implementation in 2000. It separately published a Model Code for Public Infrastructure Procurement in 2007, which extracted those portions of the 2000 Model Procurement Code that relate to the procurement of construction. The Model Procurement Code is widely considered to be a model for best practice in public procurement. The American Bar Association designated the Model Procurement Code as a model code and not as a uniform code, so that states might recast parts of its provisions to fit their needs.

The development of the Model Procurement Code, along with its implementing model regulations and the Model Procurement Ordinance for Local Governments and the Model Code for Public Infrastructure, remains a major event that affects both the present and future conduct of state and local government procurement.

Terminologies may have changed over the years since the Model Procurement Code was first issued in 1979. For instance, the term *best value*, relating to the evaluation of bids and proposals, took hold in some sectors in the 1990s and is discussed in this edition. Additionally, the term *sourcing strategies* is often used in public procurement circles to describe the development of nonstandard approaches to purchasing commodities, services, or construction, particularly of IT.

The key benchmark for any law such as the Model Procurement Code is whether, despite its age, its language is flexible enough to permit the approaches that are reflected in those new terminologies. So far, the Model Procurement Code's language holds up well. It continues to be a starting point—a model law and not one seeking uniformity—for finding good language from which a public entity may draft a solid procurement law or ordinance.

NEW TO THIS EDITION OF THE *PRACTICAL GUIDE*

Terminology Used

One improvement that this *Practical Guide* strives to make is to ensure that certain terms are used uniformly throughout the text, avoiding the confusion that arises when different terms are used to mean the same thing. The following is a directory of those terms:

- *Chief Procurement Officer* means the person who heads the central procurement office of a state or local government
- *Central procurement office* means the procurement office within a state or local government that is responsible for conducting all or most of the procurements for that government
- *Public entity* and *state and local government* are used interchangeably, although in fact, the term *public entity* is broader since it encompasses entities such as public universities that are not generally deemed to be governments

State and Local Government Procurement: A Practical Guide, 3rd Edition

CHAPTER 1: INTRODUCTION

- *User agency* means the agency, board, or department within a state or local government that is one of the following, depending on the context:
  ◊ The agency for which the central procurement office conducts a procurement
  ◊ The agency that has authority to conduct its own procurements outside of the central procurement office
  ◊ The agency requesting that the Chief Procurement Officer approve its request to engage in a limited or no-competition procurement such as a sole source or emergency procurement
- *User* means the public agency employee
- *Commodities* means all tangible things such as products, equipment, software, and hardware—in contrast to services and construction
- *Supplier* means any entity that sells commodities, services, or construction

The chapters of this *Practical Guide* also use the following shorthand terms:

- *NASPO* means the National Association of State Procurement Officials
- *NIGP* means National Institute of Governmental Purchasing: The Institute for Public Procurement
- *NIGP Dictionary* means the NIGP Online Dictionary of Procurement Terms[3]
- The *Model Procurement Code* means the American Bar Association Model Procurement Code for State and Local Governments

Negotiation Callouts Used

A final element that is new to this edition of the *Practical Guide* is the use of callouts to highlight important concepts related to contract negotiations. Effective negotiations have become a critical part of the modern public procurement process. In lieu of a new chapter on negotiations, callout boxes were used to discuss negotiations within existing chapters to emphasize how negotiation planning and execution touches multiple areas of the procurement process. Callouts discussing negotiations can be found in Chapters 4, 9, 20, and 21.

CONCLUSION

Throughout this *Practical Guide*, the kinds of decisions faced by public procurement officers and Chief Procurement Officers illustrate the importance of developing knowledgeable and skilled procurement professionals. NASPO and other organizations, as well as some colleges and universities, have launched initiatives aimed at creating sustained training programs to support state and local government procurement offices. The fact that this *Practical Guide* has been revised only four years after publication of the last edition further highlights the importance of the knowledge and training challenges that are facing procurement offices today.

Preserving the integrity of the procurement system and making it fair and equitable is an objective that is unique to public procurement. Public procurement officers have responsibilities that sometimes cause friction between user agency satisfaction and compliance requirements. The speed of change has refocused the profession on the need for continual growth of knowledge and skills. This *Practical Guide* is intended to help practitioners focus their own learning on the topics of most importance to the profession.

ENDNOTES

1. https://www.naspo.org/Publications/PID/8806/CategoryID/207/CategoryName/Survey-of-State-Procurement-Practices
2. A copy of the Model Procurement Code, along with various versions of it including the Model Procurement Ordinance is available at: http://apps.americanbar.org/dch/committee.cfm?com=PC500500
3. https://www.nigp.org/home/find-procurement-resources/dictionary-of-terms

CHAPTER 2: PROCUREMENT LEADERSHIP, ORGANIZATION, AND VALUE

RECOMMENDED BEST PRACTICES

- The central procurement office and the Chief Procurement Officer should define the internal purposes, goals, and objectives of the office; orienting them toward service, leadership, and management while addressing the full spectrum of procurement activities—including planning, procurement, quality assurance, contract administration, dispute resolution, property management and disposal, supplier relations, procurement consulting and training, and procurement data and technology management.
- The central procurement office and the Chief Procurement Officer should establish measurements for assessing the performance of the procurement process, such as processing times, supplier performance data, and client survey responses.
- The central procurement office should publish and maintain appropriate manuals for procurement personnel that set forth public entity-wide procurement goals and objectives and establish day-to-day procurement procedures in simple, concise language.
- The central procurement office should create programs and written *how-to* guides for non-procurement personnel at all levels of government and also for suppliers, instructing them in the procurement process.
- The Chief Procurement Officer should delegate, but closely monitor, procurement functions that can be logically, effectively, and efficiently performed by others. The delegation should be in writing and the scope of the delegation should be commensurate with the expertise and resources of the agency, department, or person to whom the delegation is to be made.
- The central procurement office should establish mechanisms such as focus or advisory groups and cross-functional procurement teams to encourage coordination and cooperation in order to unite the technical expertise of procurement and program staff and suppliers in carrying out its procurement mission.
- The central procurement office should encourage the use of internal teams as an effective technique for providing specialization, experienced back-up assistance, and group decision making.
- The central procurement office should ensure that consistent and uniform legal advice on public procurement and contract law issues is readily available—to everyone in their own office as well as to all procurement personnel within the public entity.
- The central procurement office should publish and maintain an internal procedures manual, a policy manual for agency personnel, and a supplier manual. These may be in hard-copy or electronic form, whichever most effectively meets the reader's needs. Composition control should reside with the Chief Procurement Officer.

This chapter promotes the strategic leadership of the state and local public procurement process. To implement that vision, this chapter advocates that procurement authority must be placed in a single leader—an experienced Chief Procurement Officer—whose position is at a high executive level within government.

This chapter will demonstrate that a strong central leader is essential to a public entity's procurement system. State and local governments cannot leave it to chance that their procurement processes, through which billions of dollars are spent, will achieve the following: ensuring the best use of public resources; allowing innovation, flexibility, and discretion; promoting professionalism; and providing a uniform and consistent way of offering contracting opportunities to encourage competition.

The *Harvard Business Review* describes strategic leaders as persons who "*. . . are constantly vigilant, honing their ability to anticipate by scanning the environment for signals of change.*"[1] Unless a Chief Procurement Officer sits at the table alongside the public entity's highest executives to gain the best knowledge of the future plans of the public entity, he or she cannot, in turn, anticipate and be vigilant in finding ways for the procurement process to support such plans.

Investing authority in a single, strategic leader does not mean that user agencies lose their authority to conduct procurements. Instead, central leadership and structure provide the best means of ensuring that the procurement process works seamlessly to meet the public entity's needs through collaborative development and interpretation of laws, rules/regulations, and policies. It also allows for professionalism in the process through, for instance, establishing criteria for delegating procurement authority, creating training programs, providing electronic tools for procurement officers and suppliers, and fostering cooperation among user agencies' procurement officers.

THE CASE FOR A SINGLE PROCUREMENT ADMINISTRATOR AT AN EXECUTIVE LEVEL

The National Association of State Procurement Officials (NASPO) has long professed that its members—the Chief Procurement Officer for each state—should be elevated to cabinet-level status. In fact, NASPO members ranked that issue highest in its recent annual Top Ten Priorities for State Procurement.[2]

That ranking is not a self-serving act. It reflects the benefits of investing a single leader with the authority to guide the movement of the ship in the same direction. The private sector has also recognized this as a best practice for decades, aiming to achieve many of the same objectives that this chapter sets forth as justification for creating a similar procurement structure within public entities.[3]

The argument that a public entity must designate a single strategic procurement leader who sits at an executive level within that entity is not new. The American Bar Association Model Procurement Code for State and Local Governments (hereafter referred to as Model Procurement Code), approved by the organization's House of Delegates in 1979 and revised with that body's approval in 2000, champions a state or local public procurement structure managed by one single experienced Chief Procurement Officer at a high level, with tenure and authority over all of the public entity's procurements.[4] NASPO has published several papers analyzing and promoting the benefits of this type of structure.[5] The National Institute of Governmental Purchasing (NIGP) issued a position paper on procurement authority that enumerates the benefits of central procurement leadership.[6]

Leadership means going beyond merely purchasing items. It involves developing a partnership with user agencies without sacrificing the responsibility to keep the procurement system accountable. Leadership starts with a cooperative and professional attitude. It means that instead of saying *no* to a *may we* question, the answer must be *let's figure it out*.

The treatment of the public procurement function as merely an awkward, hide-bound, and risk-averse process that is a necessary evil significantly reduces its chance of success. Public procurement officers should be viewed by user agencies as essential facilitators. However, to achieve this, procurement officers must be given appropriate access to in-depth program knowledge, well-trained personnel, and appropriate authority for decision making, along with adequate time to plan and implement a procurement solution. Recognition at the highest level of a public entity that procurement is a strategic function, with leadership at the top level where critical policy decisions are made, signals to user agencies that the procurement process should play a crucial role in its planning and program development. It also signals to procurement professionals that they are expected to provide superior service.

NASPO's members recognize that strategic leadership is a significant obligation for them. They and the public procurement officers that they manage must have a solution-focused attitude if they are to be considered of strategic value. When a government chief executive or user agency asks for solutions, the answer cannot be: "the rules won't let us do that," "we can't take that risk," "we would need a lot more time" or "we have never done it that way." The complex problems facing public entities today and a chronic lack of resources mean that chief executives are seeking creative solutions to accomplish their tasks.

Some key tasks of a central procurement office led by a strategic leader—the Chief Procurement Officer—are:

- Establish a program of professional excellence and make this competence known to executive and legislative management, using agencies and the public
- Clearly state the procurement system's obligation to provide service and value to its customers—taxpayers, user agencies, and suppliers
- Define the management role of the Chief Procurement Officer and the central procurement office in decision making, in policy making and implementation, and in oversight of the full spectrum of procurement activities
- Strive to improve employee motivation, professionalism, and productivity
- Encourage innovation and ingenuity by a commitment to training and research for the professional procurement staff and to program management within the user agencies
- Commit the central procurement office to working with user agencies and suppliers to achieve value for the funds spent in the acquisition of construction, commodities, and services
- Commit the central procurement office to communicating needed revisions in the procurement law to executive and legislative leadership
- Support the use of technology to provide faster services and current, accurate procurement information
- Encourage continuing education and professional certification for the procurement staff
- Establish programs to measure the performance of the procurement system, in terms of both quality and quantity, and require communication of those measures to customers
- Establish and maintain open communication with the public, including the news media

The vision of one strategic procurement leader with responsibility over all of a public entity's procurement may seem naïve. Public entities are often headed by executive and legislative politicians who regularly change after elections.

Long-term continuity of vision and policy direction is an aspiration that is not often met. Large and politically powerful user agencies, along with the suppliers that contract with them, can also wield influence to prevent central oversight by a single, strategic procurement leader.

Those barriers do not mean that the concept of a single leader and the data that supports it are flawed. This chapter provides a discussion of some tools for providing a solid, broadly unified procurement structure in which the Chief Procurement Officer may delegate procurement authority to others within a public entity based on objective criteria. It also includes a discussion of exemptions from a single leader's oversight and the best way in those cases to achieve collaboration, consistency, and policy development.

STAFFING FOR STRATEGIC PROCUREMENT SERVICES

The leadership tasks and strategic thinking that are described in this 3rd Edition of *State & Local Government: A Practical Guide* (hereafter referred to as this *Practical Guide*) require skilled professionals in order to carry them out. As the economy plummeted in the early 2000s, many procurement offices suffered serious staff reductions. Even though the economy has improved, some of those offices have not returned to their previous staff numbers.

Staff cuts—or maintaining those cuts after they are no longer necessary—may be done for political reasons to show a reduction in government. There should be communication with a public entity's senior leadership—governors and mayors, for instance—so that the unintended consequences of staff reduction will be clearly understood. A major consequence is the delay of contract awards, which impacts private sector business cash flow, the local economy, and tax revenue.

This is not merely a cry for more bodies. The activities that a well-run central procurement office is responsible for—for example, complex procurement, planning, market research, contract development and management, tracking procurement office performance, training, and user and supplier training—cannot be done with a skeleton staff.

One approach for calculating the number of public procurement officers that are required in order to conduct only a central procurement office's procurements—but not the rest of that office's responsibility—is described in the following steps. This is based on the hours calculated for procurements that are being conducted by public procurement officers who are not new to their jobs.

Step 1

- Study the labor hours needed to administer one invitation for bids (IFBs), two requests for proposals (RFPs), and three spot purchases[7]
- Identify the required steps for each of these methods of procurement—both pre-award and postaward
- Assign a labor-hour value to each step depending on whether the procurement was low, medium, or high complexity
- Project all procurements over a year—current and projected IFBs and RFPs, for instance—and categorize them as low, medium, or high complexity
- Total all of the labor hours, which will be the total office labor hours for the existing and projected workload

Step 2

Calculate a public procurement officer's productive work hours in a year. There is unproductive time taken up by meetings, interruptions, and other events.

Here is an example of a calculation of this number:

	Hours
365 days in a year × 8 hours a day	2,920
Less weekends	(832)
Less 11 holidays	(88)
Less annual leave	(80)
Less sick leave	(40)
Less 10% unproductive time	(188)
Total Productive Time, One Staff	1,692

Step 3

Take the total hours calculated in Step 1 and divide them by the number resulting from Step 2. Assuming that a workload of 37,000 labor hours is required as a result of Step 1, and then dividing it by the 1,692 productive hours determined in Step 2, the result will be the required number of procurement officers: 21.87, in this case. Essentially, 22 officers are needed to accomplish this workload, which is adjustable up or down for any error in calculation or increased productivity goal.

Central procurement and other public procurement offices have a strategic impact by saving governments money. The savings are much higher than any savings that are realized from not filling procurement jobs. As Chapter 4 (*Strategies and Plans*) explains, officers must track what they do and then report their successes. Those reports, along with staffing analyses like the one previously shown, will help provide the justification that is needed for any request for more staff.

DRAFTING A COMPREHENSIVE PROCUREMENT LAW

The structure and authority of an effective procurement program is rooted in the law that grants the authority of the procurement official to act. The procurement law does not need to—and indeed should not—specify every procurement activity in order to authorize it. The best procurement laws are those that offer a clear statement of legislative intent, a high-level description of the procurement structure and processes, and broad authority to the Chief Procurement Officer.

The nature of public procurement changes because the nature of what the public entity needs shifts regularly. Therefore, a procurement system must be adaptable, responsive, and flexible. This means that the law should outline the public entity's public procurement policies and procedures, while also leaving room for procurement professionals to exercise discretion.

The Model Procurement Code and Model Procurement Ordinance offer excellent starting points for statutory/ordinance language for adoption or adaptation. The general philosophical approach taken in those model laws is that the law should consist of clear, simple, broad legal parameters and authorities, leaving operational details to be filled in through separate implementing rules/regulations and guidelines.

The law should be written in such a way that it does not require legislative action to amend it when change occurs. For instance, the Model Procurement Code, in its 1979 version, did not codify anything requiring a paper process or require that notices should be published in newspapers. Thus, it was not necessary to update its provisions in 2000 to embrace an electronic process.

Appendix B offers a checklist that specifies organizational structure, leadership responsibilities, and activities that a good procurement law should authorize. Especially critical is the creation of the position of the Chief Procurement Officer and the central procurement office that he or she directs. The law, in whatever form is appropriate, should:

- Place the Chief Procurement Officer and the central procurement office at an executive level, reporting directly to the public entity's chief executive

- Authorize the Chief Procurement Officer to institute and maintain an effective program for all procurement of commodities, services, and construction within the public entity, and make that official responsible for the program
- Assign the Chief Procurement Officer and the central procurement office the responsibility for policymaking as well as for the implementation and oversight of the full spectrum of procurement functions
- Designate the Chief Procurement Officer as the sole authority to delegate procurement authority and to determine the conditions for doing so
- Authorize the Chief Procurement Officer to promulgate rules/regulations and policies to implement the procurement law
- Define the applicability of the law to include all of the public entity's procurements
- Exclude blanket exemption for the purchases of an entire user agency or department; if exclusions are considered necessary, define them narrowly by types of commodities, construction, or services sought and not so broadly as to exclude all the procurements of certain user agencies

One critical feature that the procurement law should include is a set of procurement definitions. Defining terms and using them in the law ensures that the law does not use different words to mean the same thing.

For instance, the Model Procurement Code defines the full range of things that may be purchased by using three terms and broadly defining them: *supplies* (including any interest in real property), *services*, and *construction*.[8] It then defines *procurement* as the *buying, purchasing, renting, leasing, or otherwise acquiring*[9] *[of] supplies, services, or construction*. The existence of three terms to represent the universe of things to be purchased simplifies the task of writing a solicitation and interpreting the law, among other things.

Additionally, definitions themselves can exclude an item from a procurement law's coverage. For example, the State of Arizona, in adopting its version of the Model Procurement Code, changed the term *supplies* to *materials* and specifically excluded from that definition any interest in real property, thus exempting something from the Arizona law that was covered by the Model Procurement Code.[10]

Exemptions from Procurement Law

Generally speaking, procurement laws often exempt some agencies or departments or particular types of procurements from that law's coverage or from centralized procurement management. For instance, states historically have excluded construction from their main procurement laws, particularly highway construction, and have created separate procurement laws for those types of procurements. The argument offered for exempting highway construction procurements is that they are heavily regulated through the federal highway funding authorities.

The real reason for many exemptions is that user agencies have enjoyed the exercise of procurement authority prior to the creation of a central procurement law with no central management oversight. The user agencies fear that they will be required either to cede authority to a central procurement leader who is not housed with the user agency or will have to follow standard procurement procedures. They perceive a loss of authority and power were they to have their procurements regulated through the central procurement office or subject to standard procedures.

However, legislative exemptions from a procurement law may result in negative procurement results, including:

- Losing the benefit of reducing the total public entity spend from economies of scale

- Inadvertently reducing competition as suppliers are required to meet multiple and differing sets of competition requirements among user agencies
- Diminishing adherence to procurement laws and best practices when underqualified or unqualified personnel are procuring commodities, services, and construction
- Minimizing the cultivation of strong supplier relationships that focus on performance and output due to varied processes and procedures across the public entity

An Approach to Reducing Exemptions

In the face of sometimes formidable opposition to centralized oversight, one compromise is for the law to cover all user agencies and make them subject to the law's requirements, but eliminate the Chief Procurement Officer's oversight of those procurements. The State of Utah, in adopting its version of the Model Procurement Code, took this approach when embracing one of the Model Procurement Code's proposed structures. It created a procurement policy board that develops procurement regulations and policies under the Utah Procurement Code, which is generally applicable to all user agencies. The policy board is composed of the Chief Procurement Officer as well as the leaders of the exempted user agencies, along with representatives of cities, counties, and school districts.[11]

Delegation of Procurement Authority

Rather than excluding some user agencies from the procurement law, a better approach is to make all user agencies subject to the Chief Procurement Officer's authority along with that official's agreement to delegate procurement authority. This approach recognizes a user agency's historical procurement authority while still achieving the goal of retaining central procurement leadership and management public entity-wide. The American Bar Association suggests—in its Commentary Notes to Section 2-301 (Centralization of Procurement Authority) of the Model Procurement Code,[12]—the following factors for the Chief Procurement Officer to consider in delegating procurement authority:

- The expertise of the potential delegate in terms of procurement knowledge and any specialized knowledge pertinent to the authority to be delegated
- The past experience of the potential delegate in exercising similar authority
- The degree of economy and efficiency to be achieved in meeting the state's requirements if authority is delegated
- The resources available to the office of the Chief Procurement Officer to exercise the authority if it is not delegated, and the consistency of delegation under similar circumstances

There are certain authorities, though, that a Chief Procurement Officer should never delegate. The most important of those is the approval of exemptions from competition, such as sole source or emergency procurement. Chapter 8 (*Noncompetitive and Limited Competition Procurements*) discusses these types of procurements in more detail.

PROCUREMENT RULES/REGULATIONS

The same philosophy previously discussed for the adoption of a procurement law applies as well to the adoption of rules/regulations that implement the statute. The terms *rules* and *regulations* mean the same thing but states will vary as to which term they use. Rules/regulations are generally limited to state governmental entities. A statute must authorize their creation and establish the means by which they are adopted within a state government.

Their scope is limited to what statutes explicitly direct and to matters that are reasonably inferable from the explicit statutory language. They must undergo a rigorous administrative review before adoption. Local public entities such as school boards, public universities, cities, and towns generally do not have the legal authority to adopt rules/regulations.

Rules/regulations should provide the requisite amount of detail needed to interpret the statutes authorizing them. They should direct the development of guidelines and procedures manuals without addressing every discrete step in a process. For instance, a rule/regulation may define the criteria for sole source procurements without establishing the exact format through which a user agency should make a request for one.

The Chief Procurement Officer should have the authority to institute rules/regulations under the procurement law. The Model Procurement Code offers statutory language for that approach as well as an alternative one that separates policymaking from day-to-day operations. The latter approach proposes the creation of a policy board, either of high-level outside persons with business experience or of cabinet-level employees of the public entity. Either configuration anticipates support staff.

The policy board that the State of Utah adopted (and which was discussed earlier) is responsible under the Utah Procurement Code for adopting rules/regulations.

The American Bar Association offers a list as examples of possible topics to cover in procurement rules or regulations for states adopting versions of the Model Procurement Code. Some of the topics mentioned are:[13]

- Conditions and procedures for delegations of procurement authority
- Prequalification, suspension, debarment, and reinstatement of prospective bidders, offerors, and contractors
- Small purchase procedures
- Conditions and procedures for the procurement of perishables and items for resale
- Conditions and procedures for the use of source selection methods including emergency procedures
- The opening or rejection of bids, proposals, and offers, and waiver of informalities in bids and offers
- Confidentiality of technical data and trade secrets submitted by actual or prospective bidders or offerors
- Partial, progressive, and multiple awards
- Supervision of storerooms and inventories, including determination of appropriate stock levels and the management, transfer, sale, or other disposal of publicly owned supplies
- Conducting price analysis
- Use of payment and performance bonds in connection with contracts for supplies and services
- Guidelines for use of cost principles in negotiations, adjustments, and settlements

CREATING TOOLS FOR PUBLIC EMPLOYEES AND SUPPLIERS

One of the critical components of the public procurement process is maintaining a system that is open, so that all of those who have an interest in it can see how public funds are being spent. Toward that end, it is important for the central procurement office to publish manuals that describe that process to user agencies, users, suppliers, legislative bodies, and the public. These tools should be developed in a manner that permits the greatest amount of input by those who will be using them.

Generally, these tools take the form of an operations manual as well as a supplier manual entitled, for example: *How to do Business with the* [*state, city, university, school district*]. Today, any public procurement office with a website has probably placed those manuals on that site in electronic form, making them widely available and in a format that is easy to revise.

As a rule, the manuals, particularly the *how to* manual for suppliers, should not discuss the specifics of the procurement law—primarily because the manuals need to be in plain, easily understood English and the language of laws is not known for simplicity. Electronic versions of those laws, at least at the state level, are readily available online and links to them may be provided in the manuals. NASPO maintains profiles for all states that include a link to each state's laws and procurement website. These can be accessed on the NASPO website.[14]

Operations or Procedures Manual

An operations manual establishes and describes the internal procedures of the procurement office. This manual should be a practical guide for public procurement officers. There is no need to repeat the law or rules/regulations in an operations manual.

In the case of a local public entity, there may be a need for more detail in an operations manual because there may be a procurement ordinance but no implementing rules/regulations if that entity is not bound by the state's procurement laws.

The subjects addressed in an operations manual will vary, depending on the language of the applicable procurement law and the authority that it grants to a procurement officer.

Chapter 4 (*Strategies and Plans*) outlines the critical role that the public procurement officer must play strategically in assisting a user agency toward meeting its future needs. It also notes that a procurement office must identify the role that it should play along with the procedures that are necessary to be prepared for emergencies. The operations manual should address matters relating to these issues.

The following list addresses some of the *how to* topics that it may be useful for an operations manual to discuss, but it is not exclusive:

- Establishing and maintaining supplier lists
- Locating new sources
- Monitoring and evaluation of supplier performance
- Determining bidder or offeror responsibility
- Notifying suppliers of contracting opportunities
- Receipt, opening, and tabulation of bids and proposals
- Determining responsiveness in bids and proposals
- Handling of supplier mistakes
- Handling of proprietary information and trade secrets
- Defining circumstances under which any or all bids or proposals may be or are rejected, including collusive bidding and resolution of identical bids
- Handling and return of samples
- Handling of and need for bid security
- Notifying successful and unsuccessful bidders and offerors
- Outlining small purchase procedures
- Specifying roles and responsibilities relating to contract administration and management—for example, verifying contractor compliance with metrics including service levels and milestones; enforcing provisions for price reduction; handling requests for price increases; monitoring contractor adherence to contract terms and conditions; and implementing quality assurance
- Handling protests of bidders and claims of contractors
- Handling complaints from user agencies or the public about suppliers, contractor performance, or procurement office services
- Transferring or other disposition of excess and surplus property
- Key steps and procedures for conducting different kinds of procurements

- Maintaining complete procurement/contract file documentation, retaining records, and making records available to user agencies and the public
- Reporting anticompetitive practices and suspected collusion to appropriate legal authorities
- Tracking and measuring procurement office performance and maintaining user agency communication through means such as surveys and focus groups

Supplier Manual

The manual should be brief, concise, and free of jargon. The introduction should be phrased in a friendly, informal way, setting the tone for the material to follow, which also should be written in an easily readable, nonbureaucratic style. It should offer some general information about the background, organization, and overall philosophy of the public entity's procurement program. The introduction should also include an invitation to visit or call the central procurement office for further details or a more complete understanding of topics discussed in the manual.

Here is a list—by no means exhaustive—of some of the topics that the procurement office may wish to address in the supplier manual:

- The kinds of construction, commodities, and services purchased
- A list of the public procurement officers in the offices, and a description of their responsibilities
- The location and address of the central procurement office and of procurement offices of user agencies with delegated procurement authority
- The way in which suppliers may register for inclusion on supplier lists and access any special requirements or communications
- The methods of conducting competitions for contracts including the receipt of solicitations
- The nature of basic statutory provisions, and of rules/regulations and policies, but not necessarily quotations or citations of statute or ordinance
- The manners in which procurements are conducted, for example, by competitive quotations, sealed bids, sealed proposals, multistep bidding, and under emergency and sole source conditions
- Clear statements prohibiting supplier gifts to public employees, and other ethical matters such as back-door selling or collusive bidding
- Any socioeconomic procurement programs, such as minority supplier programs or environmental procurement mandates

The NASPO website provides access to a variety of state *how to* supplier manuals.[15]

While it is a great benefit to offer a supplier manual online, it is important to provide something that a procurement officer can distribute at supplier fairs and other outreach opportunities. That may be as simple as a business card with the web address where the supplier may access the manual.

RESPONSIBILITIES OF THE CENTRAL PROCUREMENT OFFICE

The mandate to lead and to manage the public entity's procurement system is the foundation for organizing the central procurement office and assigning staff responsibilities. Even if the central procurement office and the officer in charge of it are not placed at the recommended executive level, the responsibility for leading the procurement system must still be the objective that defines the work of that office.

Policy Generation, Implementation, and Communication

While the central procurement office must be the undisputed leader of a public entity's procurement system, it should not operate in a vacuum, particularly when establishing rules/regulations or policies that will affect the work of others. The development of policies, procedures, and guidelines does not need to be consensus-driven, but the act of leading requires that the voices of those touched by the procurement system have an opportunity to be heard.

One best practice is for the Chief Procurement Officer to establish regular forums with user agencies and users, including user agency procurement officials. Doing so goes a long way toward assuring that issues are addressed in a timely and open fashion.

Training and Staff Development

Training for procurement staff and user agencies is critical to maintaining a high level of professionalism. As will be discussed in Chapter 21 (*Professional Development*), the central procurement office should devote resources toward developing training and education programs for user agency staff, in addition to assuring the professional development and certification of procurement staff. The central procurement office should also maintain a relationship with the public entity's personnel division in order to ensure that the job classifications and employee recruitment for procurement positions keep pace with changes in procurement and reflect the appropriate level of professionalism.

Technology

As Chapter 7 (*Competition: Solicitations and Methods*), Chapter 9 (*Bid and Proposal Evaluation and Award*), and Chapter 19 (*eProcurement*) discuss, the growth of eProcurement systems continues.

A FEW WORDS ON PERFORMANCE METRICS

The whole of this topic is too broad to address in this *Practical Guide*, but procurement office performance measurement is critical. As the saying goes, "What gets measured gets done." It is also important to show that procurement offices are actually providing the value that they promise. Measures must be both quantitative and qualitative.

A NASPO document entitled *Critical Success Areas and Key Performance Indicators for State Central Procurement Offices* is a resource for identifying what should be measured. It indicates key procurement performance indicators, many of which should be universal for all public procurement offices.[16]

THE VALUE OF PROCUREMENT

Today, procurement has a much greater role in a state or local government than the traditional mission of simply obtaining high-quality commodities, construction, and services for the lowest possible cost or best value. Instead, it has become a critical function within the public entity—with the potential of contributing as much as, or more than, other governmental functions toward the efficient and effective operation of public entities.

Traditional Value of Procurement

Perhaps the primary traditional value of public procurement is in its ability to reduce costs and generate savings. Procurement professionals do this by leveraging volume in the public entity's contracts, competing and negotiating contracts, and effectively using eProcurement solutions. The following paragraphs depict two examples.

Through Leveraged State Contracts

Procurement professionals strive to award long-term, high-volume contracts that leverage a public entity's buying power to obtain the best prices for commodities, construction, and services, and to reduce administrative costs. Other public entities, including institutions of higher education, use these contracts, thereby lowering the cost to taxpayers.

When a public entity does not leverage its buying power through a strong central procurement organization, user agencies must expend resources to purchase for their own individual needs and because the volume purchased is less than it would be if all user agencies' needs were combined, those purchases are often at higher prices.

Through eProcurement Solutions

Public entities that have made the investment in and then implemented robust, fully functional procurement solutions have achieved substantial savings by automating the procurement process. These eProcurement solutions have made a public entity's business opportunities more accessible to suppliers, reduced paperwork, increased competition, and made the procurement process more efficient and effective—all resulting in savings.

Creating and Sustaining Private Sector Jobs

Chapter 3 (*The Importance of Competition*) describes the economic impact that public procurement plays in the nation's economy. Many private sector businesses depend on public contracts to generate cash flow and to create or sustain jobs.

One often overlooked resource that helps directly improve competitiveness and sustain jobs is a state's Procurement Technical Assistance Center (PTAC). These centers, funded partially by the United States Defense Logistics Agency, provide free counseling to businesses in all aspects of federal, state, and local government procurement. Many state central procurement offices are involved in the strategic direction of PTACs, including educating suppliers about doing business with state governments. There are more than 300 local PTAC offices across the country.[17]

Ensuring a Fair, Open, Honest Process

Central procurement offices headed by a Chief Procurement Officer ensure that the procurement process is fair, open, and honest, with equal access for suppliers to a public entity's business opportunities. Absent their oversight, the integrity of the procurement process can break down, with potentially embarrassing or even legal consequences for public leaders.

Transparency and Accountability

Public procurement involves billions of dollars of public funds. Taxpayers believe procurement should be public and transparent. Central procurement offices ensure through oversight and use of technology (such as eProcurement systems) that the procurement process remains fair, open, and honest, and that its process and outcomes are transparent to the public. Without a strong central procurement office, the procurement process can degenerate and thus, transparency and accountability can be compromised.

Importance of Consistent Laws and Regulations

Businesses suffer when there is inconsistency in the rules/regulations that pertain to procurement laws. As an example, the introduction to the Model Procurement Code states:

> *The proliferation of "local content" procurement regulations has created a multitude of arcane differences among the thousands of public entities buying commodities and services on an annual basis.*

. . . complex, arcane procurement rules of numerous public entities discourage competition by raising the costs to businesses in order to understand and comply with these different rules. Higher costs are recovered through the prices offered by a smaller pool of competitors, resulting in unnecessarily inflated costs to state and local governments.

When public entities are removed from a state's procurement law and establish their own rules, businesses are forced to track a myriad of practices and procedures. Competitions initiated by those exempted public entities can vary significantly.

CONCLUSION

The key ingredient in an effective public procurement system is leadership through the Chief Procurement Officer and a central office, placed at a high executive level. To achieve this, executives and legislators must recognize the importance of the central procurement office. Leadership also requires that the person serving as the Chief Procurement Officer, along with those who work under that officer, adopt an attitude of professionalism, openness, cooperation, and creativity. Finally, leadership means going beyond simply acquiring things; training, outreach, planning, and contractor management are just a few of the other activities that are of equal importance.

ENDNOTES

1. P. J. Schoemaker, S. Krupp, & S. Howland. (March 25, 2015). Strategic Leadership: The Essential Skills. Retrieved September 18, 2018, from https://hbr.org/2013/01/strategic-leadership-the-esssential-skills
2. For the 2017 and 2018 lists, go to: http://www.naspo.org/Publications/PID/8806/CategoryID/215/CategoryName/Yearly-Top-Ten-Priorities
3. L. Younger & B. Umbenhauer. (March 27, 2018). The Deloitte Global Chief Procurement Officer Survey 2018. Retrieved October 1, 2018, from https://www2.deloitte.com/content/dam/Deloitte/at/Documents/strategy-operations/deloitte-global-cpo-survey-2018.pdf. The survey contains data from 500 business chief procurement officers in 39 countries.
4. See Article 2—Procurement Organization—of the Model Procurement Code. A copy of the Model Procurement Code, along with various versions of it including the Model Procurement Ordinance is available at: http://apps.americanbar.org/dch/committee.cfm?com=PC500500
5. https://www.naspo.org/Publications/ArtMID/8806/ArticleID/2208
6. See the white paper entitled *Procurement Authority in Public Entities* at: http://www.nigp.org/home/find-procurement-resources/guidance/position-papers
7. The NIGP Dictionary defines a spot purchase as "a one-time purchase occasioned by a small requirement, an unusual or emergency circumstance, or a favorable market condition."
8. See Sections 1-301(4), (21), and (24) of the Model Procurement Code.
9. See Section 1-301(16) of the Model Procurement Code.
10. Arizona Revised Statutes §41-2503-27. See: https://www.azleg.gov/viewdocument/?docName=https://www.azleg.gov/ars/41/02503.htm
11. https://purchasing.utah.gov/boards-and-commissions/procurement-policy-board/
12. See Section 2-205 of the Model Procurement Code.
13. See Commentary to Section 2-102 of the Model Procurement Code.
14. www.naspo.org
15. www.naspo.org
16. https://www.naspo.org/Publications/ArtMID/8806/ArticleID/3324
17. www.aptac-us.org

CHAPTER 3: THE IMPORTANCE OF COMPETITION

RECOMMENDED BEST PRACTICES

Every public procurement officer should:

- Be informed about competition law, that is, federal and state laws that prohibit commercial arrangements or certain behaviors that reduce economic competition.
- Understand market conditions for every procurement.
- Avoid specifications, scopes of work, or contractual relations that reduce competition.
- Be aware of anticompetitive patterns, responses, and communications.
- Develop a good working relationship with antitrust enforcers.
- Remain at arm's length from every supplier.
- Practice procurement ethics.
- Report concerns to prosecutors.
- Document everything.

CHAPTER 3: **THE IMPORTANCE OF COMPETITION**

Much of what this book addresses is competition and how it applies—or does not apply—when state and local governments make purchases. Most public procurement officials would probably agree that a critical, if not *the most critical*, aspect of what they do is to be good stewards of public funds—making sure that government users obtain good quality commodities, services, and construction that are appropriately priced through a process that is transparent and uncorrupted. But state and local laws establishing competitive procurement systems have other purposes as well. Among those noted in the American Bar Association Model Procurement Code for State and Local Governments[1] (hereafter referred to as the Model Procurement Code) are the following:

- To ensure the fair and equitable treatment of all persons who deal with the procurement system
- To foster effective broad-based competition within the free enterprise system[2]

Look at the facts. State and local governments spend hundreds of billions of dollars annually through their procurement processes. That hefty dollar amount means that state and local government contracts have significant clout within the economy of the United States. That clout, as recognized in the section of the Model Procurement Code for State and Local Governments noted previously, means that each public procurement official must keep an eye on that bigger picture.

This chapter provides a basic description of how competition drives the free marketplace. It also defines the types of conduct that restrain free trade and offers guidance to the procurement professional on how to prevent and detect anticompetitive behavior. This chapter includes a discussion of key federal and state laws relating to anticompetitive supplier behavior that is known as antitrust or restraint of trade laws.

For those who are not lawyers, it is important to define the two legal terms—*antitrust* and *restraint of trade*—and put them in context. Merriam-Webster defines *antitrust* as "of, relating to, or being legislation against or opposition to trusts or combinations; specifically: consisting of laws to protect trade and commerce from unlawful restraints and monopolies or unfair business practices."[3]

In the same vein, *restraint of trade* means:

1. *An act, fact, or means of curbing the free flow of commerce or trade . . .*
2. *An attempt or intent to eliminate or stifle competition, to effect a monopoly, to maintain prices artificially, or otherwise to hamper or obstruct the course of trade and commerce as it would be if left to the control of natural and economic forces . . . also: the means (as a contract or combination) employed in such an endeavor.*[4]

While this chapter contains practical advice for public procurement officers about how they can avoid and detect anticompetitive behavior, any discussion of competition requires some analyses of the laws that preclude price fixing and other types of restrictions on competition. Since those analyses are best provided by an attorney, the reader should understand that this chapter was written by an antitrust attorney who views competition through that lens.

WHY COMPETITION MATTERS

The United States was founded as a free market country. An essential premise of that type of economy is that unfettered markets will produce the highest quality commodities, services, and construction at the best possible prices to meet demand. Governments are large consumers in virtually every market. But governments, like any consumer, do not have unlimited funds. Additionally, governments, unlike private industry, cannot routinely pass costs on to the taxpayer. A price acceptable to a private firm may be unduly burdensome for a government.

Thus, effective competition in state and local public procurement plays a key economic role. Effective competition widely benefits the economy of a community. In turn, benefits return to the government in the form of vigorous competition for that government's contracts. Suppliers competing in a truly competitive market should be more reluctant to unreasonably elevate prices and reduce quality because of the risk of suffering a loss of customers. The ready availability of other market alternatives—created through customer demand and effective competition—isolates the unreasonably priced, poor quality goods and services.

Effective competition can also promote open access to the marketplace, induce new suppliers to enter it, promote better market performance, encourage new technology and higher productivity, and result in conservation of scarce and irreplaceable resources. Public procurement officers who promote competition provide an important public service.

While there are situations in which competition must and should be limited,[5] competition is the central premise in public procurement. Every public procurement practice should therefore have two co-equal objectives: using the power of free markets to generate the best commodities, services, and construction, along with the best prices; and ensuring the fairness and impartiality of the procurement process.

The methods by which public procurement officials have conducted competition have changed dramatically in recent years and will continue to do so in the future. More often than not, lowest price is no longer the key factor in selecting a contractor. That fact, along with the billions of dollars that state and local public entities spend, makes the role of public procurement officials even more important when it comes to preventing and detecting supplier anticompetitive practices.

DEFINING *ADEQUATE* *COMPETITION*

Adequate competition cannot be quantified in exact terms or prescribed by a particular procedure. As a rule, it generally means the level of competition that an unrestrained market produces.

A simple example can show how adequate competition varies based on the circumstances. If a government needs a modest quantity of paper clips and there are dozens of retailers actively competing on the price at which they sell these clips, then the public entity is well served to simply purchase them without a formal solicitation process from the supplier with the lowest price. This approach is efficient and takes advantage of a competitive market. Many public entities have rules that allow smaller dollar purchases for this very reason.

When the volume of commodities or the dollar amount the government is going to spend rises, however, adequate competition often requires a more formal process. Regarding the paper clip example, if the government is going to buy over a million paper clips and is willing to offer a contract to supply them for a term such as a year, a formal invitation for bids makes more competitive sense. That is because there may be another level of price competition created by the large purchase. Suppliers price their commodities based in part on volume sold. A retailer may sell 100 paper clips for a dollar, but would sell a million at fifty cents per 100 clips.

PROCUREMENT PRACTICES THAT ENCOURAGE COMPETITION

While procedural requirements may be helpful to achieve adequate competition, it is not necessarily ensured by blindly following a process. Fostering and maintaining competition requires the efforts of each public procurement official. The following paragraphs contain examples of how a procurement official's actions may encourage competition.

Preparing to Compete

Market Research and Supplier Outreach

- Performing market research to understand the scope of the marketplace
- Estimating prices and costs based on thorough market price and cost research
- If prequalification of suppliers is used, prequalifying as many suppliers as exist in the current market; and if there are too few suppliers, broadening the geographic area of qualification

Specifications and Scope of Work

- Clearly identifying in the solicitation the need to be filled with a view toward qualifying the broadest range of commodities, services, construction, and suppliers
- Avoiding the bundling of multiple unrelated commodities, construction, or services unless it is impossible to obtain the needed product without bundling
- Carefully weighing the advantages and disadvantages of partnering in long-term contracts, even if permitted by law, since markets can change rapidly
- Drafting specifications independent of any prospective supplier or brand name commodity
- Drafting specifications and scopes of work to be performed and other terms of the procurement to avoid brand or sole supplier limitations

Competing in an Open Fashion

Competitive Strategy and Sole Source

- Recompeting a commodity or service if markets change significantly
- Recompeting rather than extending contracts in response to new demands, changed needs, or changed markets
- Restricting sole source procurements to a limited, well-defined, and published set of criteria, and documenting the need for a sole source decision

Bidding Systems

- Publicly announcing invitations for bids or requests for proposals using different forms of publications (such as websites and e-mails to supplier professional groups and industry organizations) aimed at reaching the broadest possible number of potential suppliers
- Widely publishing the results of each formal competition
- Assuring that the public procurement office's website is easy to locate on the government's website so that suppliers may easily learn about contracting opportunities

Supplier Selection, Evaluation, Award, Negotiations, and Protest

- Selecting qualified bidders or suppliers inclusively and avoiding a set of limitations such as considering only three bids or proposals
- Always requiring suppliers to sign non-collusion affidavits since, even if false, they can be the basis for enforcement and debarment of colluding suppliers without the high cost of an antitrust enforcement lawsuit
- Conducting fair contract negotiations that treat all suppliers who reach this stage equally
- Handling bid protests, contract claims, and disputes fairly

Effectively Managing Contracts

Contract Administration and Monitoring

- Engaging in post-award contract changes only if unforeseen circumstances require them, and if the changes either could have

been foreseen or are significant in relation to the entire contract, competing that changed work, particularly if it adds to and does not simply change the original work
- Building into enterprise procurement and financial systems the capability of keeping records of competing supplier information (including pricing) and of analyzing that data to support detection of anticompetitive activities.

Documenting and Keeping Accurate Records

Public Records

- Documenting each stage of the process in a single procurement file or series of files
- Keeping nonproprietary procurement records open for review so that unsuccessful suppliers may become better equipped to compete in the future

Maintaining a System of Integrity

Professional Ethics

- Staffing the procurement process with truly independent, well-trained public procurement professionals and making sure that they are free to exercise their professional judgment without political pressure
- Avoiding conflicts of interest and establishing and adhering to a set of ethical principles, which are discussed in more detail in Chapter 15 (*Procurement Program Integrity and Credibility*)
- Avoiding special advantages for a supplier that are not available to others

PRACTICES AND LAWS THAT RESTRAIN COMPETITION

Overview

As a practical matter, a government restrains competition at times through its laws. Public procurement and other public officials may also do so through their own actions.

The most common government restraint of competition is regulation. Laws of the state of California, for instance, have for some time required that most vehicles sold in the state have emissions equipment that is different from and stricter than those mandated by the federal government. That kind of restraint is generally immune from antitrust and restraint-of-trade laws.

Other examples of laws that restrain competition and are familiar to procurement officials are bidding preference laws such as those aimed at local, small, or disadvantaged businesses.[6] Although these have been in use at federal, state, and local levels for decades, many of these types of laws have been and will continue to be subject to close legal scrutiny.

Other government-caused anticompetitive practices result from poor judgment, misunderstandings of markets, lack of resources to do necessary market research, blind obedience to past practices, and cronyism that is not recognized as such. In some cases, competition is compromised unintentionally through the mistaken belief that the public interest is being served by the action taken or by a misguided albeit sincere effort to be helpful to suppliers.

There are also political pressures. Some elected officials are notorious, at least according to the media, for implementing costly government programs that involve lucrative contracts between the government and campaign contributors. It is often difficult for appointed public officials to resist pressure from elected public officials.

Procurement Practices that Hinder Competition

Here are some procurement activities that may diminish competition:

- **Accepting a late bid because it is low.** By accepting a late bid, the public procurement officer is changing the rules of the game. This practice can also appear to be unfair since the late bid is received after the bids of the other bidders have been publicly announced, and the bidder submitting that late bid has possible knowledge of the other bids before providing its bid.

- **Using evaluation criteria not stated in the solicitation as the basis of award.** This is a practice that stands competition on its head. True competition cannot occur where the suppliers do not know the real specifications, the scopes of work, or the evaluation criteria.

- **Unnecessary sole source purchases.** In today's global economy, it is rare that only one supplier can supply whatever the government needs. Sole source procurement, which is viewed skeptically by auditors and by the public, may occur due to a lack of market research. Sole source procurement may also reflect an improper relationship, such as in the case of a pilot program managed by a supplier that leads to a set of specifications authored by that supplier or favoring that firm. The sole source procurement could also be the result of political pressure and cronyism.

- **Improper communication with suppliers.** Public procurement officers need to communicate with suppliers to understand relevant markets. However, communications should always be open to all possible suppliers. A good rule is that if the public procurement officer calls one supplier, that officer must call all of the suppliers known to him or her. Calling one supplier, particularly for help in writing specifications, leads to leaking of inside information and gives that supplier an unfair advantage. All communications should avoid the appearance of favoritism.

- **Restrictions on supplier qualifications.** While experience may be useful, requiring too much experience eliminates all new suppliers from competition. Requiring too much stock on-hand generally favors big suppliers and eliminates small suppliers who may, given the chance to bid, be able to provide the product needed. Another example of restrictive requirements is a solicitation calling for delivery within 24 hours, which may be unnecessary and frequently favors larger suppliers.

- **Bundling and other specification or scope of work restrictions.** Bundling has several anticompetitive outcomes. First, it facilitates collusion among bidders. Deals may be cut as to who will bid as the prime contractor and who will be subcontractors. Second, the practice eliminates head-to-head competition among those who supply the prime contractor. Third, smaller suppliers, who may be able to bid on 30% of a bundled solicitation but cannot bid on the other 70% are cut out of the process. Finally, the user agency loses oversight of the subcontractors. There are times when bundling is essential or even mandated, such as in design-build contracts.[7] But every time it occurs, competition is diminished.

- **Barriers to prequalification.** The fact that large suppliers have historically been the only ones to qualify does not mean that small suppliers have not come into the market who can, through legitimate joint ventures, qualify to supply what is needed. Effective, procompetitive procurement is one that is open to every supplier who can possibly qualify in every commodity, construction, or service likely to be procured.

- **Brand names and other unnecessary restraints in specifications.** It may be that a public procurement officer believes he or she knows that Brand X copiers are better than Brand Y, but that officer may be wrong. Specifications should ask for the best possible copiers capable of producing what is needed—such as 50 copies a minute, if that is a legitimate need. If a brand has failed to perform in the past, it may be that the retailer supplying the copier serviced it poorly. Procurement officials should ask for what they need by description, and almost never by a single brand name.[8]

- **Post-bid specification changes.** If specifications must be changed materially and promptly after a solicitation is issued, it is often because of a failure to conduct appropriate market research before issuing that solicitation. The changed specifications are a new competitive opportunity, and all qualified suppliers should be allowed to participate. To do otherwise is tantamount to a sole source award to the initial successful supplier. This unquestionably eliminates competition.

- **Letters of intent.** There is no competitive justification for pre-award letters of intent where the evaluation process is not complete. Where the law prohibits price as a factor in the award of a contract, such as contracts for architects or engineers, completion of the qualifications-selection process is necessary before it is appropriate for the public entity to express its intention to award a contract to a particular supplier. After the qualifications competition and a clean selection process, a letter of intent to negotiate may be appropriate, so long as this letter does not contain an intention to procure anything not in the original specifications.

- **Post-award contract changes.** Immediate post-award contract changes are often anticompetitive and unjustified. Change orders can be rife with abuse and only warranted where the change is within the original scope of work. A post-award design change that must be made to move a wall ten inches to avoid a power line is within a design scope of work. Adding a new facility to the original design contract is sole source purchasing without justification. Another contract change that is problematic is inappropriately extending the duration of contracts where the original solicitation did not specify that there would be the possibility of extensions or renewals.

- **Most favored customer pricing.** Most favored customer pricing results from a contractual provision, also known as a *most-favored-customer clause* or *non-discrimination clause* in which the seller promises the buyer that it will not offer another buyer better terms before offering those terms, or better terms, to the first buyer. This mechanism, while appearing to limit price increases, actually sets artificial floors on prices.

- **Slow pay.** When a public entity fails to pay invoices on time, the cost of borrowing to the contractor discourages competition and may preclude participation by small businesses.

- **Preferences.** These laws—for example local supplier/commodity preferences, small/disadvantaged/minority/women-owned preferences—have already been noted earlier in this chapter.

- **Rotation of suppliers or lists.** Rotation of lists of suppliers who may bid is an artificial device that impedes market forces. It may be competitively acceptable to solicit for a multi-vendor contract and to rotate work among those two or three selected in a clean, competitive process. However, these types of awards should not result in long-term contracts and they should be competed annually since better suppliers may come into the market.

- **Long-term contracts.** Long-term contracts lock the user agency into the market at the time of contract award. Some long-term contracts may be justified in order to lock in rising prices at current levels, but the public procurement office will want to be able to avoid being locked in should prices fall. If long-term contracts are used, they should include a price escalation/de-escalation clause establishing criteria for price adjustments.

- **Disclosing the budget.** A practice that denies the taxpayers the benefit of competition is disclosing the budget for a particular procurement when soliciting bids or proposals. Once suppliers know how much the government is going to spend, they will tend to price their responses so as to earn the whole amount. Public records laws may allow clever suppliers access to the information, but it should not be announced. An even worse practice is to disclose the budget to only some suppliers and not others.

- **Confidentiality problems.** Leaks of inside information are a hallmark of bid rigging involving government personnel. If information is not public, no supplier should have it. If it is public, all should have it.
- **Proprietary information.** Companies are entitled to protect their proprietary information, but what is proprietary is limited to specialized processes that genuinely are not the business of competitors. However, prices should not be considered confidential after award since this is the taxpayer's business. The finances of a competing company, if it is publicly traded (that is, offers stock on a stock market), may be subject to public records law requests—and public procurement officers should not promise confidentiality for those types of records. But, one competitor learning about another's approach (particularly that of the winning supplier) after a completed competition is procompetitive since the losers may be better equipped to compete the next time.

COMBATING ANTICOMPETITIVE PRACTICES

Awareness is the first step toward combating bid rigging and other anticompetitive practices. For public procurement officers, it means knowing how the market works so that they may discover whether the lack of bids, unreasonably rising prices, or other suspicious behavior is a problem that requires a lawyer's attention.

To obtain that knowledge, public procurement officers should have training in how unfettered markets work according to the economic laws of supply and demand. They should also learn how to conduct market research so that they are aware of what an appropriate, non-collusive market response to a solicitation should look like. A rudimentary knowledge of antitrust law and competition policy is also essential. Finally, public procurement officers should receive training on how to spot aberrant and collusive market responses, how to report these, and how to obtain assistance when suspicions arise.

Next, well-informed public procurement officers should understand the scope of their own discretion. Procurement laws often provide public procurement officers with considerable flexibility to make awards on any reasonable basis consistent with competition.

This level of discretion can be used effectively to cancel and recompete any procurement where the response is suspicious. Cancellation of the procurement is a relatively easy way to prevent an antitrust law violation and to remedy a non-competitive market response. In cancelling a solicitation after receipt of responses, the public procurement officer can communicate the user agency's intention to examine the market or to seek enforcement assistance due to concerns about the manner of bidding. Such a communication before recompeting the procurement is a wake-up call to suppliers. A cancellation and rebid, without any other action from, for instance, the attorney general, will further place the power back where it belongs—in the procurement office.

Another weapon against antitrust and anticompetitive activities is to manage public procurement offices so as to discourage favoritism in any form. A strong Chief Procurement Officer, together with enforced ethical policies, will aid the public procurement officer in withstanding political pressure to sole source, to bundle, to hurry the contract competition, or to compromise the fairness of the selection process.

Finally, public procurement officers should consider the best practices to enhance and promote competition recommended in this chapter and elsewhere in this practical guide. Some best practices for combating antitrust violations include:

- **Identical bids.** Report identical bids to management and to the state attorney general or the county or district attorney's office. On bids using federal funds, ask that the report be passed on to the Antitrust Division of the United States Department of Justice (DOJ). On reopening competitive bidding, announce that all identical bids will be rejected and reported or, at the discretion of the procurement office, that an award will be made to the first qualified nonidentical bidder.
- **Suspicious bidding patterns.** Audit bid histories from time to time and publish reports to qualified suppliers. If patterns suggesting rotating bids appear, report these to appropriate enforcement authorities.
- **Simultaneous price increases.** Conduct market research to determine if price increases appear market driven. Reject all bids, and then rebid if there is no obvious market reason for the increases.
- **Cronyism.** Practice procurement ethics at all times, with all suppliers, in all situations. The inability of a supplier to improperly buy into a contract forces it to compete on a level playing field. Where information suggests that a fellow procurement officer has become too close to suppliers, report that information. When the offending public official is a superior, the report should go to the state attorney general, any state or local government office of inspector general, a state auditor general, or an outside auditor. Many states have whistleblower protection statutes that protect those who report such illegal behavior. In some circumstances, public employee organizations have resources to protect public procurement officers caught in this situation.
- **Post-bid and contract changes and extensions.** If a public procurement officer observes unwarranted post-bid or post-award changes, including unsupported contract extensions and claims of cost overruns, these should be reported as these practices are rarely competitively justifiable.
- **Market aberrations.** Know markets well enough to recognize if a strange-looking response to a solicitation is market driven. There are times when markets, for reasons outside the suppliers' control, change rapidly. One needs only to look at historic real estate bubbles that burst to know that sometimes markets rise beyond all economic reality, and that sometimes they collapse. For public procurement officers, a burst bubble is a tremendous purchasing opportunity of which the government may take advantage, but only if its contracts contain language that allow it to do so. Where market prices are rising unrealistically, the user agency does well to avoid locking in to rising prices.
- **Anticompetitive remarks and admissions.** Write down the date, time, identity of the speaker, witnesses to the anticompetitive or suspicious remarks, and a best recollection of what was said, as soon as possible. Report these to the appropriate authorities at once.

Public procurement officers should be mindful of the fact that user agencies are consumers. The essential purpose of antitrust laws and their enforcement is to protect consumers. An example of the consumer power that state and local government procurement represents is a case involving four national drug distributors who wished to merge into two. The United States Federal Trade Commission (FTC) had jurisdiction to investigate the mergers and their effects on competition.

Federal agencies such as the military branches are huge consumers of pharmaceuticals and these were among the potential victims of the reduction in competition—both in price and distribution—that the mergers represented. But states, counties, cities, and towns along with some special quasi-government entities also purchased mass quantities of certain drugs for facilities such as state mental hospitals and prison infirmaries.

Because the FTC sought to coordinate with the states, thirty-two states as well as local governments compiled their drug purchase costs and combined their stories into a *friend-of-the-court* brief that the FTC credited with successfully defeating the mergers in 2000. The cost to state and local governments of even a 1% price increase would be so staggering that it was clear to the federal court that government consumers and ultimately their client citizens would be irreparably harmed.

Successful enforcement requires evidence. The public procurement officer is the front-line defense against antitrust violations in this regard. By thoroughly documenting procurement decisions, keeping abreast of local markets, understanding the effect on the taxpayer of a reduction in competition, and listening closely to suppliers' discussions about changes in markets, the public procurement officer is in a unique position to gather the sort of evidence that makes an enforcement action more likely.

DETECTING ANTITRUST VIOLATIONS IN PROCUREMENTS

The first part of this chapter provided tools for avoiding and detecting anticompetitive practices. The remainder of this chapter provides information about how public procurement officers can assist law enforcement officials in enforcing antitrust laws aimed at supplier behavior that violates those laws.

Public procurement officers are in a unique position to detect suspicious pricing patterns and other supplier behaviors indicating anticompetitive practices. On detecting any of those types of activities, public procurement officers should immediately alert their superiors and the antitrust lawyers in the state attorney general's office. The attorney general's office can investigate and take appropriate action to prevent threatened illegality or to remedy anticompetitive conduct that has already taken place.

The following are suspicious practices that may suggest collusion or aberrations in markets:

- **Identical bids.** No one bidder or proposer is in an identical financial situation to any other. It costs one supplier more to produce commodities, services, or construction than another. One supplier will have more efficient systems than another. Suppliers do not have identical processes, supply costs, or overheads. It is economically impossible for competition to produce identical bids. Unless there has been a leak of a desired price by the user agency, market conditions will generate different prices.
- **Alternating bid patterns.** A rotation pattern in which one of the same group of suppliers is the low bidder strongly suggests collusion. In such a case, the record might show that, although the bids appeared to be competitive for each single procurement, the awards fell into a suspicious pattern. For example, the price range top to bottom over time is B-C-A, A-B-C, or C-B-A. Since every contract is different, at least in time, from every other, consistent rotations do not reflect real market conditions.
- **Rotating territorial or product bidding patterns.** Analyzing bids and awards can show that A only bids in Zone 1, B only bids in Zone 2, and C only bids in Zone 3. A map can be used to portray such patterns. Where A only bids on Product 1, B only bids on Product 2, and C only bids on Product 3, the pattern suggests a market allocation scheme.
- *No-bid* **responses from expected bidders.** Occasionally a supplier decides it

does not wish to sell to the government. A *no-bid* response from a single expected bidder may reflect one company's circumstances. Two or more *no-bids* are suspicious. Knowing who is likely to bid, who bid on the last solicitation, and who is absent from the current bid can also reveal a bid rotation scheme where the suppliers agree to rotate chances at winning contracts, reducing price competition.
- **Simultaneous price increases.** If every bidder's price goes up in a uniform way, that uniform increase is one indicator of price collusion. If the bids go up by the same amount as a percentage or amount over the last bids, the increase is very strongly suggestive of price collusion. There are times when the price of global products used by suppliers in their processes increases. An obvious example is gasoline price increases. Public procurement officers may expect some increase in prices, if gasoline is likely a large part of marginal costs. Under a truly competitive process without collusion, however, Company A's bid price in the face of rising gas prices will not reflect an identical increase to Company B's bid price, due to differences in efficiencies and other costs within the suppliers' enterprises. And, if the pool of competitors is large enough, there should be suppliers who will find efficiencies elsewhere, and not increase price at all.
- **Comments about price, territory, or product.** Public procurement officers talk to suppliers frequently since many also serve as contract managers. Supplier comments such as "the industry's prices are going up" or, "we are not allowed to bid on that product" or, "we no longer sell in this territory" are not to be taken lightly. Such comments show broad understandings among and between competitors that affect price or restrict output.
- **Manufacturer's retail prices.** If it appears from comments made or through bid analyses that multiple manufacturers are engaged in controlling resale prices at similar levels or are imposing simultaneous restrictions on discounts, this suggests a horizontal agreement among manufacturers. Since the government as the ultimate buyer is victimized by such conduct, these patterns are worth watching carefully.
- **Other suspicious patterns.** There are antitrust violations that can also be detected just by being alert. For example, public procurement officers should watch for sudden changes in the conditions of the bidding. If suppliers or contractors suddenly eliminate or cut back the period of warranty or the discount on the items installed or sold, a conspiracy may have prompted the action.

COOPERATION WITH ENFORCEMENT AUTHORITIES

Every public procurement office should have a relationship with an antitrust enforcement office. For state agencies, this is the state attorney general, who may have a designated antitrust unit or an assistant attorney general assigned to the procurement office.

Some state agencies have internal audit or investigative departments, such as an office of inspector general, that are charged with ferreting out waste, fraud, and abuse. Antitrust violations always result in waste, fraud, or abuse on some level. States also have auditor general departments that are in charge of looking for government waste and inefficiency.

Counties have district or county attorneys who may be charged with enforcing state antitrust laws since many of these are criminal laws. Counties may also have internal auditors. Municipalities have city attorneys who enforce local laws and ordinances. These officials may have the ability to prosecute fraud in procurement.

Public procurement officers are key witnesses in antitrust enforcement actions. Not only have they witnessed and documented anticompetitive conduct, but they have also seen the harm to their government and the taxpayers from a lack of competition.

One of the strongest deterrents against collusive bidding continues to be active cooperation between alert public procurement officers and a prosecutor's office. When prosecutors become involved in antitrust suits, they will need, as evidence, records of past bidding patterns and practices. Well-documented procurement files, including historical information, are essential. The prosecutors will expect to find the following in the procurement files and data:

- The pre-notice solicitation and specification documentation
- The specifications or scopes of work
- The public notice of the proposed procurement
- Lists of suppliers in the market, including prequalified suppliers
- Names, addresses, and the principal contact person of each bidder, along with commodities, services, or construction sold by suppliers who competed
- The actual bids or proposals, specifically including all prices, rates, and qualifications
- Names, addresses, principal contact person, prices, and qualifications of any subcontractors
- The selection process documentation, including who served on selection panels, when they met, evaluation sheets, and communications among and between them
- All correspondence and communication to and from the user agency and to and between bidders or proposers and subcontractors, especially including e-mails
- Any notes taken by the public procurement officer or memoranda reflecting concerns about an inadequate or unexpected response to the solicitation, or about suspicious bids or patterns
- Files concerning historical bid patterns and prior bids by the same suppliers
- Non-collusion affidavits—signed and notarized

The enforcement authority should have a voice in determining the number of years that procurement records are kept in order to provide the adequate historical data needed as evidence of collusion.

Communication with enforcement offices should be broader than simply reporting competition concerns. These officials should be included in periodic training sessions, where informal conversations can occur about competition issues. A casual conversation with a state assistant attorney general who is responsible for antitrust matters provides much needed guidance to public procurement officers, and can often allay fears by explaining that certain conduct has been determined to be procompetitive, either by the courts or by the United States DOJ or FTC guidelines.[9]

The National Association of Attorneys General publishes an antitrust report that summarizes each state antitrust case, its current status, and the final outcome.[10] The Antitrust Division of the United States DOJ also publishes statistical reports.[11] Enforcement offices may publish excerpts of successful cases, and they also often publish remarks by chief enforcement officials as to anticompetitive trends in the marketplace. Much of this material can be found online, as noted later in this text.

FEDERAL AND STATE ANTITRUST LAWS

This portion of the chapter contains an overview of federal and state laws that address anticompetitive economic behavior as well as the civil remedies and criminal penalties in place to enforce them. The discussion in the final paragraphs of this chapter provides context for the chapter's main theme, which is that public procurement officers play a critical role in the economy of the United States because of the volume that state and local governments consume.

Summary of Federal Antitrust Laws

There are three main federal laws that prosecutors use to protect customers. The FTC describes those laws as follows:

> Congress passed the first antitrust law, the Sherman Act, in 1890 as a "comprehensive charter of economic liberty aimed at preserving free and unfettered competition as the rule of trade." In 1914, Congress passed two additional antitrust laws: the Federal Trade Commission Act (FTC Act), which created the FTC, and the Clayton Act. With some revisions, these are the three core federal antitrust laws still in effect today.
>
> The antitrust laws proscribe unlawful mergers and business practices in general terms, leaving courts to decide which ones are illegal based on the facts of each case. Courts have applied the antitrust laws to changing markets from a time of horse and buggies to the present digital age. Yet for over 100 years, the antitrust laws have had the same basic objective: to protect the process of competition for the benefit of consumers, making sure there are strong incentives for businesses to operate efficiently, keep prices down, and keep quality up.[12]

Each is discussed in the remainder of this chapter. Table 3.1 is a snapshot of the laws' provisions.[13]

There is an abundance of information available online about these three key federal laws. Additionally, states have adopted their own versions of these laws, popularly called *mini* or little versions.[14]

The Sherman Act

The Sherman Antitrust Act has been the linchpin of antitrust law in the United States since Congress enacted it in 1890. The Sherman Act is enforced by the Antitrust Division of the United States DOJ. Criminal Sherman Act investigations are conducted by the Federal Bureau of Investigation. The Antitrust Division has jurisdiction whenever an antitrust crime affects interstate commerce. In today's markets, almost every transaction affects interstate trade.

Section One of the Sherman Act, 15 U.S.C. §1, states:

> Every contract, combination in the form of trust or otherwise, or conspiracy, in restraint of trade or commerce among the several States, or with foreign nations, is declared to be illegal. Every person who shall make any contract or engage in any combination or conspiracy hereby declared to be illegal shall be deemed guilty of a felony, and, on conviction thereof, shall be punished by fine not exceeding $100,000,000 if a corporation, or, if any other person, $1,000,000, or by imprisonment not exceeding 10 years, or by both said punishments, in the discretion of the court.

The felony provisions of Section One were enacted in 1974.

Section Two of the Sherman Act, 15 U.S.C. §2, makes interstate monopolies felonies:

> Every person who shall monopolize, or attempt to monopolize, or combine or conspire with any other person or persons, to monopolize any part of the trade or commerce among the several States, or with foreign nations, shall be deemed guilty of a felony . . .

Conduct that offends Section One of the Sherman Act involves conspiracies. This type of

Table 3.1 Federal Antitrust Laws Snapshot

The Sherman Act 15 United States Code (U.S.C.) §§1–7	• The Act: ◊ Outlaws "every contract, combination, or conspiracy in restraint of trade," and ◊ Outlaws any "monopolization, attempted monopolization, or conspiracy or combination to monopolize." • As interpreted by the United States Supreme Court, it only prohibits unreasonable restraints of trade. • Some acts are considered so harmful to competition that they are always illegal, such as arrangements between individuals or business to fix prices, divide markets, or rig bids. These acts are per se violations of the Act, that is, there is no defense or justification allowed for them. • Penalties are both civil and criminal. ◊ Criminal penalties are generally reserved to intentional and clear violations such as fixed prices or rigged bids. ◊ Criminal penalties may go as high as $100 million for a corporation and $1 million for an individual, along with 10 years in prison. ◊ The Act allows for fines to be increased under certain circumstances. • The United States Department of Justice enforces violations of this Act.
The Federal Trade Commission Act 15 U.S.C. §§41–58, as amended	• The Act ◊ Bans "unfair methods of competition," and ◊ Bans "unfair or deceptive acts or practices." • The United States Supreme Court has ruled that all violations of the Sherman Act also violate this Act. Thus, the United States Federal Trade Commission may institute cases under this Act against the same kinds of activities that violate the Sherman Act. • The Act also covers other practices that harm competition that do not specifically align with those in the Sherman Act. • Only the Federal Trade Commission brings cases under this Act.
The Clayton Act as amended by the Robins-Patman Act of 1936 and the Hart-Scott-Rodino Antitrust Improvements Act of 1976 15 U.S.C. §§12–27, 29 U.S.C. §§52–53	• The Act covers specific practices that the Sherman Act does not clearly prohibit. An example is the same person making business decisions for competing companies. • It prohibits mergers and acquisitions where the effect "may be substantially to lessen competition, or to tend to create a monopoly." • It also bans certain discriminatory prices, services, and other practices in dealings between merchants. • It requires companies planning larger mergers or acquisitions to notify the government of their plans in advance. • The United States Department of Justice enforces violations of this Act. • It authorizes state attorneys general, state and local governments, and private parties to sue for civil triple damages when they have been harmed by conduct that violates either the Sherman Act or the Clayton Act, and to obtain a court order prohibiting the anticompetitive practice in the future.

conduct is typically referred to as Section One conduct. Generally speaking, the Antitrust Division brings criminal Section One charges against private suppliers engaged in price fixing, territorial market allocations, or bid rigging.

No person or firm is beyond the reach of the literal language of the Sherman Act; and this includes procurement personnel. However, certain constitutional immunities have been implied by federal courts to limit the reach of the Sherman Act. (See the discussion under the *Immunities, Exemptions, Exceptions, and Defenses to Antitrust Laws* heading of this chapter.)

In interpreting the Sherman Act, the United States Supreme Court ruled in *Standard Oil Co. v. United States*, 221 U.S. 1 (1911) that although the statute's literal language prohibits every restraint of trade, only unreasonable restraints of trade may be prosecuted. This is because, while every exclusive contract excludes the unsuccessful competing suppliers from the contract through the selection process, every exclusive contract does not restrain trade.

Unreasonable restraints of trade under Section One have been held to include contracts, combinations, and conspiracies that, in fact, harm the whole of trade in a particular product and geographic market. Certain types of practices between horizontal competitors—that is, those suppliers who compete at the same level of trade, such as retail-to-retail or manufacturer-to-manufacturer—have been held to be so likely to cause harm to the relevant market that they are per se illegal.

If an agreement is per se illegal, then competitors who do nothing more than to enter into the conspiracy have violated Section One. Per se restraints are those that are illegal simply because they are shown to exist without any need for proof of any actual harm to competition.

Generally, only the following have been held to be per se unlawful:

- Price fixing
- Territorial market allocation
- Output restriction agreements
- Bid rigging
- Tying arrangements[15]

These per se offenses nearly always involve horizontal competitors only. Federal courts interpreting the Sherman Act held for many years that even vertical price fixing, where a manufacturer dictates to a wholesaler or retailer the price at which the latter must sell the commodities, was per se unlawful. However, in recent years the Supreme Court has reversed that holding.

In today's federal Section One law, only truly horizontal conspiracies with known pernicious market effects are held to be per se illegal. Thus, the type of government contract bid rigging deemed so pernicious as to be per se illegal is generally between and among bidders and would-be bidders. Only per se violations, and those solely in which there is criminal intent, warrant criminal prosecution.

The Clayton Act

Section 4 of the Clayton Act, 15 U.S.C. §15, is the central civil antitrust enforcement statute. The Clayton Act gives the United States Attorney General the right to bring a civil suit in federal court to enjoin antitrust violations, to break up unlawful monopolies, and to recover damages for the government. The Clayton Act gives state attorneys general the right to sue as *parens patriae*, that is, to sue in the name of the state, on behalf of its citizens harmed by anticompetitive activities.

The Clayton Act is used by the Antitrust Division of the United States DOJ to remedy violations of Sections One and Two of the Sherman Act. The Antitrust Division may seek to enjoin or stop a merger of two giant suppliers under Section Two on the grounds that the merger will create a monopoly. It may also seek to break up an existing monopoly that is deemed to be abusing its power. Historic cases against AT&T and Microsoft were brought via Section Two of the Sherman Act and the Clayton Act.

The Clayton Act gives state attorneys general, state and local governments, individuals, and private suppliers the right to sue antitrust violators and recover triple damages plus attorneys' fees. Such parties are considered private attorneys general, in that a private action enforces the Sherman Act as much as does a government prosecution.

However, federal courts have imposed many burdens and threshold requirements on private antitrust plaintiffs. Such parties must prove that they were, in fact, harmed by conduct that injures competition, meaning that the conduct caused harm to a relevant market. It is not enough that a party is excluded from some aspect of trade. State and local public entities have, on occasion, sued private parties for damages and attorneys' fees under the Clayton Act.

Most civil antitrust cases brought under the Clayton Act by the Antitrust Division, by state or local governments, or by private parties are per se, Section One-type cases. A government damaged by a bid-rigging conspiracy among construction contractors, for example, has a remedy in federal court under the Clayton Act.

Under Section 4 of the Clayton Act, the Antitrust Division, state attorneys general, state and local governments, and private parties may also prosecute noncriminal, non-per se cases where consumers are actually harmed under a doctrine developed by the United States Supreme Court called the rule of reason. Rule of reason cases require proof that a defined market is actually hurt by the practice challenged.

To define a market requires defining the product and the territory in which it is sold. A product market includes all of those commodities or services which consumers will generally buy, if another similar commodity or service is unavailable. A geographic market is the entire territory where the product market trades. Rule of reason cases require extensive evidence and are frequently difficult to prosecute.

State attorneys general often combine with other states to bring civil actions against antitrust violators that affect many states. State attorneys general combined to sue Microsoft, for example, after the Antitrust Division of the United States DOJ brought its civil case.

This practice, known as *multi-state* enforcement, has often been successfully used where the federal government wants one remedy, but the states want another. These cases are also often brought with claims under state antitrust laws appended to the Sherman Act claims. In national cases, private parties or consumer classes also may sue, leading to complex litigation.

Such multi-state claims are especially important where states are direct purchasers of nationally sold commodities. One example was *In re Refined Petroleum Products*, 906 F.2d 432 (9th Cir. 1990). Four states combined to sue major oil companies for retail gasoline price fixing on behalf of their government gasoline consumers. In that case, the state attorneys general sued on behalf of the individual citizen gasoline consumers as well.

The United States Supreme Court imposed an important barrier to cases brought by ultimate consumers claiming injury from price fixing in *Illinois Brick Co. et al. v. Illinois et al.*, 431 U.S. 720 (1977). The Supreme Court held that only the direct buyer from the price-fixer could claim damages. Thus, if manufacturers conspired to fix retail prices, the retail buyers could not sue the manufacturer unless they sued all suppliers in the line of distribution and proved that the illegal or fixed part of the price was in fact passed on to them.

After the *Illinois Brick* decision, the National Association of State Procurement Officials and

The Institute for Public Procurement (NIGP)[16] petitioned Congress to amend the law, but without success. Since then, many states have passed their own statutes granting indirect purchasers the right to claim antitrust damages from price-fixers.

These laws were upheld by the United States Supreme Court in *California et al. v. ARC America Corp. et al.*, 490 U.S. 93 (1989). At least one state has held that indirect purchasers may sue manufacturers for price fixing under state law, expressly rejecting the federal *Illinois Brick* doctrine. See *Bunker's Glass Co. v. Pilkington, PLC*, 75 P.3d 99 (Ariz. 2003).

For states that have not enacted such laws, state and local governments should include a standard clause in their general contract terms and conditions similar to the following:

> *The parties recognize that, in actual economic practice, overcharges resulting from antitrust violations are, in fact, borne by the ultimate purchaser. Therefore, the bidder/offeror hereby assigns to the [government] any and all claims for such overcharges.*

The Clayton Act also prohibits certain mergers and acquisitions and interlocking directorates between competing companies. Exclusive dealings and refusals to deal, the effect of which is to substantially lessen competition or to tend to create a monopoly, are also made illegal by the Clayton Act.

The Federal Trade Commission Act

Section 5 of the FTC Act, 15 U.S.C. §45, prohibits unfair methods of competition affecting commerce and unfair or deceptive practices affecting commerce. The FTC Act creates an administrative enforcement scheme under the jurisdiction of the United States FTC. Only the FTC can enforce the FTC Act by means of cease-and-desist orders and federal court injunctions. Private persons and state and local governments cannot sue under the FTC Act.

The FTC uses the law to stop mergers that may create monopolies, and has co-equal jurisdiction with the Antitrust Division of the United States DOJ in merger enforcement. The FTC also uses the act to stop practices that may not create actual economic monopolies and that do not involve Sherman Act conduct, but are nevertheless likely to injure competition and consumers in other ways.

Practices such as false advertising and marketing or contracting practices that abuse consumers fall under the FTC's jurisdiction, so long as the practice affects interstate commerce. The FTC's remedy is to enjoin or stop the practice and to recover government costs of enforcement only. The FTC Act does not authorize the FTC to seek damages.

The FTC often enlists the help of the state attorneys general in its enforcement actions. In an action under the FTC Act, states appear as *friends of the court*, urging federal courts to consider the harm suffered by the procurement offices of state and local governments as a result of unfair trade practices.

The Robinson-Patman Price Discrimination Act

The federal Robinson-Patman Anti-Price Discrimination Act, 15 U.S.C. §13 (Robinson-Patman Act), was enacted as part of the Clayton Act. The Robinson-Patman Act makes discrimination in price as between buyers at the same levels of trade and so-called tying arrangements unlawful. The Robinson-Patman Act affects transactions in interstate commerce. As part of the Clayton Act package, the Robinson-Patman Act can be enforced by the Antitrust Division of the United States DOJ, state attorneys general, and private parties.

The Robinson-Patman Act has had a convoluted history in federal courts. Its chief utility has been as a tool against so-called tying arrangements by defining this type of trade restraint. A tying arrangement occurs when a supplier having market power (equivalent to monopoly power) over one product forces buyers of the monopolized product to purchase another, less desirable product. One of the key allegations of the state attorneys general's case against Microsoft in the 1990s was that Microsoft forced buyers of its personal computer-market-dominating operating system to buy its Internet Explorer browser at a time when that product was less desirable than Netscape.

Federal Antitrust Guidelines

The United States DOJ and the FTC have issued a number of sets of guidelines to assist those concerned to understand the effect of antitrust law on proposed business relationships. These can be very helpful if a situation is covered by a guideline. Areas that the guidelines cover include cyber security, health care, intellectual property, and joint ventures.

The guidelines are sometimes heavy on economics, but in certain industries, such as health care, they have become the standard by which risk of antitrust prosecution can be both assessed and avoided. Additionally, the FTC website contains helpful information about the laws discussed in this chapter, along with other tools to assist in detecting anticompetitive activities.[17]

BUSINESS PRACTICES THAT UNREASONABLY RESTRAIN TRADE

The next few paragraphs discuss how courts apply the federal antitrust laws to business practices. They provide a window into how the laws are applied to the suppliers with which public procurement officers work.

Horizontal Restraints Affecting Price and Output

Clearly, any conduct that constitutes a Section One per se antitrust offense under the Sherman Act restrains trade, and there is little debate that horizontal agreements among competitors that affect price and output restrain trade. Even though federal cases have severely narrowed the reach of the per se antitrust doctrine, the following conduct is likely to be deemed to restrain trade without much evidence beyond the agreement itself:

- **Price fixing conspiracies**—horizontal agreements among competing suppliers affecting any aspect of price. These are per se unlawful. *United States v. Trenton Potteries Co.*, 273 U.S. 392 (1927). Price fixing includes, but is not limited to, agreements to set common prices, discounts, trade-in allowances, and price floors or ceilings. Even agreements to set cap prices for the express purpose of benefiting consumers, if they are between horizontal competitors, are per se illegal. *Arizona v. Maricopa County Medical Society*, 457 U.S. 332 (1982).
- **Bid rigging**—horizontal agreements among competing suppliers to submit rigged bids. These are a species of price fixing, because the purpose of the conspiracy is to prevent the price competition that bidding usually involves. *United States v. Gosselin World Wide Moving N.V.*, 411 F. 3d 502 (4th Cir. 2005), *cert. denied*, 126 S. Ct. 1464 (2006). Less frequent are horizontal agreements to rig procurements based on quality or experience, not price. These often involve certain competitors agreeing not to propose on the procurement. Such agreements are no less per se illegal, since they are a form of sham competition. *United States v. Reicher*, 983 F. 2d 168 (10th Cir. 1992).
- **Group boycotts**—horizontal agreements among competing suppliers to refuse to deal with another horizontal competitor.

FTC v. Superior Ct. Trial Lawyers Association, 493 U.S. 411 (1990).
- **Territorial or customer market allocation conspiracies**—horizontal agreements among competing suppliers to not trade in each other's territories, nor sell to competitors' customers.
- **Output restriction conspiracies**—horizontal agreements among competing suppliers to restrict supply of a product to a market, or not to compete in a market. *General Leaseways v. National Truck Leasing Association*, 744 F.2d 588 (7th Cir. 1984). This type of conspiracy can be a form of bid rigging, where the agreement is that certain competitors, but not others, will propose on a procurement.
- **Customer allocation conspiracies**—horizontal agreements among competing suppliers not to sell to the other's customer, or to limit what products are sold to whom. These are a form of output restriction conspiracy. *Blue Cross & Blue Shield United v. Marshfield Clinic*, 65 F.3d 1406 (7th Cir. 1995).

Other Horizontal Restraints

Any combination of horizontal competitors raises antitrust risk, unless it is necessary to deliver a product to a market, such as a joint venture. Horizontal arrangements among conspirators should be viewed as presenting high antitrust risk.[18]

Vertical Restraints

Vertical, or buy-sell relationships, are nearly universally allowed unless they actually harm markets under a *rule of reason* economic analysis. The exception is where horizontal competitors conspire to induce a seller or a buyer in a market to refuse to deal with a competitor. When the supplier or buyer refuses to deal with the victim of such a conspiracy, the vertical nature of his relationship to the horizontal conspirators may not provide much of a defense. *United States v. General Motors Corp.*, 384 U.S. 127 (1966).

STATE ANTITRUST LAWS

State Constitutions

The first level of law for states is their constitutions; for home-rule municipalities and counties, it is their enabling charter. Some states have language that protects competition built into their constitutions.

For example, a state constitution might provide that "monopolies and trusts shall never be allowed." It may also state that "no persons shall directly or indirectly combine or make any contract, . . . to fix the prices, limit the production, or regulate the transportation of any product or commodity."

Legislation creating governments—for example, counties or municipalities—may have procompetition or procurement ethics provisions built into the enabling legislation. Such legislation or charters operate as the constitution of that government. Statutes granting powers to cities, counties, and agencies may proscribe anticompetitive conduct. Even city charters may have language prohibiting the expenditure of public funds other than via a competitive process.

State *Little-Sherman* and *Mini-Clayton* Acts

Most states have adopted their own antitrust statutes that apply to trade within that state. In practice, these statutes are typically called little-Sherman Acts because the language of the state statute parrots the federal Sherman Act's Sections One and Two. Typical language of a state little-Sherman Act forbids "contracts, combinations, and conspiracies in restraint of trade or commerce, any part of which is within the state" along with "the establishment or use of monopolies and attempts to monopolize."

Most little-Sherman acts contain a mini-Clayton Act, which gives both the state attorneys general, and often district or county attorneys as well, the authority to prosecute antitrust violations in the name of the state and on behalf of consumers within the state. These public prosecutors are often empowered to seek injunctions and damages where state and local public entities have been economically harmed. These Mini-Clayton Acts also give private parties and governments the right to sue for antitrust damages and attorneys' fees.

State statutes are not always identical to the Sherman and Clayton Acts, however. Not all state little-Sherman Acts make antitrust violations criminal. Some states have enacted special statutes that make only certain types of antitrust violations criminal. Only the state attorneys general or county prosecutors may enforce these criminal provisions.

Some state statutes provide for automatic triple damages, while others require special proof, such as proof of specific intent or knowledge or proof that the trade restraint is extreme, egregious, or flagrant. These latter conditions have been construed by some state courts to mean that only conduct that is per se illegal under the federal Sherman Act is serious enough to justify the penalty of triple damages.

While some little-Sherman Act statutory schemes contain provisions that require state courts to apply federal antitrust case law in interpreting the state's antitrust statutes, other state schemes leave this decision up to the discretion of state judges. In some states, the courts may apply federal precedent, but are not required to do so. This has led to sharp departures from federal antitrust precedent. An example is the Arizona Supreme Court's decision not to apply the *Illinois Brick* indirect purchaser bar on consumer antitrust cases based on price-fixing claims, which was mentioned earlier in this text.

Most state antitrust statutes also empower prosecutors to conduct civil investigations of possible antitrust violations. Attorneys general and sometimes county prosecutors are often authorized to issue civil investigative demands or subpoenas seeking testimony and documents from suppliers.

In some states, the attorney general may investigate (or has investigated) agencies of the state or local governments when they suspect government officials are personally involved in unlawful trade restraints. This practice is fairly rare. But at least one state Supreme Court has held that even though a state attorney general represents that state's agencies and departments, he or she may investigate and even prosecute that agency or department recognizing that, although such action is a conflict of interest, the special role of attorney general as the chief law enforcement officer for the people of the state allows this sort of investigation.

For state and local government, the most important aspect of state antitrust statutes may be that their agencies have rights as victims of an antitrust offense. When procurement professionals suspect antitrust violations resulting in higher prices, fewer bidders, or lower quality commodities, they should have procedures in place to communicate these suspicions so that the attorney general may take rapid remedial action.

If the state or local government has been damaged, state antitrust laws provide remedies to recover the funds the agency has overpaid as a consequence. The attorney general can also recover his or her in-house or outsourced attorneys' fees in such a case, all of which inures to the benefit of the taxpayers. In the event of a criminal conspiracy of suppliers, an attorney general's criminal investigation and prosecution can open up rigged markets and liberate agencies from the loss of competition.

State and Local Procurement Codes

Procurement codes are a type of competition law, along with the actual antitrust laws described previously. Chapter 2 (*Procurement Leadership, Organization, and Value*) describes those types of statutes.

Conflict of Interest Statutes

Ethics laws, particularly those defining conflicts of interest and penalties, are another type of competition law. Chapter 15 (*Procurement Program Integrity and Credibility*) discusses these in detail.

Other State Competition Statutes

Many states have criminal laws that specifically prohibit bid rigging. Other special statutes often prohibit any contract, combination, or conspiracy to restrain trade in connection with a government contract, most often a government construction contract. These statutes exist because bid rigging is, unfortunately, common in government construction procurement. Sadly, at any given time somewhere in the United States, there is likely a bid-rigging conspiracy taking place in connection with public works construction.

The sordid history of public construction bid rigging also involves many cases in which organized crime enterprises have been involved. For this reason, the United States Code and many state Racketeer Influenced and Corrupt Organization statutes make bid rigging a foundational offense to a racketeering crime. This is because a bid-rigging conspiracy can be an enterprise, with separate companies acting together to rig the bid.

Most states have a number of other criminal statutes that apply to competition offenses. Bid rigging is often prosecuted by means of fraudulent scheme criminal statutes, which make it a felony to utilize an artifice or scheme to defraud any person, including a government. Fraudulent scheme enforcement does not require proof of all of the elements of an antitrust offense and applies to unilateral action where there is no conspiracy.

There are often state statutes outside the antitrust and procurement laws that affect competition in public procurement. For instance, an exemption of a type of commodity from a procurement law requiring competition may not be in the *exemptions* section of that law, but instead is buried elsewhere in a government's law.

Public procurement officers cannot assume that there is only one law or set of laws that applies to public procurement. Nor can they assume that state legislatures or city councils will be careful to enact laws that do not conflict with one another. Therefore, it is essential that public procurement personnel be trained in the statutes that apply to them and that there be an open door to appropriate lawyers in the user agency or in the state's attorney general's office to have their questions answered.

PROCUREMENT CASE LAW

Typical procurement professionals have little time to peruse the procurement decisions of their state or federal courts. Yet there are many situations in which the rules of the game are found nowhere else. Case law that is announced through decisions of judges is just as much a part of the law regulating a public official's behavior as is an actual statute, ordinance, or rule/regulation.

For example, a 2005 federal Court of Appeals decision declared statutes granting preferences based on race, sex, or national origin are unconstitutional. *Western States Paving Co., Inc. v. Washington State Department of Transportation et al.*, 407 F. 3d 983 (9th Cir. 2005). The Ninth Circuit Court ruled that unless a state agency can prove that it has, in the past, actually discriminated against the specific ethnic minority or gender being granted the preference, the preference amounts to unequal protection of the law. This case has been followed elsewhere and has caused consternation among public entities accustomed to granting preferences to businesses owned by minorities and women.

Federal court cases interpreting federal laws and regulations are often adopted by state

CHAPTER 3: **THE IMPORTANCE OF COMPETITION**

courts enunciating new (for that state) principles governing public procurement and contract law. Cases that involve similar facts are often highly persuasive to a court or administrative law judge.

Getting Help

Public procurement officers should be deeply versed in the procurement law that applies to their government and should also be generally familiar with the other competition laws that apply to their procurement transactions. Not even experienced antitrust and competition lawyers know it all, so the best course of action for public procurement officers is to keep it firmly in mind that all competition law and policy has as its sole purpose to obtain, promote, enhance, and use the power of strong competition in government procurement.

Where there is no specific statute or rule to answer the question, research and access to legal advisors is the next step. In today's Internet world, it is relatively easy to research procurement codes and rules being used with success by other similar governments. There are also trade associations who publish government contracting developments online, such as builders' associations and professional societies. In every case, the effort made to understand competition law and policy will serve procurement professionals well.

IMMUNITIES, EXEMPTIONS, EXCEPTIONS, AND DEFENSES TO ANTITRUST LAWS

There are legal defenses and immunities that affect the scope of antitrust laws. They are described briefly here to offer some perspective to the public procurement officer about the scope of liability, both to suppliers doing business with the government and to the officers themselves.

Unilateral Action

Offenses subject to Section One of the Sherman Act require a conspiracy. Thus, a supplier or government acting alone does not violate Section One. Section Two offenses require a single actor, but that actor must have market power or monopoly power.

Antitrust scholars and economists recognize that a large buyer can exert market power, which is defined as the ability to control price outside the laws of supply and demand. A buyer monopoly is called a monopsony. Some argue that social programs (for example, Medicaid) are government monopsonies that unfairly control price. Government programs that meet the United States Supreme Court's tests for state action immunity, however, cannot be successfully sued. See the discussion under the heading *State Action Antitrust Immunity* later in this chapter. Thus, unilateral action by the government, despite its strong effect on markets, is almost never prosecuted.

Vertical Buy-Sell Transactions

Buyer-seller transactions are considered vertical relationships. Even if the nature of the government-supplier contract relationship restrains trade—for example, in that it forecloses new competitors from a large segment of a market—this relationship is considered a vertical restraint and generally will be evaluated under the rule of reason, as explained previously.

Such vertical relationships are very rarely challenged due to the cost and difficulty of proving market harm. Some states have special statutes, however, that make certain vertical arrangements, such as buyer-seller conspiracies to rig public construction bids, per se unlawful. Even so, prosecution and civil litigation against government buy-sell arrangements is extremely rare, and even an overt conspiracy between a supplier and a public official to rig bids may be entitled to immunity. See the discussion under the heading *First Amendment Antitrust Immunity* later in this chapter.

Lack of Knowledge or Intent

The fact that the person accused had no knowledge of the scheme may be used as a defense to a Section One claim under the Sherman Act. To prove the existence of a conspiracy, each person must have a unity of purpose with at least one of the other conspirators.

A procurement official who participates unknowingly in some aspect of a rigged bid is not liable. However, whether the public procurement officer knew or did not know can be subject to conflicting evidence. Practicing good procurement ethics and integrity—as set forth previously in this chapter and in Chapter 15 (*Procurement Program Integrity and Credibility*)—protects procurement personnel from the appearance of collusion.

Statutory Protections

Some state statutes expressly grant immunity to public employees who are just doing their required jobs. These statutes are reassuring, but usually only cover official action. Thus, if a public procurement officer socializes publicly with suppliers, and in the course of an off-site party cuts a deal, that conduct may not be considered official action. Again, public procurement officers do well to practice complete independence from suppliers who compete for the taxpayers' dollars.

State Action Antitrust Immunity

In 1943 the United States Supreme Court recognized that the actions of a sovereign state are not subject to liability under the Sherman Act and other federal antitrust laws. In *Parker v. Brown*, 317 U.S. 341 (1943), the high court reasoned that principles of federalism prohibit the federal government from holding states and their agents who act in their official capacities liable for antitrust violations. See also *City of Columbia v. Omni Outdoor Advertising*, 499 U.S. 365 (1991).

In a now-famous case, the Supreme Court set forth a two-part test to be used by federal courts faced with state claims of sovereign immunity. *California Retail Liquor Dealers Assn. v. Midcal Aluminum, Inc.*, 445 U.S. 97 (1980) (*Midcal*) held that the state is immune if:

1. The enabling state statutes clearly articulate a legislative intent to displace competition; and
2. The legislative scheme results in active supervision of the conduct being challenged.

This so-called *two-pronged test* has been black-letter federal antitrust law since the case was decided.

The first prong of the state action test is met where the statute declares that the state, and only the state, can trade in a market. An example is a pricing board established to set prices for agricultural commodities, where the clear legislative policy is that the government, not competition, will set prices.

Proving clear legislative policy is not sufficient. In addition to the policy to displace competition, the statutory scheme must provide for active supervision of the trade. In the agricultural commodity example, the legislature must create a state entity or oversight panel whose job it is to oversee the setting of prices.

If a statutory scheme leaves the actual price setting to a panel of private traders, it will not qualify for state action. Closer cases involve oversight panels that are staffed partly by public employees and partly by industry representatives. Such hybrid oversight has, in the past, bred litigation by those who wish to price their products in the open market.

State action immunity applies only to actions of the state and at least historically has not been deemed by federal courts to immunize anticompetitive conduct by counties, cities, towns, or other public and semipublic entities. *Community Communications, Co. v. City of Boulder*, 455 U.S. 40 (1982); *Lafayette v. Louisiana Power & Light*, 435 U.S. 389 (1978).

Because of the threat of triple damage awards against local treasuries, Congress enacted the Local Government Antitrust Act of 1984, 15 United States Code §§34–36, which immunizes local governments, special districts, and school districts from antitrust damage awards. These entities can still be subjected to suits seeking injunctions.

Immunities Related to Partnering

The common practice of partnering can raise antitrust issues. Partnering is a popular term and generally means that the government joins with industry representatives to conduct some aspect of trade. Assuming there is no true collusion or bid rigging, partnering can be an efficient and cost-effective method of providing needed commodities and services. The procurement professional is wise, however, to become educated about whether the program displaces competition; and if so, whether it meets the *Midcal* two-pronged test for state action immunity.

Partnering with a single supplier would be a vertical relationship, adjudged under the rule of reason, and only unlawful if trade is, in fact, restrained—that is, if consumers are harmed because price or output competition is diminished. Partnering that involves the government and associations of suppliers who otherwise compete directly with each other poses a larger risk.

Partnering with suppliers who collectively urge the public procurement officer to refuse to deal with another competitor of theirs raises considerable risk, because it involves collusion among horizontal competitors and can be a group boycott.[19]

Outsourcing is not necessarily anticompetitive, but any time the government selects a single supplier to supply all the commodities or services in a market, the practice can restrain trade. Whether such conduct would be immune depends on many facts and, without proper legislative authority, can lead to antitrust challenges.

First Amendment Antitrust Immunity—Noerr-Pennington

In the case of *Eastern Railroad Presidents' Conference v. Noerr Motor Freight Co.*, 365 U.S. 127 (1961), the United States Supreme Court held that the Sherman Act does not prohibit two or more persons from associating together in an attempt to persuade a legislature or the governmental executive to take a particular action with respect to a law that would produce a restraint or monopoly. There are First Amendment overtones to the decision and the court indicated that it would be a stretch to think that Congress, in passing the Sherman Act, intended to circumscribe those constitutional rights.

This type of immunity, called Noerr-Pennington immunity, has been successfully used to defend private parties accused of egregious conduct—even bribery of public officials. Because of this doctrine, prosecutors rarely use the Sherman Act to criminally charge public officials who have entered into an illegal *quid pro quo* with a supplier. See *City of Columbia v. Omni Outdoor Advertising*, 499 U.S. 365 (1991).

There are exceptions to Noerr-Pennington immunity. One is the sham exception, where individuals in a government process are used by a supplier as competitive weapons against a horizontal competitor. Another exception is where the competitor supplies false information to the government.

Improper influence of a public procurement officer can be, and usually is, still criminal under criminal statutes covering bribery of a public official or a fraudulent scheme. The Noerr-Pennington doctrine provides little help in a bribery prosecution.

State conflict of interest statutes often exist, and in many states these statutes expressly give private parties the right to sue a public official or employee for damages. These statutes apply where a public procurement officer acts in his or her own economic self-interest and not in the interest of the government or the taxpayer.

Statutory Exemptions and Exceptions

The United States Code and most state statute books are full of special situations that are exempt from competition laws, particularly the Sherman, Clayton, and Robinson-Patman Acts. Among the exemptions are agricultural cooperatives and the labor of a human being, in part because these are often wholly regulated by the federal or state government.

A dramatic exemption from the operation of the Sherman Act is called the McCarran-Ferguson Act. (15 U.S.C. §§1011–15.) This act allows insurance companies to share risk and to price their products jointly. Because this act is a federal statute on par with the Sherman Act, Congress has the power to make this broad exemption. What looks like permission for anticompetitive conduct has been of concern to many government insurance buyers as they watch insurance prices rise and coverage diminish.

The government is not without a remedy if the insurance industry goes too far, however. In the 1990s, state attorneys general and the FTC successfully challenged the insurance industry's collusive withdrawal of pollution insurance products from the market. The McCarran-Ferguson Act does not immunize a restriction conspiracy among insurance providers.

Regulated Industries

Generally, industries that are regulated by the government are not subject to antitrust and competition laws. These typically include communications, common carriers, electric power, and certain financial networks. Where not specifically exempted, the extent of a state's regulation usually must be at least enough to qualify for the state action immunity defense.

Questions can arise when regulation is incomplete. For example, competing ambulance providers may be immune from setting identical prices where a state department of health regulates those prices. But they may not be immune if they conspire not to compete in fixed territories, if the state does not regulate that aspect of their business.

Of course, improper conduct by regulating public officials can still be subject to criminal prosecution and conflict of interest claims.

CONCLUSION

Public procurement officers are the first line of defense against antitrust violations and anticompetitive conduct. Their invaluable role is often more important than that of the user agency executive or prosecutor. The public procurement officer can best serve the state and national policy of maximizing competition in public procurement by:

- Becoming informed about competition law
- Understanding market conditions for every procurement
- Avoiding specifications that reduce competition
- Being aware of anticompetitive patterns, responses, and communications
- Developing a good working relationship with antitrust enforcers
- Remaining an arm's length from every supplier
- Practicing procurement ethics
- Reporting concerns to prosecutors
- Documenting everything

ENDNOTES

1. A copy of the Model Procurement Code is available at: http://apps.americanbar.org/dch/committee.cfm?com=PC500500
2. See the Model Procurement Code Section 1-101(2) (e) and (g).
3. https://www.merriam-webster.com/dictionary/antitrust
4. https://www.merriam-webster.com/legal/restraint%20of%20trade
5. See Chapter 8 (*Noncompetitive and Limited Competition Procurements*).
6. Chapter 4 (*Strategies and Plans*) addresses bidder preference laws.
7. For information about design-build contracting, see Chapter 11 (*Procurement of Construction and Related Services*).
8. See Chapter 5 (*Non-construction Specifications and Scopes of Work*).
9. https://www.justice.gov/atr/guidelines-and-policy-statements-0 and https://www.ftc.gov/tips-advice/competition-guidance/guide-antitrust-laws
10. http://www.naag.org/naag/committees/naag_standing_committees/antitrust-committee.php
11. See Endnote 9.
12. See Endnote 9.
13. See Endnote 9.
14. See *Consumer Protection in the States: A 50-State Report on Unfair and Deceptive Acts and Practices Statutes*, Carolyn L. Carter, National Consumer Law Center, Inc. (February 2009), http://www.nclc.org/images/pdf/udap/report_50_states.pdf
15. A tying arrangement is an agreement between a seller and a buyer under which the seller agrees to sell a product or service (the tying product) to the buyer only on the condition that the buyer also purchases a different (or tied) product from the seller or the buyer agrees not to purchase the tied product from any other seller. Tying arrangements can be used to tie together not only different products but also services, leases, franchises, licenses to intellectual property, or combinations of any of those things.
16. The Institute was formerly called the National Institute for Governmental Purchasing.
17. The web addresses for this information are noted in Endnote 9.
18. See the United States DOJ and the FTC documents referenced at Endnote 9.
19. See the documents noted in Endnote 9.

CHAPTER 4: STRATEGIES AND PLANS

RECOMMENDED BEST PRACTICES

- The procurement office must foster a relationship with user agencies that ensures that those agencies will elect to have procurement professionals involved with them early in the procurement planning process. This requires, in part, that the procurement office adopt a policy of keeping an eye on the *big picture* rather than solely on daily business. It also requires that the public procurement officer engage in continual outreach to those agencies and devise effective means for collecting user agency needs information and expenditure data.
- The procurement office must plan for its workload in a manner that permits regular prioritizing and reprioritizing of work; that assigns work based on the needs of the procurement, as well as on the training and experience of the public procurement officer; and that benchmarks performance through measurements, such as processing times and customer satisfaction.
- The procurement office should have an emergency preparedness plan that permits access to its contract information even when its staff does not have access to the office.
- The procurement office should budget for supporting staff access to current market information, such as subscriptions to online market research tools and attendance at trade shows.
- Public procurement officers must be encouraged to think strategically about each procurement and ensure that they have the right tools and data to make strategic decisions.

Government is confronted with the challenge of meeting the needs of a changing social and economic environment. Planning and strategic thinking allow for the introduction of improved practices necessary to meet these challenges. Chapter 2 (*Procurement Leadership, Organization, and Value*) demonstrates the importance of placing procurement leadership at the executive level to meet those needs.

At the public procurement officer level, planning and strategizing better ensures that the procurement process is seamless in implementing critical short-term and long-term government program goals. A public procurement officer should not work without a *map* or in isolation. This chapter discusses some of the activities that should be routine in a high-performing public procurement office.

Plans for emergency preparedness are not covered in this chapter. Chapter 18 (*Emergency Preparedness*) addresses that topic.

PLANNING WITH USERS AND USER AGENCIES

Many decisions that state and local governments make touch in some way on the procurement process. As previously noted, Chapter 2 of this *Practical Guide* advocates that the best procurement structure is one in which there is a strategic leader—a Chief Procurement Officer—who, among other things, participates in the executive planning process.

Similarly, it is essential that the public procurement officer be invited into the early stages of a user agency's specific program planning where that program will require the support of a contract. In turn, the public procurement officer, as part of his or her plan for a specific procurement, must initiate a collaborative and team-focused approach with user agencies and users. A public procurement officer should not be passive.

A well-informed public procurement officer can play a vital role in the planning for a complex new technology, for example. That officer must think in terms of the long view, be a problem solver, and innovate, perhaps formulating a new way of conducting a competitive procurement. His or her professional knowledge of the process provides critical information to the user agency about the source selection methods available and how flexible they may be, market conditions, and a range of other considerations.

In the example of the new technology mentioned earlier, the public procurement officer may be able to offer a modular procurement approach. NASPO's website contains a paper on modular procurement along with a description of the steps used in this process.[1] It defines the method as follows:

> The term "modular procurement" encompasses several different specific strategies for the practice of breaking up large and complex procurements into small, "tightly-scoped projects to implement technology systems in successive, interoperable increments." [Footnote omitted.] Modular procurement methods certainly do segment risks and increase transparency, but can go even further to also result in better solutions, faster delivery, and happier customers.

On the other hand, the public procurement officer is not in a position to know precisely how the user agency will utilize the commodity or service. Because the officer is not sitting in the user's seat, he or she will not understand in detail the user agency program that the commodity or service will support. The knowledge that the user agency and the users provide about the program is a key ingredient for success. Public procurement officers must reach out regularly to user agencies and users in order to develop a solid working relationship and a good means of exchanging expertise and knowledge.

The principle of collaboration early in the process applies to more than major purchases. Cooperation improves the effectiveness of any procurement, regardless of size, by providing valuable information and insights. It helps the procurement office plan its operations around the users' needs.

Forging a good relationship with users and user agencies is a key role a public procurement professional must play. A NASPO webinar entitled *Best Practices in Agency Relations and Communications* offers some suggestions for establishing such interactions.[2] Because of the important aspect of these relationships to a public procurement officer's job, a public procurement office should provide training as part of its orientation for new staff on relationship building. Additionally, employee's success in this area should be measured as part of that employee's performance evaluation.

PROCUREMENT OFFICE PLANNING

It is perhaps stating the obvious to assert that a well-run public procurement office should have a plan that sets both operational and strategic goals and objectives. If any organization does not have a *map* to direct it to its ultimate goal, there is a good chance that it will not reach that goal.

The plan must be set forth in a document that demonstrates how the procurement office will accomplish its short- and long-term goals and objectives. These must be tied to its vision and mission. It must include activities that impel both the office and its public procurement officers to be more effective. Finally, the plan must describe the methods that will be used to measure whether the plan is effective and whether employees in the procurement office are following it.

A procurement office does not have complete control over its workload. The policy directions of a state or local government, particularly after an election, will change. In turn, the procurement office's priorities may change as well, since that office serves users and user agencies affected by the policy change. Thus, the plan must be flexible and should be reviewed regularly.

Note that every public procurement office must have an emergency preparedness plan in place to define the actions to be taken during sudden crises and to assign the appropriate staff to carry them out. The best practice is for the public procurement office to craft an emergency preparedness plan separate from their overall plan. Chapter 18 (*Emergency Preparedness*) addresses the important issue of the role that a public procurement office plays in crisis situations and in planning for them.

Developing a plan requires information and data. A NASPO document entitled *Critical Success Areas and Key Performance Indicators for State Central Procurement Offices* is a useful resource for the types of data and information that should be collected. It identifies key procurement performance indicators, many of which should be universal for all public procurement offices.[3]

Once the procurement office identifies the information and data that it needs, it will need to track them. With the increasing use of eProcurement systems, tracking some types of data has become much easier than it would have been a decade ago. Chapter 19 (*eProcurement*) discusses eProcurement systems in more detail.

Tracking should also include feedback from a broad array of public personnel outside of the procurement office at all levels of employment, as well as suppliers. They can provide critical perceptions of or experience with the procurement office. It is recommended that these surveys be anonymous, to encourage forthright answers.

Data which shows that a certain procurement is taking too long may indicate that the workload of the public procurement officer assigned to that purchase is too heavy, or that the officer is struggling with the purchase and may not have the necessary expertise. Long turnaround times for procurements among several public procurement officers may mean that the office itself is struggling under the workload.

Data showing an increase in user complaints may indicate that there are personnel issues or that the office is lacking expertise in an area that a user agency requires.

Compliments from user agencies are just as important and should be tracked. Such kudos provide valuable information to the procurement office managers about the effectiveness of their procedures. Good performance should be reported, marketed, and publicly available to demonstrate the effectiveness of the public procurement office.

The development of a plan for a procurement office is critical in order to ensure that those in the public procurement office—managers, public procurement officers, and support staff—are all working toward common goals and objectives. Plans are the foundation of high-quality procurement and assure that a procurement office is offering superior service to the user agencies and users.

RESEARCH AND OTHER PRE-SOLICITATION GROUNDWORK

A key aspect of planning is research. A public procurement officer, if acting professionally, should not be a passive recipient of the information that a user agency provides to him or her for a particular procurement. That officer has an obligation to arm himself or herself with all available data relating to the needs of a user agency.

As discussed earlier, some relevant data should be available through an eProcurement system. Other data is available outside of the public entity, such as descriptions of new models of a piece of equipment on the market. Many procurements will require numerous sources of data.

Public procurement officers must be problem solvers and investigate data sources on their own initiative. Examples of some of the types of data that are critical to know are user agency buying patterns, current and future market conditions for the commodity or service, past performance information about contractors under prior contracts, and past performance of the same or similar commodities or services.

Methods of Collecting Internal Data

There are two broad categories of purchases for which a public procurement officer must plan: those that are somewhat predictable because they recur, and those that respond to a user agency's new or changing needs.

For recurring types of procurements, access to comprehensive expenditure data is essential in planning. A single set of dollar figures for a public entity's purchases, broken down by commodity and service type, with further details available such as makes and models, could lead to a consolidation of user agencies' purchases. That, in turn, would allow the public procurement officer to achieve pricing on larger quantities of a commodity or service, perhaps lowering costs.

The availability of that data is key to the successful implementation of a sustainable procurement program because it allows for the identification of commodities and services to target for that program. Chapter 6 (*Sustainable Procurement Considerations and Strategies*) discusses these types of programs in more detail.

There have been great strides made in recent years toward reaching this goal, but it is a work in progress. Without this data, the public procurement officer must be creative and find alternative sources of information.

For non-recurring types of purchases, a public procurement officer must use ingenuity to try to predict the future requirements of user agencies and users. One approach is for the public procurement officer to survey key contacts in user agencies regularly, asking them to identify what they will need, the quantities they expect to order, and the times they will need them.

Another approach is to engage a panel of users from a broad array of user agencies to meet regularly in order to discuss problems, solutions, and forecasts. The panel may consist of user advisors that a public procurement officer brings together to provide input for procurements of specific types of commodities or services. A public procurement officer may also convene a contract oversight group to assist with the management of large and important contracts, such as health insurance or office supplies. This type of collaboration allows a public procurement officer, based on user ideas and knowledge, to be innovative and to discover new or different ways to conduct future procurements well in advance of the time that the user agencies need them.

Budget data is another source of internal information that may be helpful. However, most state or local government purchases are funded out of their regular budgets, and the budget that the legislative funding body—a state legislature or a city council—approves for a user agency will not generally identify specific items to be purchased.

The exceptions to this are capital (or high-dollar) procurements such as large construction projects or complex technology systems. Legislative funding bodies specifically appropriate funds for those. Such appropriations are based on the estimated cost of the procurement. That means that a significant amount of planning for the procurement must occur before the user agency requests the funds. The public procurement officer should be part of the team that develops the plan well before a budget item goes to the appropriating body, such as the legislature or city council.

Legislative and gubernatorial-announced programs are also a source of information for a public procurement officer. A legislative appropriation and authorization to buy drones or body cameras is one example. An explicit statement by an executive government official about implementing a new initiative or technology should spur the public procurement officer to begin evaluating the market and preparing for the future.

There is no single best way for public procurement officers to ensure that they obtain the best information. In fact, the collection of internal data for planning purposes should be part of a broader outreach effort by a procurement office to its user agencies and users. If there is good communication between that office and the user before, during, and after the procurement, obtaining data about the user's needs should evolve as part of that communication.

Methods of Collecting External Data

It is easier than it has ever been for a public procurement officer to locate useful sources of external data and carry out market research through the Internet and its search engines. The time saved by having that information at the officer's fingertips means that there is no excuse for not conducting a thorough review of available resources.

Among the resources available are studies, papers, and publications of organizations of public officials. For instance, the website for the National Association of State Chief Information Officers offers a wealth of research, studies, and position papers, some developed with NASPO, about the procurement of information technology.[4]

Subscriptions to online and print publications are also critical to ensure that a public procurement officer remains current. A best practice is to set aside a dollar amount in the procurement office budget that permits its public procurement officers to have access to information about industry innovations and future products and services.

Industry trade shows are another excellent source of information, particularly concerning technology. While budgets are often scarce for travel, trade shows allow a public procurement officer to obtain information on a wide range of suppliers' commodities in a neutral setting, that is, without becoming *too close* to suppliers.

The public procurement officer should also seek information directly from suppliers. Online survey tools can provide a simple and effective method of obtaining that information in a way in which suppliers may remain anonymous.

Even more data can be obtained through the issuance of a request for information to suppliers. This is a solicitation used solely to seek supplier information and ideas. There is no contract awarded. The drawback with this approach is that, unless the open records/freedom of information laws within a state allow the public procurement officer to keep that supplier-provided information confidential, this tool may have only limited utility. Suppliers will not provide their best information in this setting if they believe that their competitors may be able to gain access to it.

There are many other external sources of information, and some require membership or other fees. It is important for there to be a commitment by the managers of a public procurement office to obtain the best external data that the budget will bear.

DEVISING PROCUREMENT STRATEGIES

As soon as the user agency requests the public procurement officer's assistance—ideally, early in the procurement planning process—that officer must think strategically and innovatively.

Public procurement officers should consider issues such as the information that they will require in order to write the solicitation, the procurement method that will be used to conduct the competition, the most appropriate method to evaluate the bids or proposals, the type of contract to be used, and negotiation strategies.

The public procurement officer must consider not only the commodity or service being purchased, but also contract terms, payment and performance measures, and risk management. In short, they must consider the entire process. The next paragraphs discuss a few of the strategies that a public procurement officer should contemplate implementing.

Cost Savings

One of the most obvious roles of public procurement professionals is to determine how best to save their state or local government money, either through obtaining the best value/price of a commodity or service or through cost avoidance.

A poorly devised procurement raises the costs to a public entity because user agencies end up with commodities or services that do not meet their needs, wasting precious dollars. A well-run procurement is based on a full understanding of the user agencies' needs. This calls for teamwork, a well-written specification/scope of work, relevant evaluation criteria, and appropriate contract terms, all of which greatly increase the chances that the public entity will receive the best value for its money.

Additionally, while state and local governments no longer purchase most commodities, services, and construction based solely on lowest price, the public procurement officer should aim to use his or her expertise, through market research and other available data, to investigate ways in which the public entity and the specific user agency may save money. That may be through locating a better performing and less costly version of a commodity than the one the user agency regularly purchases, finding a way to increase competition among service suppliers, or looking for opportunities to combine user agency purchases in order to obtain volume discounts from suppliers.

For certain types of commodity procurements, it may be appropriate to request information from competing suppliers about either their costs or the costs to the public entity of owning and operating suppliers' commodities. The best known of these costs are life cycle cost and total cost of ownership. The NIGP Dictionary defines life cycle cost as:

> *The total cost of ownership over the lifespan of the asset. An analysis technique that takes into account operating, maintenance, the time value of money, disposal, and other associated costs of ownership as well as the residual value of the item.* [5]

Burt, Dobler, and Starling (2003) define total cost of ownership as:

> *A measure of all of the cost components associated with the procurement of a product or service. The sum of all fixed and variable costs attributed to a product or service. A philosophy for understanding all supply-chain-related costs of doing business with a particular supplier for a particular good or service*[6] (as cited in The NIGP Dictionary).

Chapter 6 (*Sustainable Procurement Considerations and Strategies*) and Chapter 9 (*Bid and Proposal Evaluation and Award*) discuss these two approaches to analyzing costs in more detail.

The analyses that the public procurement officer conducts using the information that the supplier submits during a competition permits that officer to evaluate suppliers' bids or proposals in order to determine which commodity offers the best value. Those analyses may be used to determine the actual lowest price submitted in situations where that is the basis for contract award as stated in the solicitation, or to calculate which offered price should be given the highest number of points, for instance, where price is one factor for contract award as stated in the solicitation.

One of the critical tools that may assist with cost-savings strategy is the availability of comprehensive expenditure data, as discussed earlier. The public procurement officer should not be daunted by the lack of that type of data, but instead use his or her ingenuity to find other ways to achieve cost savings.

Strategic Sourcing

Strategic sourcing began as a tool used in private-sector procurement. Its use in the federal public procurement system took hold in the early 2000s. From 2003 through 2012, the United States Office of Management and Budget issued five directives relating to strategic sourcing.[7]

The United States General Services Administration maintains a website entitled *Federal Strategic Sourcing Initiative* (FSSI).[8] It offers a description of strategic sourcing:

> *Strategic sourcing is the structured and collaborative process of critically analyzing an organization's spending patterns to better leverage its purchasing power, reduce costs, and improve overall performance. The primary goals of FSSI are to:*
>
> - *Strategically source across federal agencies*
> - *Establish mechanisms to increase total cost savings, value, and socioeconomic participation*
> - *Collaborate with industry to develop optimal solutions*

CHAPTER 4: STRATEGIES AND PLANS

- *Share best practices*
- *Create a strategic sourcing community of practice*

Since most definitions of the term *strategic sourcing* tend to be vague and broad, the FSSI website provides the best idea of how that approach is used within a public procurement system. For instance, the website identifies the current commodities and services that the federal government has strategically sourced and describes the features of the contracts, including the availability of environmentally friendly items and the use of small and disadvantaged businesses.

As may be seen by the federal description of strategic sourcing, its use relies heavily on the availability of comprehensive spending information, an issue for state and local governments that this chapter has already discussed. In situations where that kind of information is available, a public procurement officer should consider launching a strategic sourcing initiative with user agencies, users, and suppliers if that spending information suggests that a long-term and different solution in purchasing particular types of commodities or services will be beneficial.

Source Selection Methods

One of the important things that a public procurement officer must determine in preparing to conduct a procurement is the method that will be used to select a supplier—the source selection method. Chapter 7 (*Competition: Solicitations and Methods*) discusses this topic in detail.

Length of Contracts

A decision about the length of a contract requires that public procurement officers weigh several objectives. They must consider the nature of the user agency or agencies' needs, the nature of the item being procured, the ongoing or long-term need for it, and the principle of competition, which creates a presumption that a purchase ought to be competed regularly.

There are good reasons, however, in certain situations, to put in place a long-term contract, the duration of which may be as long as ten years. In contracts of that length, it is critical for the contract to include special terms that will support the issues that may arise in any long-term relationship, such as: opportunities for price/cost reductions; contractor requests for price increases and the required documentation; and procedures for handling going-out-of-business or bankruptcy problems. Simply using a public entity's standard contract terms is not sufficient.

There is a barrier to longer-term contracts. Laws reserve the authority to appropriate funds only to a state or local government's legislative body—for a state, its legislature; and for a city, its city council. While some state legislatures meet every two years and thus appropriate funds for a two-year period, most appropriate funds for only one year at a time.

As a practical matter, many state and local government contracts that support that government qualify as multi-year. That is because the duration of those contracts is at least a year and the start dates of contracts vary based on when the public procurement officer awards the particular contract. All public entities have a fiscal year for budgeting purposes. If that fiscal year begins on July 1, a public procurement officer does not award all contracts of one-year duration on July 1.

The solution that governments use to resolve the appropriations issue is to insert into each contract language such as the following, which is taken from the Federal Acquisition Regulation—the body of regulations that implements the federal government's procurement laws:[9]

> *Funds are not presently available for performance under this contract beyond _____. The Government's obligation for performance of this contract beyond*

that date is contingent upon the availability of appropriated funds from which payment for contract purposes can be made. No legal liability on the part of the Government for any payment may arise for performance under this contract beyond _____, until funds are made available to the Contracting Officer for performance and until the Contractor receives notice of availability, to be confirmed in writing by the Contracting Officer.

Some version of this language should be included in every public contract and in a public entity's purchase order terms. These contract clauses are called *funding out* or *non-appropriations* clauses.

There are instances in which the legislative body of the state or local government appropriates funds for specific high-dollar projects that will take longer than a year or more to complete, such as highway or stadium construction or the procurement of an enterprise system. In those cases, a *funding out* clause does not have as important a role to play as it does in other types of contracts. However, those contracts should still include it.

This recognition of the power of the legislative body to appropriate public funds becomes an issue in contracts under which the contractor is financing something that the government will purchase by making payments to the contractor over time. Examples of these types of contracts are the lease/purchase of equipment or contracts for a construction of a public facility that the contractor will build at its cost and the public entity will occupy. While contractors that are in the business of lease/financing to governments acknowledge that governments must include *funding out* clauses in contracts, those contractors generally will want to negotiate some specific contractual protections relating to situations in which the government may need to terminate the contract using that clause.

Any strategy of a public procurement officer to compete for and enter into contracts for long terms should be supported by a law that authorizes those types of contracts. The issue of legal authorization is a separate one from that relating to the appropriation previously discussed. Contractors who are asked to enter into long-term contracts will feel more comfortable competing for them where the law sanctions them.

Here is a sample of language that may be used in a statute or ordinance for that authorization. It is taken from the American Bar Association Model Procurement Code for State and Local Governments (Model Procurement Code).[10]

§3-503 Multi-Year Contracts
*(1) **Specified Period.** Unless otherwise provided by law, a contract for supplies or services may be entered into for any period of time deemed to be in the best interests of the [State] provided the term of the contract and conditions of renewal or extension, if any, are included in the solicitation and funds are available for the first fiscal period at the time of contracting. Payment and performance obligations for succeeding fiscal periods shall be subject to the availability and appropriation of funds therefore.*
*(2) **Use.** A multi-year contract is authorized where:*
  (a) estimated requirements cover the period of the contract and are reasonably firm and continuing; and
  (b) such a contract will serve the best interests of the [State] by encouraging effective competition or otherwise promoting economies in [State] procurement.
*(3) **Cancellation Due to Unavailability of Funds in Succeeding Fiscal Periods.** When funds are not appropriated or otherwise made available to support continuation of performance in a subsequent fiscal period, the contract shall be cancelled and the contractor shall be reimbursed for*

the reasonable value of any non-recurring costs incurred but not amortized in the price of the supplies or services delivered under the contract. The cost of cancellation may be paid from any appropriations available for such purposes.

Selection of Contract Type

One of the most important decisions that a public procurement officer makes is the type of contract that he or she will award as a result of a procurement. There are many types of contracts. Selecting the right one depends in large part on an analysis of the risks that the procurement and resulting contract pose. A later portion of this chapter describes some structured ways of analyzing risks.

A good starting point in determining the contract types that may be available to the public procurement officer is to become familiar with what is authorized by the state or local government's procurement law. An example of such legal language can be found in the Model Procurement Code:

> **§3-501 Types of Contracts.**
> *Subject to the limitations of this Section, any type of contract which will promote the best interests of the [State] may be used; provided that the use of a cost-plus-a-percentage-of-cost contract is prohibited. A cost-reimbursement contract may be used only when a determination is made in writing that such contract is likely to be less costly to the [State] than any other type or that it is impracticable to obtain the supplies, services, or construction required except under such a contract.*

Cost-plus-a-percentage-of-cost contracts are universally prohibited in public procurement, including at the federal government level.[11] A cost-plus-a-percentage-of-cost contract is one in which, before completion of the work, the contractor and the public entity agree that the contractor will be entitled to a fee amounting to a predetermined percentage of the total cost of the work. Thus, the more the contractor spends, the greater its fee. It incentivizes the contractor to incur cost at the expense of the public entity.

Note that determining what is and what is not a cost-plus-a-percentage-of-cost contract is not simple. There is a good discussion of this topic on the NASPO ValuePoint website.[12]

Contract Types

The Recommended Regulations of the Model Procurement Code offer the following list of some of the types of contracts available for commodities or services contracts: fixed-price contracts (with contract-specified adjustments); firm fixed-price contracts; fixed-price contracts with price adjustment; cost-reimbursement contracts; allowable cost contracts; cost-plus-fixed fee contracts; cost incentive contracts; fixed-price cost incentive contracts; cost-reimbursement contracts with cost incentive fee; performance incentive contracts; time and materials contracts; labor hours contracts; definite quantity contracts; indefinite quantity contracts; requirements contracts; leases; lease with purchase option.[13]

If a public procurement officer finds the preceding list of contract types daunting, it is understandable. He or she is not expected to be an expert in this area. The aim of this chapter is to provide resources to that officer as he or she strategizes about the type of contract to be used in a particular procurement.

Many contracts awarded by state and local governments are some version of a firm-fixed-price contract under procurements conducted either via competitive sealed bidding or via competitive sealed proposals. Chapter 7 (*Competition: Solicitations and Methods*) describes those procurement methods in more detail.

At the federal government level, firm-fixed-price contracts or fixed-price contracts with economic price adjustment are the only contract types that may be used when a procurement is conducted by competitive sealed bidding.[14] Nash, Schooner, and O'Brien (1998) define a firm-fixed-price contract as:[15]

A type of contract providing for a price that is not subject to adjustment on the basis of the contractor's cost experience in performing the contract. [Firm-fixed-price] contracts place maximum risk and full responsibility on the contractor for all costs and resulting profit or loss. They provide maximum incentive for the contractor to control costs, perform effectively, and impose a minimum administrative burden upon the contracting parties unless changes are issued or unforeseen events occur during performance (as cited in The NIGP Dictionary).

The Federal Acquisition Regulation describes fixed-price contracts with economic price adjustment as follows:[16]

16.203 Fixed-price contracts with economic price adjustment.

16.203-1 Description.

(a) A fixed-price contract with economic price adjustment provides for upward and downward revision of the stated contract price upon the occurrence of specified contingencies. Economic price adjustments are of three general types:
   (1) **Adjustments based on established prices.** *These price adjustments are based on increases or decreases from an agreed-upon level in published or otherwise established prices of specific items or the contract end items.*
   (2) **Adjustments based on actual costs of labor or material.** *These price adjustments are based on increases or decreases in specified costs of labor or material that the contractor actually experiences during contract performance.*

(3) **Adjustments based on cost indexes of labor or material.** *These price adjustments are based on increases or decreases in labor or material cost standards or indexes that are specifically identified in the contract.*

Federal Acquisition Regulation Subpart 16.1, entitled *Selecting Contract Types*, provides valuable information that any state or local government public procurement officer may use as a guide. There is more in those regulations than a state or local government procurement officer needs, but they are a useful starting point. A theme that runs through these regulations is the importance of the risk posed by particular contract types. Because of that reality, federal regulations mandate that the decision to use a particular contract type be documented.[17]

At the outset of a procurement, a public procurement officer must understand that contract types fall into two broad categories—fixed-price contracts and cost-reimbursement contracts, with incentive contracts somewhere in between—and that they vary according to:[18]

- The degree and timing of the responsibility assumed by the contractor for the costs of performance
- The amount and nature of the profit incentive offered to the contractor for achieving or exceeding specified standards or goals

As seen from the titles of the various contract types mentioned, there is a close relationship between the type of contract and the determination of the price under a contract. Even though there are contract designations such as *definite quantity* or *indefinite quantity*, those, in reality, are a combination of contract types, in many cases a form of fixed-price contracts.

Factors in Selecting a Contract Type

The factors that Subpart 16.1, and specifically Federal Acquisition Regulation Subpart 16.104, offers to assist with the selection of a contract type include:

(a) **Price competition.** Normally, effective price competition results in realistic pricing, and a fixed-price contract is ordinarily in the Government's interest.

(b) **Price analysis.** Price analysis, with or without competition, may provide a basis for selecting the contract type. The degree to which price analysis can provide a realistic pricing standard should be carefully considered. [Citation omitted.]

(c) **Cost analysis.** In the absence of effective price competition and if price analysis is not sufficient, the cost estimates of the offeror and the Government provide the basis for negotiating contract pricing arrangements. It is essential that the uncertainties involved in performance and their possible impact upon costs be identified and evaluated, so that a contract type that places a reasonable degree of cost responsibility upon the contractor can be negotiated.

(d) **Type and complexity of the requirement.** Complex requirements, particularly those unique to the Government, usually result in greater risk assumption by the Government. This is especially true for complex research and development contracts, when performance uncertainties or the likelihood of changes makes it difficult to estimate performance costs in advance. As a requirement recurs or as quantity production begins, the cost risk should shift to the contractor, and a fixed-price contract should be considered.

(e) **Combining contract types.** If the entire contract cannot be firm-fixed-price, the contracting officer shall consider whether or not a portion of the contract can be established on a firm-fixed-price basis.

(f) **Urgency of the requirement.** If urgency is a primary factor, the Government may choose to assume a greater proportion of risk or it may offer incentives tailored to performance outcomes to ensure timely contract performance.

(g) **Period of performance or length of production run.** In times of economic uncertainty, contracts extending over a relatively long period may require economic price adjustment or price redetermination clauses.

(h) **Contractor's technical capability and financial responsibility.**

(i) **Adequacy of the contractor's accounting system.** Before agreeing on a contract type other than firm-fixed-price, the contracting officer shall ensure that the contractor's accounting system will permit timely development of all necessary cost data in the form required by the proposed contract type. This factor may be critical:

  (1) when the contract type requires price revision while performance is in progress; or

  (2) when a cost-reimbursement contract is being considered and all current or past experience with the contractor has been on a fixed-price basis. [Citation omitted.]

(j) **Concurrent contracts.** If performance under the proposed contract involves concurrent operations under other contracts, the impact of those contracts, including their pricing arrangements, should be considered.

(k) **Extent and nature of proposed subcontracting.** If the contractor proposes extensive subcontracting, a contract type reflecting the actual risks to the prime contractor should be selected.

(l) **Acquisition history.** Contractor risk usually decreases as the requirement is repetitively acquired. Also, product descriptions or descriptions of services to be performed can be defined more clearly.

Analysis of Risks Posed by Contract Types

Finally, Federal Acquisition Regulation Subpart 16.1, specifically 16.103(d), describes the documentation that those regulations require to support the selection of a contract type for a procurement. While it may be unlikely that a state or local government procurement officer will detail the procurement file to this extent, a review of the following items provides the factors, including risks, that need to be considered and weighed in order to make the best decision:

(d)(1) Each contract file shall include documentation to show why the particular contract type was selected. This shall be documented in the acquisition plan, or in the contract file if a written acquisition plan is not required by agency procedures.
(i) Explain why the contract type selected must be used to meet the agency need.
(ii) Discuss the Government's additional risks and the burden to manage the contract type selected (e.g., when a cost-reimbursement contract is selected, the Government incurs additional cost risks, and the Government has the additional burden of managing the contractor's costs). For such instances, acquisition personnel shall discuss:
   (A) how the Government identified the additional risks (e.g., pre-award survey or past performance information);
   (B) the nature of the additional risks (e.g., inadequate contractor's accounting system, weaknesses in contractor's internal control, noncompliance with Cost Accounting Standards, or lack of or inadequate earned value management system); and
   (C) how the Government will manage and mitigate the risks.
(iii) Discuss the Government resources necessary to properly plan for, award, and administer the contract type selected (e.g., resources needed and the additional risks to the Government if adequate resources are not provided).
(iv) For other than a firm-fixed-price contract, at a minimum the documentation should include:
   (A) an analysis of why the use of other than a firm-fixed-price contract (e.g., cost reimbursement, time and materials, labor hour) is appropriate;
   (B) rationale that details the particular facts and circumstances (e.g., complexity of the requirements, uncertain duration of the work, contractor's technical capability and financial responsibility, or adequacy of the contractor's accounting system), and associated reasoning essential to support the contract type selection;
   (C) an assessment regarding the adequacy of Government resources that are necessary to properly plan for, award, and administer other than firm-fixed-price contracts; and
   (D) a discussion of the actions planned to minimize the use of other than firm-fixed-price contracts on future acquisitions for the same requirement and to transition to firm-fixed-price contracts to the maximum extent practicable.
(v) A discussion of why a level-of-effort, price redetermination, or fee provision was included.

Contract Types Requiring Substantiation of Costs or Prices

As noted before, some contracts call for the contractor to substantiate the quoted cost or prices. The reasons may be related to the type of contract, such as cost-reimbursement contracts. In that category are contracts under which price is negotiated, those that reimburse any contractor costs (such as travel), cost-plus-fixed-fee contracts, and cost incentive contracts. In other cases, the need for substantiation arises because of the lack of full competition in awarding the contract. Chapter 8 (*Noncompetitive and Limited Competition Procurements*) and Chapter 9 (*Bid and Proposal Evaluation and Award*) address those situations.

The Model Procurement Code's recommended statutory language is simple and to the point in authorizing a public procurement officer to ask a supplier for cost or pricing information:[19]

§3-403 Substantiation of Offered Prices
The Procurement Officer may request factual information reasonably available to the bidder or offeror to substantiate that the price or cost offered, or some portion of it, is reasonable, if:
(1) the price is not:
  (a) based on adequate price competition;
  (b) based on established catalogue or market prices; or
  (c) set by law or regulation; and
(2) the price or cost exceeds an amount established in the regulations.

Thus, it is important for a public procurement officer to decide in advance of a procurement whether he or she may need to insert language advising suppliers that they may be asked to provide cost or pricing data during the procurement or the contract. The Recommended Regulations of the Model Procurement Code describe the types of information that the public procurement officer may seek from a supplier or contractor as follows:[20]

R3-101.01.2 Cost Analysis is the evaluation of cost data for the purpose of arriving at costs actually incurred or estimates of costs to be incurred, prices to be paid, and costs to be reimbursed.

R3-101.01.3 Cost Data are information concerning the actual or estimated cost of labor, material, overhead, and other cost elements which have been actually incurred or which are expected to be incurred by the contractor in performing the contract.

R3-101.01.6 Price Analysis is the evaluation of price data, without analysis of the separate cost components and profit as in cost analysis, which may assist in arriving at prices to be paid and costs to be reimbursed.

R3-101.01.7 Price Data are factual information concerning prices, including profit, for supplies, services, or construction substantially similar to those being procured. In this definition, "prices" refer to offered or proposed selling prices, historical selling prices, and current selling prices of such items. This definition refers to data relevant to both prime and subcontract prices.

Contract Pricing, Important Contract Terms

Overview
Among the things that a contract accomplishes, there are three that are very important, namely: (1) establish what the contractor and, in some cases, the public entity must do; (2) detail how the contractor will be paid; and (3) allocate the other risks that may possibly arise during contract performance between the contractor and the public entity. Good contract terms are those that cover those three items in a clear and unambiguous way.

For the purposes of this discussion, the term *contract terms* excludes specifications, scopes of work, and instructions for bidders or offerors in a solicitation. In fact, it is important for a solicitation not to mix contract terms—which will apply once the contract is awarded—with instructions to bidders/offerors or specifications/scopes of work. All of these parts of a solicitation address distinct matters and should be separated under distinct headings to avoid confusing suppliers.

Contract terms appear in a variety of documents for which a public procurement office is responsible. Every formal solicitation for a procurement must include them because they are an important part of the matters that suppliers take into consideration when preparing bids or proposals. Additionally, contract terms should be included in a public entity's purchase orders, which are the documents that the public entity sends to a contractor to confirm that funds are available to pay the contractor; they authorize the contractor to begin work under the contract.

Standard Contract Terms

Most public procurement offices maintain a set of standard contract terms that are used routinely in solicitations and purchase orders. These must include a wide range of remedies that the public entity may initiate if the contractor fails to perform according to the contract's terms. Just a few examples of types of contract clauses that offer a range of remedies are:

- Modification of the terms of the Uniform Commercial Code as discussed in Chapter 13 (*Quality Assurance*)
- Reservation of all legal and equitable remedies in addition to those set forth in the contract
- Explicit warranties that are additional to those provided by law
- Termination of the contract for default or breach
- The right to offset from amounts owed to the contractor any expenses that the public entity incurs due to poor performance
- Non-waiver language, providing that the failure to invoke a remedy or enforce a right on occasion during the contract does not waive that right or remedy
- Indemnification by the contractor of the public from liability associated with claims, damages, and actions
- Termination of the contract for convenience, paying the contractor for costs along with a reasonable profit for the work to that point of termination; to be used, for instance, when circumstances change, necessitating that the public entity end the contract before completion

Nonstandard Contract Terms

With the complexity of the commodities, services, and construction that a public entity purchases today, it is unreasonable for a public procurement officer to rely only on those standard terms in the procurements that he or she conducts. He or she needs to examine those terms in light of the three issues—what the contractor is supposed to do, how it is supposed to be paid, and who accepts what risk.

Many contract terms must be founded on a prior risk analysis conducted during solicitation drafting, during evaluations of bids or proposals, during negotiation with the selected supplier, or even during contract performance. Performing risk analyses is discussed later in this chapter.

An analysis of the three main issues in each procurement will consistently result in the need to draft additional contract terms that address the unique risks and requirements posed by that particular competition. Thus, as part of a public procurement officer's first thoughts about the best way to proceed with a particular procurement, he or she must develop a strategy to collect reliable information concerning the three main issues, prepare the precise contract terms to address them, and obtain any additional expertise through the public entity's attorneys or finance staff.

The attorney general's office of the State of North Dakota has prepared a manual to instruct public procurement officers in drafting contract terms.[21] Resources such as that one are excellent guides for developing contract terms.

Contract Administration Plan

For some contracts, it is critical to have a contract administration plan in place. Chapter 14 (*Contract Management and Contract Administration*) provides a discussion regarding this type of plan.

Plans for Complex Information Technology Procurements

A significant amount of planning is part of a sound procurement for complex information technologies. Chapter 20 (*Procurement of Information Technology*) covers this topic in detail.

CHAPTER 4: **STRATEGIES AND PLANS**

Network Security and Cyber Risks

Any entity—whether it be private or public—must put policies and procedures in place to protect the confidential information it holds about people. Federal and state laws specify what kinds of information must be protected.

As state and local governments gravitate toward systems solutions that include strategies such as cloud services or software as a service, or use consultants who have access to their systems, it is necessary to establish strategies to reduce the risk of unauthorized disclosure of private information. A public procurement officer along with a larger team of public entity employees (such as information technology specialists and those responsible for obtaining that entity's insurance) must strategize about how to identify, weigh, and reduce those risks in procurements where those issues are a genuine concern. Chapter 20 (*Procurement of Information Technology*) discusses this in more detail.

Negotiation

In many instances, a public procurement officer will negotiate with a supplier during a procurement. Negotiation may occur under a procurement conducted through competitive sealed proposals. It may be with those suppliers selected from the pool of suppliers competing to be finalists for a contract award or it may be with the supplier selected for contract award. A public procurement officer will also be required to negotiate contract terms where there has been little or no price competition, such as when awarding a sole source contract. Whatever the condition is that creates the need to negotiate, a public procurement officer should not initiate negotiations without a strategy and plan in place.

Construction Project Delivery Methods

There are strategies that a public procurement officer must formulate with the user agency about how best to deliver a project to construct or renovate public infrastructure. Some of those involve financing options, such as public-private partnerships. Chapter 11 (*Procurement of Construction and Related Services*) describes those possible strategies in more detail.

Strategies—Socioeconomic Programs

Overview

The fundamental purpose of state and local government procurement is to buy the commodities, construction, and services needed for the operation of that government. The objective is to acquire these items at the best value for the public entity.

It is inevitable, however, that other state and local government policies influence the procurement function. The buying power of state and local governments is frequently used to achieve socioeconomic objectives that do not directly pertain to the procurement of commodities, construction, and services. Such objectives find their way into a law or executive order, which will generally direct a public procurement office to implement those goals.

There is a wide range of possible socioeconomic objectives. Examples are procurement preferences for local businesses, for sustainable commodities, and for small and diverse businesses—often called disadvantaged businesses, which is the term used in this chapter.

The terms *disadvantaged business* or *diverse business* are often used to encompass the most common supplier diversity categories of minority business enterprise (MBE) and women's business enterprise (WBE). Some jurisdictions, such as the Commonwealth of Massachusetts, have expanded definitions of supplier diversity to add veteran business enterprise (VBE); service-disabled veteran-owned business enterprise (SDVOBE); disability-owned business enterprise (DOBE); and lesbian-, gay-, bisexual-, transgender-owned business enterprise (LGBTBE).[22]

CHAPTER 4: **STRATEGIES AND PLANS**

PLANNING FOR NEGOTIATIONS

Negotiation is a common part of everyday life and plays an important role in the procurement process. When used properly, negotiations can help achieve best value contracts for the government entity. Effective negotiations can improve quality, delivery, cost, and provide deeper clarity for all parties around contract expectations. This guide features callout boxes (like this one) on the topic of negotiation within several chapters to reinforce the need for public procurement professionals to embrace negotiation when appropriate, seek it as a skill, refine it in staff, and realize that it is often essential to achieving best value. When negotiation is practiced in public procurement environments, it must be done with the tenants of fairness and integrity in mind—in other words, it must include principled bargaining, because that is the standard owed to the public. However, negotiation also requires diligence and thought; procurement officers cannot start throwing positions and *requests* at suppliers and hope to achieve best value.

This chapter identifies the importance of establishing strategies and plans in the management of a procurement office, such as contract coverage planning, strategic sourcing, risk management, and planning the approaches to various markets. Planning for negotiations early on is also a critical aspect of procurement office planning. When planning for a negotiation with a supplier, many of the same best practices of strategic planning are involved but use different tools and resources. For example, in the book *Getting to Yes: Negotiating Agreement Without Giving Up* by Roger Fisher and William Ury,[1] the importance of planning is emphasized primarily through techniques such as identification of alternatives, promoting a focus on interests versus positions, and creating options for mutual gain. All of these techniques require time, and more important, time spent with a team of the right people.

Engaging a cross-functional team to craft a strategy for successful implementation and monitoring of contracts is critical to minimizing risk and costs when dealing with suppliers. At each major milestone of procurement—from brainstorming on requirements during an RFP, to whiteboarding possible options available to implement a new contract, to discussing the impacts of a performance issue and the corrective action to take—a consistent team and a commitment to a structured plan will increase the chance of success.

---

[1] R. Fisher, W. Ury, & B. Patton. (2011). *Getting to Yes: Negotiating Agreement without Giving Up* (3rd ed.). New York, New York: Penguin Group.

The reference to disadvantaged businesses in this chapter should not be confused with the federal government's disadvantaged business enterprise (DBE) program. That federal program flows down to state and local governments when they are issuing contracts using federal funds for things such as highways, public transportation (such as airports and light rail), concessions in airports, and equipment related to those items.

As part of the mandate that accompanies the use of those federal funds, the state or local government is required to have a certification process in place to assure that a business claiming to meet the federal definition actually does so. The upcoming discussion does not focus on federal requirements, but instead provides an overview of socioeconomic programs at the state and local government level that are unrelated to spending federal funds.

CHAPTER 4: **STRATEGIES AND PLANS**

The State of Maryland is an example of a state government that has instituted a socioeconomic program for non-federally funded procurements. In 1978, the state's General Assembly enacted legislation to create an MBE program to encourage minority-owned firms to participate in the state's procurement process. The state's current law requires user agencies to make every effort to achieve an overall minimum goal of 29% of the total dollar value of their procurement contracts directly or indirectly from certified MBE firms.[23]

The State of Maryland uses the federal government criteria for determining which businesses qualify and which do not. Since the state already has the staffing and process in place within its department of transportation for certifying businesses as disadvantaged for federally funded procurements, it uses the same staff and process to certify businesses applying for the benefits of non-federally funded state contracts. Each user agency in state government reviews and assesses its procurements for commodities, services, maintenance, construction, and architectural/engineering contracts to determine an MBE participation goal appropriate for each contract.

The definition of an MBE business used by the state of Maryland is:

> [A] Business must be at least 51% owned and controlled by one or more socially and economically disadvantaged individuals. Under current State law, an individual is presumed to be socially and economically disadvantaged if that individual belongs to one of the following groups: African Americans, Hispanic Americans, Asian-Pacific Americans, Subcontinent Asian Americans, Native Americans, and Women. Persons who own and control their business, but are not members of one of the above groups, also may be eligible for MBE certification if they establish their social and economic disadvantage. Disabled individuals may also apply for MBE certification. A determination of whether an individual meets MBE eligibility criteria is made on a case-by-case basis.

Socioeconomic Program Risks

Socioeconomic procurement programs that give some preference to small and disadvantaged businesses have risks. For example, a law establishing a preference for local businesses in state A may trigger a reciprocal preference law in state B, disadvantaging a business headquartered in state A when it competes for contracts under a procurement solicited by state B. Additionally, programs giving preferences based on race or gender raise legal issues under the United States Constitution. Legal challenges will be successful unless the programs are based on documented disparities and are narrowly tailored to address the documented discrimination. There is substantial case law that addresses this topic, but it is not covered in this *Practical Guide.*

Strategies for Obtaining Supplier Diversity in Procurements

The stated reason for small and disadvantaged business programs is that those businesses are often at a disadvantage when they compete with large businesses for procurements. To address this situation, strategies are sometimes applied to level the playing field. The following are some of these strategies:

- **Set-asides.** A set-aside is a preference, which may be total or partial, in which a procurement is reserved solely for participation by small or disadvantaged businesses.
- **Unbundling contracts.** Unbundling involves changing a previous single award, large-volume contract either by breaking out commodities or services into smaller groups and making multiple contract awards or breaking the contract up into geographical regions. By unbundling contracts, disadvantaged businesses that may

not have the capacity to compete for the entire award may be able to compete for part of the award or for a particular region of a state.
- **Evaluation points for small or disadvantaged businesses.** In negotiated procurements that use evaluation factors to identify the supplier that submits the best proposal, one approach may be to specify in the solicitation that points will be given to a supplier that is small or disadvantaged.
- **Disadvantaged business subcontracting plan.** Another strategy to promote small or disadvantaged businesses is to require suppliers competing for the contract to show their efforts to involve small or disadvantaged businesses by submitting a plan with their bid or proposal.
- **Percentage preferences.** A percentage preference allows a small or disadvantaged business to bid a higher price than the bid of a larger, non-disadvantaged business but still be considered the lowest bid if the bid of the small or disadvantaged business is no more than a certain percentage higher (such as 5% or 10%) than the actual low bid.

Arguments Made Against These Preference Programs

There are those who are opposed to small and disadvantaged business programs.

One argument is that these programs run counter to the basic tenet of public procurement, which is full and open competition. Additionally, claims are made, correct or not, that the quality of commodities and services offered by these businesses or their ability to meet requested quantities and schedules are inferior.

Another argument proffered is that many small and disadvantaged businesses conduct transactions with the private sector without any favored treatment. Preferential strategies, as the argument goes, weaken the businesses' ability to compete in the open market by making them increasingly dependent on the public sector.

Finally, concerns are raised that, unless the process for certifying a business as disadvantaged is robust and involves in-depth investigation of the information that a business submits to qualify, disadvantaged business programs are fraught with opportunities for abuse.

Documenting Program Benefits

A public procurement office is rarely given additional resources to support implementation of preference programs. All too often there is insufficient consideration of the real cost involved when public procurement is mobilized for some ancillary purpose. Those promoting these programs as good public policy must be responsible for documenting both the costs of such programs and the tangible, measurable benefits. One measure, for example, is how many disadvantaged businesses *graduate* annually from the program and are competing along with non-disadvantaged businesses for the same contracts. That cost/reward information should be detailed and made transparent.

Increasing Small and Disadvantaged Business Participation Without Sacrificing Competition and Effectiveness

There are ways in which public procurement officers and other public officials may help small and disadvantaged businesses participate without sacrificing competition, affecting quality, or making the procurement process less effective. For example:

- Make special efforts to identify small and disadvantaged businesses and to encourage them to seek public business through methods such as advertisement of opportunities in trade journals or small or disadvantaged business audience newspapers, as well as being in contact with local chamber of commerce offices
- Coordinate with state small and disadvantaged business assistance offices and

federally funded procurement technical centers
- Use technology to increase visibility of business opportunities, including mobile technology such as business opportunity apps and e-mail campaigns
- Provide special training or introductory seminars and workshops and on-demand web-based training for businesses, including those without previous procurement experience
- Provide one-on-one counseling sessions by state or local government procurement officers
- Provide forums and expositions where small and disadvantaged businesses can present their products and network with public entity procurement professionals

MANAGING RISKS

A public procurement officer is at the center of a process that requires a consistent and in-depth look at the risks posed by a procurement and contract. While the point of a contract is to obtain needed commodities, services, and construction, there are milestones all along the decision-making continuum—starting with the user agency's decision that it needs something through contract completion to fulfill that need—at which the risks of the particular activity proposed must be reviewed. As an example, the public procurement officer's selection of a contract type involves the consideration of risks, which has already been discussed in this chapter.

Effective risk analysis and management requires strategies and plans. These should be developed in a structured manner to ensure that nothing in the analysis is missed.

There are outside professionals who specialize in the use of sophisticated risk-assessment tools, including tools used for making complex financing decisions. Projects with long performance periods, complex cash flow models, significant environmental or regulatory considerations, and large capital expenditures may require quantitative risk-management modeling to assist in decision making. Moreover, some of those projects may require stand-alone risk management plans.

In most cases, a public procurement officer, user agency personnel, or an evaluation committee reviewing and evaluating supplier proposals will not have the benefit of an outside professional to assist with risk analysis. The following text includes some suggestions about how to conduct an analysis.

Steps in a Risk Analysis

For the purposes of providing an outline of the basic steps in risk analysis, this discussion offers a formal structure for conducting that analysis. It also contemplates that those involved in the risk analysis will include a public entity's personnel who are subject matter experts in the possible risks on which the activity or issue touches. However, any individual sitting at his or her desk may use the process described here for risks/benefits decisions.

It may not always be possible to include the appropriate subject matter experts at the table. If an issue that requires a risk analysis is identified by an evaluation committee during an evaluation of proposals, the confidentiality of the committee's deliberations may not provide any opportunity to include others in its risk assessment.

The basic steps in a risk analysis are:

- **Identification of the risks involved.** To complete this step successfully, there must be a clear written statement of the activity or issue to be evaluated so that there is a common understanding of the source of the possible risks. That keeps the analysis discussion on point. In some cases, it may be useful to list the benefits of the activity or issue so that they may be compared to the risks once those are identified. In some cases, there may not be any benefit, such as when a critical supplier of cloud services, for instance, does not maintain cyber insurance for its operations. Additionally, as discussed later, it is a good practice to ask the suppliers who are competing for a contract themselves to identify the risks associated with the particular service, commodity, or construction that the procurement is seeking.

- **Assessment of the risks.** Once risks are identified and a list is made, each risk is assigned a score, such as 1 through 5; or a ranking, such as low, medium, or high. The risk is given a separate score or ranking for two different factors: the probability of the risk occurring and the impact if the risk occurs. Once that is done, the overall risk, based on the two scores, is determined and may be plotted on a chart such as the one following this paragraph. Those that hover high in Quadrant 2, or perhaps medium to high in Quadrant 1 and are located near the dividing line between the two top quadrants present the highest risk.[24]

IMPACT →		
High or 5	Quadrant 1	Quadrant 2
	Quadrant 3	Quadrant 4
Low or 1	Low or 1	High or 5
	PROBABILITY →	

- **Determine the risk response, including actions to reduce risks.** After the risk assessment, handling the risks requires the public entity to determine whether the benefits of the activity outweigh the risks—its tolerance for risk. Using the example stated earlier of a critical supplier for cloud services who does not maintain cyber insurance, the public entity must determine its tolerance for taking that risk and how it might reduce the risk. For instance, if the supplier agrees to reimburse the public entity for some of the standard costs of a data breach, such as the cost of forensic experts, notification of the victims, call center services, and credit monitoring, will that suffice? Cloud service suppliers uniformly demand that the contract place a dollar cap on their responsibility for those costs, which requires the public entity to perform another risk analysis.

- **Monitor and control risky activities.** Monitoring and controlling risks during contract performance can include requirements for approvals, authorizations, reviews, reconciliations, and contract exception reporting. Mandatory security training for certain types of contractors and administrative permissions/controls relating to technology systems are other examples. Monitoring and control for risk management purposes should also be linked with other project management activities, such as weekly or monthly reviews. Effective contract administration may be the most important element of risk monitoring and control in procurements. Chapter 14 (*Contract Management and Contract Administration*) describes good contract management/contract administration in more detail. Post-award kickoff meetings, careful monitoring of project schedule and status, and aggressive resolution of contract issues as they arise become central to monitoring the risks of a procurement project and assessing the need for any adjustments.

Requiring Suppliers to Identify Risks

It is unlikely that a group of public entity employees and a public procurement officer will be able to identify all of the key risks that a procurement of a particular service, commodity, or construction poses, particularly in the case of more complicated ones. A best practice for a solicitation is to ask competing suppliers not only to address specific risks that public entity employees have identified in their risk analysis but to identify in a detailed way, from their viewpoint, the potential significant risks posed by the contract to be awarded under the solicitation. Suppliers should also be required to provide a plan to reduce and otherwise manage risks.

The solicitation should include criteria for evaluating suppliers' responses relating to risk since they may demonstrate whether or not a supplier understands the project context. It may be prudent in particular cases to require a bidder or offeror to include a risk mitigation plan enumerating the risks that the potential contract may pose from the supplier's point of view and providing steps to mitigate them.

Suppliers' responses allow the public procurement officer and the evaluation committee the opportunity to assess the risk in each supplier's proposed approach, including whether it requires excessive contract administration to maintain the schedule and to achieve a successful outcome within the proposed cost.

Risk management is an enterprise-wide concept that covers strategies and planning in all aspects of a public entity's activities, including procurement. Risk management is a tool for identifying threats to successful procurements and managing them. The process of identifying, assessing, responding to, and monitoring/controlling risk are key ingredients in procurement planning.

CONCLUSION

Participation in the overall government planning process enables a public procurement officer to provide strategic services to user agencies. As that officer and the procurement office provide those types of services on their own initiative, user agencies will recognize the importance of involving procurement professionals early in the procurement planning process.

ENDNOTES

1. *Modular Procurement: A Primer. January 30, 2018.* http://www.naspo.org/Portals/16/NASPO%20Modular%20Procurement%20Primer%20FINAL%20%282%29.pdf
2. https://www.naspo.org/Publications/ArtMID/8806/ArticleID/4493
3. https://www.naspo.org/Publications/ArtMID/8806/ArticleID/3324
4. https://www.nascio.org/#
5. Access to the dictionary is available at: http://www.nigp.org/home/find-procurement-resources/dictionary-of-terms
6. Burt, D. N., Dobler, D. W., & Starling, S. L., *World Class Supply Management: The Key to Supply Chain Management.* McGraw-Hill: NY (2003) as cited in The NIGP Dictionary at: http://www.nigp.org/home/find-procurement-resources/dictionary-of-terms
7. https://obamawhitehouse.archives.gov/omb/procurement_strategic
8. https://www.gsa.gov/acquisition/purchasing-programs/federal-strategic-sourcing-initiative-fssi
9. See Federal Acquisition Regulation 52.233.19, *Availability of Funds for the Next Fiscal Year,* at: https://www.acquisition.gov/far/html/52_232.html#wp1152919
10. A copy of the Model Procurement Code, along with various versions of it including the Model Procurement Ordinance is available at: http://apps.americanbar.org/dch/committee.cfm?com=PC500500
11. See Federal Acquisition Regulation 16.102(c) at: https://www.acquisition.gov/far/html/Subpart%2016_1.html#wp1085495
12. https://www.naspovaluepoint.org/revisiting-an-old-nemesis-cost-plus-a-percentage-of-cost-contracts/
13. See R3-501.01. A copy of the Model Procurement Code, along with various versions of it including the Recommended Regulations,

is available at: http://apps.americanbar.org/dch/committee.cfm?com=PC500500
14. See Federal Acquisition Regulation 16.102(a) at: https://www.acquisition.gov/far/html/Subpart%2016_1.html#wp1085495
15. Nash, R.C., O'Brien, K.R., Schooner, S.L., *The Government Contracts Reference Book: a Comprehensive Guide to the Language of Procurement*. 2nd ed., George Washington Univ Government, (1998) as cited in The NIGP Dictionary at: http://www.nigp.org/home/find-procurement-resources/dictionary-of-terms
16. For the web address, see Endnote 10.
17. Subpart 16.1 is at the website noted in Endnote 10.
18. See Federal Acquisition Regulation 16.102(a) at the web address in Endnote 10.
19. See Endnote 11.
20. See Endnote 11.
21. https://attorneygeneral.nd.gov/attorney-generals-office/manuals-state-and-local-government-agencies
22. https://www.mass.gov/supplier-diversity-office
23. http://www.mdot.maryland.gov/newMDOT/MBE/FAQs.html#1
24. Risk tools similar to the chart provided here are available on line by simply Googling "risk assessment tools."

CHAPTER 5: NON-CONSTRUCTION SPECIFICATIONS AND SCOPES OF WORK

RECOMMENDED BEST PRACTICES

- In preparing a specification, a public procurement officer's key duty is to provide service to the user agency; and that officer has a responsibility to be creative in finding resources to assist that agency in obtaining the right commodities and services.
- The central procurement office should develop guidelines allowing for instances in which supplier input into the solicitation process or in the preparation of initial specifications or scopes of work is useful, so that the user agencies and the central procurement office may obtain the benefits of supplier expertise without creating unfair bias or a conflict of interest. The use of supplier focus groups and pre-solicitation conferences should be encouraged.
- Specifications should be closely tailored to the appropriate level of use and quality to meet the user agency's needs, should emphasize performance rather than design, and should not recite features or quality levels that the user agency does not need.
- A specification should identify the essential characteristics of the item to be purchased.
- For commonly used commodities that are available *off the shelf*, the specification should recite the desired features of the commercial commodity being sought and not attempt to create an entire new specification. The best practice is for a procurement policy to prefer the purchase of commercial commodities over specifications that require that items be specially made. It should also stress functional and performance characteristics above design requirements in the preparation of specifications.
- Standardization of specifications is appropriate where user agencies frequently and repetitively purchase the same commodities and uniform performance and quality levels can be identified.
- To avoid favoritism to a particular supplier and increase competition, the use of a brand-name specification must include the words: *or equivalent*. To ensure that suppliers submitting an alternative to the brand-name commodity know the exact features of the brand-name commodity that make it the benchmark, it is a best practice for the specification to identify those critically necessary features significant to the specified brand.
- As a general rule, the specifications portion of a solicitation should be distinct from the other sections. Suppliers need to be able to easily identify what the state or local government seeks to buy. Mixing instructions or terms and conditions into the specifications hinders suppliers' clear understanding of what it is that the public entity is seeking.
- Specification writing is not strictly an exercise in finding the cheapest commodity or service on the market. It is a careful balance between factors related to suitability, performance and price, and overall cost effectiveness.
- Performance specifications are useful tools because they essentially ask the supplier to show that its commodity or services can meet benchmarks.

- In the absence of a law, the central procurement office should have a written policy stating that, when an agent or representative of a manufacturer or prospective bidder or offeror unofficially and significantly participates in the preparation of a specification, the procurement office will not consider bids or proposals submitted on that manufacturer's commodity.
- Procurement policies and procedures should provide for uniform formats of specification documents; that is, standard presentation of the elements, consistent types of item identifiers, and adequate reference to the kind and source of the commodity or service requirements.

The heart of the competitive source selection process is the specifications—the description in the solicitation that identifies for suppliers the characteristics of the commodity or service that the public entity wishes to buy. It is the critical statement of what the government seeks in order to meet its needs. This chapter discusses the general principles applicable to preparing those specifications.

For purposes of this discussion, the term *specification* is used in its broadest sense to include the terms *purchase description, purchase specification, purchase requirement, commercial item description, scope of work*, and *statement of work*. In practice, these terms may refer to different types of descriptions. For instance, The NIGP Dictionary uses the term *specification* to mean a description used within an invitation for bids, and the term *scope of work* to refer to a description contained within a request for proposals.[1]

Whichever term is used, the principles used to draft specifications are the same, and authority needs to reside in the Chief Procurement Officer, either to produce them or oversee their production. This chapter focuses on those principles for commodities. Chapter 10 (*Contracting for Services*) provides specific guidance on the drafting of those descriptions for the purchase of services. Additionally, Chapter 11 (*Procurement of Construction and Related Services*) addresses the preparation of designs for seeking contractors to construct public infrastructure.

As a general rule, the specifications portion of a solicitation should be distinct from the other sections. Suppliers need to be able to identify easily what the state or local government seeks to buy. Mixing instructions or terms and conditions into the specifications hinders suppliers' clear understanding of what it is that the public entity is seeking.

OBJECTIVES OF THE PROCUREMENT AND THE SPECIFICATIONS

The development of specifications demands good communication between the public procurement officer and the user agency. For commonly used commercial commodities such as pens, paper towels, and copy paper, the procurement office can prepare specifications without significant input from the user agencies in developing the actual language of the specification.

However, it is important to obtain continuous feedback from users about how those commodities are working and whether user agencies or users are actually buying them once a contract is in place. Usage information is critical so that the public procurement officer has a *heads up* if specifications need to be adjusted for the next procurement. For instance, it is important to make sure that the paper towels described in the specification fit the various towel dispensers throughout the public entity's buildings.

For more complicated procurements, the first step in the process of developing specifications requires that the public procurement officer and representatives of the user agency work closely to determine the objective of the procurement. Issues that they might address are what the user agency's needs are, whether they are short term or long term, and whether the commodity is one related strictly to an internal need, or one that the public will be using as well.

In some instances, the user agency may not have considered the public procurement officer as a strategic partner in its initial planning process. Those procurements start off on the wrong foot and can result in the public procurement officer playing catch-up on what may have been months, or even years, of prior planning. It is critical to ensure that the public procurement officer is brought in early in the planning process. Chapter 2 (*Procurement Leadership, Organization, and Value*) discusses this need for teamwork in more detail. Additionally, Chapter 20 (*Procurement of Information Technology*) outlines a team approach between public procurement officers and public information technology staff in the procurement of complex information technologies.

Some of the steps that the public procurement officer may take with user agencies to determine the objective of the procurement are:

- An analysis of the market, the competitive climate, and resources or research available on commodities and their performance, such as specifications from other public entities or associations like ASTM International[2]
- Identification of unique or atypical elements of the user agency's request
- Data gathering, including an understanding of the user agency's intended use for the item, how often it will use the item, and the quantity of the item needed
- An analysis to identify the acceptable level of performance; such as equipment speed, service performance standards, error levels, or quality of deliverables[3]
- An analysis of any outside requirements, such as federal Occupational Safety and Health Administration requirements, that may affect the user agency's request[4]
- An analysis of the tasks required to complete the specifications drafting process, including whether outside technical assistance is needed

Whether the drafting involves a commonly used commodity or service or something more complicated, specification writing is not strictly an exercise in finding the cheapest commodity or service on the market. It is a careful balance among factors related to suitability, performance and price, and overall cost effectiveness.

Specifications may eliminate some suppliers from a competitive procurement. The objective of a sound specifications-drafting process is to find a balance between what the user believes that it needs and a fair expression of those needs that is not too restrictive for the marketplace.

MANAGEMENT OF SPECIFICATIONS

In order to find that balance, it is imperative that the drafting of specifications have a central manager. That central manager is the Chief Procurement Officer, whom the law should authorize to have overall management responsibility for specification development and oversight. Users often have a valid but different perspective since their day-to-day jobs involve implementing state and local government objectives that are unrelated to the procurement process. As the person who is tasked with ensuring that the goals of the procurement law are met, the Chief Procurement Officer must have ultimate responsibility for the soundness, openness, competitiveness, and suitability of specifications.

Exercising that authority requires a delicate balance between the primary service role that a public procurement officer plays to assist his or her user agency and users, and the responsibility that the officer has to ensure, for instance, that the user agency is not buying something simply because a supplier suggested it or that it is not buying something that patently exceeds the user agency's requirements. For the most part, the debate centers not on the statement of the type of commodity or service needed, but on the manner in which it is described; that is, the text of the specifications.

This is true even where the Chief Procurement Officer delegates procurement authority to a user agency procurement office. That office has the same duties as the Chief Procurement Officer in managing specifications. But the Chief Procurement Officer must retain oversight authority as part of the terms of the delegation. In doing that, he or she is a sounding board and ultimate arbiter for user agency procurement officers who may find themselves at odds with their users.

The Recommended Regulations of the American Bar Association Model Procurement Code for State and Local Governments,[5] Section R3-103.01, supports the need for this oversight authority, stating that the Chief Procurement Officer shall have authority to return a purchase requisition to a user agency when "the request exceeds agency needs" or "the quality requested is inconsistent with the [State's] standards and usage." In order that everyone within state or local government understands their appropriate roles in the drafting of specifications, the Chief Procurement Officer must establish and communicate—through policies and manuals—clear guidelines for that task.

TYPES OF SPECIFICATIONS

There are several types of specifications from which a public procurement officer may choose when drafting a specification for a competitive procurement. Some common examples are brand name specifications, brand-name-or-equal specifications, detailed design-type specifications, functional or performance specifications, and qualified commodity lists. These types of specifications are generally used to describe a commodity rather than a service.

It is common, however, to write performance specifications for services contracts. Additionally, services specifications can describe the type of equipment that the services contractor must have available. An example is a solicitation seeking printing services in which a particular type of printing equipment is identified through a brand-name-or-equal specification to show the functionality requested.[6]

A specification may include things other than a description of the commodity or service that the government wishes to buy. It may require the submission and testing of samples or prototypes, the inspection of the supplier's production site, custom or environmentally friendly packaging, or warranties that go beyond those that the manufacturer may normally give.

The range of items that state and local governments purchase necessitates the use of all types of specifications. In solicitations covering hundreds of items of laboratory supplies or automotive parts, a brand-name-or-equal specification may be the most appropriate. For a proprietary mechanical part where no other will fit, a brand name specification is necessary, with price competition solicited from as many dealers as possible. For gasoline, a performance specification may be necessary. For an x-ray machine or an air compressor, a combination design-performance specification may work well.

These are the tools of the trade for a public procurement officer. It is critical to the success of a public procurement program that the public procurement officer have the training, knowledge, and confidence to choose the most advantageous type of specifications necessary to meet user agency's needs. The most commonly used specifications are described in the following paragraphs.

Brand Name Specification

The NIGP Dictionary of Procurement Terms defines a *brand name* specification as "a name, term, symbol, design, or any combination . . . used in specifications to describe a product by a unique identifier specific to a particular seller or manufacturer that distinguishes it from its competition."[7] There are legitimate circumstances when using this type of specification is appropriate. For instance, the original equipment manufacturer may be the only producer of a part, but it may not be the only supplier that carries the original manufacturer equipment item for sale, and thus may not be the only supplier from which a public agency can solicit a bid.

Since the use of this specification limits competition to a single commodity, it is the most restrictive.[8] A public procurement officer should use this type of specification when it is clear that it is the only way to meet a user's need. To ensure that its use is appropriate, a law or rule/regulation should require that the Chief Procurement Officer determine in writing, in advance, the propriety of its use. Even where the use of a brand name specification is warranted, competition among multiple suppliers is often possible.

Brand-Name-or-Equal Specification

A brand-name-or-equal specification consists of one or more brand names, model numbers, or other commodity designations that identify, by way of example, the specific commodity of a particular manufacturer that has the characteristics of the item that the public entity is seeking. A solicitation using a brand-name-or-equal specification invites other brands or models substantially equivalent to those named to be considered for awards, with the public procurement officer reserving the right to determine equivalency.

To ensure that suppliers submitting an alternative to a brand name commodity know the exact features of the brand name commodity that make it the benchmark, it is a best practice that the specification identify those critically necessary features significant to the specified brand. For instance, it is not likely that the color of a brand of lawnmower is going to be critical to a user agency. However, there are other key features of a brand that could make it the standard, such as deck size, engine horsepower, or available warranty.

One practical tip about writing this type of specification is to include a statement that the designated brands are for reference purposes only, and not a statement of preference. Here is some sample language:

Any manufacturers' names, trade names, brand names, or catalog numbers used in the specification are for the purpose of establishing and describing general performance and quality levels. The references are not intended to be restrictive, and bids are invited on these and comparable brands or commodities of any manufacturer.

A good way to express to suppliers that they have the opportunity to submit an equivalent may be the use of a phrase in the specification such as *or equal*, or *approved equal*, or *similar in design, construction, and performance*. Some public entities refer to this type of specification as brand name or equivalent, instead of brand name or equal to better clarify that commodities of equivalent performance and quality levels will be considered. Brand-name-or-equal specifications invite commodity and price competition across the marketplace. They have a legitimate place in public procurement, but should be used only where the brand name describes an industry standard for which there are competitors. In fact, it is best, where practical, to specify three or more brand references.

Qualified Products List

The NIGP Dictionary defines a qualified products list (QPL) as follows:[9]

A list of products identified by manufacturers' names and model numbers that are the only items that meet the minimum specifications as determined by the using entity. These products are used when quality is such a critical factor and testing so lengthy or expensive that the entity wants to stay with proven products. The list is prepared by testing products, either in the lab or in daily use. Items may be added to the list by the supplier demonstrating their quality by meeting specifications that have been defined by the using entity.

During the competitive procurement in which it is used, the list that is generated restricts suppliers to offering only commodities on that list.

The criteria and the methods for establishing and maintaining a QPL vary widely for different types of commodities. Some items require more detailed benchmarking or testing than others and dictate that the public procurement officer have access to testing facilities.

Various commodities might be tested in different ways. For musical instruments, the procurement office may establish a committee of musicians to test different brands of an instrument according to certain procedures. In another circumstance, for an item of heavy construction equipment, that office may establish the performance level desired, and then conduct field tests of similar models from different manufacturers to determine which of them meets those performance requirements. In the case of padlocks, the procurement office may test a number of brands under controlled conditions and assess their performance. For ready-mixed paints, the office may use laboratory tests to accept or reject a brand.

The Chief Procurement Officer should establish policies and procedures specifying how the qualification process works. This includes ensuring that the procurement office announces that it is establishing a QPL and the procedures for suppliers to submit their commodities. The announcement must also advise suppliers of the qualifications of the commodities sought and the means used to evaluate the commodities submitted. It should also advise suppliers that, if they do not participate by submitting commodities to qualify, they will not have the opportunity to do so until the procurement office establishes a new QPL in the future.

Using a QPL eliminates the need for samples or testing under a solicitation issued to purchase the types of commodities that have prequalified. Instead, the public procurement officer may make an award promptly since the acceptability or comparative rating of commodities is done before the solicitation is issued. Subpart 9.2 of the Federal Acquisition Regulation—the body of regulations that implement the United States government's procurement system—spells out how the QPL process works within that system.[10]

To avoid a QPL process that leads to marginal levels of quality, a best practice is for the qualifications procedures to include, where appropriate for the commodity, qualitative ratings or test scores that are tied to prices. For example, a QPL may require a truck tire to pass a use test of a minimum average of 25,000 miles to be qualified. If tests on the six brands of tires submitted pass the tests and average 25,000; 26,000; 29,000; 30,000; 32,000; and 36,000 miles, the public procurement officer may determine the lowest average cost per mile.

This qualitative or numerical test score comparison to price is critical for assuring the best use of a QPL. Since QPLs focus on commodities already on the market, they do not encourage or take advantage of innovation unless they use those performance ratings as criteria for qualification and contract award.

The actual samples and testing results have a life beyond the establishment of the QPL, and the public procurement officer should retain them. That official may use them as a contract standard so that he or she may enforce quality if a contractor subsequently delivers questionable commodities. The need for enforceability results not only from a concern over receiving substandard commodities. At times, manufacturers modify the quality of a commodity without changing its model number or other designation. The commodity may still be listed as acceptable, though it may no longer meet the specification. The public procurement officer with the sample in hand has a formidable tool in enforcing the quality level that the contract specifies.

Design Specification

Design specifications describe dimensional and other physical requirements of the item to be purchased. *Design* indicates that the specification concentrates on how a commodity is to be fabricated or constructed. It is the most traditional kind of specification, having been used historically in public contracting for buildings, highways, and other public construction. It represents the kind of thinking in which architects and engineers have been trained. It is used when a structure or commodity has to be specifically made to meet the specific need.

Additionally, large-scale technology systems require a unique set of specifications since those systems do not exist in a commercial, off-the-shelf form to meet the specific needs of a state or local government. Because of the high cost of a major construction or enterprise technology system project, it is generally the case that a public entity must ask its legislative body—a state legislature or city council, for instance—to appropriate funds for that specific project.

Consequently, the public entity must estimate that project's cost in order to request the funds. A project design provides the basis for calculating the estimate. For large technology systems, this becomes a problem. The rapid pace of changing technology creates a dilemma since the slow nature of the legislative funding process can make a design obsolete before the procurement gets off of the ground.

Detailed design specifications frequently have precise characteristics that unnecessarily limit competition. Unless the specification seeks a custom-produced item, it can be extremely difficult to draft design specifications without being unduly restrictive. Design specifications may also reflect the status quo and lag behind the state of the art, preventing consideration of the latest improvements in commodities.

Since design specifications for commodities do not accommodate rapidly changing technology and are poorly suited for the purchase of many commercial commodities, a public procurement officer should use them sparingly. In most cases, it is far better to use a performance specification alone or combined with a design specification so that suppliers select their best commodity for the functionality required.

Performance Specification

Performance specifications state the function that a user agency wishes to achieve. They do not commit the public purchaser to a set design or commodity that will presumably meet the required functionality. Instead, the specification states what the user agency needs the commodity to do and asks the supplier to demonstrate that its commodity qualifies.

A performance or functional specification is less concerned about how a commodity is made and more concerned about how well it performs, and at what cost. In contrast to the design approach, performance specifications afford the manufacturer or supplier sizable latitude in how to accomplish the end purpose.

The use of performance specifications is not limited to the purchase of commodities. They are also critical in services contracts. The best practice for a public procurement officer writing a specification for services is to establish critical minimum levels of service to which a supplier must commit in the proposal it submits. Those minimum levels become a key part of the contract for services and provide the most valuable tool for the public procurement officer in measuring contract performance. Chapter 10 (*Contracting for Services*) discusses this in more detail.

The examples that follow illustrate the use of performance specifications for services. A solicitation seeking services to administer a public agency's employee health insurance program may require that the supplier agree to respond to all telephone calls from employees within 24 hours, and to generate no more than three employee complaints per quarter. A solicitation requesting janitorial services may mandate that the supplier commit to vacuuming offices three times per week, and generate no more than one complaint monthly about breakage. For more information about contracting for services contracts management, see Chapter 10 (*Contracting for Services*), Chapter 13 (*Quality Assurance*), and Chapter 14 (*Contract Management and Contract Administration*).

Performance specifications are not new. Dated December 23, 1907, Signal Corps Specification No. 486: *Advertisement and Specification for a Heavier-Than-Air Flying Machine* was almost entirely a performance description.[11] Materials and design were left largely to the bidders, while performance requirements listed such things as takeoff and landing in a specified distance and on specified surfaces. The Wright Brothers, Dayton, Ohio, was the successful bidder at a contract price of $25,000.00 for delivery within 200 days to Fort Meyer, Virginia, with the package to be marked Order 3619.

Writing competitive performance specifications and evaluating bids or proposals submitted in response requires a different approach than one geared more toward design. For design specifications, the goal is to look for similarities and equivalencies in commodities in order to establish common denominators, and largely to ignore commodity differences. Performance specifications, on the other hand, accept the similarities, but seek to identify differences that provide equal or better performance at lower costs.

Another element of a performance specification focuses on ownership costs as a more accurate basis than initial price for achieving economy. Chapter 6 (*Sustainable Procurement Considerations and Strategies*) and Chapter 9 (*Bid and Proposal Evaluation and Award*) discuss these types of cost analyses.

Performance specifications are useful tools because they essentially ask the supplier to show that its commodity or services can meet benchmarks. Those benchmarks make contract management easier. The central procurement office's policies and guidelines should encourage public procurement officers to start their analysis of what type of specification to use by focusing on performance specifications first.

Minimal Specifications Under the Best Value Procurement Approach

There is a source selection approach that generally is conducted as a type of competitive sealed proposals called best value procurement or performance information procurement system. Chapter 7 (*Competition: Solicitations and Methods*) and Chapter 20 (*Procurement of Information Technology*) provide descriptions of this approach. Under this approach, the specifications are very minimal. The offerors are expected to provide proposals that the solicitation often limits to fewer than ten pages.

SAMPLES AND TECHNICAL DATA

Samples and commodity data questionnaires are valuable aids in the specification process. For many commodities, the comparison and testing of samples can effectively supplement a brief commodity description that is the basis for a specification.

This is how the process generally works. The public procurement officer requesting samples under a solicitation subjects them to comparisons such as visual inspection, taste testing, or chemical and physical laboratory tests. The comparison may be conducted blindly, without identification of the particular brands being tested, to ensure objectivity. Data and relative performance results are documented. Then the public procurement officer, along with a team of users, examines that documentation and determines the best commodity on a price/performance, cost-effective basis.

Examples of commodities for which this approach is useful are waxes and floor finishes, paints, disinfectants and germicides, file cabinets, surgical dressings, tires, cleaning agents, classroom furniture, and art materials, to name a few. As mentioned earlier, it is important to keep samples that are tested or reviewed to compare them to what the contractor actually supplies.

A solicitation may require suppliers to submit product questionnaires and call for technical data to be furnished to enhance the public entity's understanding of its own solicitation's specifications. In many cases, the product questionnaires and requested data may substitute for the submission of samples.

Prototypes may also be of value in assuring compliance and ultimate satisfaction with a commodity. The NIGP Dictionary describes a prototype as "an initial version or working model of a new commodity or invention. Usually constructed and tested to evaluate the feasibility of a design and to identify problems that need to be corrected." Where a solicitation requires the production and submission of a prototype, it stipulates that the successful supplier awarded the contract will be required to submit that prototype before the government orders any of the commodity.

In the purchase of truck chassis or band uniforms, for example, final award of a contract may be contingent upon the successful supplier producing a model that demonstrates compliance with the specification's requirements. The process allows problems to be resolved before the successful supplier manufactures and delivers the units. If the public procurement officer and the successful supplier do not agree on the preproduction sample, the solicitation and contract should provide that the public procurement officer may cancel the contract, perhaps paying an amount for the prototype, and then contract with another supplier that competed for the same contract. Chapter 13 (*Quality Assurance*) discusses testing in more detail.

STANDARDIZATION OF SPECIFICATIONS

Prior versions of the NIGP Dictionary defined a *standard specification* as one "that is to be used for all or most purchases of an item. . . ." Today, that dictionary no longer offers any definition of that term but provides instead definitions of two related terms:

- ***Standardization of Specifications***—*The process of establishing a single specification for an item, or range of items.*
- ***Standards (Standardization) Committee***—*Generally, an internal committee consisting of cross-functional representation including procurement, end users, and other internal stakeholders impacted by the decisions of the committee. Examples of key functions and activities may include: Developing [sic] standards through a simplification process for products and services, establish specifications, review items to determine which items should be incorporated into a standards program, approve products for the Qualified Products List.*

Standardization of specifications is appropriate where user agencies frequently and repetitively purchase the same commodities, and where uniform performance and quality levels can be identified. It reduces the varieties of items bought, simplifies inventories, facilitates the consolidation of requirements into large volume bids and contracts, and eliminates duplicative specification writing.

Law should assign the responsibility for developing a standardization program to the Chief Procurement Officer in order to ensure that all appropriate users and relevant parties are involved. The ability of a standardization program to meet its fundamental objectives, which is to achieve uniformity and keep current, depends upon flexibility—both in how it operates and in how quickly the program can develop the specifications. To reduce rigidity and obsolescence, standard specifications should incorporate performance standards wherever practical. Standardization boards and standing specification committees should avoid becoming institutionalized, too comfortable with the status quo, and inflexible. Ad hoc committees and supplier input and participation can bring fresh approaches to the process.

A central procurement office that standardizes specifications should regularly reexamine its program to ensure that it accommodates and is readily responsive to new concepts, improved commodities, and advanced applications. This calls for a focus on at least five aspects of the program:

- Identifying items for which standards currently are relatively stable, such as meats, canned fruits and vegetables, and various building materials
- Discontinuing standard specifications for items where such specifications are no longer needed or it has become impractical to update and maintain them
- Substituting, wherever possible, performance requirements for dimensional and other design-type details, especially in the case of items for which manufacturing standards tend to be unstable
- Providing a highly expeditious means of reviewing and modifying a standard specification for a current procurement
- Expanding the advisory role and ad hoc participation of user agency personnel throughout the standards process

PROCEDURES FOR DEVELOPING SPECIFICATIONS

The ability to develop specifications is a critical skill for any public procurement officer, but can be difficult and time consuming. This section will present suggestions for drafting certain types of specifications.

Identifying the User Agency's Needs

This chapter has discussed the importance of investing the overall authority in the Chief Procurement Officer to determine specifications for a competition. That principle ensures that the decision is made by someone whose duties under the procurement law are to ensure that there is an appropriate level of competition in light of the user's needs. However, it is just as critical that the public procurement officer, whether from the central office or from a user agency, maintains through his or her own initiative good communication with the user agencies. The public procurement officer's responsibility is to serve the state or local government customer within the framework that the procurement law establishes.

Chapter 14 (*Contract Management and Contract Administration*) discusses the importance of using steering or user committees in the administration of some contracts. Good contract management also requires that there be mechanisms in place for users to report supplier deficiencies to a public procurement officer. Chapter 13 (*Quality Assurance*) offers some guidance about identifying deficiencies early and resolving them. Another means of tracking whether a contract is working is through data showing purchasing patterns, that is, that the contract is being used.

These contract management tools and the information that they generate become critical to drafting specifications for the next competition for the repurchase of those or similar items. For complicated items, such as technology integration or health insurance coverage, another important factor in preparing reliable specifications is ensuring that the public procurement officer is part of the strategic planning for the purchase. Procurement planning with users is discussed further in Chapter 4 (*Strategies and Plans*).

For a procurement that aims at a specific user's need, it is important for the public procurement officer to request that the user express its requirements in terms of functional or performance requirements. The public procurement officer should also design questionnaires for the user agencies to complete detailing their use of those items. The thrust of the questionnaires should be on how the requested commodity or service is to be used, and the results expected.

This planning helps to accomplish two important objectives: diverting the attention of user agency program personnel from a particular brand preference by directing it to describe a purpose for which the item is required; and providing the central procurement office with the kind of information needed to invite broader competition from prospective bidders and offerors and establish valid criteria for evaluating responses.

Aids in Preparing Specifications

As noted earlier, it is not the purpose or role of the central procurement office to write all specifications on its own. The central procurement office, public procurement officers in user agencies, and in some cases the user agencies themselves must assist in preparing specifications.

Here are some examples of resources that are available to the public procurement officer:

- Commodity information from industry
- Standards and test information from national professional societies
- Example specification information from other federal, state, and local governments, whether from the entity itself or through online database services that aggregate this type of data across multiple entities
- Knowledge and expertise from personnel of the user agencies
- Specification assistance for complex items through services contracts to assist in drafting specifications (and possible assessment and recommendations in the award process)

A procurement office staff must establish and maintain open communications with these resources in a manner that systematically gathers, culls, classifies, and makes use of the information available.

In using any resources or evaluating information, the public procurement officer is obligated to exercise his or her professional judgment, and not be a passive recipient of the data provided. As emphasized in Chapter 2 (*Procurement Leadership, Organization, and Value*) a key duty of the public procurement officer is to provide service to the user agency; and that officer has a responsibility to be creative in finding resources to assist that agency in locating commodities and services.

Once the public procurement officer has an initial understanding of the user's needs, he or she should make a plan (such as conducting market research) to investigate the resources available. The public procurement officer should only begin writing the specification once the information gathered has been thoroughly weighed, analyzed, discussed, and vetted with the user agency or agencies.

Specification advisory committees or focus groups involving various commodity areas and consisting primarily of knowledgeable program people from various user agencies are a necessary and invaluable part of a successful specification development process. For some critical contracts, these committees should stay intact beyond the contract award process to assist the public procurement officer in monitoring contract compliance and in making decisions (for instance, on renewal price increases).

The expertise and testing capabilities of colleges and universities, especially technical institutions, are particularly useful as a resource for specifications. Outside the state and local government community there are many industrial trade associations and independent research and testing organizations that can supply up-to-date technical information on a regular basis across a full range of commodity areas.

Direct Supplier Marketing

The marketing programs of many suppliers are geared to sales efforts made directly to user agencies rather than to or through the central procurement office. In addition to creating demand for needs that may not exist and stimulating unwarranted preferences for particular brands or suppliers, the practice frequently may result in a supplier improperly drafting or writing a specification.

In the absence of a law, the central procurement office should have a written policy stating that, where an agent or representative of a manufacturer or prospective bidder or offeror unofficially and significantly participates in the preparation of a specification, a procurement office will not consider bids or proposals submitted on that manufacturer's commodity. It should further state that a bid or proposal will not be accepted or considered from that supplier under a solicitation based on those specifications.

While information and advice are needed from industry and suppliers, a supplier who drafts specifications unofficially for the user agencies prejudices the rights of other prospective competitors and the public. Acceptance of bids or proposals from suppliers that have had significant input into specifications raises the risk of protests and litigation in which the supplier's *unofficial role* in specification development is rightfully revealed. That, in turn, reduces confidence in the procurement process by the public and legislative bodies.

There can be situations where the public procurement officer seeks out supplier input or where a supplier is under contract to provide a needs assessment or a design. In those cases, the issue concerning whether the supplier may participate in a competitive procurement that may follow is not clear cut. There needs to be balance to ensure fairness.

If the public entity issues a solicitation seeking a contractor for the first phase of a project that involves preparing data or specifications to be used in a follow-on competitive procurement, the solicitation should advise prospective bidders and offerors that they may be barred from competing on future phases of the project. Note that the Common Rule relating to procurement using federal funds, which is discussed more thoroughly at the end of this chapter, precludes any outside party assisting with drafting specifications from competing for the procurement using those specifications.

It is important to note that public chiefs of information technology believe, with valid reasoning, that a complete arms' length from suppliers makes it very difficult to quickly identify new technologies on the market. Chapter 20 (*Procurement of Information Technology*) provides further insights into this issue.

Commercial Product Preference

The best practice is for a procurement policy to prefer the purchase of commercial commodities over specifications that require items to be specially made. It should also stress functional and performance characteristics above design requirements in the preparation of specifications. Procurement policies and procedures should provide for uniform formats of specification documents; that is, standard presentation of the elements, consistent types of item identifiers, and adequate reference to the kind and source of the commodity or service requirements.

Alternatives and Optional Items

Alternatives and optional items in a solicitation describe commodities or services that are not the main object of the solicitation. Specifically, they describe items that the user agency may buy in addition to the item that it definitely intends to buy.

Occasionally, suppliers offer their own alternatives or optional items in their bids or proposals, even though the solicitation has not requested them. These are problematic. One of the foundations of the public competitive process is that competing suppliers have a level playing field. When suppliers unilaterally try to sweeten the pot by offering different terms than those requested, the user agency's consideration of those items gives an advantage to the offering supplier that competing suppliers do not have. The best practice is for the public procurement officer not to evaluate those items. Any alternatives or options that the user agency may wish to consider should be clearly requested in the solicitation.

Alternate specifications are sometimes needed in the public interest to compare costs or to keep an award within the funds available. They can be used to obtain wider competition (alternative commodities), quicker deliveries (alternative delivery requirements), and other advantages.

Optional items will have the same effect. Optional items are features that may be adapted to a piece of basic equipment such as an automobile or communication product in order to enhance performance or capacity. They may be needed under certain circumstances or may represent only luxury accessories. Optional items can significantly affect the total price of the commodity.

To ensure that the use of alternatives and options is not abused, a public procurement officer should not permit a user to make decisions concerning how alternatives or optional items will be evaluated until bids or proposals are open or are being evaluated for award. Careful planning and proper structuring of specifications and solicitations are critical to the successful inclusion of alternates and the purchase of optional items.

A WORD ABOUT SPECIFICATION REQUIREMENTS WHEN USING FEDERAL FUNDS

In 2013, the federal government issued the Uniform Administrative Requirements, Cost Principles, and Audit Requirements for Federal Awards, 2 Code of Federal Regulations Part 200 (Common Rule). Any non-federal public entity whose procurements are funded with federal monies must comply with the Common Rule.

The Common Rule requires the precise, accurate, and open process for developing specifications that this chapter discusses. For instance, the Common Rule states:[12]

> *(c) The non-Federal entity must have written procedures for procurement transactions. These procedures must ensure that all solicitations:*
> *(1) Incorporate a clear and accurate description of the technical requirements for the material, product, or service to be procured. Such description must not, in competitive procurements, contain features which unduly restrict competition. The description may include a statement of the qualitative nature of the material, product, or service to be procured and, when necessary, must set forth those minimum essential characteristics and standards to which it must conform if it is to satisfy its intended use. Detailed product specifications should be avoided if at all possible. When it is*

impractical or uneconomical to make a clear and accurate description of the technical requirements, a "brand name or equivalent" description may be used as a means to define the performance or other salient requirements of procurement. The specific features of the named brand which must be met by offers must be clearly stated; and

(2) Identify all requirements which the offerors must fulfill and all other factors to be used in evaluating bids or proposals.

(d) The non-Federal entity must ensure that all prequalified lists of persons, firms, or products which are used in acquiring goods and services are current and include enough qualified sources to ensure maximum open and free competition. Also, the non-Federal entity must not preclude potential bidders from qualifying during the solicitation period.

The Common Rule also states that outside parties assisting with procurements, including drafting specifications, "must be excluded from competing for such procurements."[13]

The Common Rule reflects the best practices for all procurements relating to drafting specifications, whether or not federal funds are paying for the purchase.

CONCLUSION

Specifications are the lifeblood of the procurement process. They must be broad enough to allow for fair competition, yet be precise enough for the public entity to acquire the quality commodities and services it needs for its essential programs. Balanced specifications require thorough planning and communication between the public procurement officer and all stakeholders involved, and function best when they are the result of a partnership between the public procurement officer and the user, formed from the moment that the user identifies its need.

ENDNOTES

1. Access to The Institute for Public Procurement: NIGP Dictionary is available at: http://www.nigp.org/home/find-procurement-resources/dictionary-of-terms
2. The ASTM was formerly known as the American Society for Testing and Materials. See: https://www.astm.org/
3. The NIGP Dictionary defines *deliverables* as: "1. Expected work product as defined in a contract . . . 3. The completion of a milestone or the accomplishment of a task that can be measured and verified, and may be a unit by which a contractor or consultant may be paid."
4. https://www.osha.gov/
5. A copy of the Model Procurement Code along with the Recommended Regulations is available at: http://apps.americanbar.org/dch/committee.cfm?com=PC500500
6. Designs for construction projects may also include brand name or brand-name-or-equal specifications in them relating to equipment that the project design requires to be installed, such as heating/air conditioning/ventilation systems or windows. The same cautions that this chapter discusses about using them for commodity procurements applies to their use in construction procurements as well.
7. See Endnote 1.
8. The Common Rule, the set of regulations establishing procurement and accounting requirements for the expenditure of federal funds by non-federal entities, explicitly states that a brand name specification restricts competition. See 2 Code of Federal Regulations §200.319(2)(6). The Common Rule is discussed at the end of this chapter.

CHAPTER 5: **NON-CONSTRUCTION SPECIFICATIONS AND SCOPES OF WORK**

9. See Endnote 1.
10. https://www.acquisition.gov/far/html/Subpart%209_2.html
11. The Wright Story. (n.d.). Retrieved September 1, 2018, from http://www.wright-brothers.org/History_Wing/Wright_Story/Showing_the_World/Back_in_Air/Signal_Corps_Spec.htm
12. See 2 Code of Federal Regulations §200.319, *Competition*, at: https://www.gpo.gov/fdsys/pkg/CFR-2017-title2-vol1/pdf/CFR-2017-title2-vol1-part200.pdf
13. 2 CFR §200.319(a). The regulation may be found at: https://www.gpo.gov/fdsys/pkg/CFR-2017-title2-vol1/pdf/CFR-2017-title2-vol1-part200.pdf

CHAPTER 6: SUSTAINABLE PROCUREMENT CONSIDERATIONS AND STRATEGIES

RECOMMENDED BEST PRACTICES

- Sustainable procurement programs should be developed with the cooperation and input from persons representing a wide range of users, using agencies, organizations that certify commodities and services as sustainable, and suppliers—all of which have ideas to contribute.
- That broad input in the development of the program will help provide support from both inside and outside the public entity.
- Foundational to a program is a policy that clearly outlines the program's purpose, legal authority establishing that policy, the commodities and services covered, and the external certifications and other verification tools used to make it credible. The policy should also identify the roles and responsibilities of the staff responsible for implementing it and the conditions under which waivers from the program will be granted.
- The benefits and effectiveness of the program must be tracked and measured, including the use of techniques such as total cost of ownership and life cycle costing. Available online calculators should be utilized to assist with demonstrating benefits.
- Reporting on the public entity's usage of sustainable commodities and services is critical, either through expenditure information if available or, if not, through reports that contractors provide.

CHAPTER 6: SUSTAINABLE PROCUREMENT CONSIDERATIONS AND STRATEGIES

This chapter offers insights and provides guidance regarding the role of public procurement in implementing state and local government sustainability programs. This chapter also provides tools and resources to assist public procurement officers in carrying out sustainability mandates. The NASPO website contains several helpful resources; including an interactive map of sustainable purchasing programs across the country.[1] NASPO's 2018 Survey of State Practices identifies states that have implemented green purchasing programs or initiatives, as seen in Figure 6.1.

The focus of this chapter is on commodities and services. Sustainability programs for construction projects are discussed in Chapter 11 (*Procurement of Construction and Related Services*).

OVERVIEW OF SUSTAINABLE PROCUREMENT

Definitions of Key Terms

To begin this chapter's discussion, it is important to define key terms. Over recent decades, environmental procurement has evolved to become part of what is known as sustainable procurement. As may be seen in the following definitions, the term *sustainable procurement* is broader than the term *environmental procurement*. Sustainable procurement includes environmentally friendly procurement along with social and economic factors. For clarity, both of these terms are defined below.

The NIGP Dictionary defines *sustainable procurement* as:

- Procurement and investment process that takes into account the economic,

FIGURE 6.1 | GREEN PURCHASING POLICIES, CONTRACTS, AND PROGRAMS

Has your state implemented any of the following green purchasing programs or initiatives?
Please select all that apply.

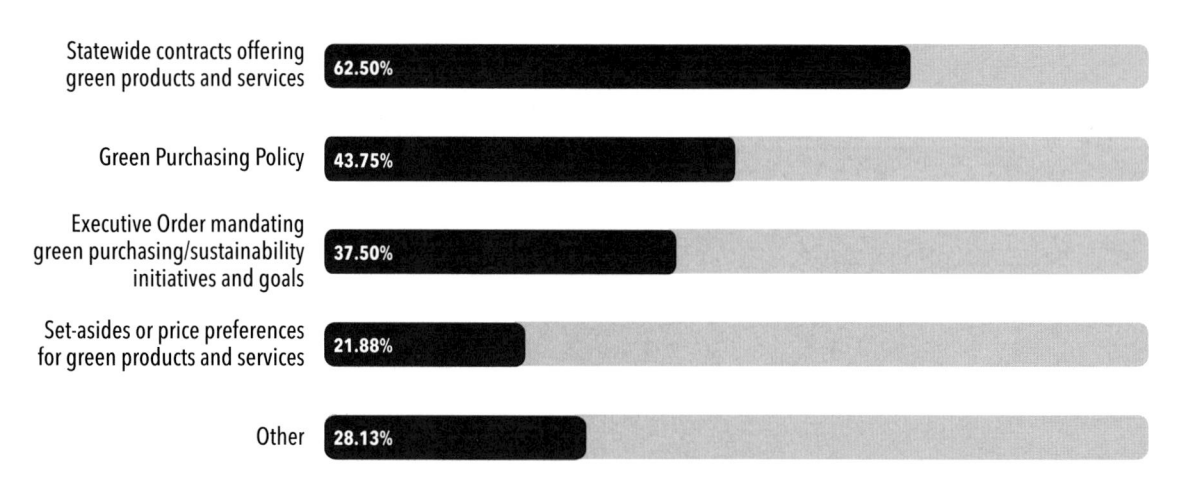

Category	Percentage
Statewide contracts offering green products and services	62.50%
Green Purchasing Policy	43.75%
Executive Order mandating green purchasing/sustainability initiatives and goals	37.50%
Set-asides or price preferences for green products and services	21.88%
Other	28.13%

Total of respondents: 48   Statistics based number of response: 32   Filtered: 0   Skipped: 16

environmental, and social impacts of an entity's spending.[2]

In comparison, Martin and Miller (2006) define *environmentally preferable procurement* as: *an attempt to address environmental challenges by taking advantage of the government's vast procurement power to create strong markets for environmentally friendly products and services. Procurement of commodities and services in a way that does not harm the environment; also known as green procurement*[3] (as cited in the NIGP dictionary).

For the purposes of this chapter, the broader term *sustainable procurement* will be used.

The language of the law or other state or local government mandate, such as an executive order that creates a program, will determine whether the program is strictly an environmentally friendly one or instead is one of sustainability.

Sustainable Commodities and Services

State and local governments that mandate the purchase of sustainable commodities and services have determined that doing so provides environmental, social, and economic benefits. That determination also recognizes that sustainability programs protect human health and the environment over the course of the commodity or service life cycle, ranging from extraction of raw materials to end-of-life disposal of a commodity. A sustainable service or commodity has a lesser or reduced negative effect on human health and the environment when compared with competing commodities or services. Examples include commodities that:

- Conserve energy or water
- Contain recycled or reused materials
- Minimize waste
- Consist of fewer toxic substances
- Reduce the amount of toxic substances disposed of or consumed
- Lessen the impact on public health
- Protect open space
- Are socially responsible

Sustainability Criteria Focused on Social Considerations

Institutional—public and private—purchasers are increasingly interested in procuring commodities that are not only environmentally preferable but have also been produced in a socially responsible manner. In a global supply chain, sourcing decisions that the public procurement officer must make can affect individual lives and communities far from the point of purchase.

Transparency throughout supply chains is still an aspiration and not a reality. Pressure is being applied to supply chains by stakeholders such as investors, customers, employees, and citizens who are increasingly expecting that public and private entities take steps to ensure that their procurement decisions do not enable or promote human rights abuses.

It is a challenge to learn what questions to ask suppliers regarding how they address negative labor and human rights impacts and to determine what constitutes credible supporting documentation from a supplier. Though additional work is still required in this area, new resources and case studies are available to state and local governments interested in learning more about how to address these issues. An example is the Green Electronics Council's *Purchaser Guide for Addressing Labor and Human Rights Impacts in IT Procurement.*[4] Several other resources that highlight the application of socially responsible procurement tools are available on the websites of the Sustainable Purchasing Leadership Council,[5] the International Labour Organization,[6] and the Responsible Business Alliance.[7]

PUBLIC POLICY REASONS FOR THE PROCUREMENT OF SUSTAINABLE COMMODITIES AND SERVICES

Laws and executive orders may mandate sustainable procurement. In many cases, procurement of sustainable services and commodities is simply a good practice. Purchasing sustainable commodities and services frequently saves money or reduces costs, promotes the more efficient use of government resources, and protects the health and well-being of vulnerable populations who work in or visit government or government contractor facilities. Sustainable procurement programs may also strengthen relationships between a state or local government and members of the community and create new opportunities for partnerships with suppliers. Finally, the buying power of governments can convince manufacturers and service providers to produce or offer reasonably priced sustainable commodities or services that do less harm to public health and the environment.

Some critics of sustainable procurement assert that sustainable commodities are more expensive than their non-sustainable counterparts. While this is true in some instances, many sustainable commodities are either cost neutral or save money when considering the total cost of using or owning them. They often have a short payback period, after which they provide a significant ongoing cost savings in the form of reduced maintenance, operation, and disposal expenses. A simple example is a ball point pen that may be more expensive, but which lasts significantly longer than a lower-priced pen.

Sustainable commodities are becoming increasingly cost competitive in high-volume markets such as information technology, janitorial supplies, personal care products, paints, lighting, and appliances. Beyond the initial purchase cost, savings can be realized through reductions in the purchase of protective equipment used with hazardous materials, in energy use and in non-recyclable waste. Sustainable commodities also offer the added value of reducing toxins introduced into the environment through manufacturing, use, or both.

Some examples of direct and indirect cost-saving opportunities that the purchase of sustainable commodities offers include reductions in:

- Material and energy consumption
- Operational costs through energy savings from more efficient equipment
- Disposal costs of hazardous and solid waste
- Repair and replacement costs when using more durable and repairable equipment
- Employee safety and health concerns
- Hazardous materials management costs through the use of less toxic commodities

CREATING A SUSTAINABLE PROCUREMENT PROGRAM

When developing a sustainable procurement program, success is predicated upon the public entity's commitment to involve key people and to create benchmarks and reporting that make user agencies and suppliers accountable for sustainable procurement goals. This section outlines core questions, considerations, and steps that state and local governments may take when laying the foundation for a procurement program focused on sustainability.

Participation of Key Stakeholders

Like all purchases, procuring sustainable commodities and services relies upon cooperation and input from a host of both internal and external stakeholders. Key participants to consider are:

- **Public procurement officers**—They play a prominent role in the development of a sustainable procurement program. They may coordinate procurements among various user agencies within a state or

local government to optimize supply chain performance and cost efficiency. Public procurement officers frequently work with user agency personnel to build sustainable specifications. Finally, they can encourage current suppliers or new ones to improve the sustainable performance of their operations and of their commodities or services.
- **Public entity program managers and other user agency personnel**—They play a large role in determining the specifications for commodities and services they need, and frequently own the budget that will pay for those commodities and services. These individuals look to the public procurement officer to obtain critical information and education regarding sustainable commodities and services.
- **Manufacturers, suppliers, and contractors**—This group can be encouraged to change the design, manufacturing processes, and supply chain of current commodities or services to minimize environmental impacts. Suppliers may provide feedback regarding new and innovative approaches to sustainable commodities and services. Contractors that provide required reporting on the types of sustainable commodities and services purchased by a public entity, the volumes purchased, and the dollars spent offer significant data for measuring the success of the program and for future planning.
- **Environmental or sustainable subject matter experts**—These persons within state and local governments are subject matter experts on priorities and strategies, and may advise on environmental laws that must be met through the procurement process. They may assist user agencies in identifying and assessing more sustainable alternatives to currently used commodities and services.
- **External organization certifiers and standard setters**—These outside organizations play a role in the process since they provide standards, certifications, and government labeling programs (called *eco labeling* or *ecolabels*) to show that the commodity is manufactured according to recognized environmental standards.

It is also essential that there be a person designated as the sustainable procurement program advocate to lead the effort, most likely from the stakeholder group. The law establishing the program may specify the user agency tapped to lead the program, which will narrow the search for the right person to be that advocate. Whether the law provides that guidance or not, the person designated as the advocate must have significant leadership skills as well as the backing of the state or local government's executives.

Building Stakeholder and Executive Buy-In

When enlisting the support of the stakeholders, the program advocate must recognize that sustainability is one of a multitude of topics vying for stakeholders' attention. As part of the effort to launch the program successfully, he or she will need to educate and advocate to the stakeholders about why they should invest their time and energy into establishing and maintaining a sustainable procurement program.

Some tips for preparing to engage with sustainable procurement stakeholders include:

- Consider how sustainability requirements for a commodity or service might overlap with existing laws, rules/regulations, policies, and strategic goals of the public entity's internal programs and users. If none exist, create a plan that details the need for the resources needed to implement the program.
- Quantify benefits whenever possible. Use benefit calculation tools that highlight program effects such as reduced or eliminated environmental impact, enhanced benefits to human health, and realization of cost savings. Benefit calculation tools are discussed later in this chapter.

State and Local Government Procurement: A Practical Guide, 3rd Edition

- Emphasize the value that a sustainable procurement program can add to the public entity's brand and reputation in the community.

Educating Versus Mandating

Sustainable procurement programs effect change through a combination of laws and efforts that encourage state and local government personnel to implement sustainability directives.

While legislation mandating the procurement of a specific sustainable service or commodity may be the most effective way of jumpstarting or growing sustainable procurement programs, enacting a law can be a long process and difficult to achieve. At the state and local government level, the issuance of executive orders by governors, mayors, and others is likely to be a more rapid method and is easier to keep current. Executive orders do not have the same legal weight that a law does but they do provide high-level directives, guidance, and support that serve as a foundation for initiating action.

The success of a sustainable procurement program can be attributed in part to comprehensive education and outreach to public procurement officers within the state or local government. That effort should include information about the sustainability issues associated with specific commodities and services, detailing both economic and sustainability benefits that can be achieved, and providing easily available tools. While this process of educating and reaching out may take more time than imposing a mandate, the program tends to do a better job of engaging both the user agencies within the state or local government and the suppliers into the process by providing them with a sense of ownership. Once the benefits are clearly understood and the performance of the sustainable commodity or service demonstrated, sustainable procurement becomes the preferable choice.

DRAFTING A POLICY FOR A SUSTAINABLE PROCUREMENT PROGRAM

Any sustainable procurement program should be codified in a single document. Many state and local governments maintain sustainable procurement policies and they are often available online.

Environmental Factors and Other Sustainable Considerations

A key step in establishing a sustainable procurement program policy is to identify the environmental or societal *ill* that the program seeks to ameliorate in preparing and using specifications for sustainable commodities and services. Though public entities may choose to emphasize or focus upon specific sustainability impacts, policies often address some or all of the following sustainable considerations:

- Pollutant releases
- Toxicity, especially the use of or release of persistent bio-accumulative toxic chemicals, carcinogens, and reproductive and developmental toxins
- Waste generation and waste minimization
- Disposal considerations such as reusability, recyclability, or compostability
- Greenhouse gas emissions
- Energy consumption, energy efficiency, and the use of renewable energy
- Water consumption
- Depletion of natural resources
- Impacts on biodiversity
- Environmental practices that manufacturers and suppliers have incorporated into their production processes or operations
- Minimized packaging
- Social responsibility, including efforts to address labor rights, human rights, and community engagement across the life cycle of the commodity

Writing a Sustainable Procurement Policy

The following points identify and describe important elements that should be included in most policies:

- **Clear statement of purpose**—Most policies begin with a statement setting out the reasons that the state or local government is developing a sustainable procurement policy, a brief statement establishing the principles of the program, and identification of the internal stakeholders that the policy will involve and affect. This statement should always address environmental and sustainability considerations as previously described, which may include social factors such as sweatshop labor or local sourcing options.
- **Legal authority and relevant laws, regulations, and policies**—A policy will have added weight and authority if it is supported by existing laws, executive orders, rules/regulations, and mandates already in effect in a state and local government. References in the policy to relevant laws and rules/regulations will provide an important context and also stimulate the user agencies' efforts to comply with the policy's directives.
- **External standards, certifications, and ecolabels for commodities and services**—External standards, certifications, and ecolabels are a key element of any sustainable procurement policy. They are discussed later in this chapter. Use of these tools allows a state and local government to easily identify the important sustainable attributes of a commodity or service, then substantiate and verify them. Additional information about the importance of external sustainability standards appears later in this chapter in the section entitled *Understanding External Sustainability Standards*. Policies should include references to any specific external standards or certifications that a state or local government recognizes.

Due to the wide range of the use of ecolabels and the ongoing proliferation of "green" marketing claims, policies should also include general guidelines and common criteria that standards, certifications, and ecolabels must meet to be deemed credible. The United States Federal Trade Commission publishes *Green Guides* to provide guidance on "green" claims.[8] Similarly, many policies require that credible standards, certifications, and ecolabels be developed in accordance with resources such as the International Organization for Standards (ISO) Standard 14020:2000, *Environment Labels and Declarations—General Principles*,[9] United States Office of Management and Budget Circular A-119, *Federal Participation in the Development and Use of Voluntary Consensus Standards and in Conformity Assessment Activities*,[10] or the ISEAL Alliance, *Credible Sustainability Standards*:[11]

- **Identifying the types of commodities and services to target**—Although the goal should be a policy that establishes sustainable criteria for almost every type of commodity or service, prioritizing those routinely used or representing large expenditures is important at the outset of the program. Examples of common high-volume commodity categories might include: appliances, automobiles, cleaning products, computers, copier/multifunctional devices, food, furniture, industrial supplies, landscaping, lighting, mobile phones, office supplies, paper, playground equipment, printing services, transportation products, and servers.
- **A description of roles and responsibilities**—The policy should define the roles and responsibilities of all program stakeholders. This facilitates implementation of the policy and avoids confusion as the policy is implemented. Depending on how a procurement office is structured and its

relationship to the sustainability program stakeholders, it is important to spell out the process by which sustainable specifications are developed and enforced, the scope of the application of sustainable specifications, available training and other tools, and the means by which implementation and benchmarking, including cost savings, will be tracked.
- **Price preferences and waivers**—A state or local government may wish to use price preferences and waivers in its sustainable procurement program. The conditions for the use of those should be spelled out in the policy.

Price Preferences

Public entities may employ the use of a price preference to give sustainable commodities and services leeway to cost more to purchase than their non-sustainable competitors, but still be the commodity or service selected to be bought. Preferences most often apply in *low bid* situations and generally require that the law authorize them if that law requires that a contract be awarded based on low price. A standard preference allows the bid submitted by a supplier offering a sustainable commodity or service to be the winning low bidder if it is no higher than five to ten percent of the low bid of the supplier offering a non-sustainable commodity or service. Due to the disparate nature of commodities and services, not every commodity or service to be purchased based on low price requires the application of a price preference. Therefore, in instances where the law authorizes preferences, policies should provide a procurement office with the flexibility to apply preferences on a commodity or service category-specific basis.

A request for proposals process where price is not the only or most important contract award factor permits the public procurement officer to establish evaluation criteria that favor sustainable commodities or services. In those situations, the solicitation establishes a minimum specification favoring sustainable commodities or services along with evaluation criteria offering the greatest number of points for sustainable commodities or services, corporate practices, and solutions proposed by the supplier.

Waivers

Due to the dynamic nature of the sustainable commodity and service marketplace and the unique needs of user agencies, sustainable procurement program policies should outline scenarios in which the purchase of a sustainable commodity or service is not necessary.[12] Waivers should be documented and incorporated into purchase expenditure reports and future programmatic decisions.

Examples include:

- The sustainable commodity does not meet the required form, functionality, or utility
- The sustainable commodity is prohibitively expensive or cannot be competitively priced
- An emergency or compelling public health or safety reason exists that requires the purchase of a specific non-sustainable commodity

IMPLEMENTING A SUSTAINABLE PROCUREMENT PROGRAM

Specification Development and Use

As discussed earlier in this chapter, it is important to create an inclusive and thoughtful process for creating a sustainable procurement program, including the development of specifications. Successful sustainable procurement programs start with a core group of commodities and services to develop specifications using broad input.

The following are suggestions to consider when developing and using sustainable specifications.

- Look at what the public entity is already buying. Often, sustainable commodities or

services are already being purchased but the data has not been centrally collected and reported. Take credit for good work that is already being done.
- Look at what other state and local governments are doing, particularly the sustainable specifications being used.
- Solicit input from the supplier community, but do not show a preference. Create an open and neutral mechanism to gather information about available sustainable commodities and services on the market. Hold *sustainable product fairs* or focused public meetings on sustainability.
- Trust and value input. Be prepared to waive use of specifications for sustainable commodities or services if following investigation, a sustainable commodity or service will not perform adequately or will cost too much.

Selecting Targeted Commodities and Services

When building a sustainable procurement program, it is important to be strategic about the commodities or services that the program stakeholders choose to concentrate on first. Procuring commodities that are easily found in the marketplace, credibly address environmental issues, and save money at the point of purchase are cost neutral. These commodities and services represent the greatest opportunities for early success.

Some commodities that are ideal as the focus of a sustainability program are:

- **Energy efficient commodities and appliances**—Two United States government entities, the Environmental Protection Agency (EPA) and the Department of Energy, sponsor the Energy Star program.[13] It is a universal and credible means of verifying a commodity's energy efficiency. The Energy Star program covers numerous commodity categories including: copiers, faxes, other office equipment, mail machines, computers, lighting (including traffic), appliances, air conditioners, heating, ventilation equipment, and more. In their solicitations, public procurement officers commonly include requirements in solicitations that commodities meet the most recent Energy Star standard available in order to reduce electricity consumption and decrease the volume of pollution related to their use.
- **Computers and office equipment**—Procuring products that are energy efficient, less toxic, pollute less, and can be disposed of responsibly creates a unique opportunity to drastically reduce the environmental impact of an organization's day-to-day activities. Public procurement officers frequently use the EPEAT—Electronic Product Environmental Assessment Tool,[14] ecolabel of the Green Electronics Council, to ensure they are obtaining sustainable commodities. The EPEAT registry offers a list of thousands of commonly purchased information technology items and office equipment from many manufacturers. EPEAT-rated commodities meet full life cycle environmental criteria, including Energy Star, and may also meet social impact criteria.
- **Environmentally preferable paper**—Paper commodities are particularly important in a sustainability program because of their frequent use and because paper production has a substantial impact on forests, water, and energy consumption. The EPA has established Comprehensive Procurement Guidelines for recycled content for various types of paper, and those are good starting points.[15] Many state and local governments seek paper with even higher levels of recycled content. Third-party commodity certifications are available to assist in creating specifications for these commodities, such as those offered through the Forest Stewardship Council.[16] Depending on the volume of paper purchased and the region of the country, many public procurement officers are

CHAPTER 6: SUSTAINABLE PROCUREMENT CONSIDERATIONS AND STRATEGIES

able to procure environmentally preferable paper without increasing costs. Other public entities implement paper reduction strategies to offset differences in price by, for instance, encouraging the setting of office equipment to default to two-sided printing, reducing margin widths, and instituting paperless practices. Another sustainable procurement best practice is to require that suppliers for contracts to print publications and other items use chlorine-free paper to the maximum extent possible.

- **Green cleaning commodities**—As many as one in three cleaning chemicals may be hazardous due to their flammable, corrosive, or toxic properties. There also may be safety, health, and cost concerns in the handling, storage, and disposal of these chemicals. Some of the chemicals may not cause immediate injury, but rather are associated with cancer, reproductive disorders, respiratory problems, skin damage, and other health conditions. As a result, many public entities including schools require the use of less toxic but equally performing cleaning products. Some tools for locating these types of commodities are available through third-party organizations such as Green Seal[17] and UL's ECOLOGO Product Certification.[18]
- **Post-consumer recycled content commodities**—Requiring post-consumer recycled content in specifications for commodities strengthens markets for recyclable materials, reduces the waste stream going to landfills and incinerators, and works to create economic development opportunities within emerging industries. Usable post-consumer content includes paper, plastics, metals, and petroleum-based products. Commodities using that content include office papers and envelopes, packaging, plastic lumber, traffic cones, re-refined motor oil, antifreeze, and toner cartridges.
- **Services suppliers**—Public procurement officers may establish sustainability requirements in service contracts by specifying that materials that the contractors use in performing the contract meet established sustainability standards. The contracts may also mandate the use of particular processes or methods that are less harmful to the environment. Some examples of services that can use sustainable practices include landscaping, custodial, pest control, and printing. To illustrate, printing contracts may require the use of water- or vegetable-based lithographic ink to the maximum extent practicable, which will reduce the amount of volatile organic compounds released into the environment.

Using the Power of the Procurement Process and the Contract

Sustainability considerations should be an essential part of the early stages of a procurement process. State or local governments can use that process to encourage or require competing suppliers to offer sustainable commodities or services, or to follow sustainability practices.

Below are some recommendations on utilizing the power of the procurement process and the contract in support of a sustainable procurement program.

- **Incorporate sustainable specifications and utilize ecolabels**—In addition to mandating minimum sustainable specifications for commodities or services, as already discussed, explore other options such as specifying in the solicitation that suppliers must provide a sustainable alternative along with a conventional commodity or service. Consider stating a scoring preference in the evaluation criteria under a request for proposals to discourage suppliers from providing conventional items, which may increase the number of sustainable options available to the public entity.
- **Require reporting on sustainable purchases and practices**—Require suppliers

seeking contract awards to offer reporting on the volumes and types purchased and dollars spent by the public entity for sustainable commodities or services. Provide additional points in the evaluation of suppliers' proposals if they have the ability to supply those types of reports.

- **Allow suppliers to recommend alternative solutions**—Encourage suppliers to submit information identifying all environmental attributes of the requested commodity or service, even when such attributes have not been required. Public entities may use this information to develop specifications in the future that incorporate sustainability criteria. Ask suppliers to provide a sustainable alternative (or replacement) for their conventional commodity wherever possible. Such requests serve to reveal new sustainable commodities in the marketplace.
- **Evaluate suppliers' sustainability programs**—Include a supplier sustainability questionnaire in every formal solicitation, giving suppliers the opportunity to describe their sustainable operations. Provide additional evaluation points for the proposals of suppliers that can prove they have programs in place. Doing this sends a clear message to the suppliers that the public entity takes sustainability into consideration when awarding contracts.
- **Write contract language to allow the substitution or addition of sustainable commodities in an existing contract**—Include language in solicitations that permits the public entities to negotiate with the contractor during the contract term to substitute and add sustainable commodities when such commodities become available at a competitive price, are readily available, and satisfy the buying entity's performance needs.
- **Green the market basket**—As a way of obtaining discounts for sustainable commodities, make sure they are among commodities listed in the market basket on the pricing sheet that suppliers must submit during a formal competition for a contract. A *market basket* is a representative sample of routinely purchased, generally high-volume commodities for which the formal solicitation asks competing suppliers to provide discounted pricing. This market-basket pricing is used to evaluate the pricing that suppliers provide in their bids or proposals.
- **Write the contract to permit sustainable planning**—Incorporate language that requires potential contractors competing under a formal solicitation to agree to work with the public entity to explore the feasibility of implementing a sustainability plan. The objective of this requirement is to encourage suppliers to incorporate sustainable practices in their business operations, and then market those practices. It also allows the public entity to encourage contractors to expand their sustainability initiatives or add new initiatives during the contract term, depending on the interests of the public entity.

Selecting Contractors Using Total Cost of Ownership or Life Cycle Cost Factors

In the evaluation of suppliers' submissions to a solicitation, public procurement officers are increasingly using methods that are focused on selecting commodities and services through source selection methods that allow for the consideration of factors other than the low purchase price. Chapter 9 (*Bid and Proposal Evaluation and Award*) discusses these methods, including the idea of *best value*. There are some non-price factors that are often taken into consideration when evaluating the sustainability of a commodity or service; including quality, risk, performance, durability, local production, and environmental impacts. The analysis of these factors is often called *total cost of ownership* or *life cycle cost*.

The NIGP Dictionary defines life cycle cost as:

The total cost of ownership over the lifespan of the asset. An analysis technique that takes into account operating, maintenance, the time value of money, disposal, and other associated costs of ownership as well as the residual value of the item.[19]

Burt, Dobler, and Starling (2003) define total cost of ownership as:

A measure of all of the cost components associated with the procurement of a product or service. The sum of all fixed and variable costs attributed to a product or service. A philosophy for understanding all supply-chain-related costs of doing business with a particular supplier for a particular good or service[20] (as cited in The NIGP Dictionary).

With the rising costs of fuel and electricity, maintenance and operation, handling of toxic substances, pollution remediation, and insurance claims, some state and local governments require contractors to take responsibility for the safe operation and end-of-life management of their commodities. Therefore, a slightly higher purchase price may easily represent the best value when it provides an opportunity for significant cost avoidance throughout the entire life of the commodity.

Even if a public entity's laws require a contract award to a low bidder, sustainable requirements within the specifications that are founded on a TCO means than the responsive bidder submitting the lowest price will meet those requirements. Depending on the language of the public entity's law, an invitation for bids seeking a lowest price commodity may include factors such as a suppliers' healthy work environment and resource conservation. Public entities should consider using the TCO of sustainable commodities over the life of the commodity to determine their true cost.

Purchasing Sustainable Commodities and Services Through Cooperative Agreements

Cooperative agreements and cooperative purchasing are essential and valuable tools for public procurement officers. Chapter 12 (*Cooperative Purchasing*) discusses this topic in more detail. Use of cooperatives encourages competitive pricing on a wide range of commodities and services due to the promise of large volumes of business for suppliers that are awarded contracts.

To encourage the procurement of sustainable commodities and services, public procurement officers should ask cooperatives to make information easily available about the sustainable commodities and services offered through their contracts.

USING CREDIBLE STANDARDS, THIRD-PARTY CERTIFICATIONS, AND ECOLABELS

Understanding External Sustainability Standards

As noted in this chapter under the heading *Writing a Sustainable Procurement Policy—External standards, certifications, and ecolabels for commodities and services*, the use of external standards, ecolabels and certifications can assist public procurement officers in locating commodities and services that have met rigid testing requirements as well as the specifications for those commodities.

The most credible, respected standards and certifications are those that have been developed in a balanced, open, transparent process by organizations that do not have a vested interest in the outcome. They usually focus on a balance of multiple sustainability attributes or considerations throughout a commodity's or service's life cycle.

Some standards and certifications require comprehensive third-party audits, while others may simply permit manufacturers to determine or self-certify whether they comply with a standard. Both can be valuable and effective, but public entities need to recognize the distinction. The following resources for research on this topic, already mentioned in this chapter, are: International Organization for Standards (ISO) Standard 14020:2000, *Environment Labels and Declarations–General Principles*,[21] United States Office of Management and Budget Circular A-*119, Federal Participation in the Development and Use of Voluntary Consensus Standards and in Conformity Assessment Activities*,[22] or the ISEAL Alliance, *Credible Sustainability Standards*.[23]

Avoid *Greenwashing*

Sustainable commodities are a rapidly growing market and suppliers have responded with *green* marketing, touting the environmental benefits of what they are selling. But sometimes what companies think their sustainable claims mean and what consumers really understand are two different things. This practice is commonly referred to as *greenwashing*.

Characteristics of modern greenwashing are:

- **Fibbing**—false claims that a commodity meets a specific standard.
- **Unsubstantiated claims**—commonly known as *just trust us*, occur when manufacturers are unable to prove their environmental claims.
- **Irrelevance**—making factually correct environmental statements that are no longer current.
- **Hidden trade-off**—making claims about a single environmental attribute, leading consumers to think that this single attribute is the only environmental one of concern associated with the use of the commodity or service.
- **Vagueness**—broad environmental claims such as *100% natural, earth smart*, and *ozone safe*, for instance.
- **Relativism**—a commodity, as compared to other commodities of the same type, may be environmentally friendly, but still a poor choice.

Incorporating requirements such as the following into solicitations and contracts can clarify how suppliers label commodities, which in turn, can assist in the consistency of and benefits from the sustainability reports that contractors must supply:

- Environmental benefit claims concerning commodities or services must be consistent with the United States Federal Trade Commission's *Green Guides.*
- Contractors providing sustainable commodities or services must explicitly identify the industry standard, certification, or ecolabel that those commodities or services meet in both the paper and online catalog descriptions available to public entity agencies and departments purchasing from those catalogs. For example, all Energy Star commodities should be labeled with the Energy Star logo and the words *Energy Star*.
- The solicitation and contract should include language that authorizes public entities to remove *green* labels and claims that constitute *greenwashing* or are determined to be weaker than the standard, such as vague claims that something is recyclable or biodegradable.
- Solicitations and contracts should require that the suppliers provide copies of the certifications they claim upon request if the public procurement officer cannot otherwise verify the certifications.

EPA Recommendations for Standards and Ecolabels

The EPA maintains guidance to assist federal government purchasers in sorting through

CHAPTER 6: SUSTAINABLE PROCUREMENT CONSIDERATIONS AND STRATEGIES

hundreds of ecolabels and identifying credible and effective standards and ecolabels that best fit their needs. That guidance is titled *Recommendations of Standards and Ecolabels for Use in Federal Procurement*[24] and it covers six broad categories of commodities with many subcategories. The EPA assesses ecolabels against the guidelines.

MEASURING AND MARKETING EFFECTIVENESS

It is often difficult to measure the effectiveness of a program or even of individual contracts. However, it may be the single most important factor in establishing and maintaining a strong and robust sustainable procurement program. Measuring success highlights both the environmental and cost-saving benefits of sustainable procurement efforts. Credible data creates opportunities to recognize and reward outstanding achievers, identify problem areas that may need correcting, and meet reporting and record-keeping requirements.

State and local governments should consider sharing and documenting achievements and challenges through the issuance of annual reports and share them with other public entities. This also offers the opportunity to discuss progress and potential barriers relating to specific commodities and services.

When drafting an annual report or an assessment of a program, there are four elements for measuring and tracking results:

1. **Identify key metrics, and then establish goals to meet those metrics**—Metrics may include an annual increase in purchase volumes or in dollars spent involving sustainable commodities or services, the number of contracts and items involving them, costs and savings, energy reduction, and other environmental benefits. Goals for the future can be defined based on the desired metric, the number of new sustainable commodities and services available, or sustainable expenditure targets. Performance measures for contractor services (such as timely delivery or response time for complaints) will also enable public procurement officers to track high- and low-performing contractors.

2. **Establish a current baseline on which to measure future progress**—The information to be used in calculating the baselines will depend to some degree upon the goals established for the sustainable procurement program. The baseline generally will include such data as: the type and number of commodities or services currently purchased, the cost of those commodities or services, and environmental data and impacts associated with those purchases. Environmental data used in a baseline may include the percentage of recycled content, the current process and cost to dispose of or recycle a commodity, and the commodity's energy and water requirements. Baselines can also include contractor performance.

3. **Determine the means of recordkeeping used to document measurements**—State and local governments that maintain a central single accounting system through which all transactions are processed offer a reliable means of collecting expenditure data. In those cases, the central procurement office should identify within that system the sustainable commodities or services so that the information can be broken out for reporting purposes. Many state and local governments have e-procurement solutions that may include the means of tracking expenditures on sustainable commodities and services.

   If this reporting is not available, many state and local governments rely upon supplier reports. However, as not all contractors are as timely in submitting their reports as others, it is helpful to have assistance in following up with the contractors.

CHAPTER 6: **SUSTAINABLE PROCUREMENT CONSIDERATIONS AND STRATEGIES**

In an effort to ensure that contractors provide complete and comprehensive information in a user-friendly format for analysis, states may want to provide a template for contractors to use when submitting this data.

4. **Publicize and reward achievers**—When data is available and shows good results, reward internal participants and publicize success. Recognition can be as simple as a thank you letter, credit toward an employee's performance review, or more publicly via a special awards program. Piggybacking on the annual meetings of various organizations (such as school business managers and public procurement officials) and offering a *sustainable procurement award* at annual events can be one way to increase visibility. In addition, featuring the success story of an agency or department in a case study can be an excellent peer-to-peer example of how to implement sustainable procurement.

BENEFITS CALCULATORS

Benefits calculation tools may be used to build the case for pursuing sustainable commodities and demonstrating project success to management, co-workers, and stakeholders outside of the public entity. Benefits calculators are most useful when they are credible and easy to use. Some calculators offer the ability to convert hard-to-understand metrics such as kilowatt hours or greenhouse gas emissions into vivid equivalents, such as numbers of cars removed from the road, or energy consumption for a given number of households.

Some examples include:

- COOL Climate Calculator, University of California at Berkeley[25]—an online decision-making tool that helps public entities estimate greenhouse gas emissions or carbon footprints from purchases of home or business commodities

- EPA Waste Reduction Model (WARM)[26]—tracks greenhouse gas (GHG) emission reductions from several waste management practices, and calculates and totals GHG emissions from baseline and alternative waste management practices, including source reduction, recycling, anaerobic digestion, combustion, composting, and landfilling

- Energy Star website[27]—contains a number of calculators created to estimate potential savings and payback of energy efficient commodities

- EPA Electronics Environmental Benefits Calculator[28]—estimates the environmental benefits of improving the purchasing, use, and disposal of computer products; specifically computer desktops, liquid crystal display and cathode ray tube monitors, and computer notebooks/laptops

A more complete list of links to useful calculators is available on NASPO's webpage.[29]

MAINTAINING YOUR SUSTAINABLE PROCUREMENT PROGRAM

Sustainable procurement programs are successful in the long term when proper resources are dedicated to them and steps are taken to promote and highlight their successes. The most successful approaches result from the work of dedicated staff.

Some specific examples of steps that individual states can take to maximize the success of a sustainable procurement program include the following:

- Create a dedicated sustainable procurement website that: features statutory language, publicizes sustainable specifications, demonstrates the benefits of purchasing sustainable commodities and

services, and provides other appropriate guidance.
- Make sure that procurement training tools and curricula include core competencies relating to the sustainable procurement program and sustainable commodities and services, such as lessons in how to draft specifications for those sustainable items.
- Highlight the achievements of public entity individuals, agencies, departments, or divisions who embrace sustainable procurement efforts through newsletters, press releases, and other forms of recognition. Whenever possible, utilize benefits calculators that can convert sustainable procurement activities into understandable environmental or human health impacts and then share the results publicly.
- Tie sustainable procurement efforts to individual and organizational performance metrics and key performance indicators.

CONCLUSION

Taking steps to ensure that sustainable purchasing considerations are a part of the procurement process is an increasing priority among procurement divisions across the states. Understanding sustainable procurement concepts and utilizing the tactics and tools described in this chapter can increase a procurement office's ability to be a responsible member of the local and global community through buying high-performing, cost-effective, and competitive commodities and services that support sustainability.

ENDNOTES

1. https://www.naspo.org/greenresources
2. http://www.nigp.org/home/find-procurement-resources/dictionary-of-terms
3. Martin, L. L., Miller, J. R. *Contracting for Public Sector Services.* Herndon, VA. National Institute of Governmental Purchasing, Inc. (2006) as cited in the NIGP Dictionary.
4. http://greenelectronicscouncil.org/wp-content/uploads/2018/02/Purchasers_Guide.pdf
5. https://www.sustainablepurchasing.org/
6. http://www.ilo.org/global/lang—en/index.htm
7. http://www.responsiblebusiness.org/
8. https://www.ftc.gov/news-events/media-resources/truth-advertising/green-guides
9. https://www.iso.org/standard/34425.html
10. https://obamawhitehouse.archives.gov/sites/default/files/omb/inforeg/revised_circular_a-119_as_of_1_22.pdf
11. https://www.isealalliance.org/credible-sustainability-standards
12. See the State of New York, Executive Order 4 (2008), *Establishing a State Green Procurement and Agency Sustainability Program,* regarding waivers at: https://www.dec.ny.gov/energy/71389.html
13. https://www.energystar.gov/
14. http://greenelectronicscouncil.org/epeat/epeat-overview/
15. https://www.epa.gov/smm/comprehensive-procurement-guidelines-paper-and-paper-products#01
16. https://us.fsc.org/en-us
17. http://www.greenseal.org/
18. https://industries.ul.com/environment/certificationvalidation-marks/ecologo-product-certification
19. Access to the dictionary is available at: http://www.nigp.org/home/find-procurement-resources/dictionary-of-terms
20. Burt, D. N., Dobler, D. W., & Starling, S. L., *World Class Supply Management: The Key to Supply Chain Management.* McGraw-Hill: NY (2003) as cited in The NIGP Dictionary http://www.nigp.org/home/find-procurement-resources/dictionary-of-terms
21. https://www.iso.org/standard/34425.html
22. https://obamawhitehouse.archives.gov/sites/default/files/omb/inforeg/revised_circular_a-119_as_of_1_22.pdf

23. https://www.isealalliance.org/credible-sustainability-standards
24. https://www.epa.gov/greenerproducts/recommendations-specifications-standards-and-ecolabels-federal-purchasing
25. https://coolclimate.berkeley.edu/calculator
26. https://www.epa.gov/warm
27. https://www.energystar.gov/
28. https://www.epa.gov/smm-electronics/assessment-tools-electronics-stewardship
29. https://www.naspo.org/greenresources

CHAPTER 7: COMPETITION: SOLICITATIONS AND METHODS

RECOMMENDED BEST PRACTICES

- Public procurement officers must have at hand a wide range of source selection methods in order to be able to meet user agencies' and users' needs.
- For a public procurement officer, acting professionally means, in part, exercising the full discretion and flexibility that a procurement law permits.
- Use of eProcurement systems does not change the steps or standards for using various source selection methods, but instead frees the public procurement officer to concentrate on substantive matters rather than paperwork.
- The standard for contract award under competitive sealed bidding should not merely be lowest price but also lowest cost to the state or local government.
- A procurement law should describe the competitive bids and proposals methods broadly enough to allow for best value as a standard for contract award as well as to authorize best value procurements.

CHAPTER 7: COMPETITION: SOLICITATIONS AND METHODS

While technology is revolutionizing the way in which the public procurement officer conducts competition for a contract, the principles governing the process remain the same. This chapter supplies a basic overview of the competitive source selection methods—that is, the methods that a state or local government uses to select a supplier for a contract—that are currently in use. It describes the tools that a public procurement officer uses to announce, solicit, and receive responses for a competitive procurement.

Procurement of construction services and what are called *alternative delivery methods* for building public infrastructure differ from the source selection methods described in this chapter. Chapter 11 (*Procurement of Construction and Related Services*) discusses those variations.

Note that this chapter provides an overview of the traditional methods of procuring commodities, services, and construction. It also offers a look at some different methods that may be used to purchase highly complex items. To understand those methods *in action*, Chapter 20 (*Procurement of Information Technology*) offers a useful discussion.

Also, be aware that the issuance of a solicitation and the decision about which source selection method to use are only part of the planning for the procurement. That planning requires the public procurement officer to think ahead about what happens after the contract is awarded. The solicitation must contain the essential tools for managing the contract that results from it. In fact, the time before issuing a solicitation is the point at which contract management needs to be considered and, where appropriate, the drafting of a contract plan begins. Chapter 4 (*Strategies and Plans*) and Chapter 14 (*Contract Management and Contract Administration*) offer insights on this issue.

TERMINOLOGY AND OVERVIEW

Informal and Formal Competition

It is important to start with the basics. Source selection methods are divided into two categories based on the level of competition that a public entity conducts.

The first is *formal competition*. It means that all suppliers who are able to supply the commodity, service, or construction that the procurement seeks must be invited to participate in the competitive procurement. Most often, the law applicable to the public entity sets a maximum expected dollar amount below which a contract may be exempt from formal competition. If the expected contract price or cost of the procurement meets or exceeds that dollar amount specified in the law, full—or formal—competition is required.

As discussed later in this chapter, announcing a *public* invitation does not mean that the public procurement officer must, for instance, take out an advertisement in the *Wall Street Journal*. Instead, the invitation to participate—called the solicitation—must be readily available, for instance, on the public entity's website.

The source selection methods that are used for procurements that are expected to cost below the dollar amount set for formal competition are in the category called *informal competition*. Those methods are often called *small purchase procedures*.

Definitions of Key Terms

Understanding a public procurement system requires comprehension of its terminology. The following definitions are of key terms that the chapters of this 3rd Edition of *State and Local Government: A Practical Guide* (*Practical Guide*) use relating to source selection methods. Apart from *competitive sealed proposals*, these definitions are provided by The NIGP Dictionary.[1] The definition provided for competitive sealed proposals was developed based off of language from the American Bar Association Model Procurement Code for State and Local Governments (Model Procurement Code).[2]

The first set of definitions is made up of the terms that designate the primary source selection methods used for formal competition.

> **Competitive sealed bidding**—Method for acquiring goods, services, and construction for public use in which award is made to the lowest responsive bid and responsible bidder, based solely on the response to the criteria set forth in the invitation for bids; does not include discussions or negotiations with bidders.
> **Competitive sealed proposals**—The process of inviting and obtaining proposals during which discussion and negotiations may be conducted with responsible offerors who submit proposals. The process concludes with the award of a contract to the offeror whose proposal is determined to best meet the criteria or factors specified in the solicitation for contract award. Price is generally one criterion or factor, but is not the only one. Thus, low price or cost is not the basis for contract award unless the proposal also demonstrates that it best meets the other evaluation criteria above all of the other proposals submitted. The solicitation used for this source selection method is a request for proposals.

The following terms are the *supporting cast* for those defined previously.

> **Invitation for bids (IFB)**—A procurement method used to solicit competitive sealed bid responses, sometimes called a formal bid, when price is the basis for award.
> **Request for proposals (RFP)**—The document used to solicit proposals from potential providers (proposers) for goods and services. Price is usually not a primary evaluation factor. Provides for the negotiation of all terms, including price, prior to contract award. May include a provision for the negotiation of best and final offers. May be a single-step or multi-step process.
> **Offeror**—A person or entity who submits an offer in response to a solicitation.
> **Bidder**—A person or entity who submits a bid in response to an invitation for bids

Some public entities may use different terms; however, the terms defined here are fairly standard.

ePROCUREMENT SYSTEMS

Many states and some local governments have eProcurement systems in place that support many of the steps outlined in this chapter. Chapter 19 (*eProcurement*) discusses these systems in more detail.

As Chapter 19 demonstrates, eProcurement systems have allowed the public procurement officer to concentrate on the substance of what needs to be done, rather than on paperwork and hand-created documentation. On a grander scale, the state and local governments that have instituted such systems have saved great sums of money. For a deeper understanding of how a particular source selection method works, state central procurement office procurement manuals are available. NASPO maintains profiles for all states; and each profile includes a link to that state's laws and procurement website where manuals are posted. They can be accessed on the NASPO website.[3]

OVERVIEW OF FORMAL COMPETITION SOURCE SELECTION METHODS

There is still a perception among the media, state legislators, the public, and even the supplier community that the lowest price should always be the sole basis for the award of a contract by a public entity. That simply is not the case. Because of the complexity of commodities, services, and construction that public entities buy today, price or cost is most often only one of several factors in determining which supplier is awarded a contract. It is not even the most important one in many cases.

At the time that the American Bar Association issued its first version of the Model Procurement Code in 1979, state and local governments almost exclusively used only competitive sealed bidding to conduct procurements, focusing on low price or cost. As those governments' requirements grew more complicated, trying to satisfy all of those needs based only on the consideration of low price or cost was not an effective approach.

The Model Procurement Code offered—and still offers—a range of source selection methods in addition to competitive sealed bidding. The most important contribution of the Model Procurement Code is that it provides sample language for a state legislature or city council to adopt to authorize the use of the competitive sealed proposals method. In addition to providing that price or cost need not be the sole basis for contract award, the Model Procurement Code's language also authorizes negotiations with suppliers (offerors) submitting proposals under the competitive sealed proposal method.

The Model Procurement Code provides a starting point for understanding the conditions for using the competitive sealed bidding and competitive sealed proposals methods.[4] Note that the following discussion analyzes the conditions for use based on the specific language in the Model Procurement Code's provisions. Different language in a law might result in a different analysis:

> Under competitive sealed bidding, judgmental factors may be used only to determine if the supply, service, or construction item bid meets the purchase description. Under competitive sealed proposals, judgmental factors may be used to determine not only if the items being offered meet the purchase description, but may also be used to evaluate the relative merits of competing proposals. The effect of this different use of judgmental evaluation factors is that under competitive sealed bidding, once the judgmental evaluation is completed, award is made on a purely objective basis to the lowest responsive and responsible bidder. Under competitive sealed proposals, the quality of competing products or services may be compared and trade-offs made between price and quality of the products or services offered (all as set forth in the solicitation). Award under competitive sealed proposals is then made to the responsible offeror whose proposal is most advantageous to the [State].
>
> Competitive sealed bidding and competitive sealed proposals also differ in that, under competitive sealed bidding, no change in bids is allowed once they have been opened, except for correction of errors in limited circumstances. The competitive sealed proposal method, on the other hand, permits discussions after proposals have been opened to allow clarification and changes in proposals provided that adequate precautions are taken to treat each offeror fairly and to ensure that information gleaned from competing proposals is not disclosed to other offerors.

COMPETITIVE SEALED BIDDING

The following are definitions provided by The NIGP Dictionary[5] of key terms related to the competitive sealed bidding method:

> **Responsive bid**—A bid that fully conforms in all material respects to the Invitation for Bids (IFB) and all of its requirements, including all form and substance.

Responsiveness can be a difficult concept to understand at first. The determination rests on whether a bid demonstrates an absolute commitment to the material requirements of the IFB. What is *material* and what is not is discussed in the upcoming paragraphs.

> ***Responsible bidder or offeror***—*A business entity or individual who has the financial and technical capacity to perform the requirements of the solicitation and subsequent contract.*

Note the difference between the two terms: responsiveness and responsibility. *Responsiveness* applies to the bid submitted and whether it complies with all of the important items set forth in the IFB, including the specifications and the contract terms. *Responsibility*, on the other hand, applies to the bidder (or offeror under competitive sealed proposals) and requires a determination that the bidder is, for instance, financially solid and has not been convicted of fraud.

The essential elements for award of a contract under the competitive sealed bidding method are the responsibility of the bidder, the responsiveness of the bid, and the lowest price.

In some cases, it may be lowest cost that is the basis for contract award. Through factors such as the cost to the public entity of owning a commodity, using life cycle costing or total-cost-of-ownership calculations, a higher-priced commodity may be, overall, the best value for the public entity. Where that is the case, it is deemed to be the lowest priced. Chapter 9 (*Bid and Proposal Evaluation and Award*) and Chapter 6 (*Sustainable Procurement Considerations and Strategies*) address the use of those calculation tools in more detail.

Content of the Invitation for Bids

An effective IFB should generally contain:

- General and special instructions to bidders, including the date and time when bids are due, the location where they are due if bids are not submitted electronically, the process for handling information in a bid that the bidder marks as proprietary and confidential, and the date/time/location for any pre-bid conference
- A general description of the commodity, service, or construction to be purchased
- Specifications, design, or scopes of work identifying the features of the commodity, service, or construction needed—prepared using the suggestions offered in Chapter 5 (*Non-construction Specifications and Scopes of Work*), Chapter 10 (*Contracting for Services*), or Chapter 11 (*Procurement of Construction and Related Services*)
- The criteria for evaluating bids
- A statement of the basis on which award will be made, which generally must be consistent with the language of the public entity's law or procedures that announce the standard for award, discussed later in this chapter
- The standard and special contract terms and conditions including the type of contract to be awarded as described in Chapter 4 (*Strategies and Plans*)
- Price sheets on which the bidders can submit prices for the items requested along with any price increases for renewal years
- A non-collusion affidavit as described in Chapter 3 (*The Importance of Competition*)
- A sheet on which the bidders sign their bid

It is important for there to be sufficient time between the date when the public procurement officer publicizes the IFB and the due date. Factors that will affect the amount of time between publication of the solicitation and the bid due date include the complexity of the commodity, service, or construction being purchased and whether the public procurement officer schedules a pre-bid conference, which is discussed later in this chapter.

Basis or Standard for Contract Award

If the public entity's law or policies contain language specifying the basis or standard that the public procurement officer must use in determining who is awarded the contract, that officer may not deviate from it. Doing so is an invitation for bidders who were not awarded the contract to file bid protests. Chapter 17 (*Protests, Disputes, and Claims*) discusses bid protests and provides tips for avoiding them.

Examples of the language of such laws or policies help illustrate this. For instance, the Model Procurement Code's award basis or standard under its competitive sealed bidding provision is:

> The contract shall be awarded with reasonable promptness by written notice to the lowest responsible and responsive bidder whose bid meets the requirements and criteria set forth in the Invitation for Bids.[6]

The Model Procurement Code's language is broad enough to allow for the use of life cycle costing or total-cost-of-ownership calculations in determining the lowest bid. It is also broad enough to permit the use of other evaluation criteria in selecting the winning bidder.

Other laws or policies may state a standard that is slightly different. If the law or policies state that award must be based on the responsible bidder submitting the lowest price—without the mention of the language in the Model Procurement Code related to *criteria*—it may be that the law or policies do not allow the consideration of anything but price.

The term *best value* as a standard for award arose in the 1990s, primarily to change the manner in which some public entities were evaluating proposals under the competitive sealed proposals method. The term developed in opposition to the practice of some public entities of awarding a contract based on the lowest-priced, technically acceptable proposal. A best value award standard as used in the competitive sealed proposals method is discussed later in this chapter.

The term also took hold in some laws as a standard for award of a contract using the competitive sealed bidding method to counter the practice of strict *low-bid* awards.[7] Generally speaking, *best value* as used in the competitive sealed bidding method allows for factors other than lowest price or cost to be considered so long as those factors are objectively measurable. Chapter 9 (*Bid and Proposal Evaluation and Award*) discusses these evaluations in more detail. Without using the term *best value*, the Model Procurement Code permits that type of evaluation.

Today, the term *best value* is often used, even in this *Practical Guide*, to refer to awards both under the competitive sealed bidding method and the competitive sealed proposal method, although the evaluations of bids and proposals using *best value* are different. Evaluation criteria for bids must generally be objectively measurable; those for proposals are both objectively measurable and subjective.

Essentially, the winning bid must be responsive, as defined earlier in this chapter. The bid may not—as of the date that the bidder submits it, which must be before the due date and time—deviate from the critical requirements of the IFBs.

If the deviation is only minor—or immaterial—the bid is still responsive. The NIGP Dictionary provides some guidance on what is immaterial:

> **Immaterial defect**—*A tangential flaw having no material body or form that may be corrected without prejudice to other bidders. Example: Submission of two copies of a catalog when three copies were requested.*

The concept of responsiveness and the basis or standard for award are also discussed in Chapter 9 (*Bid and Proposal Evaluation and Award*).

Receipt and Control of Bids

As a part of making sure that a public procurement process is fair, the time and date established when bids are due are hard deadlines. That is because, among other things, it is inappropriate to give bidders who did not plan well the same consideration as those that did.

Additionally, most public entities—either because it is required by law or simply due to practice—open bids publicly and announce or provide access to bidders' prices immediately after the date and time that bids are due. It would be highly unfair to allow a bidder to submit a bid after seeing or hearing the other bids.

If the bidding process is a paper one, it is critical for the envelopes in which the bids are submitted to be date and time stamped. The public procurement officer must keep them in a secure place to prevent them from being misplaced, lost, or tampered with until the date and time of bid opening.

Since formal bids must remain sealed until the bid opening, proper identification on the outside of the bid envelope is important. The IFB should require the bid envelope to show the solicitation number, opening date, and bidder's name or supplier number.

eProcurement systems, discussed in Chapter 19 (*eProcurement*), allow for the electronic submission of bids, including date/time stamping, sealed bid folders, and electronic opening of bids.

Bidder Request to Modify or Withdraw Bid

There are occasions when bidders ask that they be permitted to modify or withdraw their bids after they have submitted them to the public procurement office but before bids are due. As a general rule, it is appropriate to accommodate the request if an authorized representative of the bidder submits a request in writing before the date and time that bids are due. Any modified bid must be submitted by the due date and time.

After bids are opened, the general rule is much harsher, as discussed later in this chapter.

Public Opening and Confidentiality

The requirement for public opening of bids has long been a practice—if not a requirement in law—in state and local government procurement. It is aimed at reducing the potential for collusion and favoritism and to foster public confidence in the procurement system.

The best practice is for the opening to take place immediately after the date and time when bids are due. The prices submitted in the bids and the names of the bidders should be announced and available publicly at that time. Additionally, the public procurement officer should make a written record—often called an abstract—of the bidders and the bid prices, or any *no bid* that a supplier may have submitted, and place it in the procurement file. If the competition was performed electronically, the eProcurement systems will likely make that record automatically.

Bidders will ask questions about and request to examine competitors' bids. The bids themselves—along with all of the documentation about the evaluation of bids and bidders—should be confidential until after contract award. A state's open records/freedom of information law, though, may require that bids be public at that time, except perhaps for proprietary information or trade secrets that a bidder has marked as such in its bid. The best process for handling these bidder requests for confidentiality of proprietary information or trade secrets is discussed in more detail in the section of this chapter entitled *Competitive Sealed Proposals*.

After contract award, the documents in the procurement file—the bids, their evaluation, and any other information that played a role in the public procurement officer's selection of the winning bid—should be made public, except for proprietary information.

Late Bids

When a bidder submits its bid late, that is, after the deadline, the best practice is for the public procurement officer to refuse to accept it. There is one narrow exception to that hard approach. That exception arises from instances where the tardiness is due solely to the public entity's fault or inaction.

An example of a rule/regulation that specifies this treatment of late bids is in the Recommended Regulations of the Model Procurement Code, which provides:[8]

> No late bid . . . will be considered unless received before contract award, and [unless] the bid . . . would have been timely but for the action or inaction of [State] personnel directly serving the procurement activity.

The rule/regulation or policy on exceptions must also be clear on three additional points: the bid must have been out of the hands of the bidder or its agent before the time/date set for bid opening; the delay occurred out of the bidder's hands and is not the bidder's fault; and evidence of these facts is available and is documented as a public record. For instance, the failure of a delivery service to deliver as promised would not fall into the exception. However, the closure of the public entity's mail room might.

Mistakes in Bids

Claims by bidders that they made mistakes in their bids are common. The following paragraphs describe a common approach.

Before the deadline for receipt of bids, a bidder may correct a mistake or withdraw its bid in writing. After the bids are opened, but before award, a public procurement officer may waive a mistake, or permit a bidder to correct it, only if it is minor and the true intent of the bid is obvious from the information in the bid itself. The bidder may not provide any outside documents or other evidence to show the error.

An example is an arithmetic error in totaling up a column of numbers to arrive at the bid price on the bid sheet submitted with the bid. If the mistake is clear by looking at the bid alone and the bid is otherwise responsive as defined earlier, the public procurement officer may permit the correction so long as doing so does not improve the bidder's competitive position in view of the other bids, such as changing its bid from third-lowest price to lowest price.

On the other hand, a bidder that claims, for instance, that it mistakenly failed to agree to the insurance requirements in the invitation to bid has made a material mistake that may not be corrected. Its bid is nonresponsive since insurance coverage relates to price because it is an added cost for the bidder. It does not matter whether insurance cost was part of the bidder's pricing in this particular instance. Responsiveness is determined based on the theoretical effect of a bid defect on price, quantity, quality, or delivery.

All mistakes other than the minor ones previously cited that surface after bid opening and before contract award are not correctible. Any remedy for a mistake becomes more difficult after award of a contract. The universal legal view is that a mistake in a bid that comes to light after award does not relieve the bidder/contractor from contract performance in accordance with the contract award.

COMPETITIVE SEALED PROPOSALS

Similarities and Differences Compared to Competitive Sealed Bidding

Generally

The essential difference between the competitive sealed bidding method and the competitive sealed proposal method is that the latter permits negotiations with offerors and revisions of their proposals, with contract award based on a variety of factors, which may include price.

Many of the steps that are part of the competitive sealed bidding method apply also to the competitive sealed proposals method. For example, there should be public notice of the contracting opportunity. Additionally, the receipt of proposals within the procurement office should be subject to the same tracking and security procedures that are applicable to bids.

As with competitive sealed bidding, a public procurement officer opens proposals publicly. However, he or she only reads or provides access to the names of the offerors. Neither prices nor other information contained in the proposals is public until after a notice of intent to award a contract is announced or, depending on the public entity, actual contract award has occurred. This is seen as preserving the soundness of the process by avoiding situations in which offerors change their proposals in their best and final offers, which are discussed later, based on other offerors' proposals.

The law of the State of Montana takes a different approach. It requires open access to proposals shortly after their submission except for proprietary information or trade secrets. That law says:

> ***Section 18-4-304. Competitive sealed proposals.***
> *(4) After the proposals have been opened at the time and place designated in the request for proposals and reviewed by the procurement officer for release, proposal documents may be inspected by the public, subject to the limitations of:*
>   *(a) the Uniform Trade Secrets Act, Title 30, chapter 14, part 4;*
>   *(b) matters involving individual safety as determined by the department; and*
>   *(c) other constitutional protections.*

Additionally, the deliberations of evaluation committees reviewing the bids and negotiations with offerors are open and not confidential in that state.

Offerors often designate large portions of their proposals as proprietary and confidential. The law or policy of some public entities protects offerors' true proprietary information and trade secrets from public disclosure.

Because so much of a proposal may be designated as proprietary and confidential, it becomes a problem once a public procurement officer has made a contract award or has issued an intent to award a contract. It is at that point that the offerors who did not receive the award will ask to see the winning offeror's proposal.

If the public procurement officer disagrees with an offeror's claim of confidentiality, the best approach is for him or her to advise the offeror and give it the opportunity to explain the reasons it believes the information to be proprietary. That officer should make the final determination with the assistance of legal counsel.

Responsiveness of Proposals

In describing the legal standard for the award of a contract under the competitive sealed proposal method, the laws of some public entities have added a requirement that the proposal be *responsive* to the request for proposals. The laws of the State of Utah and the Commonwealth of Pennsylvania are two of those. Since the concept of responsiveness mandates compliance in all material respects to the solicitation, it is somewhat difficult to apply to proposals, where procurement laws allow for discussions with offerors and the submission of best and final offers in which offerors are allowed to make some changes to the proposals.[9]

Drafting the Request for Proposals

Overview of the Request for Proposals

The basic contents of the RFP, the solicitation document used for the competitive sealed proposals method, are similar to those of an IFB. The solicitation should include general and special instructions to offerors; the time and date for any pre-proposal conference; the deadline—date and time—for submission of proposals, and the place to submit them if submission is in paper form; the format in which offerors should submit their proposals; pricing or costing requirements, including price or cost increases for renewal periods; the specifications; the non-collusions affidavit; and the general and special contract terms and conditions.

Other chapters of this *Practical Guide* provide guidance on aspects of the planning process and the development of specifications or scopes of work that are key to a well-written RFP. Those chapters are: Chapter 4 (*Strategies and Plans*); Chapter 5 (*Non-construction Specifications and Scopes of Work*); Chapter 6 (*Sustainable Procurement Considerations and Strategies*); Chapter 10 (*Contracting for Services*); and Chapter 20 (*Procurement of Information Technology*).

Developing Evaluation Criteria

One critical difference between the content of an IFB and an RFP is that the latter must state the criteria on which the evaluation of each proposal will be measured. Since contract awards made using the competitive sealed proposals method are not generally made based on low price, the listing of the evaluation criteria informs the offerors about the methods used by the public procurement officer for organizing the evaluation of the proposals and keeping it on track.

The NIGP Dictionary offers the following definition of the term *evaluation criteria*:

> *Generally used in the Request for Proposals (RFP) method. Qualitative factors that an evaluation committee will use to evaluate/score a proposal and select the most qualified proposer(s). May include such factors as past performance, references, management and technical capability, price, quality, and performance requirements. (Harney, 1992)*

Depending on the law or policy of the public entity, the RFP must list the criteria in order of importance or provide some indication of the weight that they will be given during the evaluation. The Model Procurement Code requires that the RFP list evaluation criteria and any sub-criteria in order of their importance. It does not require that a solicitation offer further information, such as ascribing to each criterion a percentage (for instance 35%) or a description (such as *critical*).

It is imperative that the evaluation factors be set and not changed once proposals have been submitted. Making changes to them after the proposal submission deadline opens the process to an accusation that changes favored a particular offeror, since they occurred once the names of the offerors and their proposals were available to the public procurement officer and the evaluation committee.

Evaluation and evaluation committees are discussed in Chapter 9 (*Bid and Proposal Evaluation and Award*).

Discussion and Negotiation

Another key difference between an IFB and an RFP is that, under the latter, the public procurement officer may engage in discussions or negotiations with offerors whose proposals, after a first review, are generally deemed to be eligible for contract award. The RFP should advise offerors of this in language such as the following:

> *The procurement officer may enter into discussions or negotiations with offerors whose proposals that officer determines, after an initial review and based on the offeror's initial proposal, to be acceptable or potentially acceptable based on the requirements of the solicitation.*

Chapter 9 (*Bid and Proposal Evaluation and Award*) offers additional information about discussions and negotiations. Additionally, Chapter 4 (*Strategies and Plans*) advocates that there be a negotiation plan in place. Finally, the *call outs* in some of the chapters of this *Practical Guide* offer negotiating tips.

Basis or Standard for Contract Award

As in the case of an IFB, the RFP must inform offerors of the basis on which a contract award will be made. If that basis or standard is embedded in the public entity's law or policy, the statement of that basis or standard must be the same in the RFP.

The basis or standard for award under the Model Procurement Code is:

> Award shall be made to the responsible offeror whose proposal conforms to the solicitation and is determined in writing to be the most advantageous to the [state], taking into consideration price and the evaluation factors set forth in the Request for Proposals.[10]

The standards or basis for award are also discussed in Chapter 9 (*Bid and Proposal Evaluation and Award*).

A term that appears regularly in this *Practical Guide* and in some laws as a standard for award is *best value*. The NIGP Dictionary defines the term as:

> **Best value**—1. A procurement method that emphasizes value over price. The best value might not be the lowest cost. Generally achieved through the Request for Proposals (RFP) method. 2. An assessment of the return that can be achieved based on the total life cycle cost of the item; may include an analysis of the functionality of the item; can use cost-benefit analysis to define the best combinations of quality, services, time, and cost considerations over the useful life of the acquired item.

Use of the term several decades ago signaled a movement against a type of competitive sealed proposals process that required the contract to be awarded to the lowest-priced, technically acceptable proposal. Since the Model Procurement Code version in 1979, its language, cited earlier, has always permitted best-value contract awards.

Given the complexity of many state and local government procurements today, a public procurement officer must take advantage of all of the discretion that a procurement law offers, and not always rely on the way that competitive sealed proposals have been conducted in the past. As Chapter 2 (*Procurement Leadership, Organization, and Value*) demonstrates, being a strategic leader means envisioning future needs and trends and finding ways to address them.

Development of Evaluation Criteria

Development of the criteria that will be the framework within which proposals are evaluated requires that the public procurement officer work closely with the user agencies for which he or she is conducting the procurement. That officer should also work with the evaluation committee, if one is used, to refine those criteria. This ensures that the committee will have a full and common understanding of the details to consider in relationship to each of those criteria.

In many cases, the criteria will fall into three broad categories: technical capability and the approach for meeting the specifications or scope of work; competitiveness and reasonableness of price or cost; and managerial and staffing capability, including experience and past performance. Some public entities have a *stock* set of criteria, stated in broad terms, that they use in nearly every RFP. That is not a recommended professional approach. Evaluation criteria should be tailored to meet the requirements of each specific procurement.

The task of identifying evaluation criteria for the procurement of complex information technologies is part of an entire project structure in which the public procurement officer and a representative of the public entity's chief information officer are co-equal managers of the procurement process. Chapter 20 (*Procurement of Information Technology*) provides insights on this topic.

Using and Selecting Evaluation Committees

It is a standard practice to use an evaluation committee, comprised of subject matter experts, usually from the user agency, to assist the public procurement officer in evaluating proposals. Additionally, in some complex procurements, such as the selection of a health insurance plan, the procurement office may employ an outside consultant to assist in the evaluation.

The independence of the evaluation committee is essential to its fairness. To ensure that it is independent, the public procurement officer should make the final decision about who sits on the committee. It is also a best practice for the public procurement officer to chair the committee.

In the real world, the governor's or mayor's office or a large user agency may demand that they select the persons to sit on an evaluation committee for a highly visible and important procurement. If a public procurement officer cannot dissuade them from their position, that officer should insist upon naming at least some members of the committee.

Another problem occurs when a supervisor and his or her subordinate sit on the same committee and are from the user agency requesting the procurement. To avoid any possibility of intimidation, these situations should be avoided.

Before offerors submit their proposals, the committee must have an opportunity to discuss the evaluation criteria, identify any sub-criteria, and come to an understanding of how those will be applied. It must also decide how the committee will operate. Finally, the public procurement officer and, if appropriate, the committee must determine whether to use a scoring or ranking process, a consensus approach, or a combination to evaluate proposals.

As noted before regarding the preparation of evaluation criteria, this preparation must occur before the names of the offerors and their proposals are available to the public procurement officer and the evaluation committee. In fact, evaluation committee members and other technical advisors who will assist in the evaluation of proposals should be asked to sign a conflict of interest/confidentiality statement before receiving copies of or gaining electronic access to proposals.

Clearly, the unbiased deliberations of the evaluation committee are critical. Since the evaluation process using the competitive sealed proposals method frequently involves subjective judgments, the flexibility it affords requires that those participating in contractor selection bring open minds to the process.

Some of the standard rules previously noted may be problematic for procuring complicated information technologies. While the procurement process for such technologies needs to be unbiased, that complexity requires more persons to be a part of the entire project preparing for the actual procurement. Chapter 20 (*Procurement of Information Technology*) provides insights on this topic.

Conducting Discussions

After an initial evaluation of the proposals, the procurement officer and the evaluation committee may determine that discussions and negotiations with offerors are warranted. As noted earlier in this chapter, the solicitation must advise offerors of the possibility for discussions and negotiations.

As far as the offerors who should be afforded this opportunity are concerned, the Model Procurement Code offers some guidance. It states that a procurement officer must present the opportunity to all offerors whose proposals are found to have a reasonable possibility of being selected for award under the terms of the RFP. This is a useful standard.

Chapter 9 (*Bid and Proposal Evaluation and Award*) focuses on discussions in more detail.

Best Value Procurements

One approach for conducting procurement is called a performance information procurement system, more recently also known as best value procurements. In the early 1990s, Dean Kashiwagi at Arizona State University started to develop what is now known as the best value procurement/performance information procurement system (BVP/PIPS). This approach focused initially on procurements of construction but it has expanded since then. Chapter 20 (*Procurement of Information Technology*) provides a case study from the State of Alaska in which its central purchasing office used this approach to purchase information technology.

The best value procurements described here are different from the *best value* used to describe the standard for contract award, which this chapter has already discussed. Depending on the language of procurement law of the specific public entity, this approach may easily be used through a competitive sealed proposal process. It would be authorized under the Model Procurement Code's language.

On the *Governing* magazine website, in a 2017 article entitled *Most Government Procurement Has Got It All Wrong, These Advocates Say*,[11] the approach is broadly described as follows:

> Kashiwagi's approach, which he calls Best Value Performance Information Procurement Systems (PIPS), essentially reorders the traditional process of putting out requests for proposals, accepting bids, and then awarding a contract. Instead, PIPS begins with buyers or purchasing agents identifying what they think they want, and then vendors compete to provide services to meet the buyer's intent. It's up to the vendors to explain the process of what good or service they will deliver, as well as the risks. Vendors are ranked on a series of metrics; after one is chosen, it delivers regular reports on how it's meeting agreed-upon goals. The process is more collaborative between buyer and vendor, and it better utilizes the established knowledge of the experts (the vendors) rather than relying on the non-experts (the buyers), says Jacob Kashigawi, Dean's son and business partner.

An overview of the steps in this procurement process with a flow chart appears in an article published in *Government Procurement* magazine in June/July 2013.[12] Here is a summary:

- The selection phase:
  ◊ In response to a solicitation that provides a minimal description of what the state or local government is seeking—the objective of the work under the contract—offerors submit one-page surveys completed by their past clients, a cost submission, a milestone schedule, and a six-page project capability submission without any marketing information or information that would identify the offeror.
  ◊ Evaluation team members complete an evaluation of the project capability submissions without knowing who the suppliers are.
  ◊ Evaluation team members interview offerors' personnel who will be responsible for delivery of the commodity or service that the public entity is requesting.
  ◊ Scores for the offerors' submissions are tabulated and a best value offeror is identified.
- The clarification phase:
  ◊ Offeror submits a detailed plan to accomplish the objective stated in the solicitation:
    ▪ Since the selected offeror was chosen based in large part upon its expertise in accomplishing the public entity's objective, the offeror must identify risks, defined as anything outside of its control. Risks outside

of the offeror's control will be the public entity's responsibility.
- Offeror prepares a risk mitigation plan that describes potential risks and how they will be mitigated.
- Offeror must clearly identify what is within the scope of the proposed contract and what is not.
◊ The clarification phase is complete and contract award made when: past performance is verified; offeror provides a detailed delivery plan and a risk mitigation; management and reporting metrics are in place; and the public entity has reviewed all of these documents and has had its concerns addressed.
- Management by risk mitigation:
◊ Contractor submits weekly risk reports.
◊ Those reports track risks and impacts on the project, and make both contractor and public entity personnel accountable.

MULTI-STEP BIDDING

Another source selection method offers the best of two worlds—adherence to the lowest bid principles of competitive sealed bidding while offering an opportunity for some of the discretion and negotiation associated with competitive sealed proposals. This is called multi-step bidding.

The NIGP Dictionary defines *multi-step bidding* as follows:

> **Multi-step bidding**—*A method of source selection involving two competitive steps, combining the elements of both Invitation for Bids and Request for Proposals. The first step may require the submission of technical and price proposals with only the technical proposals being evaluated and scored. The second step involves the opening of price proposals of those firms who have achieved the highest technical scores.*

This method is used most often for formal competitions, but may be used as well for a small-dollar purchase or informal competition. The solicitation used is an IFB to which bidders will submit two things in response: a technical proposal offering the bidders' response to the specification—often a performance specification seeking a solution to a problem—and a price proposal.

There are two basic approaches to conducting a multi-step bidding procurement:

- **Approach one**—The first approach asks in the IFB that bidders submit technical proposals and bid prices separately on the date that the IFB establishes as the deadline. Once the public procurement officer evaluates the technical proposals, he or she opens only the price responses for those bidders whose technical proposals are found to be responsive. From the pool of those responsive proposals, the public procurement officer makes an award on price alone.
- **Approach two**—The second approach offers an opportunity to add elements of negotiation into the process. The public procurement officer requests only technical proposals in the solicitation that he or she issues. Once they have been received, he or she evaluates them. In accordance with the language of the IFB, the public procurement officer may then enter into discussions with all the bidders or only with those whose technical proposals are considered to have merit after evaluation. The public procurement officer sends another IFB to those bidders with whom discussions have been held. The lowest price offered by the bidder submitting an acceptable technical proposal becomes the basis for contract award.

The flexibility that the second approach provides makes it preferable. Whether a public entity may adopt that approach may depend on what its procurement law provides. Figure 7.1 highlights

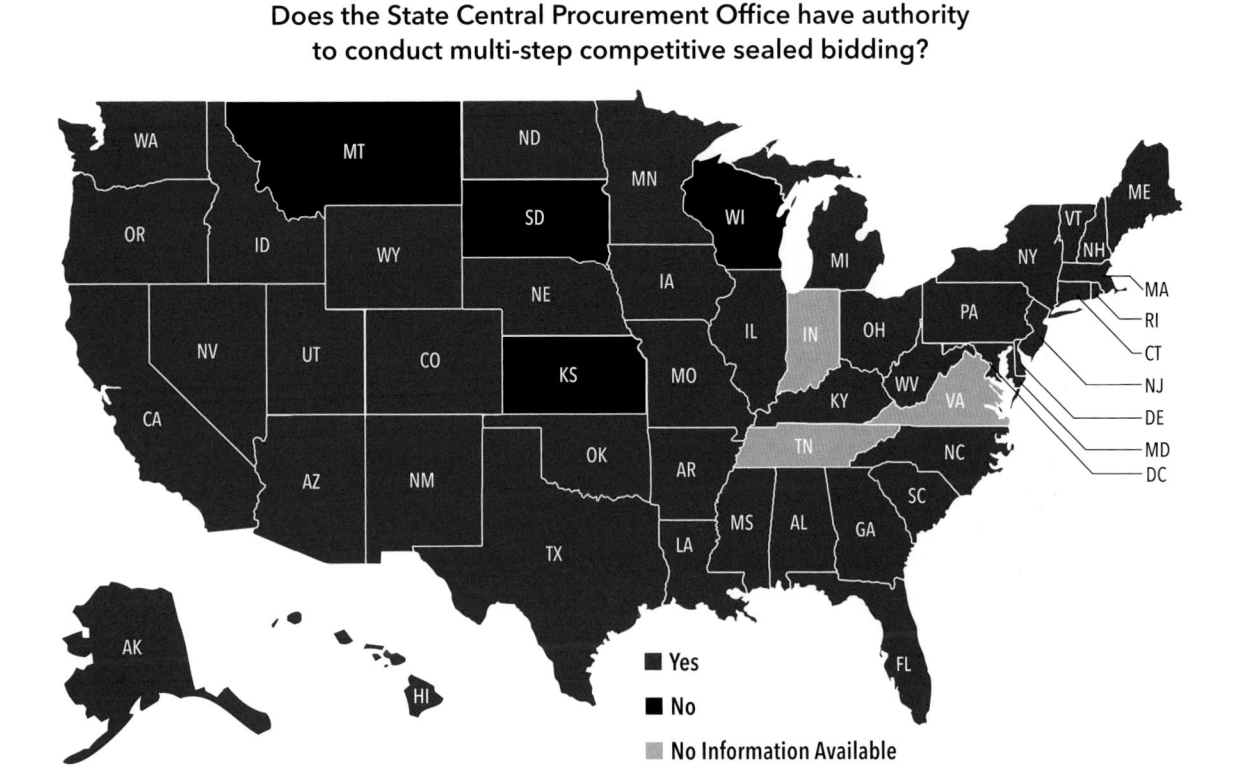

CHAPTER 7: **COMPETITION: SOLICITATIONS AND METHODS**

FIGURE 7.1 | MULTI-STEP COMPETITIVE SEALED BIDDING

Does the State Central Procurement Office have authority to conduct multi-step competitive sealed bidding?

- Yes
- No
- No Information Available

which state central procurement offices have authority to conduct multi-step competitive sealed bidding.

REVERSE AUCTIONS

The NIGP Dictionary defines *reverse auctions* as follows:

> ***Reverse auction**—An online auction in which sellers bid against each other to win a buyer's business. Typically used to purchase commodities from multiple pre-qualified providers.*

Chapter 5 (*Non-construction Specifications and Scopes of Work*) discusses prequalification in more detail.

In a reverse auction, the public procurement officer posts an online description of what it needs, and bidders bid online. Their bids, but not their identities, are public during the competition. Bidders may change their prices up to the time that the bidding closes.

Not all commodities and services are suitable candidates for reverse auctions. They are foreign to some industries, and market research is essential to assessing the viability of reverse auctions as a sourcing strategy. Problems with the value and integrity of reverse auctions have been attributed to factors such as errors in supplier data, post-auction negotiation, changes in specifications or quantities, and resulting problems from poor quality, late deliveries, and supplier performance. Reverse auctions are only one tool in the portfolio and should be used judiciously.

State and Local Government Procurement: A Practical Guide, 3rd Edition

CHAPTER 7: **COMPETITION: SOLICITATIONS AND METHODS**

FIGURE 7.2 | EXPERIENCE WITH REVERSE AUCTIONS

If the State Central Procurement Office has authority to conduct reverse auctions, what is your state's experience using reverse auctions? *Choose the option that best applies.*

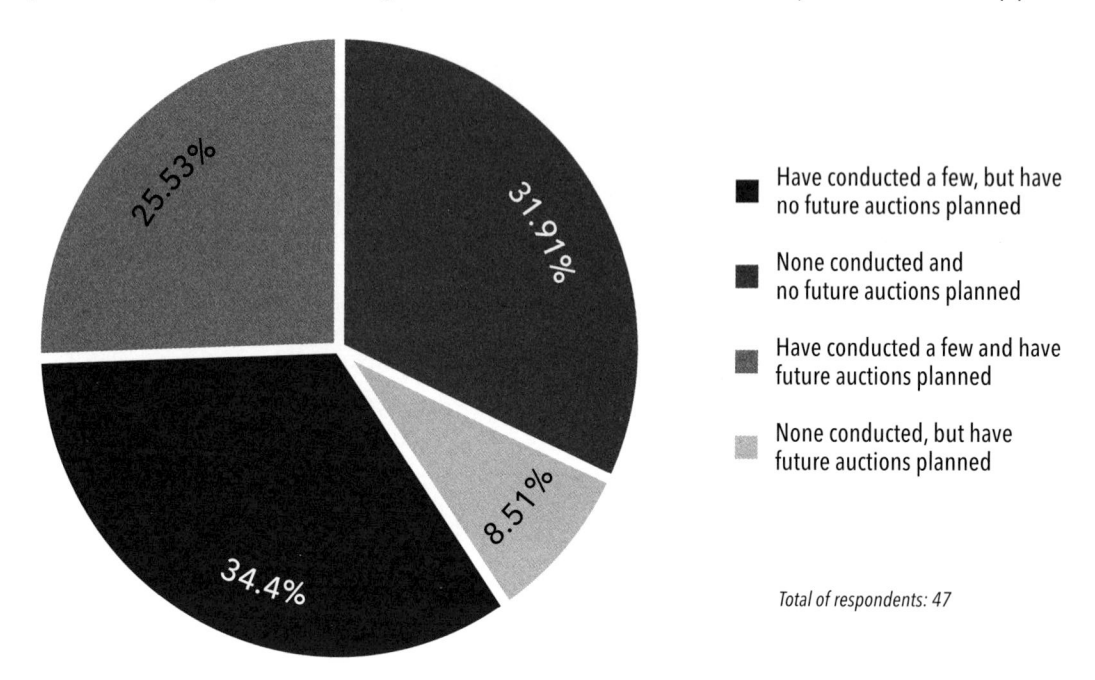

- 31.91% Have conducted a few, but have no future auctions planned
- 34.4% None conducted and no future auctions planned
- 25.53% Have conducted a few and have future auctions planned
- 8.51% None conducted, but have future auctions planned

Total of respondents: 47

The majority of states have authority to conduct reverse auctions. There is a more detailed discussion of this method in Chapter 19 (*eProcurement*). Figure 7.2 shows state's experience in using reverse auctions.

SMALL PURCHASES

Rules/regulations or policies should describe minimum levels of competition for procurements at dollar levels below the dollar amount required for formal competition, but leave the means of competition to the discretion of the public procurement officer. They should also warn that a user agency's requirements may not be split up into small-dollar purchases to avoid the requirements for formal competition.

Reasonable and adequate competition should be the norm, while some purchases are too small to justify the time and expense of soliciting any competition. The introduction of purchase cards[13] provides for control of both the procurement and accounting functions while giving users more flexibility.

Higher-dollar small purchases should not require formal competition; but they should preserve the openness of the procurement system so that any supplier that has requested to quote on a particular type of purchase is invited to do so. Additionally, there should be some competition consistent with the dollar level of the purchase contemplated.

The solicitation document most closely associated with small purchases is a request for quotation. The NIGP Dictionary defines it as follows:

Request for quotation (RFQ) — *Purchasing method generally used for small orders under a certain dollar threshold, such as $1000.00. A request is sent to suppliers along with a description of the commodity or services needed and the supplier is asked to respond with price and other information by a predetermined date. Evaluation and recommendation for award should be based on the quotation that best meets price, quality, delivery, service, past performance, and reliability.*

The principles governing evaluation of quotations and award of contracts for small purchases should follow those for fully competed procurements. For instance, the purchase description that the public procurement officer provides to suppliers must avoid favoring a particular product. Records should be maintained confirming the manner in which each procurement was made and the basis for contract award.

BIDDER AND OFFEROR CONFERENCES

Conferences with prospective bidders or offerors—either before or after a solicitation is issued—help any formal competition. Often operating as a type of focus group of suppliers, they provide an excellent source of information for the public procurement officer. Additionally, they allow suppliers to obtain a better understanding of the needs of the user agency, increasing the quality of responses to the solicitation.

As the use of technology expands, some public entities are using webcasting, and other electronic means to broadcast these supplier conferences. The use of these technologies in the procurement process increases the real-time exchange of information between public procurement officers and suppliers. They enhance the chances for a positive outcome for procurements in which they are used.

Pre-solicitation Conferences

A pre-solicitation conference is often convened through a document called a request for information. This tool may be useful to gather information before preparing a solicitation for a formal competition. The NIGP Dictionary defines "request for information" as follows:

Request for information (RFI) — *A nonbinding method whereby a jurisdiction publishes via newspaper, Internet, or direct mail its need for input from interested parties for an upcoming solicitation. A procurement practice used to obtain comments, feedback, or reactions from potential responders (suppliers, contractors) prior to the issuing of a solicitation. Generally, price or cost is not required. Feedback may include best practices, industry standards, technology issues, etc.*

There are some built-in limitations to the utility of a pre-solicitation conference. Suppliers generally do not like to share information that they believe is proprietary with their competitors. Even where they provide information in writing, they understand that the public procurement officer may not have the authority to keep that information confidential under open records/freedom of information laws.

Pre-Award Conferences

A public procurement officer convenes a pre-award conference after the solicitation has been issued but before bids or proposals are due. Its purpose is to provide an opportunity for suppliers to ask questions about specific parts of the solicitation and to ensure that the suppliers understand its requirements.

It also serves to alert the public procurement officer to parts of the solicitation that may not be clear—requiring the issuance of a solicitation amendment correcting or clarifying the solicitation text.

CHAPTER 7: **COMPETITION: SOLICITATIONS AND METHODS**

The solicitation should contain the date, time, location, and information about web access for the pre-award conference. In terms of the conference agenda, the best approach is for the public procurement officer to review the solicitation paragraph by paragraph, permitting questions limited to the paragraph at hand. That prevents *shotgun* questioning that may confuse the attendees. After the conference, the public procurement officer, by way of a solicitation amendment, should disseminate the questions and answers generated during the conference, along with any solicitation modifications made as a result.

Written Questions and Answers

Some public entities allow prospective bidders or offerors to submit questions relating to a solicitation. Both the questions and the answers are made available to all interested bidders. The solicitation should clearly explain this process, including a deadline for submitting questions and an estimated time frame for responses to be publicly posted. The public procurement officer must take pains to assure that this process is complete and made public a sufficient time before the bid or proposal is due, so that interested bidders or offerors may consider this when preparing their bid or proposal.

NOTIFYING SUPPLIERS

Notifying suppliers of a pending procurement is an important step in encouraging open competition. With eProcurement systems in use today, the suppliers who have registered in those systems to supply specific commodities, services,

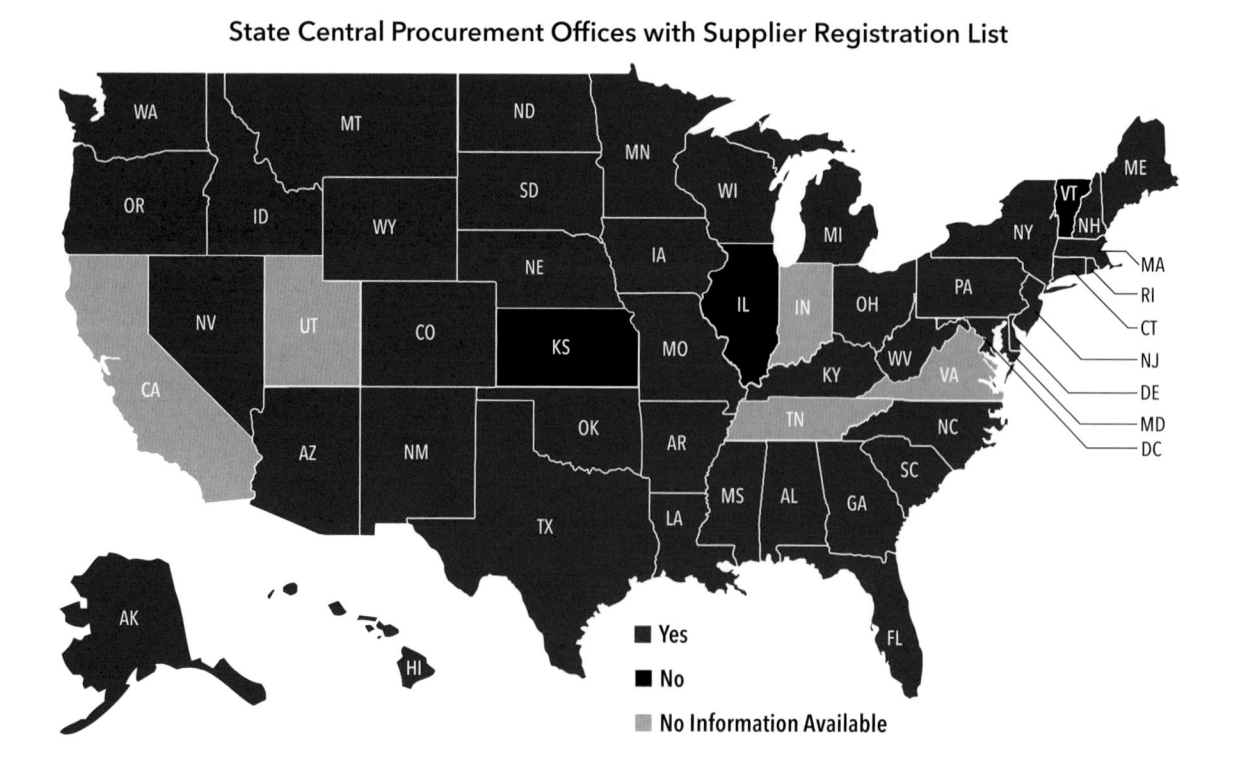

FIGURE 7.3 | SUPPLIER REGISTRATION LISTS

State Central Procurement Offices with Supplier Registration List

CHAPTER 7: **COMPETITION: SOLICITATIONS AND METHODS**

or construction will often be notified automatically of contracting opportunities relating to the items for which they have registered. Chapter 19 (*eProcurement*) discusses these systems in more detail, including supplier registration and notification.

The procurement office website should post contracting opportunities prominently. Those sites should allow suppliers to download the solicitation directly or to e-mail a request for a copy.

Registering Suppliers

Registering suppliers is a common method that state and local government procurement officers use to notify suppliers of contracting opportunities as previously discussed. In many cases, those supplier registrations link to the public entity's financial system to allow for payment to the supplier if it receives a contract.

Registration requires a supplier to select the types of commodities, services, or construction that they wish to supply. Those breakdowns and categories of commodities, services, and construction are generically called *commodity codes*. Chapter 19 (*eProcurement*) discusses the types of commodity codes that public entities use. Figure 7.3 illustrates the state central procurement offices with a supplier registration list.

In some public entities, suppliers must pay to register. Charging for registration, at least at the state level, requires statutory authorization. Note that a fee may be a barrier for small and minority businesses. Figure 7.4 shows states that charge suppliers a registration fee.

FIGURE 7.4 | SUPPLIER REGISTRATION FEES

Please indicate if your state charges a supplier registration fee and the frequency of the fee.

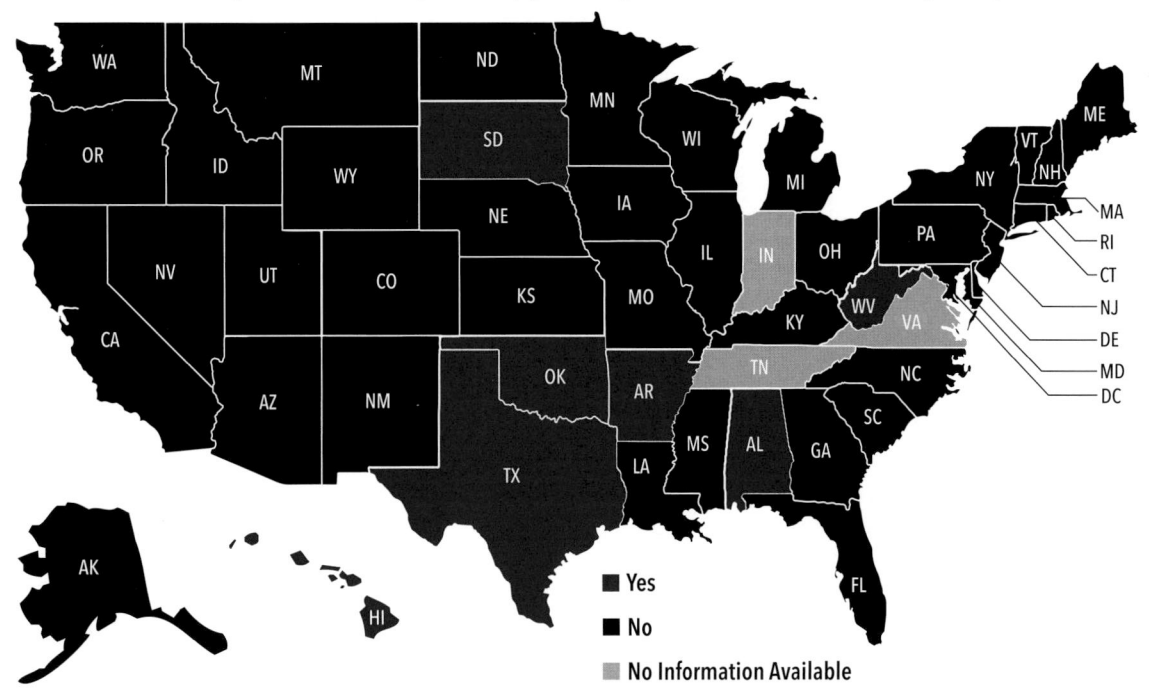

State and Local Government Procurement: A Practical Guide, 3rd Edition

AFFIRMATIVE RESPONSIBILITY CRITERIA

This chapter has already described the obligation of a public procurement officer to determine the responsibility of a supplier that is about to be awarded a contract. In many cases, that determination turns out to be perfunctory and based, in large part, on the reputation of the supplier and perhaps a financial statement that it submits. This is not the appropriate approach.

Establishing what are called *affirmative responsibility criteria* in a solicitation is a powerful tool for a public procurement officer. In essence, it allows him or her a means for requesting documentation that will assist in an evaluation of a supplier's past performance, where lowest price is the basis for contract award such as under the competitive sealed bidding methods. It permits the public procurement officer to reject the bid of a bidder whose past performance simply does not provide an adequate level of confidence that it will provide the needs identified in the solicitation.

Affirmative responsibility criteria are not as useful in procurements conducted using competitive sealed proposals since past performance and other responsibility measures may be among the evaluation criteria noted in the solicitation. However, the items listed in the following regulations as supplier capabilities for an affirmative responsibility criteria analysis are useful starting points for preparing evaluation criteria in this area.

The Recommended Regulations of the Model Procurement Code describe the breadth of the factors that a procurement officer may consider in examining responsibility as follows:

> *R3-401.02* **Standards of Responsibility.**
> *R3-401.01.1* **Standards.** *Factors to be considered in determining whether the standard of responsibility has been met include whether a prospective contractor has:*
> *(a) available the appropriate financial, material, equipment, facility, and personnel resources and expertise, or the ability to obtain them, necessary to indicate its capability to meet all contractual requirements;*
> *(b) a satisfactory record of performance;*
> *(c) a satisfactory record of integrity;*
> *(d) qualified legally to contract with the [State]; and*
> *(e) supplied all necessary information in connection with the inquiry concerning responsibility.*
>
> *R3-401.03* **Ability to Meet Standards.** *The prospective contractor may demonstrate the availability of necessary financing, equipment, facilities, expertise, and personnel by submitting upon request:*
> *(a) evidence that such contractor possesses such necessary items;*
> *(b) acceptable plans to subcontract for such necessary items; or a documented commitment from, or explicit arrangement with, a satisfactory source to provide the necessary items.*

The solicitation must describe the affirmative responsibility criteria and require the bidder or offeror in line for contract award to supply documentation showing that it can meet those criteria. The language in the solicitation should also allow the discretion of the public procurement officer to use other data in making an affirmative responsibility determination, including his or her own experience with the bidder or offeror.

OTHER TYPES OF SOURCE SELECTION METHODS

Pilot Projects

Finally, a reading of Chapter 20 (*Procurement of Information Technology*) shows the challenges posed in purchasing information technology. One of the methods it promotes as helpful to performing the critical market research is the use of pilot projects. Those projects are ones in which the public entity uses a particular commodity or service at no cost and without any financial obligation to the supplier for the sole purposes of evaluating the commodity or service.

As Chapter 8 (*Noncompetitive and Limited Competition Procurements*) explains, these types of projects often pose some ethical issues for public procurement officers. Additionally, a procurement law, if the public entity is under one, must specifically authorize them.

One state whose law permits pilot or demonstration projects is Arizona. The Arizona Revised Statutes state:

> 41-2556. **Demonstration projects**[14]
> *A. A demonstration project may be undertaken if the director determines in writing that the project is innovative and unique. This state shall not be obligated to pay the contractor, or to procure or lease the services or materials supplied by the contractor. However, on the written request and justification by the agency and written determination by the director that it is in the best interest of this state, this state may pay the contractor for the demonstration project. The contract term shall not exceed two years. A request and written determination of the basis for the contract award shall be included in the contract file.*
> *B. A contract to procure or lease services or materials previously supplied during a demonstration project shall be conducted under this article.*
> *C. Except as otherwise provided by law, a contractor for a demonstration project shall not be precluded from participating as a bidder or offeror in a procurement for the services or materials supplied during a demonstration project.*

Chapter 20 makes a case for the use of this type of market research tool.

Special Procurement Methods

Finally, the Model Procurement Code provides language that a state or local government may adopt to permit a procurement officer to devise new source selection methods when circumstances dictate a need to do so. It provides:

> §3-207 **Special Procurements.**
> *Notwithstanding any other provision of this Code, the Chief Procurement Officer or the head of a Purchasing Agency may with prior public notice initiate a procurement above the small purchase amount specified in Section 3-204 where the officer determines that an unusual or unique situation exists that makes the application of all requirements of competitive sealed bidding or competitive sealed proposals contrary to the public interest. Any special procurement under this Section shall be made with such competition as is practicable under the circumstances. A written determination of the basis for the procurement and for the selection of the particular contractor shall be included by the Chief Procurement Officer or the head of a Purchasing Agency in the contract file, and a report shall be made publicly available at least annually describing all such determinations made subsequent to the prior report.*

The American Bar Association inserted this language into the 2000 version of the Model Procurement Code. It is based on a statute that is in the version of the Model Procurement Code that the State of Alaska adopted which states:[15]

> AS 36.30.308. **Innovative Procurements.**
> *(a) A contract may be awarded for supplies, services, professional services, or construction using an innovative procurement process, with or without competitive sealed bidding or competitive sealed proposals, in accordance with regulations adopted by the commissioner. A contract may be awarded under this section only*

when the chief procurement officer, or, for construction contracts or procurements of the state equipment fleet, the commissioner of transportation and public facilities, determines in writing that it is advantageous to the state to use an innovative competitive procurement process in the procurement of new or unique requirements of the state, new technologies, or to achieve best value.

(b) The procurement officer shall submit a procurement plan to the Department of Law for review and approval as to form before issuing the notice required by (c) of this section.

(c) A procurement under this section is subject to the requirements of AS 36.30.130.

(d) Nothing in this section precludes the adoption of regulations providing for the use of bonuses instead of preferences in a procurement of construction.

CONCLUSION

The Recommended Best Practices and this chapter identify the concepts and methods that the public procurement officer applies when procuring commodities, services, and construction, and emphasizes the discretion and flexibility that he or she must exercise. These concepts and methods have been used for decades and will likely be practiced for decades more. It will be the responsibility of the public procurement officer to use them in a creative way to meet the needs of a public entity, its user agencies and its users.

ENDNOTES

1. https://www.nigp.org/home/find-procurement-resources/dictionary-of-terms
2. A copy of the Model Procurement Code, along with various versions of it including the Model Procurement Ordinance is available at: http://apps.americanbar.org/dch/committee.cfm?com=PC500500
3. www.naspo.org
4. See the commentary to Section 3-203(1) of the Model Procurement Code.
5. https://www.nigp.org/home/find-procurement-resources/dictionary-of-terms
6. See Section 3-202(7) of the Model Procurement Code.
7. See Kentucky Revised Statutes 45A.070 at: http://www.lrc.ky.gov/statutes/statute.aspx?id=22340
8. See Section R3-202.11.2 of the Model Procurement Code.
9. Pennington, R. (February 1, 2011). Problems in applying concepts of responsiveness in RFPs—Go Pro article. Retrieved October 9, 2018, from: http://www.americancityandcounty.com/2011/02/01/responsive-or-not/
10. See Section 3-203(7) of the Model Procurement Code.
11. Wyllie, J. (December 4, 2017). *Most Government Procurement Has Got It All Wrong, These Advocates Say*. Retrieved August 15, 2018, from: http://www.governing.com/cityaccelerator/blog/lc-pips-procurement.html
12. Hagar, S., (June/July 2013) A Case for Achieving Best Value Through PIPS, *Government Procurement*. Retrieved from: https://www.nigp.org/docs/default-source/New-Site/govpro/govprojunejuly2013.pdf?sfvrsn=809cca46_0
13. A purchase card "is a type of Commercial Card that allows organizations to take advantage of the existing credit card infrastructure to make electronic payments for a variety of business expenses (e.g., goods and services). In the simplest terms, a P-Card is a charge card, similar to a consumer credit card." https://www.napcp.org/page/WhatArePCardsc
14. See: https://www.azleg.gov/viewdocument/?docName=https://www.azleg.gov/ars/41/02556.htm
15. http://www.akleg.gov/basis/statutes.asp#36.30.308

CHAPTER 8: NONCOMPETITIVE AND LIMITED COMPETITION PROCUREMENTS

RECOMMENDED BEST PRACTICES

- Balancing the flexibility provided by exceptions to full competition with the need for proper administration requires central oversight, including the authority to establish strict conditions for the use of exceptions. That authority and oversight must reside solely with the Chief Procurement Officer.
- Central decision making by the Chief Procurement Officer means that there is a central repository for the documentation supporting the decision on the exception to competition. This, in turn, offers one place for auditors and others to find data about these types of procurements, including the justification for limiting or eliminating competition.
- A request for an exception to competition should be in writing and meet the conditions that are spelled out in the laws, rules/regulations, or policies establishing the conditions and procedures for these types of procurements.
- The Chief Procurement Officer should provide some public notice of sole source procurements, as notice can provide an excellent method for testing the user agency's request for a sole source against the supplier community-at-large, who may have a different view.
- When conditions necessitating an emergency procurement arise and the Chief Procurement Office is unavailable to provide approval, procedures should permit user agencies to conduct those procurements and require them to report the circumstances to the Chief Procurement Officer within a short period of time to obtain approval after the fact.
- The Chief Procurement Officer should review and approve his or her public entity's purchase of another government's property, including the advisability of the purchase and its price, along with the terms and conditions in any written agreement.

Circumstances can sometimes make it difficult or impossible to conduct a formal competitive procurement. There are source selection methods for conducting noncompetitive and limited competition procurements when conditions are appropriate. In order to provide a public procurement officer with a full range of tools, a public entity's procurement law should authorize the use of these methods where that law otherwise requires competition.

This chapter discusses the conditions and methods for awarding procurement contracts where there is limited or no competition.

AUTHORITY AND CENTRAL OVERSIGHT

A very small dollar purchase is one example of a type of procurement that a public procurement officer conducts with limited or no competition. Chapter 7 (*Competition: Solicitations and Methods*) addresses those types of procurements.

High dollar noncompetitive or limited competition procurements can be controversial and may become fodder for newspaper headlines. But these can also be legitimate procurements that offer a public entity a means of buying what it needs in situations where full and open competition does not make sense. The authority to conduct these types of procurements rests in a public entity's law establishing its procurement processes. In some cases, there may not be a law mandating competition or the law may simply give full discretion to a state or local governmental official to establish procurement processes. However, that is not the best practice.

A public entity's law should require full competition above a certain dollar level or authorize that dollar level to be established in rules/regulations. Once the law has established the mandate for competition, it must then define the specific authority of a public procurement office to make exceptions. Balancing the flexibility provided by exceptions to full competition with the need for proper administration requires central oversight, including the authority to establish strict conditions for the use of exceptions. That authority and oversight must reside solely with the Chief Procurement Officer.

That is the case even if the Chief Procurement Officer delegates authority to a user agency to conduct procurements. Chapter 2 (*Procurement Leadership, Organization, and Value*) discusses delegations in more detail.

Central oversight achieves several important public policy goals. For instance, it takes the decision to limit or eliminate competition away from the user agency requesting an exception. Public procurement officers within that user agency will often feel political pressure, real or imagined, to accommodate the request. Removing the decision from within the user agency provides a more objective and neutral process for evaluating that request.

Additionally, central decision making means that there is a central repository for the documentation supporting the procurement decision. In turn, that offers one place for auditors and others to find data about these types of procurements, including the justification for limiting or eliminating competition.

The following paragraphs address the types of procurements that fall into the limited competition or no competition categories. They also examine the kind of due diligence that is necessary to verify the reasonableness of price and the record keeping required to support the decisions being made.

A WORD ABOUT COMPETITIVE REQUIREMENTS WHEN USING FEDERAL FUNDS

In 2013, the federal government issued the Uniform Administrative Requirements, Cost

Principles, and Audit Requirements for Federal Awards, 2 Code of Federal Regulations Part 200 (Common Rule). Any non-federal public entity whose procurements are funded with federal monies must comply with the Common Rule.

The Common Rule states:[1]

> **§200.319 Competition.**
> *(a) All procurement transactions must be conducted in a manner providing full and open competition consistent with the standards of this section.*

The Common Rule does not address or authorize the use of exemptions from full competition for procurements funded with federal monies.

INVESTIGATION AND PRESERVATION OF RECORDS

For some limited competition or noncompetitive procurements, the central procurement office itself initiates the process. More often than not, however, such a procurement begins when a user agency makes a request to the Chief Procurement Officer. That request should be in writing and must meet the conditions that are spelled out in the laws, rules/regulation, or policies establishing the conditions and procedures for these types of procurements. The written request for this type of procurement is inadequate if it merely cites a need for waiver of competition without supporting information and justification.

In many cases, the Chief Procurement Officer will not have any real means to examine independently the user agency's determination of its need for these types of procurements. In other instances, the basis for exempting the procurement from full competition is clear, such as in emergencies, in instances where formal competition has previously failed, for commodities that are needed for over-the-counter sale, or when a commodity is available from correctional industries.

Whether the basis of the user agency need is obvious or not, the procurement file must demonstrate that the Chief Procurement Officer's decision to approve the purchase was based on all of the information available. For instance, the file should show that the Chief Procurement Officer independently studied the market to determine whether the commodity was, in fact, the only commodity available. It should also demonstrate that the Chief Procurement Officer took steps to substantiate that the price offered was reasonable. This is discussed later in this chapter, as well as in Chapter 4 (*Strategies and Plans*).

What is obvious to those within the executive branch of a state or local government is not always readily evident to those outside of it, such as journalists, legislators, and other suppliers. The key point is that the file should leave a satisfactory audit trail demonstrating that the Chief Procurement Officer conducted an appropriate independent analysis of a user agency's request and that he or she documented those efforts.

TYPES OF NONCOMPETITIVE OR LIMITED COMPETITION PROCUREMENTS

There are many circumstances where the opportunity for competition is limited or not practical. Some of these are discussed in the following text.

This does not suggest that the law must use the exact wording employed in this chapter for a public procurement officer to have the authority to limit or eliminate competition. The Chief Procurement Officer should interpret the law with reasonable flexibility while also considering the advice of the public entity's attorneys. However, the ultimate decision as to whether the law

Sole Source Procurements

Sole source procurement is a commonly referenced designation. However, there is not one single universally accepted definition. A good one is found in The Institute for Public Procurement: NIGP Dictionary:[2]

> **Sole source procurement**—A situation created due to the inability to obtain competition. A procurement method where only one supplier possesses the unique ability or capability to meet the particular requirements of the solicitation. The purchasing authority may require a justification from the requesting department within the agency explaining why this is the only source for the requirement.

Competition is not available in a sole source procurement situation simply because there is only a single source for the procurement or no reasonable alternative source exists.

The American Bar Association Model Procurement Code (Model Procurement Code) for State and Local Governments addresses the issue in its model statutory language and the commentary to it as follows:[3]

> **§3-205 Sole Source Procurement.**
> A contract may be awarded for a supply, service, or construction item without competition when, under regulations, the Chief Procurement Officer, the head of a Purchasing Agency, or a designee of either officer above the level of the Public Procurement Officer determines in writing that there is only one source for the required supply, service, or construction item.
>
> **COMMENTARY:**
>
> (1) This method of procurement involves no competition and should be utilized only when justified and necessary to serve [State] needs. This Code contemplates that the [Policy Office] [Chief Procurement Officer] will promulgate regulations which establish standards applicable to procurement needs that may warrant award on a sole source basis.
>
> (2) The power to authorize a sole source award is limited to the Chief Procurement Officer and the head of an agency with purchasing authority, or their designees above the level of Public Procurement Officer. The purpose in specifying these officials is to reflect an intent that such determinations will be made at a high level. The permission for these officials to authorize a designee to act for them should be subject to regulations.

The term *sole source* refers to the source, not the commodity or service. The ability of a supplier to meet a necessary condition dictated by circumstances such as immediate delivery date or repairs at a particular location can create a sole source situation in which there is a single available supplier. Some examples of sole source procurements are:

- Equipment for which there is no comparable competitive commodity, for example, a one-of-a-kind oscilloscope that is available from only one supplier
- Public utility services from regulated monopolies
- A component or replacement part for which there is no commercially available substitute and which may be obtained only directly from the manufacturer
- An item where compatibility is the overriding consideration, such as computer operating software enhancements for an existing system
- A used item, for example, a television transmitter tower that becomes immediately available

Best practice is for the law authorizing the use of sole source procurement to require that the

Chief Procurement Officer provide some public notice that he or she is embarking on this type of procurement. Even if the law does not require it, notice can provide an excellent method of testing the user agency's request for a sole source against the supplier community-at-large, which may have a different view.

NASPO has published sole source procurement information on its website.[4] That information provides a more thorough look at what constitutes a sole source, how to reduce the use of unnecessary sole source procurements, and how to maximize competition. It also offers sample justification forms and templates for sole source requests.

Emergency Procurements

Another circumstance in which competition may be limited or not practical is in an emergency. The focus here is not on the rarity of the item or service sought, but on expediency instead. As noted for sole source procurements, there should be some authority in a state or local government's law to permit this type of procurement when that law otherwise requires procurements to be conducted through full competition.

An *emergency* for procurement purposes is an unexpected and pressing situation requiring swift procurement action outside of normal procedures. The NIGP defines the term as follows:

> **Emergency purchase**—*A purchase made due to an unexpected and urgent request where health and safety or the conservation of public resources is at risk. Usually formal competitive bidding procedures are waived.*

In addition to threats to life and property, an emergency may include circumstances such as an unexpected delay in delivery or an unanticipated volume of work. It never includes a situation created by poor planning on the part of user agencies.

The Model Procurement Code addresses the issue in its model statutory language and the commentary to it:[5]

> ***§3-206 Emergency Procurements.***
> *Notwithstanding any other provision of this Code, the Chief Procurement Officer, the head of a Purchasing Agency, or a designee of either officer may make or authorize others to make emergency procurements when there exists a threat to public health, welfare, or safety under emergency conditions as defined in regulations; provided that such emergency procurements shall be made with such competition as is practicable under the circumstances. A written determination of the basis for the emergency and for the selection of the particular contractor shall be included in the contract file.*
>
> ***COMMENTARY:***
>
> *(1) This Section authorizes the procurement of supplies, services, or construction where the urgency of the need does not permit the delay involved in utilizing more formal competitive methods. This Code contemplates that the [Policy Office] [Chief Procurement Officer] will promulgate regulations establishing standards for making emergency procurements and controlling delegations of authority by the Chief Procurement Officer or the head of a Purchasing Agency. Such regulations may limit the authority of such officials to delegate the authority to make procurements above designated dollar amounts.*
> *(2) While in a particular emergency an award may be made without any competition, the intent of this Code is to require as much competition as practicable in a given situation. When the amount of the emergency procurement is within that adopted for Section 3-204 (Small Purchases), the competitive procedures prescribed under that Section should be used when feasible.*

(3) Use of this Section may be justified because all bids submitted under the competitive sealed bid method are unreasonable, and there is no time to re-solicit bids without endangering the public health, welfare, or safety. As with other emergency conditions, regulations will further define these circumstances, and any procurements conducted pursuant to this authority must be done so as to treat all bidders fairly and to promote such competition as is practicable under the circumstances.

It is a best practice for rules/regulations and procedures to address situations where prior approval of the Chief Procurement Officer is not feasible, such as when emergencies occur on weekends. In those cases, the rules/regulations and procedures should permit user agencies to conduct emergency procurements but require them to report the circumstances to the Chief Procurement Officer within a short period of time to obtain approval after the fact.

In an emergency procurement, the quantity to be purchased should only be that necessary to meet the circumstance. If time, the nature of the requirements, and other circumstances permit, verbal price quotations should be sought from more than one potential source.

For certain commodity or service needs, the Chief Procurement Officer may consider putting in place indefinite quantity contracts[6] for a period of time (such as a year) through a formal competition in anticipation of certain emergency situations, with the understanding that the user agencies will purchase from the contract only if an emergency need exists. For example, one emergency might be for helicopter services for forest firefighting work. Major disasters require prompt action and these types of contracts allow the procurement process to meet an urgent need in a competitive yet timely manner.

Procurement of Government-Produced Services or Commodities

Many state laws mandate that state user agencies use commodities or services produced by correctional industries and sheltered suppliers, such as industries for the blind. In some cases, the Chief Procurement Officer may have the authority to establish the prices that user agencies will pay for those commodities and services.

In most cases, however, the public procurement officer will not have that authority. Under those circumstances, the public entity's law must provide a mechanism for the Chief Procurement Officer to determine whether the price charged is reasonable; and if it is not, to seek to purchase the services or commodities through normal competitive processes or existing contracts.

Procurements of Other Governments' Property

Some purchases may take place between two different governments. For instance, a state highway department may rent out a road grader to a county government, or a small town may ask a larger city to provide hosting services for its website and e-mail services. A state university may wish to buy a piece of research equipment from a university in another state.

The best practice is for the Chief Procurement Officer to review and approve the transaction, including the advisability of the purchase and its price, along with the terms and conditions in any written agreement.

Procurements with or from Other Governments' Contracts

Chapter 12 (*Cooperative Purchasing*) discusses cooperative procurement in detail. When a public entity purchases services, commodities, or construction from the contract competed and awarded by a second public entity—a cooperative contract—the first public entity's purchase from the cooperative contract is an exception to any requirement in its law to compete that procurement opportunity. Therefore, it is important for the public entity to have the authority in its law to purchase from another public entity's cooperative contract.

In most cases, the public entity awarding the cooperative contract fully competes it. Typically, there are requirements in the law that have to be satisfied for a public entity to be able to purchase from a cooperative contract. For instance, there may be a requirement that the public entities—the one purchasing and the one competing and awarding the contract—have a written agreement for cooperative purchasing.

There is one issue related to cooperative purchasing that may be problematic for some public entities. In some cases, a public entity's law may authorize that entity to make purchases from a cooperative contract only if the solicitation for that cooperative contract explicitly names that entity as a potential purchaser. If a public entity who wishes to purchase from the cooperative contract is not named as a potential purchaser, it cannot purchase from, or piggyback onto, a cooperative contract.

Many governments below the state level freely purchase commodities and services from other public entities' cooperative contracts whether or not the solicitations that resulted in those contracts specifically named them or not. While the naming of every participating public entity in the solicitation at the procurement's initiation is ideal, particularly if the competing suppliers are trying to project potential volume in their pricing strategies, suppliers awarded contracts generally do not object to the additional business. It is convenient for the cooperative contract to allow the contractor the option of providing commodities or services under that contract to public entities that were not originally named in it.

Laws authorizing cooperative purchasing vary widely. As Chapter 12 explains, the specific legal authority in a particular public entity must be understood before it attempts to purchase through cooperative contracts.

Unsolicited Offers

If a supplier submits an unsolicited offer to a state or local government, acceptance of the offer constitutes a waiver of competition. It is best for a law to authorize acceptance of such offers while directing that rules/regulations and procedures be put in place to govern the conditions for considering, accepting, or rejecting them.

Generally, the rules/regulations and procedures should require that the offer be made entirely upon the initiative of the offeror; that it be submitted in sufficient detail to evaluate its need and usefulness; that it be proprietary or unique to the extent that competitive solicitations are not practicable; and that its evaluation be subject to comparisons and tests as determined by the public entity receiving the offer. In addition, procedures should require that an unsolicited offer not be evaluated, nor any commitment be made by a user agency with respect to such an offer, without written approval of the Chief Procurement Officer.

The Recommended Regulations of the Model Procurement Code address the issue in the following way:[7]

> R3-104.01 **Unsolicited Offers.**
> R3-104.01.1 **Defined.** *An unsolicited offer is any offer other than one submitted in response to a solicitation.*
>
> R3-104.01.2 **Processing of Unsolicited Offers.** *The Chief Procurement Officer or the head of the Purchasing Agency shall consider the offer as provided in this Section. If an agency that receives an unsolicited offer is not authorized to enter into a contract for the supplies or services offered, the head of such agency shall forward the offer to the Chief Procurement Officer who shall have final authority with*

respect to evaluation, acceptance, and rejection of such unsolicited offers.

R3-104.01.3 Conditions for Consideration. *To be considered for evaluation, an unsolicited offer:*
(a) must be in writing;
(b) must be sufficiently detailed to allow a judgment to be made concerning the potential utility of the offer to the [State];
(c) must be unique or innovative to [State] use;
(d) must demonstrate that the proprietary character of the offering warrants consideration of the use of sole source procurement; and
(e) may be subject to testing under terms and conditions specified by the [State].

R3-104.01.4 Evaluation. *The unsolicited offer shall be evaluated to determine its utility to the [State] and whether it would be to the [State's] advantage to enter into a contract based on such offer. If an award is to be made on the basis of such offer, the sole source procedures in Regulation 3-205 (Sole Source Procurement) shall be followed.*

R3-104.01.5 Confidentiality. *Any written request for confidentiality of data contained in an unsolicited offer that is made in writing shall be honored. If an award is made, confidentiality of data shall be agreed upon by the parties and governed by the provisions of the contract. If agreement cannot be reached on confidentiality, the [State] may reject the unsolicited offer.*

Pilot or Demonstration Projects

Public procurement professionals are often asked by a user agency to permit it to put a commodity or service through a practical test to see if that type of commodity or service might meet the user agency's critical needs. Pilot or demonstration projects are exceptions to competition, although some might argue that if the supplier provides the commodity or service without charge, the transaction does not qualify as a procurement. Given the effect on future possible competition of allowing one supplier access to test its commodity or service, this type of arrangement should be reviewed thoroughly and require the approval of the Chief Procurement Officer.

Additionally, the public entity's law should specifically authorize that entity to engage in this type of arrangement. One state whose law permits pilot or demonstration projects is Arizona. The Arizona Revised Statutes state:

> 41-2556. **Demonstration projects**[8]
> A. A demonstration project may be undertaken if the director determines in writing that the project is innovative and unique. This state shall not be obligated to pay the contractor, or to procure or lease the services or materials supplied by the contractor. However, on the written request and justification by the agency and written determination by the director that it is in the best interest of this state, this state may pay the contractor for the demonstration project. The contract term shall not exceed two years. A request and written determination of the basis for the contract award shall be included in the contract file.
> B. A contract to procure or lease services or materials previously supplied during a demonstration project shall be conducted under this article.
> C. Except as otherwise provided by law, a contractor for a demonstration project shall not be precluded from participating as a bidder or offeror in a procurement for the services or materials supplied during a demonstration project.

Supplier arrangements such as this one pose a dilemma for a Chief Procurement Officer. On the one hand, a pilot or demonstration project allows the public entity to *kick the tires* of something that may solve a serious public problem without committing the public entity to a costly contract in situations where the contractor may try to resolve the problem but not be able to perform if the solution does not work. On the other hand, the pilot project supplier will clearly have *inside information* for any formal competition that may be conducted based on the outcome of the project. Among other things, competitors of the pilot supplier will tend to be discouraged from competing based on that fact, to the detriment of the public entity.

CONCLUSION

The public procurement function must be flexible enough to allow for exceptions to the requirement for full competition. Approval of these exceptions must be within the sole authority of the Chief Procurement Officer. The key is that the special circumstances justifying the exception must be described in the public entity's law. Additionally, all steps in the process of conducting a noncompetitive or limited competition procurement must be documented.

ENDNOTES

1. See 2 Code of Federal Regulations §200.319, *Competition*, at: https://www.gpo.gov/fdsys/pkg/CFR-2017-title2-vol1/pdf/CFR-2017-title2-vol1-part200.pdf
2. Access to the NIGP Dictionary is available at: http://www.nigp.org/home/find-procurement-resources/dictionary-of-terms
3. A copy of the Model Procurement Code, along with various versions of it including the Model Procurement Ordinance and Recommended Regulations is available at: http://apps.americanbar.org/dch/committee.cfm?com=PC500500
4. http://www.naspo.org/solesourceprocurement/index.html
5. See Endnote 3.
6. The NIGP Dictionary defines an indefinite quantity contract as follows: A type of a contract that provides for the delivery of indefinite quantities, within stated limits, of supplies or services. These supplies or services are to be furnished during a fixed period, with deliveries or performance to be scheduled by placing orders with the contractor.
7. See Endnote 3.
8. See: https://www.azleg.gov/viewdocument/?docName=https://www.azleg.gov/ars/41/02556.htm

CHAPTER 9: BID AND PROPOSAL EVALUATION AND AWARD

RECOMMENDED BEST PRACTICES

- The evaluation of bids and proposals must conform to the procurement law.
- The evaluation must also be consistent with the criteria and requirements specified in the solicitation.
- There should be a plan in place for how the evaluation is to be conducted before the due date for bids or proposals.
- The public procurement officer should conduct the cost or price evaluation with any needed assistance from a public entity's fiscal personnel, leaving the technical evaluation to the evaluation committee, where one has been appointed.
- The analysis of the bids or proposals must be documented in writing. Documentation is important, not only to show that the evaluation conformed to the law and the solicitation, but also to show that the process was fair and unbiased.
- The solicitation should specify a time (such as three months) during which a bidder or offeror must keep their bids and proposals open—that is, keep their pricing firm.
- It is imperative that those involved in the evaluation of bids or proposals be completely unbiased in whatever role they play in the evaluation.
- There should be a rigorous determination of a bidder's or offeror's responsibility as part of the evaluation process. Responsibility should not be presumed because the bidder or offeror has previously been a contractor for the public entity.
- The documentation of the selection of the winning bidder or offeror must demonstrate compliance with contract award standards stated in the law and the solicitation. It should also be consistent with the procurement procedures and guidelines, such as internal procurement manuals, that exist to assist the public entity's public procurement officers.

CHAPTER 9: BID AND PROPOSAL EVALUATION AND AWARD

The evaluation of bids and proposals is a key point in the procurement process. It is where the needs of the user agency, as reflected in the solicitation, are compared side-by-side with the response of suppliers heeding the call to meet those needs. This chapter discusses the process of making that comparison—the evaluation of bids or proposals—and awarding a contract.

At the outset, it is important to say a word about who should make the award decision. A procurement law should confer that authority solely on the public procurement officer. In many state and local governments (primarily cities, counties, and districts), applicable laws grant that authority to an elected official or bodies of elected officials.

The awarding of a contract and the maintenance of a truly professional procurement system do not fit well within a political, often legislative-type process. Lobbying and other normal characteristics of the deliberations of a political body such as an elected city council or board of supervisors run counter to the promise that suppliers' responses to a solicitation will be judged fairly by those most knowledgeable about the procurement process and the subject matter of the procurement.

Thus, where the public political body has the authority to give away or delegate its authority to award contracts, it should do so to the Chief Public Procurement Officer in the interest of sound management. This also allows public officials to devote their time to the important policy and budgetary issues for which they were elected.

EVALUATIONS AND AWARDS

At the outset of this chapter, it is appropriate to set forth some overarching principles that should drive any evaluation of a bid or proposal and subsequent contract award. Important principles are:

- **Alignment of the evaluation to the law**—The evaluation must conform to the procurement law. If that law, for instance, does not explicitly permit the public entity to take into consideration evaluation criteria in considering bids but requires that the contract award be made to the lowest responsible bidder, then it is doubtful that evaluation criteria may be used. If the law allows criteria other than low price to be used in evaluating bids but limits them to those that are objectively measurable, then it is critical to limit criteria to factors that fit that requirement. Similarly, if the law says that price or cost must be one of the criteria in evaluating proposals, then the solicitation must list price or cost as an evaluation factor. Chapter 7 (*Competition: Solicitations and Methods*) discusses these legal standards in more detail.
- **Alignment of the evaluation to the solicitation**—The evaluation must also be consistent with the evaluation criteria and requirements specified in the solicitation. If the evaluation is based in part on whether a bid or proposal meets certain minimum requirements, then those requirements must be clearly identified as such in the solicitation. Additionally, the evaluation criteria must be those that will allow whoever is weighing bids or proposals—a public procurement officer or an evaluation committee—to measure how well a particular bid or proposal fares against the criteria. Finally, a mismatch between the solicitation requirements and the evaluation criteria is unfair to suppliers who may be misled about what is required or important.
- **Evaluation plan**—The plan for how the evaluation is to be conducted must be in writing and in place before the due date for bids or proposals. That precludes any criticism that the plan was crafted after bids or proposals were in the public procurement officer's hands and that it was skewed in a particular supplier's direction.

- **Evaluation of price or cost**—The public procurement officer should evaluate cost or price with any needed assistance from a public entity's fiscal personnel, leaving the technical evaluation to the evaluation committee where one has been appointed.
- **Written documentation**—The analysis of the bids or proposals must be documented in writing. The formal procurement process, and even the informal one at some dollar levels, is a written one, with a written solicitation asking for written responses. Documentation is important, not only to show that the evaluation conformed to the law and the solicitation, but also to show that the process was fair and unbiased. The importance of thorough documentation is outlined in Chapter 17 (*Protests, Disputes, and Claims*).
- **Timelines**—The solicitation should specify a time (such as three months) during which a bidder or offeror must keep their bids and proposals open—that is, keep their pricing firm. Therefore, before the solicitation is issued, it is necessary for the public procurement officer to have in mind a good estimate of the time that evaluation of bids or proposals will take. The evaluation sometimes takes longer than anticipated and stated in the solicitation. In those situations, the public procurement officer should ask each bidder or offeror to extend its bid or proposal for another specific amount of time.
- **Impartial evaluators**—It is imperative that those involved in the evaluation of bids or proposals be completely unbiased in whatever role they play in the evaluation. Chapter 7 (*Competition: Solicitations and Methods*) emphasizes this point.
- **Determinations of responsibility**—There should be a rigorous determination of a bidder's or offeror's responsibility as part of the evaluation process. Responsibility should not be presumed because the bidder or offeror has previously been a contractor for the public entity.
- **Alignment of the contract award with the law and the solicitation**—The documentation of the selection of the winning bidder or offeror must demonstrate compliance with contract award standards stated in the law and the solicitation. It should also be consistent with the public entity's procurement procedures and guidelines, such as internal procurement manuals, that exist to assist public procurement officers.

EVALUATION OF BIDS AND PROPOSALS GENERALLY

The following discussion focuses on some steps in the formal procurement process that apply to the evaluation of both the bids and the proposals.

Initial Review for Compliance

After opening bids or proposals, a public procurement officer must verify that they contain all the required documents and information and that they are properly signed. The point of that exercise is to determine whether there is any omission or defect in a bid or proposal that requires rejection before formal evaluation even begins. A public procurement officer should not waste time on an incomplete or defective submission.

Bids

For bids, the determination is whether they are responsive, that is, whether they demonstrate an unequivocal commitment to the material requirements of the solicitation. Chapter 7 (*Competition: Solicitations and Methods*) discusses this concept in more detail. Nonresponsive bids should be set aside and not evaluated.

Proposals

For proposals, the determination is more complicated. Problems may be obvious, for instance, only to technical persons assisting with the procurement or sitting on the evaluation committee.

CHAPTER 9: BID AND PROPOSAL EVALUATION AND AWARD

It may be the case in reviewing proposals for initial compliance that the public procurement officer reviews them for the most obvious non-compliance problems and that an evaluation committee composed of users with technical knowledge assists with what is often called determining technical acceptability. Proposals that are technically acceptable or may become so during clarifications or discussions, if any, with the evaluation committee are kept in the pool, and those that are too flawed to be within reasonable parameters are eliminated. No matter how that sorting is carried out, it must be reasonable, based on any requirements in the law and the solicitation, and documented.

Sending Bids or Proposals to Users for Evaluation

At the start of the formal evaluation process, some procurement offices refer bids or proposals to the user agency for its review and recommendation. That process is generally informal and unstructured.

While input from the user agency may be helpful, the informality of that approach results in at least part of the evaluation being placed outside of the hands of the public procurement officer. That means that there may not be a complete record of how the award decision was made, exposing the process to accusations that it was suspect.

The better approach is for the public procurement officer to conduct and maintain control over the evaluation of bids and proposals. There is room in that approach for user agency input without the public procurement officer losing oversight of the process. Use of an evaluation committee is one method, and it is an approach that is structured, formal, and a matter of record. The public procurement officer exercises control of the process so that the evaluation effort does not go astray or gravitate toward consideration of factors not announced in the solicitation.

Evaluation of Price or Cost

One matter that a public procurement officer needs to resolve before assigning evaluation responsibilities to a committee is whether that group will evaluate price or cost. It is the best practice for the public procurement officer to make that decision with appropriate fiscal personnel assistance, if necessary. In many instances today, price or cost requires some calculation, such as life cycle costing or total-cost-of-ownership analysis. While the public procurement officer may need help in performing the cost or price analysis, this analysis should not be within the purview of any committee evaluating bids or proposals.

The laws of some public entities specifically require that price or cost be evaluated only by the public procurement officer. The law of the State of Utah is an example.[1]

Documentation

Because the evaluation process focuses on subjects such as responsiveness in the case of bids and subjective evaluation criteria in the case of proposals, suppliers and the public may understandably think that the evaluation process is a mystery. It is common to see bid protests that challenge, for instance, the application of the evaluation criteria, an evaluation committee's interpretation of a proposal, or the determination that a bid is materially defective. It is critical, therefore, that the written record of each key step in the procurement be sufficient to demonstrate how that decision was made.

The amount of documentation will depend on the type of evaluation conducted and the complexity of the commodity, construction, or service being purchased. The public procurement officer must look at the documentation in the procurement file from the view of competing bidders or offerors, the public, the press, and auditors. The question that the review must answer is whether the procurement file tells a reasonable story about the process—particularly about the basis for award. In preparing documentation, the public procurement officer must be aware of one of the laws of contrariety: if something can be misinterpreted, it likely will be.

EVALUATION OF BIDS

Most public entities utilize a spectrum of criteria for evaluating bids and awarding contracts under competitive sealed bidding. Price is always a criterion in that spectrum, either as a principal determinant or as an element of overall cost.

Price/Performance Evaluation

For a procurement in which a price/performance evaluation will be carried out, the invitation for bids must notify suppliers that price/performance factors will be used and require them to submit technical performance and other data with their bids to allow for this evaluation. Today, price/performance analysis relies on strategies such as life cycle costing or total-cost-of-ownership calculations, which are discussed in detail in Chapter 6 (*Sustainable Procurement Considerations and Strategies*).

Whether or not the public entity has a sustainable procurement program, it is important for the public procurement officer to consider price/performance in determining which bid offers the lowest price or cost.

If the public procurement officer needs outside expert assistance to make the necessary technical assessments, that expertise should be made available. Additionally, as Chapter 6 notes, there is an abundance of information available online about energy use, maintenance, and other costs related to owning many brand-name commodities.

Types of Non-Price Evaluation Criteria

Non-price evaluation factors used in selecting the winning bid under competitive sealed bids are generally limited to those that are objectively measurable. The State of Utah's Administrative Code defines *objective criteria* as follows:[2]

(19)(a) "Objective Criteria" means the quantifiable requirements, standards, and specifications set forth in a solicitation by which solicitation responses from vendors will be evaluated and scored by evaluators based on the measurable and verifiable facts, evidence, and documentation provided in each vendor's solicitation response.
(b) Objective criteria [are] not evaluated and scored based on the personal judgement, interpretation, or opinion of evaluators. Objective criteria [are] evaluated and scored strictly on the observable, verifiable and measurable facts, evidence, and documentation provided in each vendor's solicitation response.
(c) Examples of objective criteria that may be included in a solicitation:
  (i) Vendors must document that they have a minimum of five years of experience on similar projects;
  (ii) Vendors must have three licensed technicians on the project; and
  (iii) Vendors must certify that they have an "A" rating from an accredited rating agency.

Table 9.1 lists some examples of objectively measurable criteria offered by the State of Utah and the Commonwealth of Kentucky for the evaluation of bids. The Utah Administrative Code also lists those same criteria as well as others when addressing competitive sealed proposals. The difference is that what is measured in evaluating a bid must be objectively measurable in contrast with criteria used in evaluating proposals under the competitive sealed proposals method, which may require measuring subjective criteria as well. The State of Utah's definition of *subjective criteria* is discussed under the heading *Evaluation of Proposals* in this chapter.

Objectively measurable criteria rely heavily on whether a number can be used to define baseline compliance for each criterion, such as the

CHAPTER 9: **BID AND PROPOSAL EVALUATION AND AWARD**

Table 9.1 Examples of Objectively Measurable Criteria

State of Utah[1]	Commonwealth of Kentucky[2]
(1) A procurement unit that conducts a procurement using a bidding process shall evaluate each bid using the objective criteria described in the invitation for bids, which may include: a) experience; b) performance ratings; c) inspection; d) testing; e) quality; f) workmanship; g) time and manner of delivery; h) references; i) financial stability; j) cost; k) suitability for a particular purpose; l) the contractor's work site safety program, including any requirement that the contractor imposes on subcontractors for a work site safety program; or m) other objective criteria specified in the invitation for bids.	Suggested evaluation criteria for commodities, establishing minimums and maximums for scoring purposes • Delivery: time, number of delivery equipment • Price: lowest price • Product(s): these are general measurable and quantifiable criteria. The agency is responsible for developing measurable criteria that best suit the agency's business need. Remember, use only relevant, objective, and measurable criteria. If product best value criteria are not important to your agency's business needs, use the ranking approach and other appropriate criteria • Product training • Supplier responsibility: years in business, amount of inventory, personnel (number of dedicated employees required for the contract); experience—years of combined experience; qualifications such as a minimum of one (1) year in an (applicable) accredited educational institution is required. • Service: response time • Warranty: period of warranty

1. See Utah Code 63G-6a-606-(1) at: https://codes.findlaw.com/ut/title-63g-general-government/#!tid=NFD 2F9190A04B11E1A5BEF191D2B004BD
2. https://finance.ky.gov/services/eprocurement/Documents/FAQ's and Presentations/BestValueOverview.doc

number of years of experience for each bidder personnel assigned to the contract, commodity performance ratings provided by a specified outside certifying organization, or expected delivery times in hours or days.

Evaluation of Price Discounts

It is a good practice to ask bidders to offer discounts, particularly under indefinite quantity/indefinite delivery contracts. Three common types of discounts are: a percentage off of the price deductible from an established catalog list price; a percentage off of an invoice amount deductible for payment of an invoice within a specified time; or a percentage off of the price based on volume purchased.

If the solicitation asks bidders to supply discounts, it must specify if and how the public procurement officer will evaluate them. By doing that, the procurement office prevents the bidders that do not offer discounts from claiming that they did not know that the public procurement officer would accept them.

A discount from an established list price is the only one that can be considered in evaluating bid prices. A discount based on future volume purchases will not occur until the contract is in place and thus is too speculative to consider during the procurement process. The same may be said of the discount offered for prompt payment of an invoice.

Determining Responsibility

As noted in Chapter 7 (*Competition: Solicitations and Awards*), a universal requirement for the award of a contract through a public procurement process is that it be made to a responsible supplier.

In many instances, the determination of a supplier's responsibility is given short shrift where the supplier has been a contractor for the state or local government for many years, or is well known within the community. In other cases, some of the criteria related to a supplier's responsibility, such as past performance of contracts, are made a part of the evaluation of a bid or proposal, requiring the supplier to demonstrate compliance in its bid or proposal with that criteria.

Neither of those situations, however, excuses the public procurement officer from making a specific determination that a supplier is responsible separate from the evaluation of its bid or proposal.

An example of a comprehensive responsibility determination process is that of the State of New York. The Office of the New York State Comptroller has established a precise and detailed process for examining a supplier's integrity and capability to perform a contract. The following information is part of a description from that office's website:[3]

In making a vendor responsibility determination, you must assess whether the vendor has:
- *appropriate financial, organization, and operational capacity and controls;*
- *appropriate legal authority to do business in New York;*
- *a satisfactory record of integrity; and*
- *an acceptable performance record on past contracts.*

You should consider any information that comes to your attention and work with the vendor to address any negative information.

Things to keep in mind:
- *Determinations must be made on a case-by-case basis.*
- *No specific response or piece of information from the vendor should automatically trigger a determination.*
- *A previous non-responsibility finding does not necessarily ban the vendor from future State contracts.*

Reviewing supplier information
When reviewing a vendor, you should rely on the scope of the contract to help guide you in determining what information is most relevant. However, your review must address the four categories listed here before you can make a determination:

Category	Factors to be considered include, but are not limited to:
Financial and Organizational Capacity	Assets, liabilities, recent bankruptcies, equipment, facilities, personnel resources and expertise, and proper auditing and accounting controls.
Legal Authority	Authority to do business in New York State, licenses, and registrations.
Integrity	Criminal indictments or convictions, civil fines and injunctions imposed by other agencies, antitrust investigations, ethical violations, tax delinquencies, or debarment by federal, state, or local governments.
Previous Contract Performance	Reports of less than satisfactory performances, early contract termination for cause, contract abandonment, court determinations of breach of contract.

[. . .]

Evaluating a supplier's past performance
It's good practice to require the vendor to provide references and identify other government contracts it has received, particularly those similar in scope to the contract at hand. You should contact these references and use the information obtained as part of the review process.

We encourage you to use quality control and consumer satisfaction measures, especially for human services contracts.

[. . .]

Addressing potentially negative information
Before you make a determination, you should contact the vendor to address any information that appears unfavorable. This provides an opportunity for the vendor to explain or even resolve the issue to your satisfaction.

However, there are valid causes that may warrant a finding of non-responsibility. These include, but are not limited to, the vendor having:
- committed fraud, such as anti-trust violations, embezzlement, theft, forgery, bribery, or tax evasion;
- made false statements or similar offenses;
- breached contracts resulting in their termination; or
- failed to show its financial capacity to perform the work.

If you become aware of information that calls into question a vendor's responsibility after you've awarded the contract, you may do one of two things:
- review the issue and determine no action is warranted, or
- require the vendor to correct the problem or implement a corrective action plan.

The information from the New York website reflects best practices. Since the information that a public procurement officer needs to make a responsibility determination is uniform regardless of the type of procurement involved, it should not be too difficult to establish templates and checklists for collecting the needed information from suppliers and analyzing it.

Contract Award

As noted earlier, the contract must be awarded to the responsible bidder whose bid is judged to meet the requirements that the law dictates. Additionally, there must be an in-depth scrutiny of a bidder's responsibility before awarding it a contract.

EVALUATION OF PROPOSALS

Under a request for proposals (RFP), non-price/cost evaluation factors generally play a much greater role in the selection of a winning proposal than they do in selecting a winning bid. Additionally, criteria used to evaluate proposals may include ones that rely on the evaluators' subjective judgments, and are not limited to criteria that are objectively measurable. Finally, unlike the competitive sealed bidding method, there are opportunities for offerors to modify their proposals within limits, and for discussions and negotiations to take place.

As noted earlier in this chapter, the Utah Administrative Code contains a definition of *subjective criteria*:[4]

(28)(a) "Subjective Criteria" means the open-ended requirements, standards, and specifications set forth in a solicitation by which solicitation responses from vendors will be evaluated and scored by evaluators based on the personal judgement, interpretations, and opinions of the evaluators after reviewing and analyzing the information presented in each vendor's solicitation response.

(b) Subjective criteria [are] not evaluated and scored strictly on the observable, verifiable and measurable facts, evidence, and documentation provided in each vendor's solicitation response. Subjective criteria [are] also evaluated and scored based on the personal judgement, interpretation, and opinion of the evaluators after reviewing and analyzing the information presented in each vendor's solicitation response.
(c) Examples of subjective criteria that may be included in a solicitation:
  (i) Vendors must describe how they will manage the project to meet the deadline;
  (ii) Vendors must demonstrate that they have the knowledge, skills, and ability to accomplish the scope of work; and
  (iii) Vendors must explain how their product complies with the specifications.

The Evaluation

Instructions to the Evaluation Committee

At the outset of the evaluation, the evaluation committee members should be advised of their roles in the process and the requirement to exercise independent judgment. The State of Utah Administrative Code sets out a good process for doing this, requiring a meeting at which the public procurement officer does the following:[5]

- Explains the evaluation and scoring process;
- Discusses requirements and prohibitions pertaining to socialization with suppliers, financial conflicts of interest, personal relationships, favoritism or bias, disclosure of confidential information contained in proposals or the deliberations and scoring of the evaluation committee, and ethical standards for an employee of a user agency involved in the procurement process;
- Reviews the scoring sheet and evaluation criteria set forth in the RFP; and
- Provides a copy of procedures for scoring non-priced technical criteria to the evaluation committee, employees of the procurement unit involved in the procurement, and any other person that will have access to the proposals.

That administrative code also emphasizes that the evaluation committee must "exercise independent judgement in the evaluation and scoring of the non-priced technical criteria in each proposal."[6] The steps outlined here are all good approaches.

The separation of the analysis of price/cost and the analysis of the technical aspects of proposals is a best practice. The evaluation of price or cost should be a mathematical one based on the importance of price or cost as an evaluation factor. The public procurement officer may need to ask for assistance from financial personnel within the public entity because the application of accounting principles may come into play. Removing the evaluation of a price or cost from an evaluation committee frees it to concentrate on the more important non-price portions of the offeror's proposals and whether they suit the public entity's business needs as stated in the solicitation.

Once the public procurement officer completes his or her evaluation of price or cost, that officer combines it with the evaluations of the committee. Since the committee is likely to conduct more than one evaluation during a procurement, the timing of when the public procurement officer provides the total evaluation, including price or cost, to the committee depends on the public entity.

Methods of Evaluation

It is the general practice in state and local government procurement processes to use numerical scoring to evaluate proposals—either points or rankings. That practice is even embedded into the procurement laws and procurement handbooks of various governments. For instance, the Utah Administrative Code directs each evaluation committee independently to assign a *preliminary draft score* to proposals, and states that evaluation will be based on *a one through five point scoring system*.[7] The Commonwealth of Pennsylvania's *Procurement Handbook* also requires the evaluation committee to use the *scoring sheets* provided to it.[8]

Numerical scoring is often perceived as the most objective means of evaluating criteria, including those that are subjective, such as an offeror's references. In contrast, the federal government uses a variety of ways to evaluate proposals. Table 9.2 lists some, with their pluses and minuses.

The best practice is to allow flexibility in the manner in which the evaluation is conducted.

Sequence of Evaluations

After the initial review of proposals, the sequence of the evaluation will vary, depending on the evaluation plan. If there are oral presentations, site visits/demonstrations, discussions/negotiations, and best and final offers, the evaluation committee will not make its final evaluation until these activities have occurred. It may make multiple evaluations before conducting a final one.

The Utah Administrative Code mandates the following best practice:[9]

(d) In order to score proposals fairly, an evaluation committee member must be present at all evaluation committee meetings and must review all proposals, including, if applicable, oral presentations. If an evaluation committee member fails to attend an evaluation committee meeting or leaves a meeting early or fails for any reason to fulfill the duties and obligations of a committee member, that committee member shall be removed from the committee. The remainder of the evaluation committee members may proceed with the evaluation, provided there are at least three evaluation committee members remaining.

Table 9.2

Type of Evaluation Method	Advantages	Disadvantages
Numerical scoring	• Calculating a total score for each proposal is easy • Evaluators often feel that they are being precise by using numbers	• Too easy to focus on the score without in-depth analysis of a proposal's strengths and weaknesses and potential impact of success under the contract • Numbers do not automatically transform the evaluation into an objective or precise one
Color coding (assigning colors to designate evaluation decisions such as blue = exceptional, green = acceptable)	• Allows the evaluators to focus on the strengths, weaknesses, and risks of each proposal	• Hard to identify the most technically superior proposal where each proposal evaluated has a mix of colors • More difficult to consider the relative importance of evaluation factors and subfactors
Adjectives (such as exceptional, outstanding, acceptable, weak, unacceptable)	• Same as color coding	• Same as color coding • If many adjectives are used, distinction between those adjacent to each other becomes difficult

Discussions and Negotiations

Identifying proposals for discussions—If the evaluation committee engages in discussions with offerors about their proposals, it must use some reasonable basis to decide which offerors will be afforded that opportunity. The American Bar Association Model Procurement Code for State and Local Governments (Model Procurement Code) states that those offerors "who submit proposals determined to be reasonably susceptible of being selected for award" should be given that opportunity.[10]

Another commonly used standard employed to sift through proposals is to determine which of them is within a *competitive range*. The NIGP Dictionary defines that term as follows:[11]

> **Competitive range**—That group of proposals, as determined during the evaluation process for competitive negotiation, that includes only those proposers considered to have a reasonable chance of being selected for award and who are, therefore, chosen for additional discussions and negotiations. Proposals not in the competitive range are given no further consideration.

Clarifications versus discussions/negotiations—Evaluation committees talk to offerors for two purposes. One is to obtain clarifications of offeror's proposals. The other is to enter into limited negotiations with offerors. The public entity's law should authorize both.

Federal procurement law makes a clear distinction between clarifications on the one hand and discussions and negotiations on the other.[12] Meetings with offerors during an evaluation process for purposes of clarifying proposals are quite limited and occur where the contract award will be made without discussions/negotiations "to clarify certain aspects of proposals (e.g., the relevance of an offeror's past performance information and adverse past performance information to which the offeror has not previously had an opportunity to respond) or to resolve minor or clerical errors." They are limited to a narrow set of issues.

Under federal law, discussions and negotiations are the same and allow the agenda for the meetings between offerors and the evaluation committee to be more substantive. In fact, it is generally the best practice for the public procurement officer to seek revisions of proposals after discussions/negotiations have occurred so that the substantive issues raised in those meetings may be reflected in writing and evaluated.

The agenda for discussions/negotiations is described aptly in the federal procurement regulations:[13]

> At a minimum, the contracting officer must . . . indicate to, or discuss with, each offeror still being considered for award, deficiencies, significant weaknesses, and adverse past performance information to which the offeror has not yet had an opportunity to respond. The contracting officer also is encouraged to discuss other aspects of the offeror's proposal that could, in the opinion of the contracting officer, be altered or explained to enhance materially the proposal's potential for award. However, the contracting officer is not required to discuss every area where the proposal could be improved. The scope and extent of discussions are a matter of contracting office judgment.

The federal government approach is a good one since it affords flexibility in the evaluation process.

It is critical that any meetings with offerors during the evaluation process not reveal information about the proposals of competing offerors. This is essential to ensuring that the process remains fair.

THE NEGOTIATION PROCESS

The need for negotiations will often begin to take shape during bid and proposal evaluations. For most states and government entities, the ability to negotiate and at what time that entity is allowed to negotiate will vary, and is almost always explicitly authorized in statute. The following paragraphs describe the seven major steps in the basic negotiation process.

Step 1—Receive and Evaluate Offers

The negotiation process begins with receipt and evaluation of bids and proposals. During evaluation, entities may need to confirm responsive and responsible proposals by verifying financial statements, contacting references, or conducting site visits. With offers that are evaluated and determined to be equal or almost equal, negotiation can help reduce the price or get additional features the government entity values.

Step 2—Determine Need for Formal Negotiation

The purpose of this step is to determine if formal negotiations will be needed, and if so, what approach will be taken. Statutes and policies will almost certainly influence this decision, along with the amount of time negotiations might take, the impact to resources, the amount of benefit expected from negotiating, and other factors that may be unique to the solicitation can all influence the decision to negotiate.

Step 3—Select Negotiation Team

The negotiation team will prepare for and execute the negotiations. It is therefore critical to select the right individuals to be on this team. Team members should be chosen and assigned roles based on their skill sets and personalities in relation to the specific needs of the negotiation. Especially for large contracts, it is important to have a cross-functional team representing all key stakeholders. Individuals representing central procurement, finance, using agency, legal, subject matter experts, management, and others should all be considered for the team where needed.

In the State of Wisconsin's *IT Procurement Best Practices Playbook*, Play #4 provides an acronym for those who should be involved—TEAM: T for technical staff; E for an expert in procurement or purchasing; A for attorney; M for management of the program.

Step 4—Research and Plan a Negotiation Strategy

Planning is the most important step in the negotiation process. This step involves gathering information and developing a plan to be followed during the actual negotiations. It begins by identifying the overall objectives of the negotiation and allowing those objectives to drive the resulting plan. Research and preparation should include market research and performing cost/price analysis, analyzing the negotiation positions of each party, identifying potential areas of compromise, and understanding the vendor's potential negotiating strategy, among many other things. Each negotiation is unique, therefore it is important to plan for the unexpected and remain flexible throughout the negotiation process to increase the likelihood of success.

Step 5—Strategy Meeting and Finalization of Negotiation Plan

A strategy meeting allows the team one final opportunity to prepare for the negotiations. While finalizing the negotiation plan, the team should look to review how the negotiation will be conducted, the roles of each member, and any guidelines, protocols, or policies everyone should be aware of. Team members may also engage in role playing and scenarios to further prepare for the negotiation.

Step 6—Negotiate

During the actual negotiation meeting, it is important that both sides work to identify areas of agreement, focus on interests of both parties, and identify alternatives to areas of disagreement. An agreement should be reached on all contract terms. Depending on the complexity of the project, negotiations may take additional meetings to come to a full agreement. Keep in mind that each negotiation meeting will be different.

Step 7—Document the Negotiation Process and Outcomes

Documentation of negotiations should be made and retained in accordance with laws and statutes. All required documentation should be included in the contract file, which will be a part of the official record. This step ensures transparency of the entire process.

Best and Final Offers

After discussions/negotiations, a best practice is for the public procurement officer to request that those offerors who engaged in discussions/negotiations submit revisions to their proposals—often called best and final offers. The submission of revised offers after discussions/negotiations is required under federal procurement law[14] and under the Model Procurement Code.[15]

This gives the offerors the chance to modify their proposals to reflect the issues discussed in negotiations, including price. The request should be in writing and should instruct offerors that, in the event that they choose not to submit a revised offer, the public procurement officer and the evaluation committee will consider their initial proposal as their complete submission.

The principles that apply to the evaluation of initial proposals also apply to the revisions that offerors submit in their best and final offers. The evaluation must stay within the criteria outlined in the solicitation and the plan that the public procurement officer and the evaluators put into place at the outset of the evaluation process.

Determining Responsibility

The responsibility determination process is the same for any supplier or suppliers in line for contract award, whether the procurement was conducted through competitive sealed bidding, or competitive sealed proposals, or for that matter, any other selection process. The section of this chapter entitled *Evaluation of Bids* discusses responsibility determinations in more detail.

Contract Award

As noted earlier, the contract must be awarded to the responsible offeror whose proposal is judged to best meet the requirements that the law dictates.[16]

CHAPTER 9: BID AND PROPOSAL EVALUATION AND AWARD

PRICE AND COST ANALYSIS

The award of certain kinds of contracts requires scrutiny of a supplier's prices or costs. Those contracts include sole source contracts and contracts in which the public entity will reimburse any of the contractor's costs, such as contracts in which pricing is based on the contractor's costs plus a fixed fee. What is sometimes absent in the situations where a price or cost analysis is appropriate is head-to-head competition with other suppliers on what the public entity will be required to pay the contractor. The NIGP Dictionary defines the key terms as follows:

> **Price analysis**—*Evaluation of readily available information in the marketplace. The process of examining and evaluating a prospective price without performing a cost analysis; that is, without evaluating the separate cost elements and profit of the offeror included in that price. The end result of price analysis is to ensure fair and reasonable pricing of a product or service. Price analysis may include a variety of techniques such as comparing proposed prices with prices of same or similar commodity or services obtained through market research. (Nash, Schooner, and O'Brien, 1998)*
> **Cost analysis**—*The review and evaluation of cost data for the purpose of arriving at costs actually incurred or estimates of costs to be incurred. A cost analysis should be employed when price analysis is impractical or does not allow a purchaser to reach the conclusion that a price is fair and reasonable. Cost analysis is most useful when purchasing nonstandard items or services. (Burt, Dobler, and Starling, 2003)*

Conducting a price analysis is less complicated than conducting a cost analysis. Price analysis may be based on market research focused on pricing. Cost analysis, on the other hand, involves applying government accounting standards. The regulations that implement federal procurement law are quite detailed regarding this subject.[17] It is beyond the scope of this 3rd Edition of *State & Local Government: A Practical Guide* to provide an in-depth discussion of this topic, but here are some good practices relating to these types of analyses:

- The solicitation must reserve the right of the public procurement officer to conduct a price or cost analysis.
- The public procurement officer, in evaluating prices or costs, must go beyond the simple numbers that suppliers offer and, in appropriate circumstances, must scrutinize them to ensure that they are reasonable.

MULTIPLE SOURCE AWARDS

There are times when it is beneficial for a public procurement officer to award a contract to more than one supplier. In the case of definite quantity contracts, this is called a progressive or incremental award. For indefinite quantity contracts, it is called a multiple award.

Conditions are right for a progressive award when two or more suppliers are needed to supply the required definite quantity specified in the solicitation or to meet the delivery requirements. A multiple award is the award of a contract to two or more suppliers to furnish an indefinite quantity of a commodity or service.

To guard against carelessness and abuses in using multiple source awards, a public entity's law or rules/regulations should specify that: they must not be made when a single award can meet the contract requirements; the number of suppliers awarded a contract is limited to the minimum number necessary to reasonably satisfy the needs of the user agencies; and awards shall not be made for the purpose of dividing the business or providing a selection of commodities, services, or suppliers to satisfy user agency preferences instead of actual needs.

EVALUATIONS USING ePROCUREMENT SYSTEMS

As eProcurement systems become more common among state and local governments, many are able to conduct a good portion of their procurement processes online, including the evaluation and award processes. Chapter 19 (*eProcurement*) discusses the state of these systems in more detail.

CONCLUSION

The bid and proposal evaluation process must be flexible, but must also stay within the boundaries of principles that ensure equitable treatment of all bidders and offerors. The public procurement officer and any evaluators who are assisting must ensure that the evaluation criteria are broad enough to permit a range of responses from competitors, but are also precise enough for those suppliers to submit their best ideas and products in response. Additionally, they must leave a clear and easy-to-follow written trail of how decisions have been made. Good management of this process should assure public confidence in the fairness of the procurement function.

ENDNOTES

1. See Utah Code 63G-6a-707-(6)(b) at: https://codes.findlaw.com/ut/title-63g-general-government/#!tid=NFD2F9190A04B11E1A5BEF191D2B004BD
2. R33-1-1. Definitions at: https://rules.utah.gov/publicat/code/r033/r033-001.htm#T1
3. https://www.osc.state.ny.us/vendrep/info_vresp_agency.htm
4. R33-1-1. Definitions at: https://rules.utah.gov/publicat/code/r033/r033-001.htm#T1
5. R33-7-703(2)(a). https://rules.utah.gov/publicat/code/r033/r033-001.htm#T1
6. R33-7-703(4)(b). https://rules.utah.gov/publicat/code/r033/r033-001.htm#T1
7. R33-7-703(5) and R33-7-704(1). https://rules.utah.gov/publicat/code/r033/r033-001.htm#T1
8. Part I Section 06-B-3-b. https://www.dgs.pa.gov/Documents/Procurement%20Forms/Handbook/Pt1/Pt%20I%20Ch%2006%20Methods%20of%20Awarding%20Contracts.pdf
9. R33-7-703(5)(d) https://rules.utah.gov/publicat/code/r033/r033-001.htm#T1
10. Section 3-203(6). A copy of the Model Procurement Code is available at: http://apps.americanbar.org/dch/committee.cfm?com=PC500500
11. http://www.nigp.org/home/find-procurement-resources/dictionary-of-terms
12. Federal Acquisition Regulation 15-306 at: http://farsite.hill.af.mil/reghtml/regs/far2afmcfars/fardfars/far/15.htm#P286_46346
13. See Endnote 14.
14. Federal Acquisition Regulation 15-307 at: http://farsite.hill.af.mil/reghtml/regs/far2afmcfars/fardfars/far/15.htm#P286_46346
15. Section 3-203(6). http://apps.americanbar.org/dch/committee.cfm?com=PC500500
16. Chapter 7, *Competition: Solicitations and Methods*, describes problems associated with evaluations for public entities whose laws require them to award a contract based on a *responsive* proposal.
17. FAR Subpart 15.4. https://www.acquisition.gov/far/html/Subpart%2015_4.html

CHAPTER 10: CONTRACTING FOR SERVICES

RECOMMENDED BEST PRACTICES

- A services contract creates a human-to-human relationship between government employees and the contractor, with the aim of achieving a specific end. The words used to describe the services sought must be precise, since features that are found in specifications for commodities, such as equipment output minimums or life cycle standards, are not applicable.
- A well-written solicitation for the procurement of services includes a profile of the user agency and the specific program to which the services are directed.
- The procurement of services that are considered *professional services* dictates that the service provider supply professional liability insurance instead of the standard commercial general liability insurance that contractors are generally required to have.
- A service provider who is going to have access to the public entity's network must be asked to provide network security and cyber security insurance.
- A contract for services should include some means of measuring contractor performance such as milestones, performance measures, deliverables, and service levels.
- Unless payment is going to be made to the contractor only at the end of the contract after the public entity has received the contract deliverables and accepted those deliverables, periodic payments to the contractor during the contract term must be tied to service levels, performance measures, milestones, or sub-deliverables that the contract specifies.
- There should be ramifications in the contract for the failure of the contractor to meet one or more service levels. A contractor's service fees should be docked based on a formula that the solicitation and the contract set out.
- Contracts may offer an incentive to a contractor where it consistently exceeds the established service levels.
- Even in contracts for routine services, there should be more than one activity within the total services provided that the public entity considers important. Thus, every service contract should contain more than one service level.
- Service levels must be based on a careful examination of service data detailing a solid service baseline as well as an understanding of what service suppliers can provide.
- If the service is a complicated one and the contractor's performance depends in part on the public entity's actions, there should be service levels in the contract for that public entity to meet as well.
- A contract for services must explicitly establish services warranties.
- Outsourcing, or privatizing government services to outside contractors, is complicated and should be subject to a precise and in-depth analysis of critical information, such as the cost of providing the services through government employees; a detailed and specific set of contract requirements; and a detailed plan for implementation, including the establishment of performance measures and continuous assessment of contractor performance.

CHAPTER 10: CONTRACTING FOR SERVICES

- The selection of a service contractor to provide a government service or manage a government facility is complicated. The best practice is for such procurements to be under the authority of the Chief Procurement Officer working closely with the user agency that will have oversight of the contractor.
- Contracting for human services providers is one example of the alternative delivery of government services. Funding for these services is different from most other state and local government procurements. It can consist of a complex mixture of federal and state government dollars along with, in some cases, charitable donor funds. The supplier community delivering these types of services is also atypical. A significant portion of them are nonprofit entities.
- The process for obtaining human services contractors must permit the user agency to maintain and grow a steady stream of good providers. In many cases, competing and awarding contracts every year or every five years does not work.

Contracting for services is often an exercise in subjectivity. Unlike buying tangible things with a defined outcome, such as office supplies or the construction of a new building, the procurement of services requires the public entity to think carefully about what it wants from the service provider and how best to describe it. It may sometimes seem easy, such as producing a description of courier services. In other cases, the service requested is more complicated, such as the delivery of services that public employees previously provided. Even in the case of simple services, there is no *brand name* or *brand-name-or-equal* specification or architect's design to use as a starting point. The words used in the solicitation's scope of work need to be precise, clear, and well written.

This chapter focuses on issues relating to contracting for services and the use of those contracts as alternative methods for delivering government services. It also focuses on the procurement of one unique type of service—delivery of human services. It does not address services related to construction. That topic is covered in Chapter 11 (*Procurement of Construction and Related Services*). This chapter also does not discuss the purchase of services that are closely linked with information technology (IT), such as software as a service or hosting services. Those are covered in Chapter 20 (*Procurement of Information Technology*).

A well-written solicitation for the procurement of services includes a profile of the user agency and the specific program to which the services are directed. It is also useful for the solicitation to feature a narrative answering the questions, "What is the user agency seeking to procure?" and "What problem is the user agency seeking to solve?" Other components of a well-thought-out solicitation for services are:

- The user agency's program philosophy and/or mission statement
- Major components of service sought and the desired outcome
- Service elements and service delivery, setting forth specific aspects of the services requested and those items that the agency wants the supplier to address
- Desired contract outcomes, including quantifiable objectives, which may be performance based
- Technology standards that identify the entity's data security, handling, and ownership guidelines
- A statement that payment will be tied to performance and deliverables, and based on documentation that the contract requirements have been met

DEFINITION OF TERMS

The American Bar Association Model Procurement Code for State and Local Governments[1] (Model Procurement Code) provides a definition of the term *services*, and distinguishes those from two other general types of items that a procurement officer purchases under the Code—supplies and construction. Section 1-301(21) of the Model Procurement Code states that *services* means:

> . . . The furnishing of labor, time, or effort by a contractor, not involving the delivery of a specific end product other than reports which are merely incidental to the required performance. This term shall not include employment agreements or collective bargaining agreements.

At times, there is confusion between a contract for services and a grant of public funds. A grant, as defined in Section 1-301(12) of the Model Procurement Code is:

> . . . The furnishing by the [State] of assistance, whether financial or otherwise, to any person to support a program authorized by law. It does not include an award whose primary purpose is to procure an end product, whether in the form of sup-

plies, services, or construction; a contract resulting from such an award is not a grant but a procurement contract.

The Model Procurement Code is written in language appropriate for a statute or ordinance. A practical working definition of *services* in plainer language is found in the NIGP Dictionary:[2]

> **Service/Services contract**—*1. An agreement calling for a contractor's time and effort. 2. The furnishing of labor, time, or effort by a contractor or supplier, which may involve to a lesser degree the delivery or supply of products. The Uniform Commercial Code (UCC)/state commercial codes only apply to a procurement of a product, while state common law would apply if it is considered a procurement of a service.*

The key concept to draw from both the aforementioned definitions is that while a services procurement may require the delivery of something tangible like a report, the procurement is still one for services.

There is another observation about services procurements that is important. The procurement of services that are considered *professional services* demands that the service provider supply professional liability insurance instead of the standard commercial general liability insurance that contractors are generally required to have. The NIGP Dictionary defines "professional services" as:[3]

> **Professional services**—*Services rendered by members of a recognized profession or possessing a special skill. Such services are generally acquired to obtain information, advice, training, or direct assistance.*

The two categories of services for which professional liability insurance is necessary are: services to be performed by a licensed professional such as an engineer, lawyer, or doctor; or services where the contractor will provide a recommendation on which the public entity will rely in order to make a decision.

Finally, a service provider who will have access to the public entity's network must be asked to provide network security and cyber security insurance. There are other insurance products that a contractor should be required to provide if it will have routine access to offices where sensitive documents may reside. The services where that type of insurance may be appropriate can be as innocuous as heating/ventilation/air conditioning/electronic controls maintenance, temporary employment services, janitorial services, and document storage/shredding services. Contracts under which a contractor supplies temporary employees must ensure that the contractor not only has the appropriate data security insurance but is also responsible for the employees' acts that are not specifically directed by the public entity.

PREPARATION OF SERVICE DESCRIPTIONS AND STATEMENTS OF WORK

Both Chapter 5 (*Non-Construction Specifications and Scopes of Work*) and Chapter 7 (*Competition: Solicitations and Methods*) address in a general manner the preparation of specifications and statements of work. This portion of the chapter focuses on three areas relating to the preparation of services descriptions for a solicitation or for a statement of work issued under a contract:

- The appropriate level of specificity in the description of the service sought
- Measurement of performance
- Establishment of a general legal standard with which the contractor must comply

Preparing the Service Description

Drafting a description—a specification or scope of work—for a solicitation seeking a services contractor requires a close collaboration between the user agency and the public procurement officer, particularly if the services are complex. Technical experts and lawyers may need to be part of the team.

While it may seem to be stating the obvious to point out the necessity for a close working relationship, it is important to keep in mind that a services contract creates a human-to-human relationship between government employees and the contractor, aimed at achieving a specific end. The words used to describe the services sought must be precise, since features that are found in specifications for commodities, such as equipment output minimums or life cycle standards, are not applicable.

The precision of the services description relies heavily on an understanding of the user agency's needs and wants, even if the services sought are seemingly simple. For instance, in a description for janitorial services, does the user wish to require that the contractor use eco-friendly products?

The service description will depend in part on whether:

- The service sought is complicated or routine
- There are a specific and limited number of deliverables (such as a report) that the contractor must provide during or at the end of the contract, or the contract calls instead for the contractor to provide the same services regularly during the term of the contract (such as landscaping services)
- The solicitation seeks a contractor or contractors to provide multiple types of related services from which a user agency may choose during the contract as the user's need arises

There is no magic set of principles that will ensure that a service description is a good one. Here are some basic tips:

- Make sure that the description is broad enough to cover all of the services sought. Use examples of types of services desired under the general service description to illustrate what is intended, making sure to state that the examples are not all-inclusive of the desired services.
- Concentrate in the description on the service output rather than itemizing individual tasks. Detailed itemizing of individual tasks may restrict the effectiveness of the contract.
- If the service description is for a consulting report, particularly where a recommendation is being requested that will be the basis of a public policy decision, include as an *output* requirement that the contractor must provide all of the underlying data or other information that served as the basis for the report or recommendation.
- Tie the service description to the measurements in the solicitation by which the contractor's performance will be evaluated. If the service description and the measurements do not fit well, something is awry and needs to be fixed. Measuring performance is discussed in the next part of this chapter.
- Read the service description as someone who knows nothing about the user agency's needs would read it. Ask whether the service description is clear and precise, allows flexibility, and paints a vivid picture of what the solicitation seeks.

Where state and local government procurements utilize federal funds, the Uniform Administrative Requirements, Cost Principles, and Audit Requirements for Federal Awards, 2 Code of Federal Regulations Part 200, known as the Common Rule, provide that solicitations:[4]

- Must incorporate a clear and accurate description of the technical requirement for the service to be procured;
- Must not unduly restrict competition;
- May include a statement of the qualitative nature of the service to be procured; and

- Where necessary, must set forth those minimum essential characteristics and standards to which it must conform if it is to satisfy its intended use.

In complex procurements for services, a procurement office may contract with an outside party to assist in the development of the service description and other parts of the solicitation. The Common Rule states that those outside parties "must be excluded from competing for such procurements."[5] That reflects the best practices for all procurements on which outside assistance is used, whether or not federal funds are paying for the purchase.

Best Value Procurements

There is a source selection approach that generally is conducted as a type of competitive sealed proposals called best value procurement or performance information procurement system. Chapter 7 (*Competition: Solicitations and Methods*) and Chapter 20 (*Procurement of Information Technology*) provide descriptions of this approach. Under this approach, the specifications are very minimal. The offerors are expected to provide proposals that the solicitation often limits to fewer than ten pages.

MEASURING AND PAYING FOR PERFORMANCE

Overview

There is a variety of terms that are used to describe the ways in which a contractor's performance may be measured.[6] As defined by the NIGP Dictionary, four common terms are discussed in the ensuing paragraphs.

Deliverable

The NIGP Dictionary defines this term as follows:

1. Expected work product as defined in a contract . . . 3. The completion of a milestone or the accomplishment of a task that can be measured and verified, and may be a unit by which a contractor or consultant may be paid.

Deliverables under a services contract are something that the contractor provides. For a services contract, a *deliverable* may be a desired report or recommendation, which may include *sub-deliverables* such as progress reports at specified intervals of the contract term. In other types of services contracts, for instance a contract for a call center, the deliverable may be the actual ongoing services themselves, with additional performance measures tied to that deliverable, such as maintaining the ability to handle a certain number of phone calls per day.

Milestones

The NIGP Dictionary defines this term as follows:

Designated steps of the planned acquisition that usually signify a completion of a requirement or delivery of materials. Payments may be targeted to the completion of milestones. (Harney, 1992)

Milestones are the points in time when the contractor needs to complete a portion of its contract work in order to be on schedule so that it can finish the contract's tasks on time. A milestone is important and more likely to be used in a services contract where there is a specific deliverable such as a report to be provided.

Performance Measures

The NIGP Dictionary defines this term as follows:

Tools used to measure performance and quantitatively evaluate progress toward planned targets

Although this definition may suggest that a performance measure is strictly a quantitative one—that is, how much of the work was accomplished, it may also be a qualitative measure—that is, how well the work was performed.

Service Level Agreement (SLA)

The NIGP Dictionary defines this term as follows:

1. An agreement between the Application Service Provider (ASP) and the end user to determine the scope of work to be provided by the ASP. 2. An agreement between a customer and a service provider that details the level of service and the quality of the service to be provided. May be a legally binding agreement. (Business, 2002)

Service levels are a type of performance measure that developed originally as a means of measuring services—and assuring a certain level and quality of them—in the IT sector. Today, service levels are an essential part of services contracting, particularly where the contractor is providing services on an ongoing basis. Service level measurements are critically important in instances where the contractor is performing services that public employees used to perform.

Some benefits in using service levels in contracts are:

- They provide the contractor with a clear picture of what is considered good performance
- Problems with performance may be identified early and amicably and be solved before the contractor is considered to have breached the contract
- Agreed-upon penalties for failure to meet a service level eliminate the possibility of a contentious situation in which a contractor seeks damages
- Service levels avoid the need to quantify loss, which can often be difficult
- They assist in aligning requested services with their delivery
- They improve an understanding of the services requested and the interdependent relationships involved in their delivery
- They provide a framework for effective communication between parties

Service levels should be set forth as part of any solicitation for services. The public entity may need to change them as a result of additional information gathered from prospective bidders or offerors who wish to respond to the solicitation. However, defining service levels at the point of negotiating with a selected contractor leaves the public entity with less bargaining power.

Measurements Tied to Payments

Unless payment is going to be made to the contractor only at the end of the contract after the public entity has received the contract deliverables and accepted those deliverables, periodic payments to the contractor during the contract term must be tied to service levels, performance measures, milestones, or sub-deliverables that the contract specifies. For instance, payment under services contracts where there is a major deliverable to be presented at the end of the contract should always be tied to milestones that are established at the start of the services contract. If the contractor does not meet a milestone, the services contract should, at a minimum, authorize the public entity to withhold some or all of the payment due on that milestone date. Tying payment to performance is discussed further in the next section of this chapter.

The importance of tying payment to performance is reflected in part in the Common Rule. Those requirements define an *improper payment*, among other things, to include incorrect payments (including overpayments and underpayments), and any payment where insufficient or lack of documentation prevents a reviewer from discerning whether a payment was proper.[7] The requirements also mandate that recipients of federal awards relate financial data to performance accomplishments, and that federal agencies awarding federal funds provide recipients with *clear performance goals, indicators, and milestones*.[8]

As noted earlier, these federal requirements reflect good practice. A public procurement officer, as well as the user agencies assisting that officer, should keep them in mind as they work together to develop a solicitation for a services procurement.

Developing Service Levels

Service levels require the services contractor to perform specified outputs to a particular, measurable level to bring certainty to what it delivers. Examples are:

- The percentage of the time that the service is available
- How long it takes to contact someone on the phone
- The total number of complaints about a service for a period of time, often categorized by ranking or severity
- The average or total time to complete a particular activity related to the service, such as maintenance
- The reasonably determined, hoped-for increase in the use of the service over the period of the contract, particularly where the contractor is providing services to the public on the public entity's behalf

If the service is a complicated one and if the contractor's performance depends in part on the public entity's actions, there should be service levels in the contract for that public entity to meet as well.

As noted earlier, the service levels established for the contractor to meet must relate directly to the services description in the solicitation. Service levels may not be pulled out of the air. They must be based on a careful examination of service data detailing a solid service baseline as well as an understanding of what the service contractor can provide. Here are some basic rules for writing service levels:

- Focus on specific outputs rather than tasks.
- Make the outputs measurable. If the public entity will not have access during the contract to all of the data needed to determine whether levels have been achieved, the contract must require the contractor to report its service level performance on a regular basis, reserving the right of the public entity to audit the contractor's records.
- Avoid making service levels complex, as those are more difficult to monitor.
- Allow for improvements in the service and provide a mechanism in the contract for revising the service levels to fit those improvements in the service.
- Review any historical data and entity-specific examples as well as current industry trends.

Even in contracts for routine services, there should be more than one activity within the service to be delivered that the public entity considers important. Thus, every service contract should contain more than one service level.

Finally, there should be ramifications in the contract for the failure of the contractor to meet one or more service levels. In this case, contractor's service fees should be docked based on a formula that the contract sets out. For instance, the formula might provide that a failure to comply with two of four service levels in one month results in a reduction in the fee for that month of $XX. A specified number of months of failures to meet a set number of service levels might result in a greater reduction of fees, again by a dollar number detailed in the contract. The contract should further define that the failure to meet set numbers of service levels over a period of time results in the contractor defaulting on its contractual obligations. Keep in mind that there is a point at which contractor failures result in such degraded service that the contract may no longer meet the public entity's needs.

Contracts may also offer an incentive to a contractor that consistently exceeds the established service levels. The formula for both incentive and *disciplinary* measures related to service level achievement or failure must be part of the solicitation that the entity publicly distributes seeking a services contract.

A Word About Service Warranties

As a general rule, warranties are most often associated with the sale of goods. The Uniform Commercial Code (UCC), which is discussed in more detail in Chapter 13 (*Quality Assurance*), codifies the standard implied warranties—that is, warranties that are not expressly in a contract's language—that arise under the law in the sale of goods. But the UCC does not apply to the sale of services.

Warranties for services contracts arise from the language of the contract itself. The contract must explicitly establish them, which is a key factor in drafting a professional solicitation or contract for services. Performance measures, milestones, deliverables, and service levels assist with contract performance by providing both the public entity and the contractor with a means of measuring, evaluating, and demanding the improvement of performance. Explicit services warranties, that is, those set forth in writing in the solicitation or contract, provide the public entity with another set of overarching standards with which the contractor must comply. They can be the critical validation for a public entity's decision to terminate the contract for default if the contractor continuously fails to meet performance measures, milestones, deliverables, or service levels. The following are some examples of explicit service contract warranties:

- The contractor will provide the services within the highest standards of its profession
- The contractor will provide the services with reasonable skill and care according to best industry practices
- The contractor will provide the services in compliance with all applicable laws, rules, and regulations
- The contractor will provide the services in compliance with the code of conduct of (for instance, some industry, national, or international standard-setting organization)

ALTERNATIVE DELIVERY OF GOVERNMENTAL SERVICES

When the government finds an alternative means of delivering its services, some terms used for those alternative methods include contracting out, outsourcing, and privatization.

Privatization is different from the other two, which are basically synonymous. *Privatization*, as the NIGP Dictionary defines it, means:

> *The divestiture of both management and assets of a public function to the private sector in order to change the status of a function formerly performed by the public entity to one that is privately controlled and owned including the transfer of real and personal property.*

The critical factor in privatization—the divestiture of both government assets and services—is not present in outsourcing or contracting out. The NIGP Dictionary defines *outsourcing* as occurring "when an organization makes an informed decision to contract out a product, service, or business process that was previously provided by internal (in-house) resources."

An Overview of the Outsourcing Process

The process of either privatizing or outsourcing government services is complicated. In fact, there are a host of nonprofit organizations devoted to reducing the size of government that advocate for and track instances of government privatization and outsourcing.

It is beyond the scope of this book and chapter to describe in detail the precise reasons for a government to consider allowing the private sector to offer the public services that the government used to provide. Those reasons may vary greatly. Some can be purely political and others may be based on data suggesting that the private sector is able to provide the service at a lower cost. As a matter of practice, a well-conducted procurement for privatizing or outsourcing a government service should be determinative. That is, it should be the point at which the public entity decides—based on the information in proposals received under the solicitation—that private industry can or cannot provide the services in a manner that fulfills the original objective for considering privatizing or outsourcing.

There is a good short set of recommendations by experts outlining the key steps in the outsourcing/privatization of state and local government services. They are contained in a report called *Government Outsourcing: A Practical Guide for State and Local Governments, The Report of an Expert Panel*, School of Public and Environmental Affairs, Indiana University, January 2014.[9]

Recommendations from the report are enumerated below. Where the recommendation provides guidance related to the procurement process, the text from the report is provided in full.

Recommendation #1. Determine initial motivations for outsourcing.

Recommendation #2. Thoroughly assess the feasibility, potential costs, and potential benefits of the outsourcing initiative.

Recommendation #3. Scope and plan the outsourcing project early on in the process.
The second and third recommendations are closely related, since an adequate assessment of costs requires full understanding of the scope of the project. The more decision makers are clear about the goals and expected outcomes, the better they can plan major processes, tasks, and milestones, as well as identify associated costs. Proper scoping and planning is also important to attracting the right suppliers and setting reasonable expectations. Importantly, ample time must be allowed to accurately describe the service or function, especially when no precedent exists. The timing for scoping and planning is important. Planners should try to seek advice from potential providers (e.g., at a pre-solicitation public meeting where all interested vendors are welcome) and other technical experts before drafting the solicitation document. The earlier this occurs in the process, the better. Officials are encouraged to develop Most Important Requirements (MIRs), which reinforce the goal of maintaining competition and serve as guiding principles for the entire source selection process. A useful practice is to publish requests for information (RFIs), which can provide the government with good understanding of the capabilities of the supplier community. When adequate planning and scoping occurs before the solicitation, a more diverse group of stakeholders is likely to weigh in, including possible vendors, public employees, elected officials, citizens, and consultants. The wider the range of input, the greater the likelihood that any potential issues and problems will surface early and can be dealt with before the solicitation document is issued. Planners should also set up information systems to facilitate frequent and systematic feedback, for example, by scheduling public forums and designing websites to send comments and responses.

Recommendation #4. Develop clear, specific, and effective contract requirements.
Contract requirements should reflect organizational goals and mission. To the extent possible, clearly and precisely describe key aspects of a project (inputs, processes, technologies, outputs, and/or outcomes) that are essential to its success. Consider developing a summary contract term sheet with key contract principles and requirements to include in the solicitation documentation. Contract

requirements should balance the needs for specificity and flexibility, and opportunities for mutual adjustment. When drafting contracting specifications, look for opportunities for operational efficiencies from the existing method of delivery. In addition, be sensitive to contract requirements that inadvertently encourage delays or indirectly transfer unnecessary costs to the government by shifting risks and uncertainties to the vendors that get priced back to taxpayers. Finally, the contract type (e.g., fixed-price, cost plus, and time and materials) should be determined with due consideration for such factors as service type, price, labor certainty, available suppliers, acceptable levels of risk, and the adequacy of structures in place for monitoring and accounting.

Recommendation #5. Encourage competition at different stages of the project.
Gains in efficiency are premised upon attracting competition and optimizing the supplier base. There are many ways that competition can be encouraged at the early stages of project planning as well as in the contract negotiation, specification, and implementation phases. Match the scope of the contract to the market and to supplier availability to attract the highest number of quality bidders. Avoid developing contract specifications that are too narrow and unnecessarily exclude potential providers from bidding. Consider using a mix of public, private, and nonprofit providers to avoid "thinning the market" during the contract term. Limit the use of excessively long contract terms while providing opportunities for contract renewal based on performance. Release a draft solicitation document and request feedback from vendors during a reasonable period of time, revise the solicitation document using that feedback, and issue a final document. Finally, consider using indefinite delivery/indefinite quantity (IDIQ) contracts that foster an ongoing competitive environment by promoting competition for task orders that are part of a larger contract, motivating contractors to be innovative and deliver superior performance, and providing the government entity the leverage needed for changing requirements and workload. Policymakers should be engaged on an ongoing basis to reduce regulatory barriers associated with sustaining markets. They must also ensure that sufficient rules are in place to reduce the likelihood of collusion among suppliers and/or improprieties between procurement staff and bidders.

Recommendation #6. Select the "best" suppliers and partners.
There are several steps to selecting the "best" suppliers and partners. After optimizing the supplier base and prior to awarding the contract, there should be a rigorous and objective evaluation of potential suppliers and partners. Seek all relevant information about the reputation, capabilities, and past performance of potential suppliers. A method for evaluating responses and selecting the winner should be in place, including clearly identified and ranked or weighted evaluation criteria. Evaluation criteria should reflect such considerations as capability and approach, proposed service levels, price, the adequacy of the contractors' management team, and the contractors' past performance.

Recommendation #7. Spend adequate time negotiating and crafting the contract document.
Once partners and suppliers are selected, the final terms of the contract must be negotiated and specified. Policies should be in place to ensure probity of negotiations. Assess the government's capacity to gather relevant information, negotiate the contract terms, and adequately specify the contract. If government does not have the right skill sets on hand, con-

sider bringing in outside consultants to augment the expertise of procurement staff. Identifying and complying with all the relevant procurement requirements takes time. Contracts should establish clear expectations, roles, and responsibilities. Review the appropriate contract term with due consideration for the level of partners' investments, performance expectations, risk tolerance, prior performance, and cost associated with timing of renegotiation. Plan for an assessment of performance at the end of a contract term and make contract renewals contingent upon satisfactory performance. Finally, identify and plan for challenges during transition between providers when designing contract terms.

Recommendation #8. Assess contract performance both during and at the end of the contract.

The prior recommendations provided some prerequisites for performance monitoring and assessment. Policies should be in place up front to insulate performance evaluations and contract disagreements from undue political influence. The contract should clearly identify milestones, expectations for service levels, output measures, and standards. Monitoring performance should be considered an iterative and dynamic process, where learning, change, and innovation can occur. Especially with high-value procurements, a periodic project review should be implemented where both parties can discuss challenges with execution as well as identify additional cost savings that could be achieved through a collaborative approach. Optimize monitoring with technology by making it frequent and by relying on multiple sources of feedback. Leverage information technology to facilitate data collection and evaluation. Obtain feedback from contractors' managers and employees, as well as from citizens, consultants, and community groups. Collect performance data that is meaningful to decision makers and can be acted upon to improve performance. Share performance information with internal managers, external stakeholders, and contractor staff and their principals. Finally, take advantage of less adversarial approaches to resolving disputes and handling performance issues, like mediation or arbitration.

Recommendation #9. Minimize service disruptions and other difficulties associated with transitioning at the end of the contract.

In addition to designing the contract with end-of-contract challenges in mind, other planning can facilitate smooth transitions. Planning for contract transition cannot wait until 12 months before the end of the performance period. Successful transitions are addressed in the original proposal submission and updated throughout the contract period. Governments must anticipate capacity issues and costs if they must resume activity, for example, by ensuring access to and transfer of all relevant information, materials, and technologies. The contracting entity is cautioned to carefully craft and review contract clauses that may affect transition, including rights to documents, successors in interest, and any proprietary rights to knowledge and equipment. Government officials should ensure that the initial contract includes provisions regarding government ownership of all data and intellectual property related to the project. Particular attention must be given to penalty, early termination, and buy-back clauses that commit the government to a long-term relationship. If the government decides at some point that a better approach makes sense (e.g., switching suppliers or insourcing), it needs to have an unfettered hand to undertake such a change. It is also important that contracting officers maintain contact information for alternative suppliers and key employ-

ees should the need arise to prematurely terminate a contract.

Chief Procurement Officer Authority

As previously illustrated, the process of the selection of a service contractor to provide a government service or manage a government facility is complicated. The best practice is for such procurements to be under the authority of the Chief Procurement Officer working closely with the user agency that will have oversight of the contractor. That team approach ensures that the handing over of a government service is conducted with the expertise needed for success—procurement professionalism and the experience and knowledge of the subject matter that the user agency offers.

A LOOK AT HUMAN SERVICES CONTRACTING

Contracting for human services providers is one example of alternative delivery of government services. There are many unique aspects to this kind of contracting. One of them is that they involve human subjects with the objective of making life better for the individuals receiving the services.

Another unique feature is that there are, in most cases, a significant number of federal laws that apply to the delivery of these types of services. In fact, the requirement of state and local governments to provide these services generally started with the United States Congress's passage of the Social Security Act in 1935. One of the subsequent drivers toward contracting out to provide these services was the increased unionization within the public sector that made contracting out more cost effective.

Funding for these services is also different from most other state and local government procurements. It can consist of a complex mixture of federal and state government dollars along with, in some cases, charitable donor funds. Examples of services that the federal government funds through state and local governments are: child welfare; health services to the aged, the disabled, and individuals and families with low incomes; and a variety of services to individuals and families with special needs relating to conditions such as mental illness, addiction, and developmental disabilities.

The supplier community delivering these types of services is also atypical. A significant portion of them are nonprofit entities.

The methods through which state and local governments determine payments to providers also vary from the manner that payments are determined for other types of services. Some of the standard payment methods are: cost reimbursement based on government accounting standards; unit cost based on a fixed cost that the government establishes for a particular service; and payment for performance or outcomes.

In many cases, competing and awarding contracts every five years does not work. The state or local government needs some flexibility to add providers and modify levels of service after contracts are awarded because the services are based, in part, on a fluctuating population. Another unique characteristic of the procurement of human services is the need for the state or local government entity to ensure the maintenance and growth of a steady stream of good providers. Maintaining a robust set of potential providers is essential because the demand is so high. Good human services procurement is creative enough to permit a continuous competition for and addition of new contractors on a regular basis.

Thus, the competitive process that state and local governments use to select providers must involve a careful balance. The process must set high standards for a provider to qualify, including financial soundness; but must avoid being so complex that it bears heavily on the supplier community, particularly the small nonprofit providers who do not have the same monetary resources that the for-profit providers have. Ultimately, a well-functioning procurement/contracting process for human services should be characterized by:

- The ability to create and manage a competitive process among providers in a manner that results in competitive prices with high-quality privatized or outsourced services
- The creation and successful negotiation of a legally binding contractual agreement that requires the provider to deliver the service at the levels of quality and comprehensiveness specified
- The capacity to effectively monitor performance of the provider, ensure accountability, and require corrective action when necessary and appropriate
- The ability to critically analyze contract outcomes and incorporate what is learned into successive contracts with providers to improve future services and results

CONCLUSION

Contracting for services can present a challenge to procurement officers. Human talent is never generic, often elusive to define, and can be difficult to evaluate objectively. The procurement officer can employ procurement strategies to make the process successful, but should do so in close partnership with the using agencies.

ENDNOTES

1. A copy of the Model Procurement Code is available at: http://apps.americanbar.org/dch/committee.cfm?com=PC500500
2. Access to the NIGP Dictionary is available at: http://www.nigp.org/home/find-procurement-resources/dictionary-of-terms
3. See Endnote 2.
4. 2 CFR §200.319(c). The regulation may be found at: https://www.gpo.gov/fdsys/pkg/CFR-2017-title2-vol1/pdf/CFR-2017-title2-vol1-part200.pdf
5. 2 CFR §200.319(a). The regulation may be found at: https://www.gpo.gov/fdsys/pkg/CFR-2017-title2-vol1/pdf/CFR-2017-title2-vol1-part200.pdf
6. See also the importance of the concept of *accepting* the services delivered, which is discussed in Chapter 13, *Quality Assurance*.
7. 2 CFR 200.53. The regulation may be found at: https://www.gpo.gov/fdsys/pkg/CFR-2017-title2-vol1/pdf/CFR-2017-title2-vol1-part200.pdf
8. 2 CFR 200.301. The federal requirements define a *performance goal* as "a target level of performance expressed as a tangible, measurable objective, against which actual achievement can be compared, including a goal expressed as a quantitative standard, value or rate." 2 CFR §200.76.
9. https://datasmart.ash.harvard.edu/sites/default/files/2018-02/IU_SPEA_Government_Outsourcing_Report.pdf

CHAPTER 11: PROCUREMENT OF CONSTRUCTION AND RELATED SERVICES

RECOMMENDED BEST PRACTICES

- The responsibility for procurement of all construction should be separate and independent from the user agency and under the authority of the Chief Procurement Officer.
- Public procurement officers, under the leadership of the Chief Procurement Officer, must be trained and be prepared professionally to conduct procurements using a wide range of project delivery methods and contract types for the construction or renovation of public infrastructure.
- While there are helpful starting points for contract language in contract forms prepared by the construction industry, the public entity should prepare its own contract forms to ensure that the terms of the contract are fair and balanced, and contain the key terms that are important to that public entity.
- Public entities with a strong commitment to sustainable procurement may wish to establish a framework that meets the requirements for the U.S. Green Building Council's program entitled *Leadership in Energy and Environmental Design* (LEED).

CHAPTER 11: PROCUREMENT OF CONSTRUCTION AND RELATED SERVICES

This chapter provides an overview of state and local government procurement for construction. It includes a description of: project delivery methods, the kinds of solicitations used to purchase construction and related services, the types of contracts used, and the range of collaborations possible with the construction contractor.

In 2017, the American Society of Civil Engineers projected that it would cost $4.6 trillion over a five-year period to repair the country's aging infrastructure. That figure represents a funding gap of more than $2 trillion.[1] Even without addressing all of those needed repairs, public construction spending is a significant expenditure in state and local government budgets. For the year ending in October 2017, those expenditures amounted to approximately $267 billion.[2] These figures suggest that the procurement of public construction (and how to pay for it) will continue to be a critical area of focus for state and local government procurement offices across the country.

DEFINITION OF *CONSTRUCTION*

Procurement of construction essentially involves contracting with a contractor to build something and with an architect or engineer to design the facility to be built. The American Bar Association Model Procurement Code for State and Local Governments[3] (Model Procurement Code) defines *construction* as follows:

> *Construction means the process of building, altering, repairing, improving, or demolishing any public infrastructure facility, including any public structure, public building, or other public improvements of any kind to real property. It does not include the routine operation, routine repair or routine maintenance of any existing public infrastructure facility, including structures, buildings, or real property.* Section 1-301(4).

Typical public construction projects or public works involve the building or renovation of public infrastructure such as highways, bridges, dams, commuter rail, prisons, shipyards, office buildings, schools, canals, tunnels, wastewater systems and sewers, power generating systems and lines, pumps, wells, and water treatment facilities. Construction activities include planning and budgeting, architectural and engineering design, project management, actual construction, and construction management.

At times, determining whether a project meets a law's definition of *construction* can be difficult. That determination is important because construction contracting requires, for instance, that the contractor obtain performance and payment bonds. The hiring of a remediation contractor to remove some asbestos in a wall is an example of a project that might fall into a gray area. If the contractor needs to demolish the wall to do the job, that may qualify as construction under the definition. A fix for this type of ambiguity might be to add the words *routine demolition* to the category of activities that are considered outside of the definition in the Model Procurement Code of *construction*. Construction and professional services licensing statutes and ordinances may also help in distinguishing what qualifies as construction and design services.

AUTHORITY TO CONDUCT CONSTRUCTION PROCUREMENTS

State and local laws governing procurement of infrastructure facilities and related services are often different and separate from other public procurement laws. Procurement of construction may be the responsibility of the Chief Procurement Officer, or it may be within the purview of a separate public works division or highway department. It may also be divided among various state or local government agencies. In the State of Arizona, the Chief Procurement Officer, who is housed in the Department of

Administration, is responsible for construction services except for construction of public highways, which is under the authority of the transportation department.[4]

Many public works projects involve the blending of federal funds with state and other sources. Federal funds require compliance with a variety of federal laws and regulations, including procurement of architectural and engineering design services using the Brooks Architect-Engineer Act selection process,[5] which is discussed later in this chapter, along with payment of prevailing wages, use of disadvantaged business enterprises, compliance with the federal Buy America provisions, and other requirements.

As with public procurements for commodities and services, the National Association of State Procurement Officials (NASPO) recommends that the responsibility for procurement of all construction be separate and independent from the user agency and under the authority of the Chief Procurement Officer. Because of the complexities of contracting for construction and related services, the best approach is to place this type of procurement under the authority of a single procurement official who has the expertise and project management team to conduct competitions for, and administration of, these contracts.

In reality, at the state level, the procurement official authorized to oversee contracting and management of the construction of highways has nearly always been separate from the procurement official who conducts procurements for other types of construction projects, with entire state departments devoted to transportation issues. The separation of state-level construction projects for highways from other construction procurements constitutes a long-term practice, and it is likely to continue. One of the reasons is the significant role that federal funding plays in those procurements with many federal requirements flowing down with those funds.

SELECTING THE APPROPRIATE CONSTRUCTION PROJECT DELIVERY METHOD

In the construction industry, there are various methods for delivering a completed project from start to finish. They are better understood as designations of what the contract requires the contractor to do and are called *project delivery methods*. The term *alternative project delivery methods* means a method other than the standard and long-used one called *design-bid-build*, where a public entity initiates a competition for, and contracts with, an architect or engineer for a design, and based on that design, subsequently competes for a contractor to build the facility. Contract award is made to the lowest price bidder.

Conceptually, project delivery methods may be divided into two categories that relate to the type of commitment that the public entity requests of the contractor. Some involve short-term, initial delivery strategies. There is no long-term relationship with the project delivery contractor. Others reach beyond initial delivery of the project and can be considered long-term delivery strategies. Long-term strategies may also embrace funding mechanisms in which the public and private sector share the cost of the project, or the private sector bears the entire cost.

The website of the National Council for Public Private Partnerships lists 18 different types of alternative project delivery methods.[6] This resource includes information about projects in which public entities have used these methods, along with sample solicitations.

SHORT-TERM PROJECT DELIVERY METHODS

There is a wide range of project delivery methods, and some are used more frequently than others. Short-term project delivery methods are those where the contractual relationship between the public entity and the contractor only lasts until construction is complete.

Types of Common Short-Term Methods

The most common short-term project delivery methods as identified by the Association of General Contractors are:[7]

- Design-bid-build
- Construction manager at risk
- Design-build
- Integrated

Design-bid-build is the method that is most familiar to the public. It consists of awarding a contract to the bidder submitting the lowest price based on a design prepared by a design professional under a separate contract with the public entity.

There needs to be some authority under law—that is, statute or local ordinance—to use a project delivery method, regardless of type. Given the historical and consistent use by public entities across the country of the design-bid-build approach, the authority to use this method is likely to already exist. Relatively speaking, public entities have only recently advocated the use of the other methods. Without legal authority to use them, however, they are out of reach.

In Arizona, for example, a state public university used the design-build method for the renovation of its student center when state law did not grant public entities the authority to use anything but the design-bid-build approach. As is the case for any public entity, the fact that a statute or ordinance is silent on an issue does not mean that the activity is permissible. When a dispute arose during the renovation of the student center, one of the challenges made against the university was that its use of an alternative project delivery method was not permitted. The Arizona legislature had to enact a law and make it retroactive in order to correct that problem.

The American Bar Association Model Code for Public Infrastructure Procurement[8] provides statutory language authorizing the aforementioned methods, but it does not separately treat the job order contracting method, which it considers a type of design-bid-build or design-build method, as the case may be. The Model Code for Public Infrastructure Procurement is a resource available to those searching for statutory language to authorize these methods.

The following are descriptions of the standard project delivery methods in which the contractor does not continue its relationship with the public entity once it completes its work on constructing or renovating a public infrastructure project (short term).

Design-Bid-Build

Under the design-bid-build method, the public entity competes and awards a contract to the architect or engineer to perform design services. The completed design is used to solicit bids under an invitation for bids for a contractor to build from that design. The construction contract is awarded to the responsible bidder who submits the lowest responsive bid. During construction, the architect or engineer assists the public entity with administration of the construction contract.

The NIGP Dictionary defines this delivery method as follows:

> *The traditional project delivery method, which customarily involves three sequential project phases: design, procurement, and construction; and two distinct contracts for the design and construction (build) phases.*

Job Order Contracting

Job order contracting is a variation of the design-bid-build method that may be used for smaller construction projects, such as remodeling or repairs. The NIGP Dictionary defines this type of delivery method as follows:

Based on a competitively bid indefinite delivery-indefinite quantity (IDIQ)[9] contract between a [public entity] and a construction contractor. The contract typically has a base year with 2 to 4 option years. The contract sets parameters such as the types of work that can be done, location of work, design criteria, and maximum amount of work to be awarded. The contract also has a unit-price book (UPB) that establishes a unit price to be paid for each of a multitude of construction line items. The contract's price is put in terms of a coefficient, which is a multiplier that covers the contractor's overhead and profit as well as any adjustments between the UPB and actual local prices. (Burt, Dobler, and Starling, 2003)

Construction Manager at Risk

The NIGP Dictionary defines construction manager at risk as follows:

A construction delivery method in which the [public entity] enters into separate contracts with the designer and builder, often at or about the same time so that both parties can collaborate. Selection is based on an evaluation of qualifications and price, and the contractor offers a Guaranteed Maximum Price (GMP) instead of a fixed bid. The Construction Manager at Risk (CMAR) is responsible and accepts risk for constructing the entire project for the GMP, and the contractor is responsible for assembling the team of suppliers and subcontractors.

The Water Design-Build Council describes the construction manager at risk project delivery method as follows:[10]

With the CMAR delivery method, the [public entity] first selects and retains the design firm, similar to a design-bid-build project. Selecting the design firm can be based on price, qualifications, and any other criteria desired by the [public entity]. . . . CMAR projects require the contractor to provide a Guaranteed Maximum Price (GMP) somewhere within the 60 to 90 percent design phase of the project.

It is at this point in the project that the "at risk" portion of CMAR comes in. The CMAR assembles a GMP largely based on subcontractor bids, plus contingencies and allowances. The CMAR then communicates the anticipated cost of the project based on the design in hand, but they are financially liable if the project exceeds that amount. If the project is completed for less than the GMP, there is generally a cost-sharing agreement in place.

There is also the possibility that the project could encounter scope changes which could result in a change order leading to an increase in the GMP, but this would be discussed collaboratively by the [public entity] and CMAR Project Team.

There can be variations on the role of the construction manager under this method. The Dallas Area Rapid Transit (DART) uses a construction manager/general contractor delivery method. Under this method, DART selects the construction manager/general contractor through a request for proposals (RFP) solicitation and the construction manager is paid a fee for services up through the completion of 65% of the design process. If DART and the construction manager/general contractor are unable to reach agreement on the fees for the remainder of the project, DART uses the project design to seek competitive bids for construction.

Design-Build

The NIGP Dictionary defines this project delivery method as follows:

A delivery method for construction projects that combines the architectural, engineering, and construction services required for a project into a single contractual agreement. (ISM, 2000)

Under the design-build project delivery method, a single contractor is responsible for both design and construction services.

There are a number of design-build variations that are generated in the design and construction industry. Under the progressive design-build approach, the design builder is selected during the earliest stages of the project and price and schedule are determined as the design progresses. The Design-Build Institute of America describes progressive design-build as follows:[11]

> While a project design is usually 35 percent complete (or more) by the time a design-builder is procured in the traditional two-step design-build process, [Progressive Design-Build] adds the design-builder to the [public entity]'s team even earlier in the design phase. When the design is somewhere between 50 and 75 percent complete, the design-builder issues a Guaranteed Maximum Price (GMP).

Integrated Project Delivery

Some may view the integrated project delivery (IPD) method as another design-build variation. However, it deserves its own category. On its home website, the AGC defines IPD as:

> IPD as a Delivery Method is a delivery methodology that fully integrates project teams in order to take advantage of the knowledge of all team members to maximize the project outcome. Integrated Project Delivery is the highest form of collaboration because all three parties ([public entity], Architect, Constructor) are aligned by a single contract.[12]

Currently, there is a great deal of enthusiasm about this method in the construction industry. In fact, the Lean Construction Institute exists to promote this delivery method as Lean construction.[13]

The National and California Councils of the American Institute of Architects offers a comprehensive document entitled *Integrated Project Delivery: A Guide*.[14] Another useful resource is a document entitled *Integrated Project Delivery for Public and Private Owners* published by a group of construction and architectural industry organizations.[15] That document describes the philosophy and principles behind IPD, among other things. Under this type of project delivery method, the public entity, the architect, and the contractor are all parties to one contract. The contract contains behavior principles to which all of the parties agree—such as mutual respect and trust, willingness to collaborate, and open communication. The contract also follows these contractual principles:

- Key participants bound together as equals
- Shared financial risk and reward based on project outcome
- Liability waivers between key participants
- Fiscal transparency between key participants
- Early involvement of key participants
- Intensified design
- Jointly developed project target criteria
- Collaborative decision making

A SNAPSHOT OF THE RISKS AND BENEFITS OF SHORT-TERM PROJECT DELIVERY METHODS

Before comparing short-term project delivery methods for a particular project, the public entity must first determine which delivery method works best, considering the budget and schedule, technical requirements and complexity, environmental factors, project risks, business and political environment, and other factors. For a complex wastewater facility project with a very tight schedule, design-build might be the best choice, or construction manager at risk might work best.

Table 11.1 lists some of the advantages and disadvantages to consider for each approach.

Table 11.1

Delivery Method	Advantages	Disadvantages
Design-bid-build	• Preferred or only authorized project delivery method for some states • Designer serves as the public entity's advocate during construction • Competitive pricing based on completed design	• No or little opportunity for contractor input into design • Slow linear process • Award based on price only • Greater risk of disputes between public entity, designer, and contractor • More opportunity for change orders and claims
Job order contracting	• Needs can be responded to in a *just-in-time* and *as-needed* manner • Work needs and outcomes are not subject to interpretation or negotiations • Increase in flexibility to meet staffing resource needs for priority or emergency work • Predicted types of work can be outsourced thus reducing full-time staffing requirements and costs.	• Poorly defined performance outcomes or measures • Possible higher unit bid prices, escalation costs for materials, labor, and equipment • Uses of the contract for inappropriate projects • Work flow or labor shortage conflicts • Potential bonding capacity impacts for the contract term
Construction manager at risk	• Selection of contractor through competitive proposals • Combined expertise of contractor and designer during design • Faster concurrent schedule with some opportunity for fast-tracking • Proponents claim higher quality and lower price	• Requires advanced level of public entity expertise and administration • Can result in higher total cost • If guaranteed maximum price is not a selection factor, there is no assurance that the price is fair and reasonable • Fewer contractors may be capable of competing for construction manager at risk contracts
Design-build	• Selection of contractor through competitive proposals • Combined expertise of contractor and designer during design • Single source of responsibility for design and construction • Faster concurrent schedule, ability to fast-track, and elimination of construction contractor sourcing process • Proponents claim higher quality and lower price	• Public entity has less control over design • Requires advanced level of entity expertise and administration • Public entity does not have the benefit of an independent designer during construction • If guaranteed maximum price is not a selection factor, there is no assurance that the price is fair and reasonable • Fewer contractors may be capable of competing for design-build or integrated project delivery contracts
Integrated project delivery methods	• Same as design-build	• Same as design-build

Long-Term Project Delivery Methods

In addition to short-term delivery methods, there are various long-term delivery methods that involve an extended contractual relationship between the public entity and the contractor. Given the complexities of these types of approaches, this chapter will only highlight some of them to illustrate how they differ from the ones discussed as short-term delivery methods.

Long-term project delivery methods are akin to instances in which a state or local government leases out the operation and management of some complicated technology, placing the responsibility and cost on the contractor for updating the software and hardware and training its employees to run the system.

Successful use of many of these project delivery methods requires careful planning and detailed fiscal analyses. In addition to materials available from the National Council for Public Private Partnerships and other organizations promoting these types of approaches, there are technical articles and books available for those who are interested.

Here are a couple of examples of term methods:

Operations and Maintenance (O&M)
A public entity contracts with a private partner to provide and/or maintain a specific service relating to the upkeep of a public facility. Under the private operation and maintenance option, the public entity retains ownership and overall management of the public facility or system.

Design-Build-Operate-Maintain (DBOM)
The DBOM model is an integrated procurement model that combines the design and construction responsibilities of design-build procurements with operations or maintenance or both. These project components are procured from the private sector in a single contract with financing independently secured by the public entity. This project delivery approach is also known by a number of different names, including *turnkey* procurement and build-operate-transfer (BOT).[16]

Public-Private Partnerships

The term *public-private partnerships* (P3s) is often used to describe the contractual relationship that occurs as a result of some types of long-term project delivery methods described above. There is no universally accepted definition, and some may focus solely on whether the contractor/private partner is providing some sort of financing for the infrastructure project.

In its publication, *A Guide to Public-Private Partnerships (PPPs): What Public Procurement Specialists Need to Know*,[17] NIGP describes P3s as follows:

> Typically, a PPP is conceptualized as a contractual agreement between one or more state or local governments/public agencies and one or more private sector or nonprofit partners for the purpose of supporting the delivery of public services or financing, designing, building, operating and/or maintaining a certain project for the public good. These types of partnerships are usually developed with the implicit and explicit objectives of leveraging additional financing resources and expertise, which otherwise might not have been available for public purposes through traditional procurement practices.

Note that the description of P3s above includes instances in which a state or local government outsources or privatizes some of the services it provides. Chapter 10 (*Contracting for Services*) discusses the outsourcing or privatizing of state or local government services.

In the case of privatizing public infrastructure, the design-build project delivery method forms the foundation for a P3, as can be seen in the definitions of long-term project delivery methods described in this chapter. Other elements may be combined, including financing, operation, and maintenance.

Combining a financing element for a P3 is commonly employed to facilitate project completion when other traditional forms of financing may not be available. The financial element could take the form of private investment, loan or lease, or other vehicles, and may be combined with state or local government financing sources such as appropriations, bonds, and grants. Adding operation and maintenance elements to a P3 over a specified period of time serves as a form of extended warranty and can provide the contractor with a revenue stream for recovery of its investment in the project.

There is a wide variety of publications and information about P3s, including a joint report by NASPO, the National Association of State Facilities Administrators, and the National Association of State Chief Administrators entitled *Considerations for Public-Private Partnerships*.[18]

SOURCE SELECTION METHODS FOR ARCHITECTS AND ENGINEERS

The source selection method for awarding contracts to architects and engineers relating to the construction of public infrastructure is a controversial one. As the American Bar Association was drafting the Model Code for Public Infrastructure Procurement for State and Local Governments in the 1970s, this issue received the most public input and outcry from the various constituencies—public procurement officials and architect and engineer professional organizations.

Federal procurement laws and most state procurement laws require use of the Brooks Architect-Engineer Act (Brooks Act) method for procurement of architectural and engineering services. This is the approach that the professional organizations representing architects and engineers prefer.

The Brooks Act requires selection of the architect, engineer, land surveyor, and other related services based only on qualifications. Comparison of competing prices or fees is not permitted under the Brooks Act. A fair and reasonable price is negotiated only with the most qualified firm. If the state or local government and the selected firm are unable to agree upon a fair and reasonable price, the state or local government may terminate negotiations and proceed to negotiate with the next most qualified firm in succession until an agreement is reached. The procurement officer, however, may not negotiate again with firms for which negotiations failed the first time.

Some procurement professionals disagree with this approach. They believe that it is problematic not to consider fees as one of the criteria for the selection process. A small *rebellion* against the qualification-based approach is found in the State of Florida law, which exempts some contracts for services with construction professionals from its version of the Brooks Act.[19]

Even in states with laws similar to the Brooks Act approach, many award indefinite quantity/indefinite delivery requirements contracts[20] to architects and engineers for small-dollar projects. Specifically, the public entity awards contracts to more than one architect or engineer. The contract does not specify any projects or promise the suppliers on the contract that the public entity will use them. The contract essentially creates a type of master list from which user agencies may select an architect or engineer when small projects come up. This approach avoids the need to compete each of those projects separately. To comply with the mandate to award to the most qualified firm, the procurement officer awards contracts to perhaps three or four firms within a particular architectural or engineering specialty, and advises user agencies to discuss each project with the top-ranked firm first, unless it is not available.

SELECTION METHODS FOR PROJECT DELIVERY METHODS

Next is a short description of the source selection methods that are generally used for specific short-term project delivery methods.

Design-Bid-Build Method

Most state laws require selection of the design architect or engineer through a qualification-based selection process. The contractor is typically procured through competitive bids. However, some state laws permit sourcing of the contractor through competitive proposals, including negotiation.

Construction Manager at Risk Method

Like design-bid-build, the design architect or engineer is procured through a qualification-based selection process. Depending on specific state laws, the construction manager (CM) may be procured through either a qualification-based selection as in the Brooks Act or through competitive proposals with price as a selection factor. The CM receives a fixed fee for work as the design progresses. The CM may be invited to submit a guaranteed maximum price or fixed price for construction when the design is sufficiently defined (50–65% complete). The public entity may accept the price, negotiate, retain the contractor for CM services, or terminate the CM contract and seek bids.

Under the Construction Manager/General Contractor variation that DART uses, as discussed earlier, a not-to-exceed or guaranteed maximum price is part of the initial proposal and is a factor in selection. This price is refined as design progresses, and the public entity may retain any savings or share savings with the designer and CM.

Design-Build and Integrated Project Delivery Method

The public entity procures both the designer and the builder under one contract. The public entity's requirements may be stated as a performance-based specification or as the preliminary design (10–30% complete). Design-build contracts are most often sourced through an RFP and price is a factor in the selection decision. Depending on the applicable laws, integrated project delivery contracts are procured either through an RFP or qualification-based selection method such as that found in the Brooks Act.

SOURCES OF CONTRACT FORMS

There are many organizations that provide form contracts for construction contracting, including the following:

- The American Institute of Architects provides a wide range of contract forms for both design and construction services.[21]
- The Design Build Institute of America is another source of contract forms.[22]
- A collaboration of 20 national construction-related associations have recently developed and published consensus contract documents under the name *ConsensusDOCS*.[23]
- The Construction Owners of America also maintains a library of documents and offers a wide range of training.[24]

Many of these are good starting points. However, they are drafted with the private sector in mind. In places within the contract text, they can tend to favor their particular constituency.

The best practice for a public entity is to avoid adopting any of these forms verbatim. Instead, they should carefully consider the language and make sure that it protects the public investment. While the contract language does not need to unfairly shift risks to the contractor, it should make sure that procedures for items such as modifying the design or submitting accurate progress schedules are clearly spelled out so that the entity has something to enforce if things go wrong.

TYPES OF CONTRACTS

There is a wide range of contract types used in construction contracting, although some are used less frequently in public construction than others. The key to categorizing them is to consider how those forms treat pricing. Chapter 4 (*Strategies and Plans*) discusses contract types in more detail.

BONDING REQUIREMENTS

Chapter 7 (*Competition: Solicitations and Methods*) discusses the matter of requiring bid bonds in competitions for commodities and services and advises that a procurement officer should not use a bid bond as a means for determining a bidder's responsibility. When a competitive sealed bidding method is used to select a contractor for a construction project, the procurement law will likely mandate that the solicitation require a bid bond from each bidder.

Bid bonds have been standard fare historically in invitations for bids for a construction contractor. These have been under attack because they pose a barrier to small and disadvantaged businesses. Construction is an area where participation by these types of businesses is low for a number of reasons.

The bid bond usually must be in an amount equal to a certain percent of the bidder's bid price. The purpose of the bond is to ensure that if the lowest bidder balks at entering into a contract for some reason, the public entity will still get the dollar benefit of that low bid by calling on the bonding company to pay the difference between the low bidder's bid and that of the next lowest bidder. Generally speaking, a procurement officer must reject a bid that fails to provide a bond.

Performance and payment bonds issued by surety companies are also mandatory in public construction contracting, usually by law. These types of bonds apply only to the winning contractor.

A payment bond is for 100% of the contract price and provides assurance that there is a mechanism to pay subcontractors and suppliers on the project if the contractor does not pay them.

A performance bond is for the protection of the public entity. It also is for 100% of the contract price. Under a performance bond, the public entity may ask or demand that the surety step into the contractor's shoes if the contractor defaults or is struggling to complete the work.

CONTRACT ADMINISTRATION

Chapter 14 (*Contract Management and Contract Administration*) addresses this topic in more detail. The difference between contracts for commodities or services and those for construction is that laws generally direct the management of a public construction contract while saying nothing or very little about commodities or services contracts.

For instance, they often require that the public entity pay the contractor promptly—defined as a number of days after the entity approves a payment request. Because construction of a public project is performed over many months, the law usually authorizes progress payments to the contractor for work performed and material purchased and delivered to the site. That law also permits the public entity to retain a certain percentage of each progress payment to ensure completion of the work. The public entity pays the contractor that accumulated retention after accepting the contractor's work at the end of construction.

The public entity also requires different types of insurance for construction than it does for commodities and services suppliers. A contractor providing design services must have errors and omissions coverage. A contractor's commercial general liability policy must include builder's risk insurance and completed operations coverage to guarantee recovery of damages to the work in progress during construction.

For large construction projects, state or local governments may elect to insure the project themselves through a special owner controlled insurance program (OCIP) that provides umbrella coverage to contractors and subcontractors. Through an OCIP, they may benefit from a better insurance program and lower costs by requiring contractors and subcontractors to exclude insurance from their bids.

One frequent challenge for a public entity is receiving bids that are much higher than the independent cost estimate or budget. If the state or local government is unable to negotiate down to the original estimate or budget, design revisions and new bids may be required, incurring considerable delay and additional cost. To mitigate the impact of such a situation, the public entity should include a provision in the designer's contract that requires the designer to redesign for no additional cost or fee.

Changes to the design can occur during construction as a result of unforeseen site conditions—as required by the public entity or as recommended by the designer. Even though design changes are only addressed in this paragraph, this should not be interpreted to suggest that they are rare. They occur quite regularly in public construction work and are often fodder for disputes. These changes may require an adjustment to the price or time to perform the contract. Changes are issued to the contractor through change orders, which provide for uninterrupted performance of the work while the contract modification is being negotiated.

A WORD ABOUT ENVIRONMENTALLY FRIENDLY CONSTRUCTION

Chapter 6 (*Sustainable Procurement Considerations and Strategies*) addresses sustainable and environmentally friendly purchases of commodities and services. It focuses on establishing a public-entity-wide program focusing on sustainability using the procurement process.

There is increasing interest in and legislation requiring environmentally friendly construction. There is a process for certifying buildings as constructed with the environment in mind. The U.S. Green Building Council offers a program entitled the Leadership in Energy and Environmental Design (LEED) Green Building Rating System. As explained on the council's website:[25]

> *LEED, or Leadership in Energy and Environmental Design, is the most widely used green building rating system in the world. Available for virtually all building, community, and home project types, LEED provides a framework to create healthy, highly efficient and cost-saving green buildings. LEED certification is a globally recognized symbol of sustainability achievement.*

CONCLUSION

Construction, and finding the means to pay for it, will be a large focus of public procurement in the foreseeable future. Public procurement officials must meet the challenge by being professionally prepared for the use of project delivery methods and contract types that speed up the construction process through collaboration, reduce costs, and share some of the cost of infrastructure construction and renovation with the private sector.

ENDNOTES

1. http://www.infrastructurereportcard.org
2. http://www.census.gov/construction/c30/c30index.html
3. A copy of the Model Procurement Code is available at: http://apps.americanbar.org/dch/committee.cfm?com=PC500500
4. See Arizona Revised Statutes §§41-2501-J and 41-2511-C-1 at: https://www.azleg.gov/arstitle/
5. See Brooks Architect-Engineers Act, 40 U.S.C. 1101 *et seq.* at: https://www.gpo.gov/fdsys/pkg/USCODE-2016-title40/html/USCODE-2016-title40-subtitleI-chap11-sec1101.htm
6. https://www.ncppp.org/ppp-basics/types-of-partnerships/
7. https://www.agc.org/industry-priorities/project-delivery
8. The Model Code for Public Infrastructure Procurement is available at: https://apps.americanbar.org/dch/committee.cfm?com=PC500500
9. The NIGP Dictionary defines an indefinite quantity contract as "a type of a contract that provides for the delivery of indefinite quantities, within stated limits, of supplies or services. These supplies or services are to be furnished during a fixed period, with deliveries or performance to be scheduled by placing orders with the contractor." An indefinite delivery contract in the context of job order contracting simply means that the contract itself does not set a time frame for the contractor to perform since the contract is for future construction work as it arises. The type of work and the time frame for it to be completed are contained in the specific job orders issued under the contract.
10. Brennan, T. (November 4, 2016). Water Design-Build Council. Retrieved August 1, 2018, from: http://info.waterdesignbuild.com/blog/what-is-construction-management-at-risk-cmar
11. The Emergence of Progressive Design-Build—DBIA. Design-Build Institute of America (May 24, 2018). Retrieved from: https://dbia.org/the-emergence-of-progressive-design-build/
12. See Endnote 7.
13. https://www.leanconstruction.org/about-us/
14. https://info.aia.org/SiteObjects/files/IPD_Guide_2007.pdf
15. https://www.agc.org/integrated-project-delivery
16. https://www.fhwa.dot.gov/ipd/alternative_project_delivery/defined/new_build_facilities/dbom.aspx
17. Published in 2015, this guide is available at: https://www.nigp.org/docs/default-source/New-Site/research-reports/guidetopublic-privatepartnerships(ppps)-whatpublicprocurementspecialistsneednowfinal.pdf?sfvrsn=4
18. http://www.naspo.org/Portals/16/Whitepapers/documents/GOV16%20WHITE%20PAPER%20P3%20FINAL%209.6.16.PDF
19. See Florida Statutes Title XIX Section 287.055-4(c) available at: http://www.leg.state.fl.us/Statutes/index.cfm?App_mode=Display_Statute&URL=0200-0299/0287/Sections/0287.055.html
20. See Endnote 9.
21. https://www.aiacontracts.org/
22. https://dbia.org/
23. https://www.consensusdocs.org/
24. https://www.coaa.org/Collaboration/COAA-e-Catalog-en
25. https://new.usgbc.org/leed

CHAPTER 12: COOPERATIVE PURCHASING

RECOMMENDED BEST PRACTICES

- Clearly understand the nature of the various cooperative participants to ensure that legal authority exists for the cooperative purchase and that the requirements for participation are satisfied. Use written cooperative purchasing agreements to ensure a common understanding among participants.
- Use a lead public entity, but involve other participating states and entities in the market research for each cooperative procurement, solicitation planning and development, and evaluation to add expertise and to better ensure use of an accepted, compliant procurement process that promotes best value through full and open competition.
- To the extent possible, limit use of preferences and varying public entity-specific terms and conditions to those absolutely essential to satisfy mandatory legal requirements.
- Build reporting into the solicitation and cooperative contract in order to collect data for future solicitations and to manage administrative fees.
- Minimize administrative fees to those essential to covering the costs of administrating the cooperative purchase program and reimbursing lead agencies and other participating entities.
- When evaluating piggybacking opportunities, analyze the terms to ensure that they represent best value and effectively leverage volume to achieve favorable pricing.
- If feasible, work with public entity finance officials to establish a separate cost center for the administration and tracking of cooperative transactions.

CHAPTER 12: COOPERATIVE PURCHASING

This chapter is designed to provide public procurement officers, elected officials, government executives, government suppliers, and citizens with an introduction to cooperative purchasing[1]—particularly its definition, purpose, authority, value, and best practices.

DEFINITIONS AND OVERVIEW

Key Definitions

In simple terms, the most common type of cooperative purchasing involves public entities sharing their contracts with other public entities. The formal definitions of cooperative purchasing vary.

The NIGP Dictionary defines *intergovernmental cooperative purchasing* as follows:[2]

> *A variety of arrangements under which two or more governmental entities pool their commodity and/or service requirements to purchase aggregated quantities thus achieving economies of scale. The process usually involves a single combined bid or request for proposals in which all of the participating entities are named or their participation implied.*

Another definition can be found in the American Bar Association Model Procurement Code for State and Local Governments (Model Procurement Code). It states:

> *Cooperative purchasing means a procurement conducted by, or on behalf of, one or more public [entities or non-profit entity comprised of one or more public entities].*[3]

The section of the Model Procurement Code that provides statutory language to authorize cooperative purchasing also authorizes the sharing among public entities of procurement officers and of informational, technical, and other services. Other examples of shared activities may include specification development, joint training programs, and advice or assistance on technical evaluation committees. Those types of cooperation are not addressed here.

Piggybacking

The definition of *cooperative purchasing* contemplates that public entities pool their needs for commodities or services before a procurement, with one of those public entities conducting the procurement for a contract from which the participating public entities may buy. Piggybacking, on the other hand, occurs when public entities that did not participate in the procurement purchase commodities or services from the cooperative contract.

The NIGP Dictionary defines *piggyback* (*piggyback cooperatives*) as follows:

> *A form of intergovernmental cooperative purchasing in which an entity will be extended the pricing and terms of a contract entered into by a larger entity. Generally, a larger entity will competitively award a contract that will include language allowing for other entities to utilize the contract which may be to their advantage in terms of pricing, thereby gaining economies of scale that they normally would not receive if they competed on their own.*

For a contract to permit piggybacking, it must explicitly say so. The public entity competing for and awarding the contract must place language in the solicitation and contract that states that other public entities may purchase from the contract at the discretion of the contractor.

It is not uncommon for a local government or public university to establish, through the procurement process, a contract for itself and insert piggybacking language in it—particularly where the contract is not for a project but is instead an indefinite quantity/indefinite delivery contract[4] for a commodity or commodities or services. Other local public entities looking for a contract vehicle with good pricing may take advantage of that language to buy commodities or services from that contract and avoid the need to conduct their own procurement.

Piggyback contracts represent the most immediate cooperative purchasing resource, especially for smaller public entities. Such contracts can benefit larger public entities by saving administrative costs and by creating pressure for lower prices.

Yet there are drawbacks to piggybacking. Due to the lack of a solid estimate of the expected quantities to be purchased, there is the potential loss of the benefits and leverage that accompany a competition for a contract. Contractors may offer minimal discounts under the contract and subsequently benefit from windfall profits when participation and usage exceed estimates. Local suppliers may view piggyback contracts as unfair because they did not have an opportunity to compete.

Finally, there are some restrictions on piggybacking when a public entity is using certain federal funds to buy the commodity or service. This chapter discusses those restrictions later.

Types of Purchasing Cooperatives

Public sector purchasing cooperatives may be comprised of similar or different levels of government with common requirements. Examples are:

- State procurement cooperatives serving multiple state and local governments
- Consortia of same-level governments (state-to-state and city-to-city) sharing similar requirements
- State and local governments participating in federal contracts
- Cooperative purchasing supporting specific government programs (for example, law enforcement or hospitals)
- Governments located within defined geographic areas
- Groups of higher education institutions

The purest form of cooperative purchasing occurs when two or more public entities combine their procurement requirements and compete them through a single solicitation. The National Association of State Procurement Officials (NASPO) refers to this form as a *true cooperative*. NASPO ValuePoint is an example of this type of cooperative.

Another type is third-party aggregator cooperatives. Those occur when a third party that is not necessarily a public entity brings together multiple entities (both public and private) to conduct a procurement and manages the resulting contract or contractor. The E&I Cooperative Services discussed later in this chapter is an example of this type of cooperative.

Most early cooperative purchasing efforts involved the purchase of bulk commodities using standard specifications, such as cleaning supplies, gasoline and fuel, or services such as the collection and disposal of hazardous waste or used oil.

Examples of commodities that are currently found on cooperative contracts include office supplies and furniture, digital copiers and printers, carpeting, computer hardware, industrial lab supplies, infant formula, electronic defibrillators, smartphones and other Internet of Things[5] devices, drones, and fleet vehicles.

Additionally, more complicated requirements, including information technology and cloud services, software, and consulting are often targeted today for cooperative purchasing contracts.

LEGAL AUTHORITY FOR COOPERATVE PURCHASING

If the law of a state or local government specifies that the government must award procurement contracts through competitive methods such as competitive sealed bidding and competitive sealed proposals, cooperative purchasing among public entities may not satisfy those legal requirements, even if a cooperative contract is formally competed by another public entity. A government's law must authorize cooperative purchasing and piggybacking as exceptions to the mandate to compete.

Foundational Legal Authority

A comprehensive law addressing cooperative purchasing does the following:

- Defines the types of public entities and other entities such as consortia of public entities or not-for-profit organizations with which the public entity may engage in cooperative purchasing
- Authorizes the public entity to participate in, sponsor, conduct, or administer a cooperative procurement so long as the procurement is conducted through full and open formal competition
- Authorizes the public entity to purchase from a formally competed cooperative contract of another public entity or consortia of public entities, even if the public entity was not an original participant in the procurement for the contract
- Authorizes the central procurement office to collect reasonable administrative fees from public entities or other approved entities who make purchases from cooperative contracts

A 2018 NASPO State Practices Survey[6] indicates that virtually all states have legislation providing some authority for cooperative purchasing, although the specific requirements vary. Some laws limit the nature of participation in cooperatives, either as a participating public entity purchasing from another public entity's contract or as a lead government conducting the procurement. Other states restrict or regulate the scope of cooperatives to exclude cooperative purchasing from the contracts of the federal government or not-for-profit organizations, or they impose administrative requirements that must precede participation in a cooperative.

It is often difficult to locate state laws authorizing cooperative purchasing. The Model Procurement Code includes an article entitled *Intergovernmental Relations* in which the authority for cooperative purchasing resides. Some state statutes treat cooperative purchasing under names such as *joint powers* or *intergovernmental agreements*. To add to the confusion, authority for cooperation sometimes resides in separate parts of a set of statutes governing specific entities.

Other Limitations

In cases where a state's statutes grant legal authority for cooperative purchasing, there may be limits on the types of entities with which a public entity may cooperate, on the specific commodity or service purchased, or on the nature of the process used by the other entity to award the contract. Moreover, some statutes require that the contract be competitively awarded by the lead public entity using procedures substantially the same as those of the entity wishing to use the contract, which excludes purchasing from the United States General Services Administration schedule contracts. This chapter discusses those schedules in more detail later.

Even states considered to have enacted statutes based on the Model Procurement Code may have added specific procedural requirements, such as publication of notices of intent to use a cooperative contract. Public procurement officers must be familiar with the laws in their own state or local government.

Finally, some laws require that the public entity seeking to purchase from another public entity's contracts first have in place an overarching written agreement with the public entity offering the cooperative contract, such as an intergovernmental agreement or joint powers agreement. Finalizing that agreement is a precursor to engaging in cooperative purchasing.

AN OVERVIEW OF COOPERATIVE PURCHASING ALLIANCES AND TRENDS

Today, cooperative purchasing has become a standard tool for most public procurement offices. The following brief account discusses how states and other public entities are organizing to carry out cooperative purchasing.

Statewide Contracts

Statewide cooperative contracts, sometimes referred to simply as statewide contracts, are generally established by a state's central procurement office and are often indefinite quantity/indefinite delivery contracts for commodities and services that user agencies regularly need. These contracts aggregate the volumes across all user agencies to increase value and reduce cost.

A state's user agencies under the control of its central procurement authority may be required to purchase from the statewide contracts, or such purchases may be optional. If use of the statewide contract is discretionary, it lessens the value of the contract, because estimates provided to suppliers of the volume that may be purchased from it are not firm.

Statewide contracts are not really cooperative contracts if they are used only by the state's user agencies. Where that state's procurement law authorizes cooperative purchasing, statewide contracts are made available to cities, counties, universities, other public entities, and non profit organizations that enter into a cooperative purchasing agreement with the state central procurement office.

Use of statewide contracts by those other public entities is typically optional. Their consistent use of statewide contracts over time allows states to track usage and volumes, enabling them to leverage those volumes with suppliers to increase pricing and other supplier-offered benefits to both the state and the participating entity.

NASPO ValuePoint Cooperative Purchasing Program

As the chief organization representing state procurement since 1947, NASPO plays a critical role today in administering state-to-state cooperative purchasing. Until 2013, cooperative purchasing was done separately through the regional NASPO structure comprising of Eastern, Southern, Midwest, and Western regions as depicted in Figure 12.1.

Historically, states making up the western region designated a name for their cooperative—the Western States Contracting Alliance (WSCA). Despite it having a separate name, the cooperative was a NASPO program. In 2013, NASPO created a single member limited liability company, the NASPO Cooperative Purchasing Organization, to meet the increasing needs for resource assistance in cooperative procurement among the states. On March 30, 2015 the cooperative's brand was launched as NASPO ValuePoint.[7] Since that date, purchases from NASPO ValuePoint cooperative contracts have reached billions of dollars annually.

NASPO ValuePoint acts as a resource to the central procurement offices of each state—the NASPO membership. The role of NASPO ValuePoint in the cooperative process is to:

- Perform market and technical research to locate commodities and services ripe for interstate cooperative opportunities
- Provide technical and procurement expertise to volunteer states leading cooperative contracting projects
- Identify and support individual volunteers from other states to join project sourcing teams
- Collect and manage administrative purchasing fees from participating suppliers for the NASPO organization

CHAPTER 12: **COOPERATIVE PURCHASING**

FIGURE 12.1 | NASPO REGION MAP

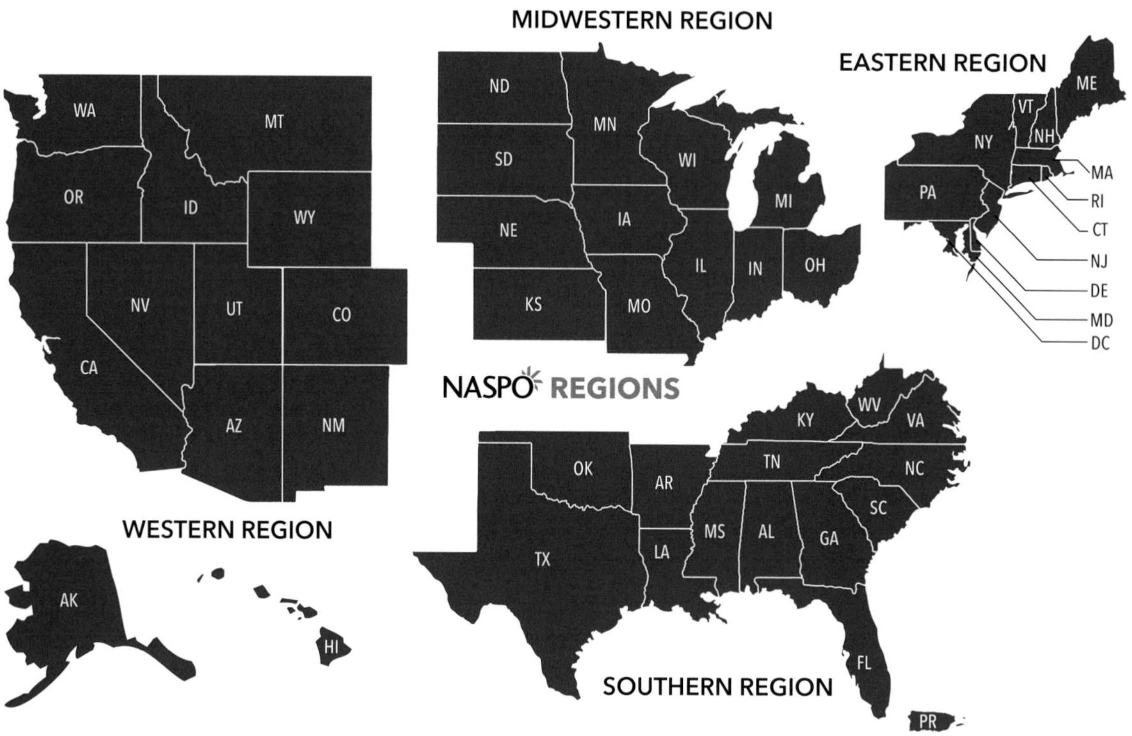

Minnesota Multistate Contracting Alliance for Pharmacy

Cooperative purchasing has dramatically reduced the prices that state and local governments pay for pharmaceuticals and medical supplies and services through the Minnesota Multistate Contracting Alliance for Pharmacy (MMCAP), established in 1985.[8]

MMCAP is a free, voluntary, group purchasing organization operated and managed by the Office of State Procurement within the State of Minnesota's Department of Administration. MMCAP's mission is to ensure best value for pharmaceutical healthcare products and services to state and local government facilities across the nation.

MMCAP's offerings include pharmaceuticals, clinical pharmacy services, medical supplies, influenza and routine vaccines, dental supplies, drug testing products and services, prescription filling services, pharmaceutical repackaging, emergency preparedness/stockpiling services, and more.

Before MMCAP was in place, most states had little chance of convincing pharmaceutical companies that those companies should provide them with favorable and discounted pricing. Today, MMCAP member facilities purchase more than $1.6 billion annually and have national account status with all the major brand name and generic pharmaceutical manufacturers.

MMCAP has over 10,000 participating facilities in all states and Washington, D.C. A list of

MMCAP current services and suppliers is available on its website.

Other Cooperative Purchasing Alliances

In June 2018, the National Joint Powers Alliance cooperative announced the launch of its new brand name, Sourcewell.[9] The alliance was originally founded in 1978 as an educational cooperative service unit under the laws of the State of Minnesota for a five-county region. Its initial focus on education and schools has continued as it has expanded to serve other government entities and nonprofits in Minnesota and across the country. There are now more than 50,000 government, education, and nonprofit organizations affiliated with Sourcewell. It is a self-funded agency with $3 billion in annual cooperative purchasing volume.

The U.S. Communities Government Purchasing Alliance (U.S. Communities)[10] was founded in 1996 as a partnership between the Association of School Business Officials International, the National Association of Counties, the National Institute of Governmental Purchasing (NIGP), the National League of Cities, and the United States Conference of Mayors. NIGP withdrew from the partnership in 2014, but U.S. Communities continues to provide a national purchasing forum for local and state government agencies, school districts, higher education, and nonprofits nationwide. U.S. Communities is currently a subsidiary of OMNIA Partners.[11]

E&I Cooperative Services,[12] a not-for-profit buying consortium affiliated with the National Association of Educational Procurement, is another cooperative purchasing organization. E&I Cooperative Services and other cooperative purchasing organizations like it conduct the procurements themselves, which is different from the process that NASPO ValuePoint, MMCAP, and U.S. Communities use, in which public entities conduct the procurements and award the contracts.

Higher education groups have also formed cooperatives. Examples are the Midwest Higher Education Compact,[13] Western Interstate Commission for Higher Education,[14] New England Board of Higher Education,[15] and the Southern Regional Education Board.[16] These cooperatives are not organized around purchasing alone, but engage in cooperative buying as a benefit to their members.

Trends

Cooperative purchasing is growing. In addition to the increasing use and choices, the organizations are beginning to re-brand, acquire, and aggregate with other cooperatives. Another trend is the development of professional organizations representing the needs and interests of public cooperatives. The National Cooperative Procurement Partners (NCPP) is one of those professional associations.[17]

The NCPP's mission is to elevate the advocacy, collaboration, and education for cooperative procurement so that its strategic value is widely recognized and promoted by government and educational leaders. Its membership is diverse and consists of national or regional cooperative organizations, suppliers, professional associations, nonprofits, state and local governments, educational entities, and public procurement professionals. While there are several associations focused on public procurement, there are few focused exclusively on cooperative purchasing. Recognizing the evolution and expanding arena of cooperatives, NCPP is currently taking the lead in education and advocacy of public-sector cooperative purchasing, and fostering a collaborative culture representing the diverse interests of the cooperative purchasing community.

CHAPTER 12: COOPERATIVE PURCHASING

BEST PRACTICES FOR INITIATING A COOPERATIVE PURCHASE

Using best practices and sound business processes is important when initiating a cooperative purchase. Adherence to these practices improves the value of contracts and makes them easier to use.

Based on experience, NASPO suggests the best practices[18] listed in the following section as a way to help public procurement officers avoid the pitfalls common with cooperative purchasing contracts. This is not an exhaustive list, but it is based on NASPO's insights into how successful cooperatives have worked at the state government level.

Joining a Cooperative and Pre-issuance of a Solicitation

- Require public entities who wish to join the cooperative to sign an agreement consenting to the terms under which the cooperative operates.
- Develop a standard set of solicitation general terms with member input.
- Develop a standard set of contract terms to which all of the cooperative members can agree, leaving aside the unique terms that a particular cooperative member's law requires.
- Identify the types of commodities or services to be procured through market research and surveys of cooperative members, including historical buying patterns and estimated requirements of the particular commodities or services.
- For each cooperative procurement, designate a lead state or local government procurement office to conduct the procurement using qualified procurement and technical staff with expertise in the commodities or services to be procured.
- Determine which of the cooperative members wish to participate in the specific procurement and have those members sign what NASPO ValuePoint calls a *participating addendum* to the contract:
    ◊ The participating addendum includes contract terms that the particular participating public entity requires in addition to those that are the cooperative's standard contract terms.
    ◊ The participating addendum becomes part of the solicitation.
    ◊ The participating addendum advises the competing suppliers of the specific contract terms of each participating public entity.
- Determine whether an administrative fee will be assessed under the particular contract based on the volume of purchases made and what the assessment will be to the contractor to reimburse the administrative expenses of the cooperative organization, the lead agency, and other procurement/sourcing team participants:
    ◊ Some cooperatives require contractors to add a specific, small percentage to their prices for each order and forward it to the cooperative, such as NASPO ValuePoint.
    ◊ In other cases, the lead government collects that fee from the contractor but must generally be authorized under its law to assess and collect that fee.
    ◊ The fee must be stated in the solicitation.
- Invite cooperative members, including technical specialists, to participate in the development of specifications or scopes of work for the particular cooperative procurement.
- Circulate draft solicitations for comments and suggestions among the public entities participating in the particular procurement, including prospective contractors.
- Permit suppliers to offer value-added services beyond those requested in the solicitation.

- Generally utilize the competitive sealed proposal source selection method to conduct the competition and use best value and similar evaluation tools, as the lead public entity's law allows.

Issuing the Solicitation

- Notify all suppliers registered with the participating public entities of the procurement and the solicitation.
- Through the lead public entity and all participating public entities, advertise the procurement according to their laws. NASPO ValuePoint uses a process that informs all state directors of the issuance of a solicitation so they can provide notice of solicitation that may be required by their individual laws.
- In all communications and the solicitation, designate one point of contact in the lead public procurement office for supplier inquiries.

Evaluating and Negotiating Offers

- Invite representatives from the lead public entity and all participating public entities to participate in technical evaluations.
- Negotiate supplier terms and conditions that conform to the legal requirements of each participating public entity or permit negotiation of more specific terms and conditions by each participating entity.
- Carefully evaluate the proposed contractor's ability to service all cooperative members.
- Evaluate and award the number of contracts needed for free and open competition and to provide best value to the participating public entities and to the cooperative organization.

Contract Award and Administration

- Notify all participating public entities of contract awards and provide them and the contractors with electronic copies of the entire contract.
- Permit each participating public entity to administer contractor performance and handle routine administration.
- Require that disputes relating to any specific purchase from a cooperative contract be handled by the public entity making the purchase.
- Provide that disputes relating to the master agreement/contract should be handled by the lead public entity.
- Establish a contractor performance reporting system for participating members.
- Require that the contractor provide periodic contract sales reports.
- Invite participating public entities to comment on proposed contract extensions.
- Negotiate deeper volume discounts in contract prices if actual purchases under the contracts exceed estimates.
- Provide plenty of time to compete for replacement contracts.

Purchasing from Cooperative Contracts

- To ensure compliance with a public entity's law where that law was not reflected in the solicitation, review the cooperative contract for conformance with applicable laws and ensure that the cooperative contract produces best value.
- If necessary, contact the cooperative's lead public entity to verify eligibility and the procedures for buying off of a contract.
- Compare what is offered under each contract if there are multiple contracts awarded for the required commodity or service.
- When buying large quantities, verify whether the contract permits negotiation of additional price concessions. In many NASPO ValuePoint master agreements, the contract prices are considered ceilings, and public entities are permitted to seek quotes that may offer more favorable pricing depending on the nature and timing of the requirement.

- If a written agreement with the cooperative contractor is required, as may be the case for piggybacking purchases, confer with legal counsel to determine whether the cooperative contract alone is acceptable.

COSTS OF ADMINISTRATION

Developing and administering a cooperative procurement usually involves added time, staff, and other resources for the lead public entity. In some cooperatives, the lead public entity charges and collects from suppliers an administrative fee based on each sale made under the contract to cover the expenses of the cooperative, the lead agency, and others participating on procurement/sourcing teams. The fee is disclosed in the solicitation and collected either by the cooperative organization or by the lead public entity, if legally authorized, on behalf of the cooperative organization.

Fees vary widely, from one-twentieth of one percent to three or more percent by some cooperatives. Higher fees can negatively affect the suppliers' final pricing, reducing the benefit of the cooperative purchase. Cooperatives should routinely review their administrative fees to ensure that revenues meet needs but do not reduce the value of the commodities and services in the eyes of potential buyers from the contracts.

In many cases, a state central procurement office will charge a fee for each purchase from a statewide contract. As stated earlier, there generally must be some authority in the state's law to allow that office to make such an assessment.

BENEFITS AND CHALLENGES OF COOPERATIVE PURCHASING

There are both benefits and challenges to engaging in cooperative purchasing. The benefits outweigh the negatives, but the challenges should not be ignored. The brief discussion that follows lists some of those benefits and challenges.

Benefits

Most of the benefits of cooperative purchasing have historically revolved around saving time and money, as previously noted. However, an added benefit today is that technical expertise may be developed and shared across public entities to deal with the many challenges that purchases of complicated commodities and services pose for individual public entities:

- Cooperative contracts generally produce lower prices due to the greater volumes purchased under them. Cooperative contracts are especially advantageous for small public entities because they benefit from the market share leveraged by larger ones.
- Cooperative contracts often provide greater assurance that commodities and services purchased under them will be of high quality. That results from using the best-suited, specialized specification writers, public procurement officers, and technical evaluation committee members through public entities' sharing their talents. Again, this is particularly helpful for small public entities.
- Cooperative contracts play a key role today in providing complex information technologies. Chapter 20 (*Procurement of Information Technology*) discusses this in more detail.
- The ability to use or share public procurement officers among public entities allows for reallocation of internal resources.
- With one procurement process and one contract serving multiple public entities, cooperative contracts reduce administrative costs by spreading them across multiple governments.
- Cooperative contracts are convenient. Instead of seeking quotes, bids, or proposals, public entities simply select commodities and services from the cooperative

contract catalog, saving considerable time and effort.
- Ultimately, citizens benefit from cooperative procurement through lower total cost of government, better application of resources, and more efficient government operations.

Challenges

Although there are many examples of successful government cooperative purchasing programs, there are pitfalls and challenges.

Legal Compliance

Most governments operate under some form of procurement law intended to: achieve best value for citizens; protect against fraud and abuse; ensure fairness, equity, and transparency; and maintain public trust. Although most procurement laws are similar, there are often subtle but significant differences in them. Some public entities require strict compliance with their own procurement laws when using cooperative contracts awarded by other public entities. Communication and active participation in the procurement process by cooperative members helps the cooperative achieve universal compliance.

Buy-Local Laws

Many public entities have laws that favor or give preference to local suppliers. These laws may interfere with the ability of a public entity to develop and award a cooperative contract, or may prevent it from using a cooperative contract.

Open Competition

Many public entities' procurement programs maintain lists of suppliers who register with them to compete for contracting opportunities. Their laws often require them to notify those suppliers of procurement opportunities and to post public advertisements when solicitations are issued. To ensure compliance with such requirements, it is best for the public entity to take those steps where it wishes to participate in a cooperative procurement being led by another public entity.

Small Business Participation

Some small businesses may be able to handle business for one state or local government, but may not be able to deal with the combined requirements of multiple governments. Encouraging local delivery and service networks and utilization of small business subcontractors under a cooperative contract provides opportunities for small businesses to continue to serve the members of the cooperative.

Cherry-Picking

The existence of multiple cooperative contracts for similar commodities and services among multiple cooperative organizations permits public entities to shop those contracts until they find one with their preferred suppliers or brand names. That activity skirts around free and open competition. In addition, public entities may compare different cooperatives and their contracts for the same commodity or service and choose the cheapest one. This can pose a challenge to contractors when customers buy only the bargain items in large quantities.

Battle of the Forms/Terms

Although most are similar, public entities use unique contract terms and conditions and purchase order terms. A cooperative contract awarded by one public entity may not conform to the terms and conditions of another.

There are several methods for addressing contractual differences, including development of standard terms and conditions among cooperative members, inclusion of public entity members' term variations in the solicitation, and negotiation of participation agreements between the particular public entity and the contractor.

Pricing

Although most cooperative contracts generate considerable cost savings for public entities, not all cooperative contracts achieve best value. Potential purchasers should be attentive to situations such as the following:

- If estimates in the solicitation are inaccurate, price may be based on an estimate that is much lower than actual usage. Pricing is much more likely to be unfavorable in contracts where significant piggyback purchasing occurs, because usage is difficult to estimate beforehand.
- Contractors may offer a high price because many of the cooperative members are small or located in remote areas.
- A contractor may price the contract high because of administrative costs associated with the cooperative, including collection of the cooperative's administrative fees.

Time and Resources

It takes more effort to award a contract that serves multiple public entities than it does for a contract that serves only one government. In theory, the time and resource investments for a cooperative procurement for the lead public entity are likely recovered when that public entity in turn uses other cooperative contracts for which it is not the lead. Time and resource requirements can also be reduced by using procurement and technical experts from other public entities to assist with the cooperative procurement.

Lack of Collaboration

For state government cooperative purchasing, it is imperative that all states belonging to the cooperative participate in a cooperative purchase to assure the best chance for success. Full participation is not always the case, and some states may even establish a competing statewide contract. Among other things, that refusal to join in a particular cooperative purchase lessens the leverage power of the resulting cooperative contract by reducing estimated volumes. It also opens the door for cherry-picking between the statewide contract and the multistates' cooperative contract. Every effort should be made to solicit full participation by state, local, and higher education entities.

Fees

As noted earlier, many cooperatives charge a fee on each purchase made from a cooperative contract. It these fees are too high, it reduces the incentive to use the contract.

FEDERAL GOVERNMENT COOPERATIVE PURCHASING ISSUES

Piggybacking Restrictions

In 2013, revisions were made to the governing regulations in federally funded programs. In these regulations, known as Uniform Guidance, the OMB *Super Circular*, or *Omni Circular*, the intent was to streamline government by integrating a variety of Office of Management and Budget circulars and federal agency regulations known as the Common Rule.[19] The following is a summary of the requirements affecting procurements and contracts funded with federal funds as they relate to cooperative purchasing.

The Common Rule prescribes specific standards for procurements of commodities and services by state and local governments using federal grant funds. Its provisions are discussed in other chapters of this 3rd Edition of *State & Local Government: A Practical* Guide, including Chapter 5 (*Non-Construction Specifications and Scopes of Work*) and Chapter 10 (*Contracting for Services*).

While the Common Rule was intended to create one set of compliance requirements for all federal grants, there may be additional requirements. Those prescribed by the Federal Transit Administration (FTA) are one example.

The FTA imposes some restrictions on the practice of piggybacking. Where local governments are not part of a state government's cooperative procurement program, procurements by local governments commonly characterized as piggybacking are treated as *assignments* under FTA regulations. Assignments are only permitted where the state's original solicitation reflected current and reasonably expected needs, but some amount of the published estimate is no longer needed. The FTA permits assignment of that unneeded contract requirement to another government; this is more restrictive than piggybacking.

On its *frequently asked questions* web page, the FTA states the following:[20]

> "Piggybacking" is defined as "the postaward use of a contractual document/process that allows someone who was not contemplated in the original procurement to purchase the same supplies/equipment through that original document/process." The circumstances when piggybacking is permissible:
>
> The solicitation and contract include an assignability clause that allows for the assignment of all or part of the specified deliverable items.
>
> The quantities to be ordered were included in the original bid and evaluated as part of the contract award decision. Note that "piggybacking" is not permissible when the action would call for an increase in quantities that were not originally bid on and not originally evaluated as part of the contract award. Such an order for additional quantities would constitute a non-competitive procurement. This practice is sometimes referred to as "tag-ons." Such non-competitive procurements would have to be processed as such and approved through the grantee's official approval chain.
>
> The contract being accessed by the piggybacking procedure must contain the clauses required by Federal regulations.[21] FTA Circular 4220.1F, Appendix D, defines the required contract clauses by type and dollar value of procurement.

The FTA publishes a *Best Practices Procurement Manual* that explains the permissible use of piggybacking. The FTA requirements emphasize the importance of being familiar with the laws relating to purchasing with federal funds, in addition to the Common Rule.

A Word about GSA Schedules

The United States General Services Administration (GSA) maintains a large list of multiple award purchasing schedules.[22] Contractors are selected for GSA multiple award schedules through an open and continuous qualification process instead of using formal competition methods—competitive sealed bids or competitive sealed proposals.[23]

If a public entity's law authorizes cooperative purchasing only where the cooperative contracts are competed through a formal competitive process, the legal authority to use GSA contracts is doubtful. In order to avoid that legal issue, some states have adopted specific laws permitting the use of GSA schedules. One is the State of Arizona, whose law is as follows:[24]

> 41-2558. <u>General services administration contracts</u>
> Notwithstanding [requirements for competitive sealed bidding and competitive sealed proposals], the director or the director's designee may evaluate general services administration contracts for materials and services. The director or the director's designee may authorize a purchasing agency to make purchases under a contract approved by the director or the director's designee without complying with the requirements [for competitive sealed bidding and competitive sealed proposals], if the director or the director's designee determines all of the following apply:

1. The price is equal to or less than the contractor's current federal supply contract price.
2. The contractor has indicated in writing that the contractor is willing to extend the current federal supply contract pricing, terms, and conditions.
3. The purchase order adequately identifies the federal supply contract on which the order is based.
4. It is cost-effective and in the best interests of this state.

If legal authority exists, public entities using GSA schedules generally seek competition from multiple GSA contractors by obtaining quotations. GSA requires most favored customer pricing, which means that GSA expects its schedule contractors to extend the price advantages they offer to the federal government to state and local governments based on federal purchasing volumes. Many states strategically use the GSA pricing as benchmarks in their own negotiations with suppliers.

GSA contractors may offer discounts for large volumes. Still, public entities having the authority to use GSA schedules should carefully analyze the GSA terms and prices and compare them to other available procurement vehicles, including contracts established by other cooperatives.

A GSA supplier is not obliged to honor a state or local government request to buy from it. A state or local government's purchase from a GSA schedule contractor may also require separate contracting arrangements between the supplier and government entity to accommodate unique legal requirements.

CONCLUSION

Cooperative purchasing is a very effective tool that public procurement officers can use to obtain effective, best-value solutions for public entities and the taxpayer. Aggregated volume creates significant price breaks—sometimes in double-digit percentages. Partnering with a lead entity can reduce time, administrative overhead, and other costs, while taking advantage of the experience and expertise of those with specialized knowledge in a sector.

Knowing and paying attention to best practices and challenges will result in a contract that is beneficial for all participants through cost savings and a reduction in time to procure items by aggregating knowledge, spend, and technology. Not only are savings achieved by combining requirements into cooperative contracts, but further cost savings are realized through a reduction in administrative expenses. Cooperative contracts may also serve as a forum for professional development and exchange and sharing of resources and technical information.

With state and local government budgets being stretched to the limit, it is essential that Chief Procurement Officers look for innovative ways to utilize taxpayer dollars efficiently and effectively. Cooperative purchasing is a logical and practical way to do this. By establishing solid cooperative purchasing processes and procedures, maintaining clear channels of communication, and working together closely, state and local governments can create a win-win situation for taxpayers and suppliers.

ENDNOTES

1. There is a type of construction contract called *job order contracting* that is often a cooperative contract, and it is covered in Chapter 11, *Procurement of Construction and Related Services*.
2. https://www.nigp.org/home/find-procurement-resources/dictionary-of-terms
3. Section 10-101(1). The Model Procurement Code uses the term *Public Procurement Unit* generally to refer to the state, any political subdivision of the state or other public entity in that state, other states and their political subdivisions, federal government

agencies, as well as to a not-for-profit entity comprised of more than one of those public entities. See Section 10-101(4).
4. "[An] *indefinite quantity and delivery* [contract] is used to establish a minimum and maximum quantity that can be ordered within a definite delivery period. This contract requirement is flexible in terms of both quantity and delivery schedule." NIGP Dictionary. https://www.nigp.org/home/find-procurement-resources/dictionary-of-terms.
5. "The Internet of Things (IoT): the networking capability that allows information to be sent to and received from objects and devices (such as fixtures and kitchen appliances) using the Internet." Merriam-Webster Dictionary. https://www.merriam-webster.com/dictionary/Internet%20of%20Things
6. https://www.naspo.org/2018Survey
7. http:// www.naspovaluepoint.org
8. http://www.mmd.admin.state.mn.us/mmcap/
9. https://www.sourcewell-mn.gov/
10. http://www.uscommunities.org/about/
11. https://www.omniapartners.com/
12. https://www.eandi.org/
13. https://www.mhec.org/
14. https://www.wiche.edu/
15. http://www.nebhe.org/
16. https://www.sreb.org/
17. https://ncppassociation.org/
18. *Strength in Numbers: An Introduction to Cooperative Procurements.* NASPO Issue Brief. (pp. 9–10). www.naspo.org/dnn/portals/16/documents/Cooperative_Purchasing 0410update.pdf
19. The Common Rule may be found at: https://www.gpo.gov/fdsys/pkg/CFR-2017-title2-vol1/pdf/CFR-2017-title2-vol1-part200.pdf
20. https://www.transit.dot.gov/funding/procurement/third-party-procurement/piggybacking
21. These clauses are discussed in the FTA Best Practices Procurement Manual, Appendix A.1. https://www.transit.dot.gov/funding/procurement/third-party-procurement/best-practices-procurement-manual
22. https://www.gsa.gov/acquisition/purchasing-programs/gsa-schedules/state-and-local-government-customers
23. The qualification process is described in *Beginner's Guide to GSA Schedule Contracts* at: http://gsa.federalschedules.com/wp-content/uploads/2017/02/Beginners-Guide-to-GSA-Schedule-Contracts-Federal-Schedules-Inc.pdf
24. https://www.azleg.gov/viewdocument/?docName=https://www.azleg.gov/ars/41/02558.htm

CHAPTER 13: QUALITY ASSURANCE

RECOMMENDED BEST PRACTICES

- There must be a quality assurance manual in place that provides an internal roadmap for user agency personnel and public procurement officers, setting forth their roles and responsibilities as well as a consistent set of quality assurance-related definitions, quality assurance procedures, and actions to take when a contractor fails to perform as the contract requires.
- Quality assurance should also be part of any contract administration plan prepared for specific contracts.
- The central procurement office should have a training program in place to assist user agency personnel in understanding their role in quality assurance.
- Quality assurance should be a topic in market research discussions with industry, so that public procurement officers may become familiar with quality standards and oversight practices that might be valuable to the government.
- Quality assurance begins with a solicitation that contains an accurate and well-written description of the item desired and, more important, what it is supposed to do.
- The solicitation must also contain relevant and precise evaluation criteria so that the best contractor may be selected. Additionally, the solicitation should in appropriate instances establish particular criteria requiring competing suppliers to demonstrate their knowledge, such as minimum experience requirements.
- To avoid confusion about what warranties apply, and to make warranties expressed and not implied, a solicitation's terms should include language that restates Uniform Commercial Code (UCC) warranty language so that the warranties become an express part of the resulting contract.
- The right to conduct testing of commodities, including first article testing, must be specified in both the solicitation for the item to be tested and in the contract along with the details of how the testing will be conducted and evaluated.
- The solicitation should contain measurable performance standards that the selected contractor must attain during performance.
- Quality assurance should be part of any written contract administration plan.

CHAPTER 13: QUALITY ASSURANCE

This chapter focuses on the quality assurance tools that must be available to a public procurement officer and a user agency. Quality assurance starts with writing solicitation terms that permit the public procurement officer to evaluate a commodity or service during a procurement, such as through testing or supplier site visits. Assuring quality also requires the development of contract terms and contract administration procedures that define some of the steps that the public entity will take to confirm that what the contractor supplies is consistent with the contract.

DEFINITIONS AND OVERVIEW

A simple definition of *quality assurance* appears in federal regulations that apply to state transportation departments' use of federal funds for highway construction:

> *All those planned and systematic actions necessary to provide confidence that a product or service will satisfy given requirements for quality.*[1]

Quality assurance consists of steps that public entities must take to *provide confidence* that quality will be obtained. Contrast that with the definition of *quality control*, which is the responsibility of the supplier:

> *All contractor/vendor operational techniques and activities that are performed or conducted to fulfill the contract requirements.*[2]

Quality assurance is an unstated but overarching objective of each step of the procurement process leading to contract award. A public procurement officer must ask the question "how may quality assurance be achieved" at the outset of every procurement.

Formal quality assurance programs, featuring quality assurance manuals and testing staff and facilities, have waned in the last 50 years, or since the earliest version of this *State & Local Government: A Practical Guide* (*Practical Guide*) was first published. Possible reasons are: budget cuts and lack of resources; increase in the purchase of commercial items over that period of time by state and local public entities; and product information available online. However, quality assurance is and will continue to be an important aspect of a high-functioning public procurement office. The example provided in the callout in this chapter entitled *Quality in the Crossfire* demonstrates that importance.

Quality assurance starts with narratives in a solicitation and contract that feature the precise description of the commodity or service sought along with the metrics by which the contractor and the commodity or service that it supplies will be evaluated. As the definition suggests, *requirements for quality* cannot be left to chance. Achieving quality requires adherence to the best practices that are discussed in several chapters of this *Practical Guide*. For instance:

- For quality assurance as a topic in market research discussions with industry in order to understand quality standards and oversight practices that might be valuable to the government, see Chapter 4 (*Strategies and Plans*).
- For guidance on writing the critical descriptions of items desired, which will serve as the basis of the competition, see Chapter 5 (*Non-Construction Specifications and Scopes of Work*).
- For a discussion on composing a solicitation that contains relevant and precise evaluation criteria and that establishes particular criteria requiring competing suppliers to demonstrate their knowledge, see Chapter 7 (*Competition: Solicitations and Methods*).
- For ideas about how to write a solicitation that contains measurable performance standards that the selected contractor must achieve during performance, see Chapter 10 (*Contracting for Services*) and Chapter 20 (*Procurement of Information Technology*).

QUALITY IN THE CROSSFIRE[1]

During the summer of 2003 in Forest Hills, Pennsylvania, a bullet resistant vest made by a manufacturer—constructed using multiple layers of fabric woven from a particular yarn—suffered a bullet penetration, injuring a police officer. The incident was the first case reported to the National Institute of Justice (NIJ) in which NIJ-compliant body armor appeared to fail to prevent penetration from a bullet it was designed to defeat. As the vest manufacturer—an ISO 9001 certified company[2]—characterized the issue in its press release, the synthetic yarn was flawed.

The objective of product assurance is to achieve an acceptable quality and the right to demand remediation when a product is defective. The NIJ recognizes the wisdom of defining inspection and acceptance protocols in large quantity purchases, but it implied in its guide that routine inspection of vests by testing is inadvisable.

Why is routine testing inadvisable? Because the attributes that define nonconformity, other than some workmanship characteristics that can be evaluated by visual inspection, are measured by destructive performance testing in accordance with a prescribed testing protocol that uses samples. Requiring NIJ testing in conjunction with each delivery of a vest would be cost prohibitive. So what the NIJ offers the law enforcement community is a qualified product list approach by publishing products on its Personal Body Armor Consumer Product List (CPL) where they meet NIJ compliance testing standards.

Compliance certification represents a finding of compliance with the NIJ standard at a single point in time. In May 2004, in response to questions about the warranties and service life of vests, the State of Colorado initiated a multistate cooperative procurement aimed at validating the acceptability of delivered vests against the criteria in the NIJ standard. The expectation was that actual finished products, e.g., *out of the box*, would be submitted for testing, instead of relying on testing of pre-production samples submitted by manufacturers. The Colorado solicitation was intended to eliminate the effect of variation between design models tested by NIJ and actual production models. But it still was unclear how samples would be tested and the effect of failures of these non-NIJ tests on acceptability of the entire, sampled lots.

Ballistic Resistance of Body Armor NIJ Standard-0101.06 was issued in 2008 to improve the testing. The certification now is based on a four-fold increase in numbers of production samples. Notably, the new standard also added environmental conditioning, including "tumbling," over 10 days at high temperature and humidity to simulate adverse field conditions as part of the certification. Colorado's Body Armor cooperative master agreement adopts and does not add to the NIJ standard.

---

[1] This example has been reproduced for use by NASPO. The content originally appeared in *Legal Aspects of Public Procurement* published by NIGP.
[2] The International Organization for Standardization establishes quality standards. It describes the 9000 series standards as follows: *The ISO 9000 family addresses various aspects of quality management and contains some of ISO's best known standards. The standards provide guidance and tools for companies and organizations who want to ensure that their products and services consistently meet customer's requirements, and that quality is consistently improved.* The ISO website address for its 9000 standards is: https://www.iso.org/iso-9001-quality-management.html

- For quality assurance that is part of a written contract administration plan, see Chapter 12 (*Contract Management and Contract Administration*).
- For information about using the contract administration tools that are part of many eProcurement systems, see Chapter 19 (*eProcurement*).

AUTHORITY TO ESTABLISH QUALITY ASSURANCE PROGRAMS

Effective public entity-wide quality assurance requires leadership. Applicable law should accord the Chief Procurement Officer the authority to create standards and tools to implement a quality assurance program within his or her public entity. The American Bar Association Model Procurement Code for State and Local Governments (Model Procurement Code) provides an example of statutory language that establishes that leadership:[3]

> **§2-204 Authority of the Chief Procurement Officer**
> (3) Duties
> Except as otherwise specifically provided in this Code, the Chief Procurement Officer shall, in accordance with regulations:
> (d) establish and maintain programs for the inspection, testing, and acceptance of supplies, services, and construction;

The Model Procurement Code also provides the authority to inspect the plant or place of business of a contractor or subcontractor[4] and to audit cost or pricing data books and records, and books and records of a contractor or subcontractor under any negotiated contract or subcontract.[5]

In the absence of language in a statute or ordinance that grants the Chief Procurement Officer broad authority to establish quality assurance programs, there is much that can be implemented through manuals, solicitations, and contract and purchase order terms. This chapter addresses those methods.

QUALITY ASSURANCE PROGRAMS

Although the authority to establish a public entity-wide quality assurance program must reside with the Chief Procurement Officer, it is often the primary responsibility of the user agency to implement the critical steps of any program, coordinating with the public procurement officer who awarded the contract when supplier problems arise. This coordination is critical.

Practical guidance on the steps to take when a user agency receives commodities under a contract can be found in the State Contracting Manual of the California Department of General Services:[6]

> Departmental receiving and/or designated staff (dependent upon the goods received and whether or not staff with specialized expertise is necessary), should, upon acknowledging delivery of an order, conduct an inspection for the following minimum conditions:
> - Verify that what was ordered conforms to purchase document documentation (Statement of Work, specifications, attachments, etc.), including the product description, model, brand, and product numbers.
> - Verify the quantity ordered against the quantity shipped or delivered.
> - Inspect for damage or breakage.
> - Check for operability/functionality.
> - Confirm instructions regarding special handling or packaging were followed.
> - Verify that the unit of measurement count is correct (e.g., if the unit of measurement on the purchase document is one dozen, count 12 in the unit package).

- *Verify that delivery documentation (packing slip, certifications, etc.) is acceptable.*
- *Verify that packaging integrity is preserved (no leakages, damages, etc.).*
- *Verify that perishable items are in good condition and expiration dates have not been exceeded.*

Under the quality assurance program of the State of Oklahoma, these are some of the verifications recommended as first steps:

- Quantity ordered versus quantity received
- Correct product received
- Contract price versus price charged on delivery
- Product damaged
- On-time delivery
- Lead-time compliance (such as where the contract called for 90 days for the police car but the supplier did not deliver until after 120 days) and risk mitigation

While these tasks may seem simple, they are not. This is the point in time that determines whether the public entity retains all of its legal and contractual rights to insist on full contract performance, thus reserving its contractual remedies for failed performance, or dissipates those rights and remedies due to a failure to monitor a contractor's performance to determine that it conforms to the contract. Quality metrics are used to ensure that user agencies receive suitable commodities or services. They directly translate the needs of user agencies into acceptable performance measures that determine a contractor's compliance with the contract.

These matters should not be left to chance or to a lawyer's interpretation of a state's laws relating to contracts. The best practice is to maintain a quality assurance manual that provides a roadmap for user agencies and public procurement officers; sets forth roles and responsibilities; and includes a consistent set of definitions, quality assurance procedures, and actions to take when a contractor fails to perform as the contract requires. The Commonwealth of Pennsylvania has quality assurance standards and procedures in place.[7] Some of the guidance provided in the handbook maintained by its Bureau of Procurement are:

- Distinguishes among nonperforming breach, a partial performance breach, and a nonconforming breach
- Defines what *delivery* means related to contracts for commodities
- Specifies the standards for the time for performance of services
- Identifies what should be done when the contractor fails to deliver or perform
- Establishes the right of the user agency to inspect the commodities or services delivered
- Specifies what the term *acceptance* means relating to receiving a commodity or service
- Sets forth the right to test the commodities
- Sets forth the right to reject the commodities or services
- Sets forth the right to revoke the acceptance of commodities or services after the time that the user agency has legally accepted them
- Sets forth the measure of damages for breach of warranty and nonconforming delivery or untimely performance

The Commonwealth of Pennsylvania has a quality assurance division that is part of the Bureau of Procurement within the Department of General Services. At the publication of this *Practical Guide*, the division is staffed by 10 persons.[8]

Another example of a state that maintains a useful set of written quality assurance standards and procedures is the State of California. Chapter 10 of the State Contracting Manual, Volume 2, addresses receipt, inspection, acceptance, or rejection of non-information-technology commodities.[9] Table 13.1 from the manual demonstrates the process of receiving commodities with quality assurance in mind.

CHAPTER 13: QUALITY ASSURANCE

Another schematic from the manual, shown in Table 13.2, outlines the steps that should be taken when the user agency receives commodities that do not conform to the requirements of the purchase document (that is, the contract or the purchase order).

Table 13.1

Term	Definition
Receiving	The act of taking possession of commodities in order to stage them for inspection or place them into inventory. *Caution*: placing commodities into inventory without inspection may waive future inspection rights and remedies.
Inspecting	The act of examining commodities that have been delivered to determine conformance to what was ordered via the purchase document. In some cases, the acquisition may require specialized skills or expertise in examining the commodities to determine conformance.
Acceptance testing	The act of testing what is purchased, either all items delivered, or the first item delivered or by random sampling of some or all items delivered. Testing determines that the commodities purchased are in conformance to the contract requirements as stated in the solicitation and purchase documents and the supplier's and/or manufacturer's published technical specification, and that the commodities perform to a satisfactory level.
Acceptance	The legal act of documenting that the commodities and/or services conform to the requirements of the purchase document terms and conditions.

Table 13.2

Stage	Description
1	The person rejecting the commodities must immediately communicate the problem(s) and rejection in writing to the buyer.
2	The buyer is responsible for notifying the supplier within a reasonable time after delivery or tender under Uniform Commercial Code (UCC) 2-602, making arrangements to hold the rejected commodities somewhere protected from damage, and taking reasonable care of rejected commodities until the supplier can take possession of the commodities and remove them from the site.
3	The buyer is responsible for providing a notice of rejection letter to the supplier describing the defect(s) that renders the delivery as nonconforming to the purchase document, what the delivery and inspection criterion was, and how the delivered product does not conform.
4	The buyer can accept any unit of measure (e.g., lot, case, and pallet) and reject the rest (UCC 2-601). Example: a department executed a purchase document for 50 cases of bond paper, but the supplier shipped 150 cases of bond paper. The receiving staff may either reject the entire shipment or accept the 50 cases of bond paper in accordance with the provisions of the purchase document. The remaining 100 cases of paper will be rejected and returned to the supplier.
5	If the supplier, within a reasonable time period or as stated in the purchase documents, does not remove rejected commodities, the department buyer may: • Ship products back to the supplier at the supplier's expense • Store the rejected commodities with reimbursement required from the supplier for any incurred costs

A WORD ABOUT ARTICLE 2 OF THE UNIFORM COMMERCIAL CODE

As can be seen from the previous discussion, quality assurance is comprised in part of *inspection*, *rejection*, *acceptance*, and *revocation*. These are terms of art with legal ramifications. These are key terms representing milestones under Article 2 of the UCC, which applies to the sale of *goods* by a *merchant* to someone or some entity.[10] Fourteen States have adopted Article 2 essentially in whole, including the State of California. Research suggests that most other states have adopted laws similar to Article 2.

The Commonwealth of Pennsylvania has adopted a law similar to Article 2. Its law uses UCC terminology despite not adopting Article 2, and goes beyond Article 2 by applying these same key terms in many cases to the purchase of both services and commodities.

For states that have adopted Article 2, the UCC provides default provisions governing inspection and acceptance, rejection and revocation of acceptance, implied warranties, and remedies for the buyer and seller, including a public entity contractor as the seller, and a public entity as the buyer. A buyer and seller can modify the UCC provisions through a contract or purchase order. Whether a state has adopted the UCC or not, it should create a quality assurance manual that includes in the narrative a clear and concise definition of the meanings of key terms.

Following the Commonwealth of Pennsylvania's lead can be advantageous, since the more the quality assurance manual can establish a common set of standards for both commodities and services, the easier it will be to utilize for the user agency. Once the quality assurance manual is created, it is important to codify the public entity's rights and remedies in the standard terms of the public entity's solicitations and in other contract documents such as purchase order terms.

As a point of reference, the following is some of the UCC's language encompassing the key terms:

§2-513. **Buyer's Right to Inspection of Goods.**
(1) Unless otherwise agreed . . . , where goods are tendered or delivered or identified to the contract for sale, the buyer has a right before payment or acceptance to inspect them at any reasonable place and time and in any reasonable manner. When the seller is required or authorized to send the goods to the buyer, the inspection may be after their arrival. . . .

§2-602. **Manner and Effect of Rightful Rejection.**
(1) Rejection of goods must be within a reasonable time after their delivery or tender. It is ineffective unless the buyer reasonably notifies the seller.

§2-606. **What Constitutes Acceptance of Goods.**
(1) Acceptance of goods occurs when the buyer:
  (a) after a reasonable opportunity to inspect the goods, signifies to the seller that the goods are conforming or that he will take or retain them in spite of their nonconformity; or
  (b) fails to make an effective rejection . . . but such acceptance does not occur until the buyer has had a reasonable opportunity to inspect them; or
  (c) does any act inconsistent with the seller's ownership; but if such act is wrongful as against the seller it is an acceptance only if ratified by him.
(2) Acceptance of a part of any commercial unit is acceptance of that entire unit.

§2-608. Revocation of Acceptance in Whole or in Part.
(1) The buyer may revoke his acceptance of a lot or commercial unit whose nonconformity substantially impairs its value to him if he has accepted it:
    (a) on the reasonable assumption that its nonconformity would be cured and it has not been seasonably cured; or
    (b) without discovery of such nonconformity if his acceptance was reasonably induced either by the difficulty of discovery before acceptance or by the seller's assurances.
(2) Revocation of acceptance must occur within a reasonable time after the buyer discovers or should have discovered the ground for it and before any substantial change in condition of the goods which is not caused by their own defects. It is not effective until the buyer notifies the seller of it.

In the interest of promoting a clear understanding of these terms and ease of use, it is better for a quality assurance manual to define these key terms in language that is user-friendly and features as little *legalese* as possible.

There is another feature of the UCC that should be part of any quality assurance program: warranties. A warranty is a promise that is legally enforceable.[11] Warranties are intended to protect a buyer against poor workmanship and defects. They come into effect once the public entity has accepted a commodity and generally require the contractor to repair or replace it without cost during the warranty's duration. Warranties may be expressly written or implied. The existence of warranties may mitigate some risk of defects that do not appear at the time of acceptance.

The UCC establishes two implied[12] warranties that apply to the sale of commodities: *merchantability* or fitness of the commodities for the use that the supplier describes generally to the public; and *fitness for a particular purpose*, that is, the commodities are suitable for the purpose that the buyer has specifically described to the seller. The UCC specifies the remedies the buyer has if the seller breaches a contract by providing commodities that do not perform according to the contract, including meeting the terms of a warranty.

To avoid confusion about which warranties apply and how they differ among suppliers, and to make warranties express and not implied, a solicitation's terms should include language that restates the UCC warranty language, so that the warranties become an express part of the resulting contract. Language similar to the following is not unusual:

By submitting a bid or proposal under this solicitation or purchase order, the bidder or offeror warrants that any commodities provided will:
- *Pass without objection in the trade under the solicitation description*
- *In the case of fungible commodities, are of fair average quality within the description*
- *Are fit for the ordinary purposes for which commodities of that description are used*
- *Run, within the variations permitted by the contract, of even kind, quality, and quantity within each unit and among all units involved*
- *Are adequately contained, packaged, and labeled as the contract may require*
- *Conform to the promise or affirmations of fact made on the container or label, if any*

Additionally, where the bidder or offeror at the time of contracting has reason to know any particular purpose for which the commodities are required and that the government is relying on the bidder's or offeror's skill or judgment to select or furnish suitable commodities, the bidder or offeror warrants that the commodities shall be fit for such purpose.

CHAPTER 13: QUALITY ASSURANCE

NON-UCC WARRANTIES

Manufacturer and Dealer Warranties

Manufacturers and dealers often offer warranties of their own. Express supplier warranties may be more limited than those under the UCC, and they often have explicit time limits (for example, 90 days or one year). Their terms typically define what the warranty covers, how the warranty is invoked, and the remedies for breach. The remedies often are made exclusive—that is, the language of the warranty states that there are no warranties other than the one provided, including none of the UCC warranties. They may also place dollar limits on the financial obligation of the manufacturer or dealer in trying to meet the warranties. Additionally, written manufacturer or dealer warranties often exclude the UCC's implied warranties of merchantability and fitness for a particular purpose.

Given those limits, express warranties may or may not be helpful in assuring quality. It is better to have a robust inspection program so that defects and nonconformities in commodities are identified when the public entity has more remedies. Remedies decrease once the public entity accepts the commodities.

Service Contract Warranties

Suppliers or contractors providing services generally do not offer warranties. Even though the UCC's Article 2 does not apply to them, they often include language in their bids, proposals, or forms stating that they are not providing any warranties, and that any warranties are explicitly excluded, often with the language in all capital letters.

It is important for the public procurement officer to include warranty language in any solicitation for services. Chapter 10 (*Contracting for Services*) discusses this subject in more detail.

OTHER WAYS OF SUPPORTING QUALITY ASSURANCE

Off-Site Evaluation of Supplier Quality Programs

Evaluation of the quality program of potential contractors during the competitive selection process may help avoid unhappy surprises once the contract is in place. In most instances, however, a public entity procurement office will not have a full-fledged quality assurance team available to examine competing suppliers' quality programs at the suppliers' sites during a competition for a contract.

Additionally, state and local public entities often purchase commercial commodities, that is, commodities that are available to the public generally, such as desktop computers. In doing so, the public entity is assuming that the public will walk away from a poorly performing product and that the supplier's or the product's track record will be commonly known and readily available during market research.

Those barriers should not hinder a public procurement office from asking competing suppliers to supply information as part of their submissions under a solicitation about both their quality programs and quality evaluations of their commodities. That may not be necessary for the procurement of pencils, for instance, but the public procurement officer should ask the question as he or she prepares a solicitation.

Quality Assurance Plans

Quality assurance plans are prepared as part of a pre-solicitation phase and focus on the item to be tested during contract performance. If there is going to be a written contract administration plan for contract performance, the quality assurance plan should be part of that larger plan.

The quality assurance plan typically answers the following questions:

- What will be inspected?
- When will the inspection take place?
- What monitoring methods will be used?
- How will performance be evaluated and assessed?
- How will performance be accepted?
- Who is responsible for each activity?

The use of quality assurance plans is not widespread by state and local public entities. But these types of plans are required in some cases for certain procurements using federal funds. The United States Federal Highway Administration and the Environmental Protection Agency are two of the funding agencies that require plans or programs.[13]

First Article Inspection or Testing

First article testing is a specific type of testing aimed at assuring that a commodity, particularly a noncommercial one, is suitable for the public entity's needs before full-scale production begins. In instances where federal funding is involved, first article testing is required for the purchase of items such as light rail cars.

The Federal Acquisition Regulation—the body of regulations that implements the federal government's procurement system—provides a good summary of the conditions in which first article testing/inspection should be used:[14]

> **9.303 Use.**
> Testing and approval may be appropriate when—
> (a) The contractor has not previously furnished the product to the Government;
> (b) The contractor previously furnished the product to the Government, but—
>   (1) There have been subsequent changes in processes or specifications;
>   (2) Production has been discontinued for an extended period of time; or
>   (3) The product acquired under a previous contract developed a problem during its life;
> (c) The product is described by a performance specification; or
> (d) It is essential to have an approved first article to serve as a manufacturing standard

Subpart 9.3—First Article Testing and Approval [of the Federal Acquisition Regulation] offers a description of how a first-article testing program operates. The right to conduct first article testing must be specified both in the solicitation for the item to be tested and in the contract, along with the details of how the testing will be conducted and evaluated.

Inspections and Testing Generally

Research suggests that supplier-site testing and testing by state and local public entities is not a general practice. With commercial product/service procurement representing a large part of the items that state and local governments purchase, the need to have those capabilities has not been considered pressing.

However, the right to do so should be preserved. The Commonwealth of Virginia has done so in its Suppliers Manual at Section 7.10, which states:[15]

> **Inspection.** All materials, equipment, supplies, and services are subject to inspection and testing. Items or services that do not meet specifications may be rejected. Failure to reject upon receipt, however, does not relieve the contractor of liability for latent or hidden defects subsequently revealed when goods are put to use or tested. If latent defects are found, the contractor is responsible for replacing the defective goods within the delivery time originally stated in the solicitation and is liable for any resulting expenses incurred by the state.

Quality Assurance Under a Best Value Procurement

There is a source selection approach that is generally conducted as a type of competitive sealed proposal called best value procurement or performance information procurement. Under this approach, quality assurance is primarily the responsibility of the contractor since the proposal that the offeror/contractor submitted to be awarded the contract was significantly limited. Chapter 7 (*Competition: Solicitations and Methods*) and Chapter 20 (*Procurement of Information Technology*) provide descriptions of this approach.

CONCLUSION

Quality assurance is both a key part of procurement planning (the process of competing to award a contract) and contract management after award. Quality considerations should be part of market research, solicitation development, writing of specifications and scopes of work, proposal evaluation, and contract administration. Both public procurement officers and user agencies must see quality assurance as a key responsibility.

ENDNOTES

1. See: 23 Code of Federal Regulations §637.203, Definition, at: https://www.ecfr.gov/cgi-bin/text-idx?SID=4f4c8515fcb6873787857e30df84a31b&mc=true&node=pt23.1.637&rgn=div5s
2. See Endnote 1.
3. The Model Procurement Code is available at: http://apps.americanbar.org/dch/committee.cfm?com=PC500500
4. See Section 3-601.
5. See Section 3-602.
6. See State Contracting Manual (SCM), Volume 2, at: http://www.dgs.ca.gov/pd/Resources/publications/SCM2.aspx
7. http://www.dgs.pa.gov/Documents/Procurement%20Forms/Handbook/Pt1/Pt%20I%20Ch%2057%20Contractor%20Performance-Legal%20Remedies%20Materials%20and%20Services.pdf
8. http://www.dgs.pa.gov/Businesses/Materials%20and%20Services%20Procurement/Documents/orgchart.pdf
9. http://www.dgs.ca.gov/pd/Resources/publications/SCM2.aspx
10. https://www.law.cornell.edu/ucc/2
11. See the definition of *warranty* at: http://www.nigp.org/home/find-procurement-resources/dictionary-of-terms
12. They are implied because under the UCC, they exist in the sale of a good even if not explicitly stated. However, they may be waived under certain conditions specified in the UCC.
13. https://arb.ca.gov/aaqm/qa/pqao/repository/qmp_final.pdf and http://www.dot.ca.gov/hq/LocalPrograms/public/QAP_Manual.pdf
14. https://www.acquisition.gov/far/html/Subpart%209_3.html
15. https://dgs.virginia.gov/globalassets/business-units/dps/documents/vendorsmanual/vendors-manual-as-of-12-01-15.pdf

CHAPTER 14: CONTRACT MANAGEMENT AND CONTRACT ADMINISTRATION

RECOMMENDED BEST PRACTICES

- Good contract management begins in the procurement planning and solicitation development stages when risks and responsibilities are identified and addressed.
- The central procurement office should offer regular contract administration training to new public procurement officers as well as users in user agencies.
- Development of a contract administration plan (CAP) is strongly recommended in appropriate instances. It should identify all pre-award and post-award activities and designate the individuals responsible for carrying out the plan.
- For contracts that serve a single user agency, the central procurement authority should ensure that there is a user agency contract administrator designated to oversee day-to-day contract activities.
- The public procurement officer and the user agency contract administrator should meet regularly to evaluate and document the contractor's performance, and to identify any issues that need to be resolved.
- The central procurement office may wish to form a contract administration team composed of the user agency's procurement officer, the user agency contract administrator, primary contract users and other public entity employees whose expertise is useful in managing the contract, such as information technology (IT) and quality assurance personnel. The contract administration team should be involved in the procurement from the development of the specifications to the closeout of the contract.
- Good contract management requires that there be specific procedures in place for making changes to a contract that arise during contract performance and for assuring that any changes are authorized by the public procurement officer.
- Depending on the duration and complexity of the contract, it may be useful to schedule regular contract progress meetings with the contractor.
- Procedures should be in place for the expedient resolution of contract disputes and claims, and should encourage informal resolution while ensuring due process to the contractor.
- User agency contract administrators will maintain their own files relating to the contract that are separate from those that the central procurement office, or even the user agency procurement office, establishes. When closing out the contract, the files of the user agency contract administrator should be provided to the public procurement officer responsible for conducting the procurement and awarding the contract. There should be only one contract file.

CHAPTER 14: CONTRACT MANAGEMENT AND CONTRACT ADMINISTRATION

Contract management and contract administration are often neglected parts of the procurement process. Once a contract is in place, a busy procurement officer may believe that *no news is good news*, surmising that a lack of complaints about contract performance from user agencies is a sign that all is well.

However, effective contract management and contract administration requires vigilance. This chapter is designed to provide public procurement officers with general guidelines and techniques for both. These guidelines offer a consistent early warning system about problems and will enhance the service that public procurement officers offer their user agencies.

Note that this chapter does not address management of construction projects, as there are many resources written on that subject. Additionally, state and local governments generally have staff devoted to the management of those types of projects. While there are some similarities in managing, for instance, a complex IT project and the construction of a bridge, they are sufficiently different to be beyond the scope of this 3rd Edition of *State & Local Government: A Practical Guide* (*Practical Guide*).

DEFINITION OF TERMS

Terminology

It is essential to understand the key terms used in this chapter. The definitions here are from the NIGP Dictionary:[1]

Contract Management
The overarching process that ensures performance in accordance with the performance standards contained within the statement of work or the performance work statement. A quality assurance plan contained within the contract. May include 100 percent inspection, random sampling, periodic inspection, customer input, as well as other methodologies.

Contract Administration
A term used to describe the functions that are performed after the parties have signed the contract (Sherman, 1996). Typical contract administration activities are goal oriented, aimed at ensuring enforcement of the contract terms and conditions while giving attention to the achievement of the stated output and outcome of the contract.

The boundary between contract management and contract administration in public procurement is not a clear one. In the public sector, both terms are often used interchangeably to refer to post-contract-award activities. While the NIGP definition of *contract management* is the oversight of the contract after the public entity awards it, the States of Oregon and Arkansas, for instance, use the term *contract administration* to refer to that oversight.[2] The differences in terms will appear within some of the examples utilized in this chapter. NASPO's *Contract Administration Best Practices Guide* includes links to those states that maintain contract management manuals as of the date that the guide was published.

Within this guide the term *contract management* will be used to describe the overall process related to ensuring the performance of a contract, including pre-solicitation activities through contract closeout. *Contract administration* will be used to specifically describe all activities taking place after the award of the contract.

Importance of Procurement Planning and Solicitation Development to Contract Management

Regardless of the term used, the successful management or administration of a contract once a public entity awards it—and the success of the contract itself—depends in large part on sound and careful planning for the procurement that should have already taken place. The importance of this is apparent in the training document that the State Procurement Office of the State of Hawaii offers, entitled *Contract Management and Administration—An Overview*, which includes the following checklist demonstrating the elements of good procurement planning and thus providing guidelines for contract management:[3]

- *Specifications/scope of work (SOW) is clear*
- *Summary of performance requirements is clear*
- *Evaluation criteria measure what is being asked for*
- *Procurement method is appropriate*
- *Payment is linked to performance*
- *Subcontracting and flow down requirements [from the solicitation/contract to the contractor and its subcontractors] are defined*
- *Performance evaluation is defined*
- *Submission as part of proposal of quality control plan—based on SOW and summary of performance requirements*
- *Risks are identified and planned for*
- *Terms and conditions (T&Cs), general and special conditions, are included in the solicitation*

Many of the chapters of this *Practical Guide* deal with procurement planning and solicitation development.

OVERVIEW OF CONTRACT MANAGEMENT

General Levels of Contract Management

Contract management may be viewed along a continuum depending on the nature of what the contractor is providing and the terms of the contract. Here are some examples:

- Small-dollar contracts will generally require less contract management than large-dollar ones.
- A one-time purchase of a commercial commodity will require less contract management than a one-time purchase of routine services because the contract duration for the latter is longer and the contractor is often on site at the public entity.
- The purchase of noncommercial, special order commodities or non-routine services requires more contract management than the purchase of commercial commodities or routine services.
- The management of a contract awarded for a specific project for a specific user agency will require user agency personnel, who will be working directly with the contractor, to participate officially in managing the contract along with the procurement office that awarded the contract.
- Contract management of indefinite quantity/indefinite delivery contracts that the central procurement office establishes for commodities and services that the public entity regularly uses, such as office supplies, vehicles, temporary employment services, and travel services, will reside primarily with the central procurement office, but with users playing the important role of alerting the central procurement office about any problems with the contractor.
- A contract in which the contractor performs over time to provide the contract end product and which authorizes the contractor to be paid portions of the total contract price during performance requires diligent contract management to ensure that payment is based on deliverables or service levels achieved.

There are other situations that will affect the level of management that a contract requires. In complex IT project procurements, for instance, governance plans include instructions relating to contract management. Chapter 20 (*Procurement of Information Technology*) discusses managing these types of projects, including the contracts, in more detail.

Additionally, a contract awarded using the best value procurement/performance information procurement system approach places the bulk of contract administration responsibilities on the contractor itself. Chapter 7 (*Competition: Solicitations and Methods*) features a description of this approach.

Focus of Contract Administration

The *Contract Administration Best Practices Guide*[4] of the State of Arkansas offers the following as a non-exclusive list of the duties that those in the public entity administering the contract will need to carry out:

- *Understanding the contract terms and conditions including the scope and performance indicators*
- *Monitoring the contractor's progress and performance to ensure goods and services conform to the contract requirements*
- *Receiving and responding to communications between the agency and the contractor*
- *Documenting all actions and maintaining contract-related documents as part of the official contract file*
- *Participating in resolving disputes in a timely manner*
- *Conducting contractor performance evaluations as specified, and closeout activities*
- *Managing changes to contracts (change orders, amendments, addenda, renewals, extensions, termination, etc.)*
- *Maintaining and closing out the contract file*

Those activities encompass more than passively monitoring contractor performance. The person or persons responsible for the administration of the contract must actively manage by taking steps such as verifying that payments to the contractor are correct and based on verified achievement of contract performance measures, and resolving any barriers to successful contract performance that may arise during the contract term. The imperative for contract administration to be actively conducted is reflected in a description in the *Michigan Procurement Policy Manual*, which states that "[c]ontract management is the process of actively managing State contracts to ensure compliance with the requirements of an executed contract."[5]

Finally, successful contract administration requires consistent communication among the public procurement officer who conducted the procurement for the contract, the user agency, the contractor, and anyone else who is part of a contract administration team for the contract.

The Role of the Contract Administrator

Published contract administration guides and manuals often differ as to whom they designate as the *contract administrator*—or the person responsible for monitoring the contract after award. In most instances, the public procurement officer who conducted the procurement and awarded the contract will perform the duties of the contract administrator as well. The *Michigan Procurement Policy Manual* defines the term *contract administrator* to always mean *the purchasing professional. . . .*[6] That manual describes the contract administrator's responsibilities to include:

- *Monitoring the contractor's performance throughout the life of the contract*
- *Scheduling and facilitating progress or performance meetings*
- *Resolving contract performance issues*
- *Maintaining the contract file*

Under that manual's provision, the *program manager* is the representative of the user agency responsible for monitoring of the contract daily. It describes the program manager and his or her responsibilities as follows:

[The program manager is] the individual identified by the business owner,[7] or designee, who is responsible for, including but not limited to, the following:
- *The technical oversight and direction of the day-to-day administration of the contract*
- *Monitoring the contractor's performance throughout the life of the contract, including ensuring that the contractor is meeting all milestones and is in compliance with service levels identified in the contract*
- *Serving as the day-to-day contact for contractor questions, and engaging Contract Administrator's assistance when necessary*
- *Understanding contract and payment terms, including payment stream, early pay discounts, applicable holdbacks, etc.*
- *Reporting to the Contract Administrator contractor's failure to meet service level agreements*
- *Reviewing and approving invoices by ensuring accuracy and alignment with contract payment stream (e.g., milestone and deliverables associated with payment stream)*
- *Understanding what is considered a Minor Contract Issue*[8]
- *Following all steps required to resolve Contract Issues*[9]

It is often a best practice to appoint a user agency employee to serve as contract administrator where the procurement and the contract are for a specific user agency. While the State of Michigan calls that person a *program manager*, the State of Arkansas's *Contract Administration Best Practices Guide* calls that person a *contract administrator* and mandates that the user agency assign one when the initial contract amount or the total projected cost of the contract is equal to or greater than $1,000,000.[10]

The remainder of this chapter uses the term *user agency contract administrator* to refer to the user agency employee designated to serve as the day-to-day administrator of a contract.

It is critical for the public procurement officer to make clear to the user agency contract administrator that he or she does not have authority to make or approve changes to the contract. The appointment of a user agency contract administrator to oversee a contract does not transfer to that employee the procurement and contracting authority of the public procurement officer.

The user agency contract administrator must be involved in the procurement planning process at the earliest stages. That person must be a key part of every step in the procurement process so that he or she has an in-depth knowledge of the contract and the user agency project or program that it supports. This principle is reflected in the State of Hawaii's procurement rules, which require that the contract administrator chair and serve as a member of each committee evaluating proposals under a competitive sealed proposal solicitation.[11]

Clearly, good contract administration requires a close working relationship between the public procurement officer and the user agency that is the beneficiary of the procurement conducted and contract awarded. NASPO's *Contract Administration Best Practices Guide* notes that the public procurement officer and the user agency should work together to determine:

- *Roles and responsibilities and who is responsible for each activity*
- *How performance will be evaluated, including milestones and performance metrics*
- *Monitoring methods*
- *Reporting tools and processes*
- *Process for resolution of disputes and claims*

CONTRACT ADMINISTRATION PLANS

The NIGP Dictionary defines a CAP as follows:

A planning tool that provides the framework for effective contract administration with an emphasis on process, output, and outcome. The length and detail of the contract administration plan depends on the complexity and potential risk of the contract.

CAPs are a must for large, high-dollar contracts for complex projects, but pared-down versions of plans are also useful for other types of contracts. For instance, the management of a large indefinite quantity/indefinite delivery contract for office supplies may benefit from a written CAP.

The CAP should be drafted concurrently with development of the solicitation. NASPO's *Contract Administration Best Practices Guide* lists the critical elements and activities of an effective CAP:

- Selection of contract administration team members
- Justification of solicitation source selection method
- Scope of work or specifications that include deliverables
- Contract goals
- Pricing structure for contract
- Delivery terms and requirements
- Key contract terms and condition to include risk mitigation and information security
- Contract monitoring methods
- How performance will be measured and accepted
- Milestones for measurement (linked to payment terms)
- Payment terms
- Reporting method and frequency
- Documentation required
- Names of contract administration team members responsible for measuring performance, reporting, documenting files, authorizing payment, approving change orders, supervising contract closeout checklist and procedures and overseeing contract closeout files

The Georgia *Procurement Manual* contains a template for a CAP.[12] There is also a checklist for developing a contract monitoring and administration plan in the State of Arkansas *Contract Administration Best Practices Guide.*

STEPS IN CONTRACT ADMINISTRATION

Use of a Contract Administration Team

For some projects, the public procurement officer may need to approach the user agency contract administrator about establishing a steering or contract administration committee to assist in contract administration. The NIGP Dictionary defines a *contract administration team* as follows:

A cross-functional team comprised of such members as the procurement contracting officer, subject matter expert, IT, engineering, legal advisers, price and cost analysts, quality assurance specialists, contracting officer's representative who all offer their expertise to the contract. Such a team is generally used on complex projects. This team may also assist in resolving conflict that arises during the contract performance.

If a team is utilized, its members should attend any kickoff conference. It is also a good practice for the committee to meet regularly and often to effectively monitor administrator contract progress. Any meaningful recommendations by the team should be made after discussions with key personnel significantly involved with the contract, including the public procurement officer, the contractor's representative, and the user agency contract administrator.

A Kickoff Conference

For certain contracts that are high risk or complex, or that affect a large number of user agencies, a best practice is to conduct a pre-performance conference or project *kickoff* meeting with interested parties to the contract. These tend to be informal discussions.

Conferences such as these are important communication tools to use after contract award and before contract performance. Subjects discussed should include roles and responsibilities in determining how contractor performance will be evaluated, documented, and reported; and how best to set performance metrics. A good understanding of the standards of performance helps establish a positive relationship between the public procurement officer, the user agency contract administrator, if applicable, and the contractor. It is imperative that all those attending the conference have an in-depth understanding of the contract.

The *Michigan Procurement Policy Manual* describes a kickoff meeting as:

> . . . a conference of the parties (Contract Administrator, Program Manager, contractor, and other individuals as determined by the parties) who are responsible for administering the contract. The Procurement Executive should decide if a Contract Kickoff Meeting is necessary. If a Contract Kickoff Meeting is necessary, it should be held after the contract award, but before the contractor begins performance.
>
> The Contract Kickoff Meeting can be held in person, by video, or conference call. The Contract Administrator is responsible for scheduling and facilitating the kickoff meeting with the contractor, and recording communications of the meeting on the "Contract Kickoff Meeting Record" form. The Contract Kickoff Meeting Record should be maintained in the contract file.
>
> Prior to the kickoff meeting, the Contract Administrator may conduct a kickoff planning session with the contract Program Manager and appropriate end users.[13]

The State of Arkansas *Contract Administration Best Practices Guide* has a checklist for these meetings that is available online.[14]

Maintaining the Contract File

Documenting activities and maintaining a contract file are good practices to ensure the delivery is in line with the contract requirements and that issues are addressed in a timely fashion. All contract performance issues should be properly documented and included in the official contract file.

The contract file must contain the essential record of contract award and performance. It should include:

- Pre-award documents:
  ◊ Solicitation document
  ◊ All responses to bids or proposals
  ◊ Copy of the contract, including all attachments and amendments
- Post-award to contract closeout documents (contract administration files):
  ◊ Copies of all correspondence with the contractor
  ◊ Notes from all meetings and verbal communications
  ◊ Documentation of performance issues/complaints, cure letters[15]
  ◊ Contract amendments
  ◊ Documentation of deliverables
  ◊ Payment records
  ◊ Contract closeout documentation

Contract Administration Tools

State central procurement offices have developed useful tools for tracking contract performance. For instance, the State of Arkansas *Contract Administration Best Practices Guide* offers the following checklists:[16]

- Contract administration file
- Contract monitoring and administration plan
- Kickoff meeting
- Contract monitoring
- Contract closeout
- Contract validation

The *Georgia Procurement Manual* has several templates for tracking contractor compliance.[17]

eProcurement systems have allowed these tools to be available and used electronically. Given the ease of completing the forms electronically and the greater availability of them to those involved in the management of a contract, the contract management process should become more efficient and effective.

Managing Contract Changes

The importance of a process for managing changes to a contract cannot be overstated. Contract changes are inevitable. The flexibility to make contract amendments for revisions to the contract such as performance times or the scope of work or specifications and associated pricing must be built into the contract language.

As noted earlier in this chapter, the public procurement officer responsible for conducting the procurement and awarding the contract must authorize and sign any contract amendment. This line of authority must always be clear.

Changes must follow these principles:

- Only changes that are within the general scope of the original contract should be accepted
- Changes should be in accordance with the terms of the contract
- Only changes that are due to legitimate unforeseen circumstances should be allowed
- A written determination should be required prior to amending a contract

The CAP should specify the steps and approvals needed to make contract changes.

Contract Progress Meetings

This chapter has already emphasized the importance of communication during the administration of a contract. One vehicle for ensuring communication is the contract progress meeting.

The *Michigan Procurement Policy Manual* describes these meetings as follows:[18]

> A "Contract Progress Meeting" is intended to assist the State and contractor in, including but not limited to, reviewing the Contract Compliance Report, addressing outstanding items on the Issue Tracking Log and Vendor Performance in [the eProcurement system], reviewing overall contract compliance, discuss[ing] market trends that will assist the State in understanding changes in the industry, and solicit[ing] contractor recommendations for increasing contract efficiency and reducing costs. Contract Progress Meetings can be held (in person or by conference call) at any time, but at a minimum the Contract Administrator should hold a Contract Progress Meeting at least yearly. The Contract Administrator, Program Manager, and any individual identified by the parties should participate.

Contract Compliance Reports and Ongoing Reporting

On a regular basis, depending on the length of the contract, the public procurement officer and the user agency contract administrator should evaluate the contractor's performance and document the evaluation. The report should summarize the contractor's performance since the last report. If the report identifies any issues, they should be addressed with the contractor before the report is placed into the contract file.

Contract Issue and Dispute Resolution

A public entity must have contractor issue and dispute resolution procedures and tools in place.

The *Michigan Procurement Policy Manual* contains a good example of an internal issue and dispute resolution process. It is not quoted below but is summarized instead.

> There are two types of contract issues:
>
> A *minor contract issue* is a contract issue that can be easily resolved with a call or e-mail. If the issue has not been resolved within 30 calendar days, or is repetitive, it then becomes a major contract issue.
>
> A *major contract issue* is a minor contract issue that has not been resolved within 30 calendar days, or is repetitive; or it is a contract issue that substantially impacts the performance of the contract, or immediately impacts the needs of the state. Each contract issue should be resolved by the contract administrator and program manager in accordance with the process described as follows:
>
> Step 1—Identify the issues and document them
> Step 2—Evaluate
> Step 3—Discuss with contractor
> *Step 4—Initiate dispute resolution activities identified in the contract*
>
> If the issue is not resolved within the time period identified in the written notice issued during discussions with the contractor, the state must consider additional dispute resolution steps such as issuing a right to cure letter or a stop work order, or terminating the contract. Dispute resolution steps required under the contract must be followed.

Additionally, those procedures must be supported by a set of contract terms that specifies to the contractor how issues and disputes must be resolved. Those terms must also contain a full array of contract remedies available to the public entity if things go dramatically wrong.

They may include:

- Informal dispute resolution through collaboration and negotiation[19]
- Alternative dispute resolution[20]
- Liquidated damages[21]
- Contract termination/cancellation:
  ◊ Termination without cause—mutual consent of both parties
  ◊ Termination for convenience when the contract no longer serves the best interest of the government
  ◊ Termination for default (termination for cause) due to failure to perform, failure to deliver on time, or failure to comply with other terms and conditions. Prior to terminating a contract for default, a cure notice must be sent to the contractor. If the contractor fails to remedy the contract deficiencies identified in the cure notice, the contract may be terminated.

The process of instituting contract remedies is not a simple one. Successful pursuit relies heavily on the existence of good documentation of both the nature of the problem and the opportunities provided to the contractor to remedy it. It also requires that the public entity demonstrate compliance with the notice and disputes procedures that the contract specifies. Unfortunately, the procurement file is often devoid of that documentation, thus the need for the development of the CAP and the quality assurance plan to help ensure the contract files will contain the appropriate documentation to handle any situation that may arise.

Additionally, as problems occur, the procurement officer and project manager must have legal counsel available to consult, an element often missing in some governments. Pursuit of valid contract remedies is a legitimate tool. However, where conflicts and problems can be avoided or resolved, the primary energies of the procurement officer and the project manager ought to be focused on effectively managing the contract.

Alternatives to termination for default that may be considered include: withholding payment until performance requirements are met, seeking an alternative source of supply, revising the contract or delivery schedule, or re-procuring the commodity or service. However, the contract should specify these remedies to make them available to the public entity.

Contract Closeout Activities

A contract is completed when all commodities or services have been received and accepted; all reports have been delivered and accepted; all public-entity-furnished equipment and material have been returned if applicable; and final payment has been made to the contractor. Before the public entity pays the final contractor invoice, the public procurement officer and the user agency contract administrator, as applicable, should ensure that all outstanding issues have been resolved and that both parties to the contract have fulfilled their contractual obligations.

User agency contract administrators will maintain their own files relating to the contract that are separate from those that the central procurement office, or even the user agency procurement office maintains. When closing out the contract, the files of the user agency contract administrator should be provided to the public procurement officer responsible for conducting the procurement and awarding the contract. There should be only one contract file.

The public procurement officer and the user agency contract administrator, as applicable, must prepare a contract closeout report which must become part of the contract file. The NASPO *Contract Administration Best Practices Guide* and the State of Arkansas *Contract Administration Best Practices Guide* contain useful checklists for conducting a contract closeout.

CONCLUSION

Contract management and contract administration are essential pieces of the procurement process. It requires that the public procurement officer exercise good procurement and contract planning, possess communication and problem solving skills, and effectively use a team approach with user agencies.

ENDNOTES

1. http://www.nigp.org/home/find-procurement-resources/dictionary-of-terms
2. https://www.oregon.gov/das/Procurement/Guiddoc/contract administration plan.docx; https://www.dfa.arkansas.gov/images/uploads/procurementOffice/OSPContractAdministrationGuide_08152018.pdf
3. https://spo.hawaii.gov/wp-content/uploads/2013/11/spo135ContractMgtAdminRev16_07.pdf
4. https://www.michigan.gov/documents/micontractconnect/Chapter_12_-_Contract_Management_516308_7.pdf https://www.dfa.arkansas.gov/images/uploads/procurementOffice/OSPContractAdministrationGuide_08152018.pdf
5. See Section 12.1 at: https://www.michigan.gov/documents/micontractconnect/Chapter_12_-_Contract_Management_516308_7.pdf
6. See Section 12.1.2.1 at: https://www.michigan.gov/documents/micontractconnect/Chapter_12_-_Contract_Management_516308_7.pdf
7. *Business owner* is defined as "[t]he agency leader (e.g., department or agency director,

or designee) who is the owner of the procurement need." Section 12.2.1.1 at https://www.michigan.gov/documents/micontractconnect/Chapter_12_-_Contract_Management_516308_7.pdf

8. *Minor Contract Issue* is "a Contract Issue that can be easily resolved with a call or e-mail. If the issue has not been resolved within 30 calendar days, or is repetitive, it then becomes a Major Contract Issue." Section 12.5 at https://www.michigan.gov/documents/micontractconnect/Chapter_12_-_Contract_Management_516308_7.pdf

9. A *Contract Issue* is defined as ". . . circumstances when the contractor and the State disagree over contract performance." Section 12.5 at https://www.michigan.gov/documents/micontractconnect/Chapter_12_-_Contract_Management_516308_7.pdf

10. https://www.dfa.arkansas.gov/images/uploads/procurementOffice/OSPContractAdministrationGuide_08152018.pdf

11. Hawaii Administrative Rules Section 3-122-45.01: http://spo.hawaii.gov/references/har/goods/

12. http://doas.ga.gov/state-purchasing/seven-stages-of-procurement/stage-7-contract-process

13. See Section 12.3 at https://www.michigan.gov/documents/micontractconnect/Chapter_12_-_Contract_Management_516308_7.pdf

14. https://www.dfa.arkansas.gov/images/uploads/procurementOffice/OSPContractAdministrationGuide_08152018.pdf

15. The NIGP Dictionary defines *cure notice* as: "A delinquency notice that must be issued prior to termination for default of a supply or service contract before the contract's delivery date. Failure to issue a cure notice when required may result in an invalid termination for default." It also defines *cure period* thus: "Following the issuance of a cure notice, the time allowed for the defaulting party of a contract to resolve the specified delinquency or default."

16. https://www.dfa.arkansas.gov/images/uploads/procurementOffice/OSPContractAdministrationGuide_08152018.pdf

17. http://doas.ga.gov/state-purchasing/seven-stages-of-procurement/stage-7-contract-process

18. See Section 12.7 at https://www.michigan.gov/documents/micontractconnect/Chapter_12_-_Contract_Management_516308_7.pdf

19. See Chapter 17, *Protests, Disputes, and Claims*.

20. See Endnote 19.

21. The NIGP Dictionary defines *liquidated damages* as follows: Damages paid, usually in the form of a monetary payment, agreed to by the parties to a contract, that are due and payable as damages by the party who breaches all or part of the contract. May be applied on a daily basis for as long as the breach is in effect. May not be imposed as an arbitrary penalty. The key to establishing liquidated damages is reasonableness. It is incumbent upon the buyer to demonstrate, through quantifiable means, that damages did exist.

CHAPTER 15: *PROCUREMENT PROGRAM INTEGRITY AND CREDIBILITY*

RECOMMENDED BEST PRACTICES

- Embrace written procedures designed to detect and prevent the circumvention of procurement and ethics laws and rules.
- Identify and use a designated person to serve as the standards of conduct counselor who can help users understand and apply the various conflicts rules.
- Make standards of conduct issues a recurring part of procurement training.
- Create standard contract terms that address ethical issues and provide that any violation of those ethical standards is a breach of contract.
- Establish a program for continuing communication and coordination with the state's antitrust attorneys, and with the appropriate law enforcement units who are responsible for dealing with organized crime matters.
- Develop contract and solicitation provisions that address organizational conflicts of interest issues where there may be competing roles of consultants and other contractors that make participation by some in a procurement unfair.

Accountability, fairness, and transparency are some of the fundamental tenets of public procurement. Unethical behavior is the antithesis of the competitive process as described in Chapter 3 (*The Importance of Competition*). Public officials who allow bias to sway their procurement decisions or who accept gifts and other compensation from persons who do, or want to do, business with a public entity are acting in a way diametrically opposed to the foundation of public procurement. Equally as damaging to a procurement structure are suppliers who conspire with each other in an attempt to control the competitive process.

This chapter examines some behaviors that may compromise the integrity of a public procurement system and how laws should address those behaviors. It also identifies some resources available to assist public officials at all levels in ensuring that public employees are trained to prevent and to respond appropriately to unethical behavior.

NASPO has published additional resources on the topic, including a research paper entitled *Ethics and Accountability*.[1] It discuss best practices for applying accountability and transparency and includes case studies.

OPENNESS AND MAINTENANCE OF RECORDS

The procurement process must be transparent. Other chapters of this 3rd Edition of *State & Local Government: A Practical Guide* (*Practical Guide*) discuss the importance of the principle of openness in a sound procurement system. For instance, Chapter 7 (*Competition: Solicitations and Methods*) addresses methods of soliciting bids and proposals broadly and in a way that invites competition, and of documenting each step and decision. Chapter 8 (*Noncompetitive and Limited Competition Procurements*) describes the need to establish clear standards for instances in which competition is limited, for centralized approval and for retention of the evidence of the circumstances of a reduced competition. Chapter 9 (*Bid and Proposal Evaluation and Award*) outlines the principles for receiving, handling, and evaluating bids and proposals in a manner that fosters confidence that the process is fair and legal. Chapter 5 (*Non-Construction Specifications and Scopes of Work*) cautions against permitting only certain suppliers to contribute to the preparation of specifications. Chapter 3 (*The Importance of Competition*) discusses the role that a public procurement officer plays in detecting supplier anticompetitive behavior.

All of the principles in those chapters obligate the public procurement officer to manage the process in a manner that withstands scrutiny. These principles are critical to ensuring that the process is seen as one of integrity and credibility.

ENSURING INTEGRITY WITHIN GOVERNMENT

In addition to what is mentioned in the other chapters of this *Practical Guide*, there are additional steps that may be taken to help maintain ethical practices within a procurement organization. Some of these are discussed in the upcoming paragraphs.

Procurement Office Ethical Standards

Creating a simple and concise list of ethical standards establishes a basis for ensuring that the public procurement officers in a public procurement organization—whether it be centralized, with all procurement conducted by a single office, or decentralized—understand their common ethical obligations. To develop such a statement, the Chief Procurement Officer should gather all of the public procurement officers within his or her administration in order to draw up a short list of standards that they believe are important. This list must be consistent with the state's relevant laws and any ethics commission guidelines to ensure there are no conflicts.

Although the standards may not be legally enforceable because they are simply guidelines, they make an important statement about the ethical principles under which all public procurement officers, by agreement, will operate. All of those who participate in the procurement process, such as evaluation committee members and using agency personnel who provide specifications, should be given copies of those guidelines as well.

The following points illustrate what those standards might look like and why they are important:

- **Be independent**—Any public procurement officer should be independent from suppliers, bidders, prospective bidders, and in a perfect world, politicians and political appointees, including their own bosses. Procurement professionals, being human, can become emotionally connected to a supplier they work with and like; someone who helps them, who flatters them, and who gives them gifts, even though these might be items of nominal value. While procurement personnel should be friendly and helpful, they must resist the temptation to accept benefits from or socialize with any supplier in order to reduce the temptation to reciprocate.
- **Act only in the public interest**—A public procurement officer must represent the public's interest exclusively. On the other hand, it is the responsibility of the supplier representative to maximize his or her employer's profit. This is not to say that it is bad to have a profit motive. The profit motive drives markets toward developing better products; and certainly, corporations can be very good public citizens. A public procurement officer should always be aware of the driving motives of the supplier.
- **Remain a trustee of the public's money**—A public employee is a fiduciary for the public's money, or in other words, a trustee. An effective government procurement program emphasizes that the money being spent was hard-earned by the taxpayers. A practical rule is for public employees to spend the public's money with the care they would demand that a bank exercise in handling their own funds.
- **Follow the law**—Most public entities are subject to procurement laws and rules/regulations that require competition. New public procurement officers should be required to undergo procurement integrity training, and all public procurement officers should have some passing knowledge of the ethics laws that apply in their own particular state or local government. They should develop close working relationships with attorneys assigned to their procurement office and those that deal with anticompetitive legal matters so that legal questions can be asked and answered. A close working relationship with these types of attorneys empowers public procurement officers, since that public entity's lawyers may be able to intercede with higher-ups when those higher-ups intend to take unlawful actions, behave unethically, or act against public policy.
- **Strive for market efficiency**—It is not easy to ensure perfect efficiency in a system of cumbersome procurement laws and rules. However, efficiencies can be realized in ways public procurement officers can control. Competition creates market efficiencies. Public procurement officers must do their own market homework, independent of any one supplier. They should study historic outcomes that reflected poor procurement choices so that they may avoid them in the future. Identifying how efficient suppliers function can serve as a guide for the next set of specifications or scopes of work. It is sometimes argued that it is efficient to permit existing or prospective suppliers to write specifications or statements of work. A market competitor should be allowed to

write specifications only when it cannot compete for, or subcontract under, the procurement for which they are drafting solicitation language.

- **Take nothing, ever**—A truly independent public procurement officer should not accept even cookies from the supplier dropping by. Why not? It could be said, "Surely no one is bought for a couple of cookies!" But if public procurement officers make it their policy to take nothing from any supplier—not even the cookies—no person can ever point to the appearance of a relationship between them. The public procurement officer who refuses to take the cookies also avoids creating witnesses who can testify against the government entity in the event of a bid protest, for example. Even where government ethical rules permit a public employee to accept lunch or anything valued under a set dollar amount, the public procurement officer should take nothing.
- **Do not socialize with suppliers**—Prosecutors often prove antitrust and procurement offenses through testimony that establishes that government officials socialized with government suppliers. If a public procurement officer has social friends who may seek or have sought business with the officer's employer, he or she should remove himself or herself completely from every aspect of a procurement process involving those suppliers. This guideline applies equally to business associations. If a public procurement officer wants to participate in a trade association, he or she should remove themselves entirely from the procurement process relating to that area of trade before any such relationship taints the process.
- **Maintain confidentiality**—The business of the government in procuring commodities, construction, and services is the taxpayer's business, not the personal business of public procurement officers, their business associates, their families, their friends, or their golf buddies. Ethical procurement practice demands that public procurement officers reveal only as much information as is necessary to ensure a clean and fair competitive process. The possession by a competitor of insider information not available to other competitors is all too common in procurement law enforcement actions. If the information is public, the best policy is to ensure that everyone who wishes to compete obtains that information. If the information is not public, it must remain confidential.
- **Do not play favorites**—Truly professional procurement personnel do not help friends, family members, or business associates to gain an unfair advantage in the procurement process. Each supplier must stand on level ground.

Ethical procurement generates clear payoffs. On a personal level, it goes a long way toward avoiding a situation in which a public procurement officer or the agency involved is named in the next headline claiming public corruption. On a practical level, the agency, the taxpayer, and the economy will be able to choose the best from among all the suppliers who have developed high-quality, well-priced commodities, construction, and services. Ethical procurement is not always easy, but it is always worth the effort.

Sole Authority for Procurement Decisions

Procurement decisions should be the sole domain of the Chief Procurement Officer or of those to whom he or she has delegated that authority. It is not a good practice for that officer's decisions, particularly contract award decisions, to be reviewable or subject to be overturned by others except through appeals of bid protest and contract claim decisions according to an established process. Chapter 17 (*Protests, Disputes, and Claims*) discusses those processes.

Oversight of Unauthorized Acts

Circumvention of a procurement system from within a state or local government often takes the form of efforts by user agencies to avoid the competitive process. These behaviors can create risk to the government because they are unauthorized. They are attempts to contract in violation of law. Circumvention can lead to protracted disputes and even litigation, since government is not generally required to pay a supplier receiving an unauthorized contract.

Examples of actions that fall within the category of unauthorized acts are: ordering an item from a supplier without proper competition or in violation of existing contracts; creating emergency procurements in situations that are not, in fact, emergencies; and dividing requirements into smaller amounts to artificially bring them below the formal competition dollar amount.

At a minimum, a contractor that was part of an unauthorized procurement should be required to file a written claim for the dollar amount it is owed and provide documentation of the work performed. Since the procurement was outside of the law and the procurement process, the user who took the unauthorized action should be required to state in writing the reasons why he or she proceeded with the particular purchase.

Depending on the validity of the claim and the innocence of the contractor in the transaction, the Chief Procurement Officer or the public employee who is authorized to settle claims may approve payment. Generally, these approvals should be at a high enough managerial level to highlight the importance of the issue and mitigate the increased risk that sometimes results from after-the-fact approvals of unauthorized acts.

Threshold questions to ask in cases of circumvention are whether the user's justification for the action rings true and whether the terms and prices were fair and reasonable. However, if either the public employee or the supplier has a pattern of unauthorized purchases, that history obviously makes a case against approving any claim. In many cases, the employee who acted outside of his or her authority may be personally liable to the contractor.

Circumvention of sound procurement principles is harmful to government. There are reasons why competition principles and other procurement practices are used. They promote integrity in the system and help ensure fair and reasonable pricing. Nevertheless, unauthorized behaviors occasionally occur. State and local governments should have well-established procedures for dealing with them.

Reviews of Delegated Procurement Authority

The Chief Procurement Officer should perform a periodic and systematic review of the procurement operations within the public entity, particularly where procurement authority has been delegated to persons outside of the central procurement office. The review may cover a range of actions, but at a minimum, should focus on compliance with the law, policies, and rules that govern the procurement program.

Reporting Suspicious Behavior

There may be several options for a public procurement officer to report suspicious behavior so that action can be taken to investigate it. It often takes courage to do so because the behavior may involve elected officials or senior managers within the public entity.

How do public procurement officers protect themselves if there is fear of retribution or retaliation for reporting suspicions? Most state legislatures have enacted what are known as whistleblower laws.

Whistleblower laws typically require the public employee who is reporting suspicious behavior to provide written notice of the issue to a specified government official before reporting the behavior further within a state or local government. In many cases, that specified government official is an elected one—such as the attorney general, the governor, or a city council member.

If the law also specifies an official who is not elected—such as a police agency official—the public procurement officer may feel more comfortable reporting suspicious behavior because it would appear, at least on the surface, to remove some of the political ramifications of invoking the law's protection. The most important thing to remember is that the public procurement officer must report the suspicious behavior to one of the specified government officials before reporting it further, in order to be protected later from reprisals or retaliation.

If the procurement office has a close and trusted relationship with its in-house attorneys—for states, the attorney general's office; for counties, the district attorney's office; for cities, the city attorney's office—that is another avenue for reporting suspicious behavior. Oftentimes, though, those attorneys have such a heavy workload that they may not be able to initiate an investigation.

Note as well that the attorney-client privilege probably does not apply to the conversations between a public procurement officer and the in-house attorney. As a result, confidentiality may be an issue. The attorney-client privilege is generally owned by high executive-level officials such as the governor.

Some states have ethics commissions or inspectors general. These entities can be found on the Internet with a search of subjects such as *state ethics commissions* or *state inspector general*. Those offices may have the authority to investigate violations of the state's laws.

Finally, some public entities have what are called ombuds officers. While the primary duty of these officers may be to help a citizen redress an issue with a governmental entity, the officers may have the authority to investigate complaints from public officials about suspicious behavior on the part of other public officials.

ENSURING SUPPLIER INTEGRITY

It is unlikely that a public entity's laws will provide a full set of tools to define and enforce ethical behavior among all of those who participate in the public procurement system. There are steps, however, that the Chief Procurement Officer and an individual public procurement officer may take in each procurement to help ensure ethical standards for suppliers.

Managing Integrity Through Contracts

One tool that a public procurement officer may use to enforce ethical standards is to insert clauses into contracts that establish those standards. For instance, the clause may state that it is a breach of contract and that the public procurement officer may terminate the contract if evidence comes to light that the contractor paid a gratuity, kickback, or contingent fee relating to the award of a contract.

The American Bar Association Model Procurement Code for State and Local Governments (Model Procurement Code) advocates the inclusion of ethics contract clauses. It specifies the following:

> *The prohibition against gratuities and kickbacks prescribed [in the Code] shall be conspicuously set forth in every contract and solicitation therefor.*

It also requires that a supplier, before being awarded a contract, represent in writing that the supplier has not retained anyone with a contingent fee for the award, and that this representation be conspicuously set forth in every contract and solicitation.[2]

There are other types of supplier behavior that a contract may define as a breach of contract. For instance, contractors often try to market equipment that they designate as a new model or upgrade of an item specified on a contract. More often than not, they are attempting to sell something that is not actually in the contract and that is more expensive than the specified item. A public procurement officer should draft contract language to address this type of behavior and specify remedies against contractors that overtly misrepresent facts or otherwise violate the competitive process.

Finally, a contract should authorize a public procurement officer to audit the books and records of a contractor and to require that the contractor retain contract records for a period of time after the contract's expiration. A good procurement law should already provide that authority, but if it does not, the public entity may gain that authority by making it clear in the contract's language.

Resolution of Supplier or Contractor Complaints

A procurement system that is truly open is not afraid to be challenged on its contract award and management decisions. This openness is achieved by establishing a publicized, workable procedure for bidders and contractors to file bid protests, appeals, complaints, and contract claims. Allowing suppliers to question a particular procurement makes it more difficult for unethical behavior to remain secret.

Chapter 17 (*Protests, Disputes, and Claims*) discusses these processes in more detail.

Suspension and Debarment

The ultimate tool in the arsenal of the public procurement officer that he or she can wield against unethical behavior is the authority to suspend or debar a supplier from competing for that state or local government's contracts. Public entities vary on the grounds for suspension and debarment, as well as on the procedures required to invoke them.

Generally, a law must explicitly grant that authority, establish procedures, and specify the supplier behavior for which suspension or debarment is appropriate. Common grounds for suspension and debarment include debarment by another government, convictions for certain offenses, and recurring breaches of contract obligations.

From a legal standpoint, there is a difference between making a decision that a supplier is not responsible[3] and suspending or debarring that supplier. A determination that a supplier is not responsible, and thus is ineligible for contract award, generally relates to a limited number of procurements conducted over a relatively short time. The essence of the responsibility determination is whether the supplier has current responsibility in terms of resources, financial capability, and integrity.

The suspension or debarment of a supplier, on the other hand, means that it may not compete for any contracts for a set period of time, potentially as long as three years. Debarment is often defined as a permanent prohibition from competing for a government's contracts, but in fact debarments are often for a set period of time.

Some state or local governments may not suspend or debar a supplier for a lengthy period of time without a full hearing, which stems from the legal argument that a suspension or debarment impairs the reputation of the supplier, and thus affects a constitutional property right.

While a public procurement officer should be able to suspend a supplier for a short period of time without a hearing, it is the best practice that longer suspensions or debarments be handed down only after a hearing. In cases where the supplier has been indicted or is being investigated by a police agency, it will be difficult to proceed with a hearing because the criminal judicial process or police investigation will take priority.

ORGANIZATIONAL CONFLICTS OF INTEREST

One final topic is relevant to the issue of program integrity. While not concerned with personal integrity and conflicts of interest, policies on organizational conflicts of interest are concerned with the roles of some government contractors and consultants that may be inconsistent with participating in competitive procurements.

In 2013, the federal government issued the Uniform Administrative Requirements, Cost Principles, and Audit Requirements for Federal Awards, 2 Code of Federal Regulations Part 200 (Common Rule). Any non-federal public entity whose procurements are funded with federal monies must comply with the Common Rule. The Common Rule also states that outside parties assisting with procurements, including drafting specifications, "must be excluded from competing for such procurements."[4]

The Common Rule sets a solid standard. It should apply even when a procurement does not involve federal funds.

First, the procurement office must advise suppliers in precise terms about the nature of the activities that bring about exclusion. This limitation should be clear and bounded by reasonable time limits that mitigate the effect of the disqualifying activity on subsequent procurements. The disqualification and the details surrounding it, such as time limits, must be stated in multiple places such as the supplier manual and the solicitation for hiring the assisting contractor who will be banned from competing for the follow-on contract.

Second, the solicitation for the follow-on contract should contain clear provisions that describe the nature of the disqualification. Competitors often know which consultants are working with public programs, and they need to know the nature of those consultants' eligibility or ineligibility to compete.

Teams of users are often formed on complex proposals. Chapter 20 (*Procurement of Information Technology*) discusses teams for those types of procurements. Those teams need to know the ground rules regarding team composition. It is not uncommon for prime contractors to ask teams to certify compliance with organizational conflict restrictions.

This issue has become more central as public procurement grows in complexity and consultants are used more in solicitation development and supporting procurements. Procurement professionals must guard against being too cautious, since there is much to be learned in market research.

LAWS ADDRESSING UNETHICAL BEHAVIOR

The behaviors that can damage the public procurement process are just as damaging when directed at influencing the decisions of public officials unrelated to procurement, such as licensing and legislating. Because this *Practical Guide* discusses public procurement, this chapter focuses only on ethics laws and unethical activities related to public procurement.

Clearly, it makes no sense to limit laws establishing ethical behavior only to public procurement officers. A public entity's law must cover the entire range of state and local government decisions and actions.

Conflict of Interest Laws

A *conflict of interest* is "a conflict between the private interests and the official responsibilities of a person in a position of trust."[5] Public procurement officers are in *positions of trust*. The decisions that they make commit public entities to spending billions of dollars.

Conflict of interest laws, as they are generally called, aim to prohibit decision making where the public's interest must or may compete with a public employee's self-interest. Such laws are most likely to do the following, with variations:

- Define what self-interest is, generally by focusing on financial or ownership interests
- Define who is a public employee covered by the law, often expansively, to include close relatives and even in-laws
- Cover not only the self-interest of the public employee, but impute the financial interest or ownership of relatives to the public employee as if it is the self-interest of the employee
- Prohibit the public employee with a self-interest from participating in any way in any decision, vote, contract, or other matter of the public entity for which the employee works and in which the employee would normally be involved
- Require the employee to:
  ◊ Declare the self-interest publicly in writing
  ◊ Recuse himself or herself or decline to participate in any decision, vote, contract, or other matter in which the employee has a self-interest
- Prohibit or establish the circumstances under which a public employee may sell commodities, construction, or services to the public entity that they serve
- Prohibit or set restrictions on whether public employees may undertake outside additional employment
- Make a public employee violating the law subject to civil and/or criminal penalties for a violation of the law

Other Laws Addressing Public Ethics

Kickbacks and Bribes

Another type of behavior that a comprehensive set of ethics laws should address is kickbacks and bribes. A *bribe* is "money or favor given or promised in order to influence the judgment or conduct of a person in a position of trust."[6] A *kickback* is "a return of a part of a sum received often because of confidential agreement or coercion."[7]

A kickback involves the sharing by a government contractor of public contract proceeds back to the public official who made the tainted contract decision. For example, a building contractor might give a portion of its contract payment to a government official who was involved in awarding the contract.

A bribe is different from a kickback. It involves a payment to the public official in advance of his or her decision regarding a government matter.

The occurrence of either of these regarding the public procurement process is disastrous.

Revolving-Door Restrictions

Ethics laws should forbid:

- Former public employees from representing or assisting someone with a governmental matter, including a contract, if the employee participated in the matter personally and substantially and if the matter was one over which he or she had significant decision-making authority
- Former government executives for a period of time from participating in a governmental matter for which the former executive was officially responsible

These laws are often called revolving-door laws because of the circular image of the former government employee being on both sides of an issue.

Prospective Employment Discussions

Revolving door restrictions do not often address the important issue of prospective employment discussions. For example, a public procurement officer or a user on an evaluation committee may be approached by an offeror—however innocently—after learning of that employee's imminent retirement. If the law does not address this situation, policies should deal with prospective employment discussions. At a minimum, the discussions should be disclosed and a determination made about whether the employee should be disqualified from involvement in a procurement.

CONCLUSION

The integrity and ethical operation of the procurement process requires an overlay of safeguards—laws that define unacceptable behavior, procedures that ensure the independence of those responsible for operating and participating in the procurement system, and a strong Chief Procurement Officer who is not subject to political whims. Unethical behavior cannot be completely eliminated, but by announcing to suppliers and public employees alike that ethical behavior is expected and by defining what precisely ethical behavior is, the likelihood of unethical behavior occurring can be reduced.

Further, sensitivity must be shown about the roles of contractors in an environment where consultants are being used more and more to assist governments with complex procurements. Organizational conflict of interest laws and policies help mitigate the problems associated with these necessary relationships.

It is important to remember that technical compliance with ethics does not always solve the problem of perception. Sometimes the appearance of impropriety can be as damaging to a procurement system as would public findings that there have been criminal violations of conflicts statutes.

ENDNOTES

1. https://www.naspo.org/Portals/16/NASPO_ATC-Ethics%20Paper_V4Final.pdf
2. See Section 12-207 (2) and (3) of the Model Procurement Code.
3. Chapter 7, *Competition: Solicitations and Methods*, discusses the term *responsibility*.
4. 2 CFR §200.319(a). The regulation may be found at: https://www.gpo.gov/fdsys/pkg/CFR-2017-title2-vol1/pdf/CFR-2017-title2-vol1-part200.pdf
5. https://www.merriam-webster.com/dictionary/conflict%20of%20interest
6. https://www.merriam-webster.com/dictionary/bribe
7. https://www.merriam-webster.com/dictionary/kickback

CHAPTER 16: *SURPLUS PROPERTY MANAGEMENT*

RECOMMENDED BEST PRACTICES

- Surplus property should be managed through a single office within a public entity.
- Processes for managing, reusing, or disposing of surplus property should be public and transparent.
- The surplus property office should have standard sales terms and conditions that disavow retailer-type responsibility for every sale or transfer and specify that a sale or transfer is *as is*.
- No employee of the user agency transferring the surplus property to the surplus property office or of the surplus property office should benefit from access to information about the property.

CHAPTER 16: SURPLUS PROPERTY MANAGEMENT

Discussion of public procurement is not complete without addressing how a state or local government uses or disposes of commodities that a user agency no longer needs. With the emphasis today on recycling and sustainability, the decision about whether to buy a new commodity or to find a use for a previously owned version is ever more important.

Chapter 6 (*Sustainable Procurement Considerations and Strategies*) focuses on the economic and societal need to purchase commodities that offer some sustainability or environmental benefit. As those programs grow and commodities are consumed through their useful life, spent commodities may put the focus on disposal rather than resale.

In many cases, particularly at the state level, the office responsible for surplus property is not the central procurement office. Where that is the case, the central procurement office should have a close working relationship with the surplus property office.

DEFINITIONS OF KEY TERMS

All but a public entity's *expendable* commodities should be managed as surplus property through a single office. The NIGP Dictionary defines the term *expendable* as "supplies or equipment that are normally consumed during use and have a very short life cycle."[1] The definition of the term *expendable supplies* in the American Bar Association Model Procurement Code for State and Local Governments (Model Procurement Code) provides more specificity by placing a dollar limit on the acquisition cost and limiting the useful life of the commodity to one year or less.[2]

There are other terms of art that are used in the area of surplus property including *excess supplies, nonexpendable supplies, obsolete supplies*, and *surplus supplies*. This chapter uses the term *surplus property* to describe all of them.

AUTHORITY OVER SURPLUS PROPERTY

The Model Procurement Code contains a simple set of statutory provisions for the management of surplus property:

§8-201 Supply Management Regulations Required.
The. . . . [Chief Procurement Officer] shall promulgate regulations governing:
(a) the management of supplies during their entire life cycle;
(b) the sale, lease, or disposal of surplus supplies by public auction, competitive sealed bidding, or other appropriate method designated by regulation, provided that no employee of the owning or disposing agency shall be entitled to purchase any such supplies; and
(c) transfer of excess supplies.

§8-301 Allocation of Proceeds from Sale or Disposal of Surplus Supplies.
Unless otherwise provided by law, the Chief Procurement Officer shall be empowered, pursuant to regulations, to allocate proceeds from the sale, lease, or disposal of surplus supplies.

State laws may take a broader approach to defining that particular state's surplus property program. For example, the State of Georgia has several statutory provisions establishing its program that are spelled out in its comprehensive *Georgia Surplus Property Manual*.[3]

THE DISPOSITION PROCESS

This section of this chapter focuses on the disposition of state and local government surplus property. A discussion of the disposition of federal surplus property through state surplus property offices appears in later paragraphs.

State surplus property supervisors generally have management responsibility for two types of surplus property: property that the state has owned and that the user agency no longer needs; and property that the federal government owned and that has been transferred to the state for further disposition under federal laws and regulations.

Disposition by User Agency

Cannibalization

Instead of transferring the commodity to the surplus property office, a user agency may decide to disassemble it so that its component parts may be used to repair or maintain a similar commodity. However, disassembly of the commodity should occur only after that agency determines that there is a greater potential value and benefit to taking the commodity apart than by trading it in or selling it.

Additionally, the user agency should notify the surplus property office and obtain its authorization before disassembly. The user agency should transfer any leftover material that remains after the cannibalization to the surplus property office for sale or disposal as scrap via one of the methods described below for disposal of other surplus property.

Trade-in

A user agency may also wish to negotiate a trade-in with the manufacturer or dealer of the commodity being disposed of. However, the outright sale of the commodity through the surplus property office may bring a higher return than a trade-in.

In instances where a user agency seeks a replacement commodity, such as a copier, it may be able to purchase the replacement from an existing contract or, if one does not exist, initiate a formal procurement for that replacement. If the user agency wants the option of receiving some reduction in price for the replacement by trading in the old one, it should ask suppliers for prices both with and without the trade-in. If a solicitation is issued for a replacement, it should state that contract award may be made based either on pricing reduced by the trade-in value or without the trade-in value.

Disposition by Surplus Property Office

If the user agency does not dispose of the surplus property, the next step is for the user agency to notify the public entity's surplus property office that the commodity is available.

Overview

The process starts when a user agency gives notice to the office responsible for surplus property that it has property that it no longer needs. The example below demonstrates how that exchange of information might work (the example below is taken from the *Georgia Surplus Property Manual*).

> *Chapter 8: Overview of Disposal Process*
> *Once a state agency decides that property is no longer needed, Surplus will work with the agency to ensure that the selected disposal method returns the most value to the state. The disposal process for all the transaction types is comprised of four basic steps:*
> *1. State Agency completes and e-mails a Property Transfer Form, signed by an authorized property signor, with market quality photos of property to [The] Surplus [Office] . . . [Citation omitted].*
> *2. Surplus reviews the submission and determines the best disposal method.*
> *3. State Agency releases/disposes of property.*
> *4. Surplus e-mails finalized Property Transfer Form to state agency to remove property from the agency's inventory.*

Here, the user agency transfers the piece of property to the office responsible for surplus property and that office authorizes the user agency to remove the piece of property from the agency's inventory to assure a proper accounting in the user agency's property inventory system of the property removed from that agency. It is then up to the surplus property office to dispose of the property via the methods described below.

Today, most public entities require user agencies to report surplus property electronically.

Transfer

One disposal method is to transfer the surplus property to another user agency that has a use for it. Transfer can be an especially effective technique when ingenuity finds new uses for commodities.

For example, an excess fire engine pump might be transferred to a user agency for use in dust control (watering dirt roads). Plexiglas drums originally purchased for lottery drawings might be useful to prison shops where the material could be used for security windows, nameplates, and shelving.

If the property does not have any use within the public entity that owns it, that entity's laws should permit the sale or transfer of the property to other public entities or charitable organizations without requiring that the property be offered for purchase to the entire universe of potential purchasers.

Sale

A public entity's law should authorize a surplus property office to use a full range of methods for selling surplus property, and grant it the discretion to choose which approach is best. To reduce opportunities for deception and to help avoid any appearances of impropriety, it is best to prohibit the sale of surplus property to any employee of the surplus property office or of the user agency that owns and is releasing the commodity.

The following are some of the sales methods that state and local governments employ:

- **Live and electronic auctions**—Auctions are widely used to sell surplus property. Today, many of those auctions occur online. Various state and local governments provide websites displaying surplus property offered for online auction. There are a number of suppliers that provide online auction or marketing services that are utilized by state and local governments.
- **Retail stores**—Public entities often have a location or locations where potential buyers may shop for surplus commodities.
- **Sealed bids**—Another sales method is sealed bids. This method operates much the same as it does when the public entity is purchasing something through competitive sealed bidding. The surplus property office issues a solicitation for the sale of the commodities and provides suppliers with notice of their availability. Bids are received and opened in the surplus property office. Award is made to the highest bidder.
- **Commercial markets**—Some types of surplus commodities, such as antiques or art pieces, are best sold through established commercial markets. The surplus property office sells the commodity through the services of a commercial seller who specializes in the sale of those commodities.
- **Posted prices**—For commodities for which there is no regular market, demand is erratic, or prices received on competitive bids or auction are unacceptable, a posted price approach offers another method of sale. In this case, the surplus property office establishes a price and the commodity is posted for purchase at that price.

Conditions of Sale

To avoid being considered a retailer of the surplus property sold and thus subject to laws that cover retailers, a surplus property office should have standard sales terms and conditions for every sale or transfer that disavow retailer-type responsibility. It should also include in all notices and other sales information and announcements, the known condition of the commodities being offered, including defects.

The following is a short list of terms and conditions for sale that are examples of subjects that are important to cover:

- It is the buyer's responsibility to remove the commodities within a stipulated time after the purchase
- The public entity makes no guarantees or warranties for the commodities
- The commodities are sold *as is*
- The obligation to inspect a commodity rests solely with the buyer
- All defects not listed are unknown and the public entity takes no responsibility regarding them
- All sales are final and the sale will not be invalidated if the buyer discovers defects in the commodity after the sale
- The public entity assumes no responsibility once the commodities are sold

Finally, the sales terms and conditions should also specify the types of payment that are acceptable.

The terms and conditions should be easily accessible. The best practice is to post them online and in all advertisements, solicitations, notices, and sales paperwork.

ALLOCATION OF SALES PROCEEDS

In general, proceeds from the sales of surplus property can go to the user agency that supplied the property, to the surplus property office for its operations, or into the public entity's general fund. The most successful surplus property programs authorize the surplus property office to determine how much of the proceeds the user agency receives and how much is kept by the surplus property office.

FEDERAL SURPLUS PROPERTY

The federal government transfers what is called federal surplus personal property and excess personal property to state agencies that it designates. The property is called *surplus property* in this discussion. In many cases, those state agencies are the same ones that state law makes responsible for managing and disposing of state surplus property.

The United States General Services Administration (GSA) is responsible for managing a program called the Federal Surplus Personal Property Donation Program.[4] The program allows certain non-federal government organizations to obtain surplus property that the federal government, other than the Department of Defense, no longer needs.

The Federal Property and Administrative Services Act of 1949, as amended,[5] provides for the transfer of surplus personal property to agencies that GSA designates as State Agencies for Surplus Property (SASP).

The following entities and activities are eligible to receive donations of federal surplus personal property through the SASPs:

- Public agencies
- Nonprofit educational and public health activities, including programs for the homeless
- Nonprofit and public programs for the elderly
- Public airports
- Educational activities of special interest to the Armed Services
- Other approved activities

Surplus property of the United States Department of Defense (DoD) is handled through the Defense Logistics Agency (DLA) Disposition

Services.[6] The SASPs may withdraw DoD property from the DLA website for direct issue to their customers who qualify.

The National Association of State Agencies for Surplus Property (NASASP) is a nonprofit organization that "maintains active leadership in establishing and promoting ways and means of acquiring and distributing equitably federal personal property to public agencies and other eligible entities."[7] The organization's mission is to save taxpayer dollars by extending the useful life of federal government surplus property.

CONCLUSION

Surplus property should not be an afterthought in strategic procurement planning for state or local governments. Robust surplus property management works to prevent fraud, theft or pilferage, facilitate reuse, and provide visibility to the assets of the government and their proper disposition.

Budget challenges and sustainability goals make the sound management and disposition of surplus property one of the ways that governments can demonstrate a commitment to resource recovery and good stewardship of public funds.

ENDNOTES

1. https://www.nigp.org/home/find-procurement-resources/dictionary-of-terms
2. See Section 8-101(2) and (3) of the Model Procurement Code at: http://apps.americanbar.org/dch/committee.cfm?com=PC500500
3. http://doas.ga.gov/assets/Surplus%20Property/NEADocumentLibrary/Georgia%20Surplus%20Property%20Manual.pdf
4. https://www.gsa.gov/acquisition/government-property-for-sale-or-disposal/personal-property-for-reuse-sale/for-state-agencies-and-public-organizations
5. 40 United States Code §§471 *et seq.* https://www.gpo.gov/fdsys/granule/USCODE-1997-title40/USCODE-1997-title40-chap10-subchapI-sec471
6. http://www.dla.mil/DispositionServices.aspx
7. http://www.nasasp.org/

CHAPTER 17: PROTESTS, DISPUTES, AND CLAIMS

RECOMMENDED BEST PRACTICES

- Processes should be in place for the filing of bid protests and contract claims, as well as initiating appeals for review of initial decisions on those protests and claims. While there are both advantages and drawbacks from the state or local government's point of view, in these processes, the advantages prevail—including ensuring a fair and transparent procedure for vetting disputes.
- The procurement office should train its public procurement officers on actions and best practices that may reduce the conditions from which disputes arise or, once they have arisen, allow them to be resolved with means less contentious than protests, claims, and appeals.

At times, suppliers may firmly believe that the public entity has acted unreasonably or has made a bad decision in a solicitation for a public contract or while managing that contract. That belief may or may not be justified.

This chapter discusses the typical legal processes that state and local governments have in place for the airing and disposition of these types of contentious matters. It also provides some suggestions on how to prevent a disagreement or controversy from leading to litigation-style contention. Finally, it offers some advice on how a public procurement office may adopt its own non-statutory, non-regulatory procedures for resolving these matters less formally than through litigation-style sets of procedures.

OVERVIEW

There are generally two types of *contention*—those relating to the award of a contract (that is, the process by which the public entity selects a contractor) described in Chapter 9 (*Bid and Proposal Evaluation and Award*) and those relating to the performance of the contract.

Bid Protests

Supplier challenges lodged during the public entity's selection of a contractor are generally called *bid protests*. The NIGP Dictionary defines *protest* as "a written objection by an interested party to a solicitation or award of a contract with the intention of receiving a remedial result."[1] There are two types of bid protests. Some protests are filed against the content of the solicitation itself before the suppliers' submissions to the solicitation are due. For example, a potential bidder or offeror may believe that the terms of the solicitation provide an unfair advantage to a competitor, such as specifications or scopes of work that seem to be slanted toward a particular competitor. The protestor in this type of protest seeks to have the solicitation revised to correct the problem that is raised in the protest.

More often, protests are of the second type. These consist of a complaint by a supplier who unsuccessfully competed for a contract award, challenging either the rejection of its bid or proposal during the evaluation process or of an award to a competitor—or both. Protests in this category usually allege irregularities in the solicitation and evaluation processes and may even include assertions of bias or claims that the winning supplier will not be able to perform the contract. Ultimately, a protester in this type of protest seeks either award of the contract—rarely granted as a remedy—or correction of the irregularity, such as reevaluation of bids or proposals consistent with the terms of an invitation for bids (IFB) or a request for proposals (RFP).

Contract Disputes and Claims

The other type of contention in public contracts involves differences of opinion between a public entity and its contractor about what the contract requires. Typically, there are two types: disputes and claims. A dispute is a disagreement or misunderstanding between the public entity and the contractor about what the contract requires the contractor to do, or about how the public entity is administering the contract. Disputes arise after the contract is signed or otherwise awarded and can involve disagreements about whether the public entity has met its contractual obligations, whether the contractor is in breach of the contract, or whether there has been a change to the scope of work or contract entitling the contractor to additional money, performance time, or both.

When the dispute cannot be resolved to the mutual satisfaction of the parties, it may become a claim. A *claim* is defined in the NIGP Dictionary as "a written assertion or demand, by one of the parties to a contract, which seeks, as a contractual right, payment of money, adjustment of contract terms, or other relief, for injury, loss, or damage arising under or relating to the contract."[2] While contract claims under public contracts are most often those that the contractor asserts against the public entity, the public entity may make claims against a contractor as well.

Administrative Procedures and *Exhaustion* of Them

Processes that are established in law and that a supplier must follow if it files a bid protest or contract claim are called *administrative procedures*. Typically, a supplier filing a bid protest (*protestor*) or a contract claim (*contractor*) must complete all of the administrative procedures—called *administrative remedies*—before it may take the matter to a court. Typically, those administrative procedures consist of two levels:

- **Stage 1:** The head of the procurement office conducting the procurement—either the Chief Procurement Officer or the user agency public procurement officer—makes a decision on the bid protest or contract claim.
- **Stage 2:** If the supplier filing the bid protest or the contractor filing the claim is not satisfied with the decision made at Stage 1, the supplier or contractor may appeal that decision to a higher-level official within the public entity:
  ◊ That higher-level official may initiate a hearing on the appeal and in order to do so, appoints a hearing officer to conduct a hearing, which is less formal than a trial but has some of the same features.
  ◊ After the hearing, the hearing officer recommends a decision to the higher-level official for his or her decision. That official may accept or reject the recommendation.

In some cases, such as in the State of Maryland, the appeal is made to an appeals board and not to a higher level official. The appeals board hears the appeal and renders a decision.[3]

Bid protests within state government for the State of Colorado consist of only one required administrative decision. A supplier must lodge its protest with the head of the user agency that awarded the contract. After a decision at that level, a protestor who does not agree with that decision has an option of either appealing to the executive director of the Department of Personnel and Administration or pursuing a court action. The first administrative step—the bid protest—must be exhausted. The second administrative step—appeal—need not be used.[4]

The Commonwealth of Massachusetts, on the other hand, has not had a general administrative bid protest process in place since the late1990s. The website for the Operational Services Division (OSD) of the Executive Office for Administration and Finance states:[5]

> *OSD's rules and regulations permit an appeal process only for procurements related to purchase of human and social services, as specifically defined. There is no protest or appeal process for other categories of bids for goods and services.*

However, the Massachusetts Attorney General's Office's Bid Unit hears allegations of violations of bidding laws relating to public construction and renders decisions regarding its findings.[6]

There is a Stage 3 for bid protests and contract claims. It consists of an appeal from the Stage 2 decision to a state court. Courts generally will not consider a bid protest or contract claim unless the protest or claim has proceeded through Stages 1 and 2 if the public entity has those procedures in place. In legal parlance, that requirement is known as the *exhaustion of administrative remedies*. The court will review the Stage 2 decision in a limited way. It will overturn the Stage 2 decision only if it concludes that the decision was arbitrary and capricious. The term *arbitrary and capricious* means that an action has been taken according to one's will or caprice and therefore conveys a notion of a tendency to abuse the possession of power.[7]

There are some laws or agreements that require state and local governments to maintain some supplier/contract dispute resolution process. Federal regulations governing expenditure of federal funds state that a non-federal recipient (for example, a state and local government) "must be responsible, in accordance with good administrative practice and sound business judgment, for the settlement of all contractual and administrative issues arising out of procurements."[8] Further, the states that have elected to be covered by the World Trade Organization Agreement on Government Procurement must provide opportunities for review of award decisions of state agencies in large procurements covered by the Agreement.[9]

The objective of this chapter is to describe both the formal and informal processes for handling bid protests and contract claims and disputes, along with suggestions about how to avoid them.

VALUE AND RISKS OF ADMINISTRATIVE PROCEDURES

It is important to recognize the value of establishing workable administrative procedures for bidders and contractors to file protests, contract claims, and appeals. A procurement system that is truly open is not afraid to be challenged for its contract award and contract management decisions.

It is in the interest of a user agency to establish an administrative process. It permits the user agency to investigate and rule on a protest or claim before the bidder or contractor can ask a court to intervene. As will be discussed in this chapter, bid protests and other administrative dispute resolution processes require resources in terms of procurement staff time—time that takes away from the staff's primary responsibilities. Still, an administrative protest or dispute resolution process can serve the interests of transparency and promote an effective procurement system that is fair to all involved in it.

Risks and Disadvantages of a Bid Protest Process

Responding to a bid protest can be a time-consuming effort. A response to a complex or lengthy set of allegations in a bid protest requires time (defined as 20 hours or more to prepare a response) and support from legal counsel, who will be required to defend a user agency at Stages 2 and 3. Those types of protests—occurring with greater frequency and requiring extraordinary costs, such as the hiring of an outside attorney—are expensive in terms of staff time required to respond. If the Chief Procurement Officer is the only available person with legal training, the response can take significant time away from his or her other duties.

In some instances, suppliers may use the process to retaliate against a competitor. Additionally, a procurement process may not have functioned *perfectly*, particularly if the service or commodity being procured is complex. The protesting supplier's assertion that a mistake or even several mistakes occurred in the process, therefore entitling it to some relief, is wrong where, even if the assertion is true, the correction of the mistake or mistakes does not change the outcome, which was the award of a contract to a supplier that is not the protestor.[10]

Another drawback to a bid protest process is that it can halt the award or performance of a contract for a critically needed commodity, service, or construction until Stages 1 through 3 are complete. The delay can often be lengthy.

Value/Benefit of a Bid Protest Process

Bid protest processes vary among states but there is a definite common understanding that the process has value. Research conducted by NASPO has found that the most frequently indicated benefits of a bid protest process were that it provides a fair process and real check on flawed or anticompetitive awards. It also offers an opportunity to identify defects in the procurement process.

Protest procedures generally allow for a supplier to protest the terms of a solicitation—an IFB or an RFP, for instance. The intention is that the suppliers who may know the most about the commodities, construction, or services being purchased will point out flaws in the solicitation, such as in the way that it describes the commodities, construction, or services. Bid protest procedures allowing these solicitation protests require the protest to be filed before the deadline for submission of bids or proposals, so that the public entity may consider the protestor's allegations and correct the problem if the allegations are true, thus improving the solicitation and the basis for the competition.

In practice, some suppliers withhold their concerns about flaws in the solicitation until after the public entity selects some other supplier for award. An attempt by the supplier to call attention to those flaws later in a protest challenging the public entity's award decision, however, will be deemed to have been made too late.

Another example of how a bid protest process may ensure fairness occurs when public entities require that notice be posted of an intended contract award without competition, such as a sole source contract. A public procurement officer, in determining whether the conditions under the law authorizing non-competed public contracts have been satisfied, relies on the facts that a user agency supplies. Announcing the intended award of a non-competed contract allows for public scrutiny of those facts and the filing of a protest if there are any flaws in determining that a non-competed contract is appropriate.

PREVENTING OR DEFUSING DISPUTES

Before this chapter launches into a more detailed description of the bid protest and contract claims processes, it is important to offer some ideas about how to prevent a contentious situation in the first place.

Tips for Avoiding Bid Protests[11]

- Ensure that all solicitation specifications and requirements are relevant, objective, and encourage competition.
- Confirm that within the solicitation, the risks and responsibilities assumed by each party are clearly outlined.
- Make sure that the solicitation addresses the process for handling information that potential bidders or offerors may claim as trade secrets or otherwise confidential information.
- Ask a colleague to review the solicitation to ensure clarity, accuracy, and objectivity.
- Avoid deviating from the written requirements of the solicitation during the evaluation of bids or proposals. Use of terms in the solicitation such as *requirements, mandatory*, or *shall* mean to potential bidders or offerors that they must comply. To make sure that mandatory items stated in the solicitation are truly mandatory, perform a review of the solicitation.
- Hold a pre-bid/proposal conference to address supplier questions and concerns. Take notes and share them with all suppliers.
- Create a simple and straightforward way for potential bidders and offerors to submit questions; then make the information available to all potential bidders and offerors. Put communication in writing to avoid an appearance of favoritism or inconsistent release of information.
- Hold a pre-bid/proposal conference to identify supplier questions and concerns. Take notes and share them with suppliers.
- Have a process for determining when a solicitation amendment is needed. This should include publishing the amendment, notifying potential suppliers, and allowing sufficient time for responses.
- After awards are issued, offer a debriefing opportunity for unsuccessful bidders or offerors.[12] The debriefing should include a discussion of why the bidders or offerors proposal was not awarded.

- Include all communication, decisions, and documents in the procurement file. An unsuccessful bidder or offeror is likely to want to see the procurement record or make a public records request for it. A well-documented procurement file may discourage that supplier from filing a protest and will be critical as evidence during any protest and appeal. Note that any deadlines for protest by an unsuccessful bidder or offeror may need to be extended in good faith until the unsuccessful bidder or offeror is able to view the requested documents.
- Remember that internal e-mails will be part of the procurement record and may be sought under a public records request. Make sure that those communications conform to what the solicitation specifies. Ensure that all persons involved with the particular procurement, including evaluation committees or teams, understand the importance of limiting communications on the procurement to only the public procurement officer and the committee or team as a whole.
- When issuing an RFP, do not use a generic set of evaluation criteria. Make sure that the evaluation criteria are suited to and specific to the commodity or service being purchased.
- Provide written rejection notices to all bidders and offerors whose bids and proposals were unsuccessful. Include specific feedback, the bid tabulation, and other information that will help the supplier understand the award decision.
- While input from technical experts and end users during the evaluation process may be helpful, remember that the final decision belongs to the public procurement officer.

TIPS RELATING TO BID PROTESTS AND PROTEST RESPONSES

In the event of a protest, here are some tips for handling the situation and developing a protest response:

- Take immediate action on numerical errors or process errors if satisfactorily brought to the public procurement officer's attention. Do not put the supplier through the time and expense of a formal appeal—admit the errors.
- Discuss any protest with the user agency or department and legal counsel when received. Ensure that each protest point is vetted and analyzed against the solicitation requirement and the way the proposal or bid was evaluated. This exercise assists in preparing the state's response to the protest, ensures that there were no errors in the evaluation, and prepares the staff for possible testimony.
- Be timely, direct, and factual. Do not minimize a supplier's position; all suppliers feel they're best suited for contract award.
- Be impartial, courteous, and responsive to the protester, regardless of how angry or weak the protest.
- Explain the policies behind statutes and administrative rules.
- Explain the standard of review and procedural requirements (in as simple language as possible).
- Carefully write a bid protest decision and imagine that the reader will be a judge or a hearing officer who does not know anything about the matter. Be concise and clear. Do not cite statutes, ordinances, or rules/regulations to explain why the protest is incorrect. Explain the facts that make the supplier's position incorrect.
- Involve legal counsel in responses to protests—the Attorney General or public agency counsel will ultimately have to defend any legal challenge.

There are resources available online discussing ways to avoid protests. One of these is offered by the Federal Acquisition Institute, an arm of the United States government under the jurisdiction of the Office of Federal Procurement Policy and managed by the General Services Administration. While the training is federally oriented, the issues are generally the same at the federal, state, and local level. This training video, called *Strategies to Successfully Prevent and Defend Bid Protests*, is available online at any time.[13]

Avoiding Contract Claims

There is no magic formula for avoiding contract claims. One of the key barriers preventing early identification and resolution of a contract dispute or claim is the fact that the public procurement officer and the procurement office do not have the day-to-day interaction that the user agency enjoys with the contractor and the contractor's work. While the public procurement officer is responsible for the process of forming the contract, understanding the contract's requirements, and making official decisions related to it, he or she is removed from the information that is needed to assess regularly the contractor's performance compared with the actual contract.

The contract should identify procedures to resolve disputes or claims, and it should require that any contract claim be filed with the public procurement officer. Those procedures are discussed later in this chapter.

There are some tools that may help in defusing a contentious situation before a contractor files a claim. For instance, an established mechanism for early communication of a problem among the contractor, the user agency and the public procurement officer is critical. Holding regular meetings among those parties during contract performance is one such mechanism. Another is language in the contract requiring that the contractor or the user agency, as applicable, provide written notice to the public procurement officer at the first point of disagreement. A third excellent tool is the creation, before the contract begins, of a written contract administration plan in which the roles and responsibilities of all persons are clearly stated and understood, including in the case of disagreements. There is more about contract administration plans in Chapter 14 (*Contract Management and Contract Administration*).

It may also be useful to create a diversion process for the early resolution of disagreements. This would be something less formal than the alternative dispute resolution procedures discussed under the next subheading. For instance, the contract might require that disagreements be referred to persons representing the public entity and the contractor who are not involved in actual contract performance and who are at an executive level. The idea behind such an approach is to refer the disagreement to persons within the public entity and contractor organization at a high level in hopes that some distance from the issue will allow for a reasonable resolution.

Using Alternative Dispute Resolution

More formal tools that are outside of the administrative steps already described in this chapter are known as alternative dispute resolution (ADR) procedures. ADR may be useful at any stage of a disagreement.

ADR is designed to increase the opportunity for relatively inexpensive and quick resolution of contract disputes. Participating in the ADR process, though, does not release the contractor from complying with the statutory or regulatory filing deadlines for claims and does not imply that the public procurement officer's previously issued decision is suspended or no longer final.

ADR can take various other forms, from third-party assisted mediation to binding arbitration, which means that the decision of the arbitrator is final. The laws of the public entity may require the use of ADR. The public entity and the contractor can agree to ADR in a dispute even where not contractually required.

The federal government has made a commitment to use ADR for disputes of all kinds. Congress passed the Administrative Dispute Resolution Act of 1996 (ADRA),[14] which requires the head of each agency to designate a senior official to be the *Dispute Resolution Specialist* for that agency. The designated Dispute Resolution Specialist is responsible for implementing ADRA and the agency policy developed under it.

A MODEL FOR ADMINISTRATIVE PROCESSES

Article 9 of the American Bar Association Model Procurement Code for State and Local Governments (Model Procurement Code) includes model language for legal and contractual remedies. Many states have adopted some or nearly all of the Model Procurement Code. Commentary included in the Model Procurement Code notes that "it is essential that bidders, offerors, and contractors have confidence in the procedures for soliciting and awarding contracts and this can be ensured by allowing an aggrieved person to protest the solicitation, award, or related decisions."[15] Even if the Model Procurement Code has not been adopted, the provisions serve as useful models for state and local governments considering the establishment of protest and dispute processes.

DETAILS ABOUT ADMINISTRATIVE PROCESSES

Timelines and Other Bid Protest Requirements

Generally, protests must be filed in writing with the public procurement officer conducting the procurement that the supplier is contesting. The procedural steps for bid protests vary among public entities.

There are time limits for filing bid protests and they are strict. Failure to comply will result in the protest not being considered. The time when the clock begins to run becomes important. This generally runs from the time that the protesting supplier knew or should have known, if it acted diligently, about the flawed decision or other issue that is the basis of its protest. The deadline is often 10 calendar days.

A public procurement officer must track that time limit and preserve all records, including e-mails, to show when suppliers were notified about not receiving the contract award. Memos of discussions with bidders are sometimes useful. Moreover, if a supplier files an open records/freedom of information act request relating to a protest, records regarding the timing of the request and the public procurement officer's offer to disclose or actual disclosure of records may be particularly important in determining timeliness of a bid protest.

There also may be formal requirements for bid protests. Often, a protest must contain a clear statement of the law and the facts supporting the protest and must be filed in a specific manner. Failure to comply with those may result in the protest being rejected without it ever being considered on its merits.

Protests and later appeals generally are limited to the issues that the supplier raised in its original protest, even if those other issues may surface later.

Stage 1: Bid Protest Decision

The first decision on a bid protest is generally written by the public procurement officer who conducted the procurement or that officer's manager. The decision should do the following:

- Summarize the nature of the procurement, combining the supplier's arguments where it has attempted to create, for instance, three issues where there is really only one

- State when the protest was filed and by whom; if the protest is filed late, a clear, factual narrative of the dates and times is important
- State the ground(s) for the protest as specified in the written protest
- Include a *Facts* section in the response, setting forth all of the facts that relate to the supplier's protest, stating where the protest misstates them and why
- Include a *Discussion* section that relates the facts to the law and describe how the law was followed or if there was a minor misstep during the procurement, state the reasons that the misstep does not change the original decision of the public procurement officer
- Avoid simply stating the law that supports the procurement decision
- To show that the law or the evaluation procedure conducted under the solicitation was followed, explain clearly why the procurement complied and if applicable, describe the mischaracterization of the actual facts by the supplier protesting
- Plainly state a *Decision*—for example, "the protest is denied"—and in cases where a protest is sustained, state the remedy (e.g., resubmission to the evaluation committee for reevaluation consistent with the RFP)
- State the appeal rights, if any, and the name and address of the official to whom appeals can be addressed

The rules/regulations in a public entity often grant authority and specify requirements for issuing protest decisions; and they must be followed. As a good practice, public procurement officers issuing protest decisions are encouraged to seek legal review of their proposed decisions.

Stopping Contract Performance

In federal government contracting, a bid protest often results in an automatic stopping—called a *stay*—of contract performance, which may remain in place until the protest is decided. The federal government stay may be overridden for compelling reasons. Automatic stays of contract award or performance are less frequent at the state and local government level. Where the laws or policies of a state or local government provide for a stay at the filing of a bid protest—such as suspending the start of contract performance—until a final bid protest decision is made, the stay may be lifted if a user agency shows that the contract must proceed without delay to serve the best interest of the public entity.

Debriefings

A debriefing, if conducted properly, is an effective tool for answering the questions of unsuccessful bidders or offerors and potentially defusing a protest. Subpart 15.5 of the Federal Acquisition Regulation,[16] the body of regulations that implements the federal procurement system, provides guidance about how to conduct debriefings, including how to avoid a point-by-point comparison of bids or proposals. It is mentioned here to provide it as a resource.

JUDICIAL REMEDIES FOR DISAPPOINTED BIDDERS

As noted earlier in this chapter, courts give public procurement officers wide discretion. The Model Procurement Code reflects this approach. Specifically, it provides that a public procurement officer's determinations are final and conclusive unless they are clearly erroneous, arbitrary, capricious, or contrary to law.[17]

That provision mirrors in many ways the reluctance of judges to substitute their judgment for that of procurement professionals. In the bid protest context, courts generally defer to procurement decisions if they are not arbitrary and capricious. As noted earlier in this chapter, the expression *arbitrary and capricious* applies to an action that has been taken according to one's will or caprice, therefore conveying a notion of a tendency to abuse the possession of power.

DISPUTES AND CLAIMS

Aside from bid protests, the other type of dispute involves issues that arise during contract performance. The Model Procurement Code uses the term *contract controversy* to describe the administrative and judicial process for resolving contract disputes. The Model Procurement Code confers specific authority on public procurement officers to resolve disputes or controversies. These can include issues such as contract breach, misrepresentation, or as is more common, claims for additional compensation and/or additional time.

Approaches to Resolution of Contract Disputes

Judicial relief usually is available to contractors relating to contract disputes or claims. Where there is a contractually mandated process for filing them or an administrative review process as discussed earlier in this chapter though, a contractor must pursue a resolution first through those processes.

For example, the State of Maryland's board of contract appeals process (already mentioned in this chapter) must hear contract claims and disputes before a contractor may go to court. Under the Model Procurement Code, the court must generally rely on the facts that an appeals board adopted regarding the claim or dispute. These boards usually prescribe procedures similar to those in courts, with written complaints and answers, rules of evidence, and the right to call and cross examine witnesses.

The alternative approach to judicial review in contract disputes or claims is known as *de novo* review. That means that the court determines facts without relying on the facts determined during the prior administrative proceeding.[18] De novo review occurs where the administrative claims/disputes processes in those state or local governments, if they exist at all, are less formal than those with the formal administrative processes described earlier. Where the court will consider a claim or dispute de novo, litigation between a public entity and contractor in court is much the same as commercial litigation between private parties.

Ideally, the parties can mutually agree to resolve contract disputes and controversies. If the issue is expected to proceed to a formal administrative process or court action, then procedural requirements will require involvement of legal counsel. Procurement professionals should consult their legal counsel early when claims are likely or contract actions (such as default termination) are being considered that could lead to litigation.

CONCLUSION

Specific procedures for resolving bid protests and contract disputes are dependent on the laws, rules/regulations, and contract provisions in each public entity. Procurement professionals must be familiar with the key procedural elements of their public entity's process. More important, the successful resolution of bid protests and contract claims depends on the quality of procurement actions and contract administration. Good record-keeping practices are essential. Finally, close and early coordination with the public entity's legal counsel is important once issues arise that may proceed to formal administrative or judicial review.

ENDNOTES

1. The NIGP Dictionary is available at: http://www.nigp.org/home/find-procurement-resources/dictionary-of-terms
2. See Endnote 1.
3. http://msbca.maryland.gov/
4. See Colo. Rev. Stat. §§ 24-109-102(1), 24-109-203 and -204 at: https://leg.colorado.gov/agencies/office-legislative-legal-services/colorado-revised-statutes

5. http://www.mass.gov/anf/budget-taxes-and-procurement/oversight-agencies/osd/legal-policy-and-compliance-faqs.html#LPC_FAQ_2
6. https://www.mass.gov/guides/bid-disputes
7. https://definitions.uslegal.com/a/arbitrary-and-capricious/
8. See 2 Code of Federal Regulations §200.318(k) at: https://www.gpo.gov/fdsys/pkg/CFR-2014-title2-vol1/pdf/CFR-2014-title2-vol1-subtitleA.pdf
9. https://www.wto.org/english/Tratop_e/gproc_e/disput_e.htm
10. This is called *harmless error* in legal parlance.
11. J. Ziegler, (March 1, 2006). Preventing Protests. *American City and County*. Retrieved September 1, 2018, from https://www.americancityandcounty.com/2006/03/01/preventing-protests/
12. A *debriefing* is defined by the NIGP Dictionary as "a practice used primarily during the Request for Proposal process, whereby the contracting authority will meet with those parties whose proposals were not deemed appropriate for award. It is viewed as a learning process for proposers who may gain a better understanding regarding perceived deficiencies contained within their submitted proposal."
13. https://www.fai.gov/media_library/items/show/48
14. See 5 U.S.C. §§570a-581 at: https://www.gpo.gov/fdsys/granule/USCODE-2011-title5/USCODE-2011-title5-partI-chap5-subchapIV-sec581
15. A copy of the Model Procurement Code is available at: http://apps.americanbar.org/dch/committee.cfm?com=PC500500
16. https://www.acquisition.gov/far/html/Subpart%2015_5.html
17. See Section 3-701 at: http://apps.americanbar.org/dch/committee.cfm?com=PC500500
18. The court will not apply an arbitrary or capricious standard when it hears a matter de novo.

CHAPTER 18: EMERGENCY PREPAREDNESS

RECOMMENDED BEST PRACTICES

- Public procurement officers and staff play an important role in their state's emergency preparedness plans. They must have copies of their state's plan and be trained in what the plan means.
- Each public procurement office should maintain its own emergency preparedness plan that addresses, for instance, roles and responsibilities during an emergency, off-site office space and resources such as computers and access to electronic procurement records, maintenance of off-hours staff contact information, and emergency purchase record keeping.
- State public procurement offices should establish indefinite quantity/indefinite delivery contracts annually for commodities, services, and construction commonly needed during an emergency.
- Public procurement offices should develop short-form contracts to be used during an emergency for suppliers who are not already under contract with the state or local government.
- There should be a purchase card in place for the purchase of needed commodities, services, and construction during an emergency.
- Documentation of purchases made during an emergency, including the amount of competition conducted and the payments made, is imperative. In addition to documentation being a standard best practice, the availability of that documentation will be required when seeking reimbursement from the federal government for emergency expenses.

An important function of government is to provide support to its citizens during emergency situations.

The need for a disaster recovery plan as part of the public procurement office's planning process is indisputable. As an example, the procurement office for the Port Authority of New York and New Jersey, located in the World Trade Center, found itself without any of its contract files after the World Trade Center was destroyed on September 11, 2001.

Luckily, the office's computerized information, consisting of the records of purchase orders that it had issued to suppliers, was stored outside of the World Trade Center. It was the only information available regarding the suppliers with which the Port Authority had contracts. Thus, the procurement office was hindered in responding to the crisis because of the destruction of most of its records.

This chapter offers an overview of the laws directing that states create emergency preparedness plans and the roles of their public procurement offices in those plans. An additional resource is the National Association of State Procurement Officials' (NASPO's) *Emergency Preparedness for State Procurement Officials Guide*, which is available on the NASPO website.[1]

FEDERAL LAW AND DIRECTIVES

To understand the part that public procurement plays in emergency preparedness, it is important to be aware of the principles and approaches that drive emergency preparedness and disaster response.

The United States Department of Homeland Security

Congress passed the Homeland Security Act in November 2002.[2] The United States Department of Homeland Security was created, combining 22 different federal departments and agencies.[3]

Federal Emergency Management Agency

The Federal Emergency Management Agency (FEMA) was placed under the Department of Homeland Security in 2002. The mission of FEMA is to "support our citizens and first responders to ensure that as a nation we work together to build, sustain, and improve our capability to prepare for, protect against, respond to, recover from, and mitigate all hazards."[4]

FEMA has a Public Assistance (PA) grant program that provides federal assistance to governments and other organizations following a Presidential disaster declaration. Through the PA program, FEMA provides supplemental assistance for state and local government recovery expenses. The federal share will always be at least 75 percent of the eligible cost.

The Robert T. Stafford Disaster Relief and Emergency Assistance Act (The Stafford Act)[5] is the federal law related to federal government emergency assistance to state and local governments and to FEMA programs. This Act constitutes the statutory authority for most federal disaster response activities, especially as they pertain to FEMA and FEMA programs.

State Plans

The Stafford Act establishes programs for disaster preparation and mitigation assistance. The federal government provides assistance and grants to states for the development of state plans and programs. Among other things, the Stafford Act directs the President to provide technical assistance to the states including: developing comprehensive plans and practicable programs for preparation of disaster plans, including hazard reduction, avoidance, and mitigation; assistance to individuals, businesses, and state and local governments following such disasters; and recovery in the case of damages or destruction of public and private facilities.

State plans are generally available online or through the state's emergency management agency. Public procurement officers should obtain a copy of their state's plan to determine what roles and responsibilities are assigned to the state procurement office in the event of a disaster.

National Incident Management System

The National Incident Management System (NIMS) was developed as a result of Homeland Security Presidential Directive 5 (HSPD-5),[6] issued by the President in February 2003. NIMS provides guidance for the management of domestic incidents (which it generally defines as terrorist attacks), major disasters, and other emergencies. HSPD-5 requires all federal departments and agencies to use NIMS for internal incident management and when providing assistance to state, tribal, territorial, and local governments.

Under HSPD-5, state, tribal, and local entities are required to adopt the NIMS as a condition of receiving federal preparedness assistance. The introduction to the NIMS guide[7] explains its role in the following manner:

> The National Integration Center[8] develops supporting guides and tools to assist jurisdictions in their implementation of the National Incident Management System (NIMS). The guides and tools align with the NIMS doctrine to provide a common and standard understanding about the tools and resources needed to sustain, build, and deliver the core capabilities necessary to achieve a secure and resilient nation.

The NIMS doctrine states, in part:

> The National Incident Management System (NIMS) provides a common, nationwide approach to enable the whole community to work together to manage all threats and hazards. NIMS applies to all incidents, regardless of cause, size, location, or complexity.

National Response Framework

The National Response Framework (NRF) is another service of the Department of Homeland Security that provides guidance for conducting all-hazards response. The Introduction to the NRF document of 2013 (2nd edition) explains:

> The National Response Framework is a guide to how the Nation responds to all types of disasters and emergencies. It is built on scalable, flexible, and adaptable concepts identified in the National Incident Management System to align key roles and responsibilities across the Nation. This Framework describes specific authorities and best practices for managing incidents that range from the serious but purely local to large-scale terrorist attacks or catastrophic natural disasters. The National Response Framework describes the principles, roles and responsibilities, and coordinating structures for delivering the core capabilities required to respond to an incident and further describes how response efforts integrate with those of the other mission areas.[9]

The NRF focuses on the following areas:

Prevention—The capabilities necessary to avoid, prevent, or stop a threatened or actual act of terrorism. Within the context of national preparedness, the term "prevention" refers to preventing imminent threats.

Protection—The capabilities necessary to secure the homeland against acts of terrorism and man-made or natural disasters.

Mitigation—The capabilities necessary to reduce loss of life and property by lessening the impact of disasters.

Response—The capabilities necessary to save lives, protect property and the environment, and meet basic human needs after an incident has occurred.

Recovery—The capabilities necessary to assist communities affected by an incident to recover effectively.

The NSF identifies *response core capabilities* toward meeting the National Preparedness Goal. The 13th core capability is logistics and supply chain management, in which procurement plays a key role to:

Deliver essential commodities, equipment, and services in support of impacted communities and survivors, to include emergency power and fuel support, as well as the coordination of access to community staples. Synchronize logistics capabilities and enable the restoration of impacted supply chains.

Under the NSF's 7th emergency support function—logistics—the function is described as follows:

Coordinates comprehensive incident resource planning, management, and sustainment capability to meet the needs of disaster survivors and responders. Functions include but are not limited to:
- *Comprehensive, national incident logistics planning, management, and sustainment capability*
- *Resource support (e.g., facility space, office equipment and supplies, contracting services)*

Generally, state and local procurement offices support the logistics function under the NRF, but may be asked to serve other functions as well. Here is a complete list of the NRF emergency support functions:

1. Transportation
2. Communications
3. Public works and engineering
4. Firefighting
5. Information and planning
6. Mass care, emergency assistance, temporary housing, and human services
7. Logistics
8. Public health and medical services
9. Search and rescue
10. Oil and hazardous materials response
11. Agriculture and natural resources
12. Energy
13. Public safety and security
14. National disaster recovery framework, long-term community recovery
15. External affairs

PROCUREMENT IN THE EMERGENCY MANAGEMENT PROCESS

With that overview, the role that state and local procurement officials play before and during emergency response efforts is evident. The responsibilities of the state's central procurement office will vary based on the state's plan and other factors such as weather, geography, and the nature of the disaster.

Factors that Determine Procurement's Role

First, the public procurement office will be responsible during an emergency response for obtaining new construction, commodities, and services that are not otherwise available through other governments or nonprofit charitable organizations. Additionally, as previously noted, a public procurement office's duties may fall within more than one emergency response function, depending on how centralized the procurement process is within a state or local government.

For instance, if the state central procurement office does not have the authority to procure construction or construction services, that office will likely not have any responsibility in a disaster for assisting in emergency response function 3, public works, and engineering. Also, the roles and responsibilities of agencies within a state government's particular structure may dictate which agencies are responsible for particular NRF functions.

The Chief Procurement Officer must coordinate with the state government entity that is tasked with being the state's emergency operation center (SEOC) in order to understand what roles and responsibilities have been assigned to the central procurement office in the state's emergency management plans. Periodically reviewing the state plan is important to make sure it is kept current.

Contingency Plan

There are some obvious steps that the central procurement office should take to ensure that it has planned for the services it will need to provide in an emergency situation. Planning and preparation for any disaster fall under a continuity of operations plan or COOP. The NIGP Dictionary defines a *continuity of operations plan* as follows:

> *A detailed strategy developed to ensure the continuation of essential functions during an emergency that results in the inability of the organization to provide essential services to its constituents. The COOP must be a fluid and dynamic plan capable of being immediately adjusted and modified depending on the situation. A well-developed COOP addresses the people, processes, systems, and infrastructure elements that will be needed to continue to perform essential functions during a disaster or emergency situation.*

The central procurement office should develop contingency plans. For instance, it needs to identify an alternate emergency facility for office staff and ensure that the office will have access to the necessary data, records, supplies, and services to support the emergency response at that remote location. It is essential to draw up a prioritized list of duties to help guide the reestablishment of operations.

The nature of the disaster may require additional personnel. The contingency plans should address communication (land phone, cell phone, and radio), computers, government systems access, and backup electrical power issues.

Identifying the procurement response team

It is important for the central procurement office to make two key assumptions when preparing for an emergency: some of its key personnel will not be available at the time of the emergency; and it may not have access to its office and the records that reside there. There are some obvious steps that the central procurement office should take to ensure that it has planned for the services it will need to provide in the next emergency situation.

As a starting point for the Chief Procurement Officer when examining his or her own operations and preparing for emergencies, it is wise to look at certain expectations that state plans use to ensure that they are ready for the worst case scenario. At a minimum, the Chief Procurement Officer needs to designate staff members to be available 24 hours per day to manage the procurement office's emergency response and to be the liaisons to the SEOC. The Chief Procurement Officer may also want to designate a member of the staff as the *incident commander* to assist in the coordination of the emergency response.

When the central procurement office is called in to support an emergency, the Chief Procurement Officer will probably have to trigger an internal emergency notification procedure. It is imperative to maintain a current list of emergency contact telephone numbers for procurement officers and other procurement staff who are emergency responders. An emergency may occur outside normal working hours, and this information is needed to contact procurement staff about when, where, and why they should report to work.

Designated personnel within the central procurement office will be required to respond to the SEOC's activation of emergency procedures, and a schedule will need to be developed for consecutive shifts of emergency responders if they are needed.

Training the Team

The central procurement office must ensure that all procurement personnel who will play roles in an emergency are trained for an emergency response. Training should be coordinated with the SEOC. The central procurement office staff should also participate in SEOC exercises to make sure that there is a clear understanding of roles/staff coordination—both internally and externally.

FEMA offers online independent study courses to help staff learn more about emergency management.[10]

Pre-Establishment of Statewide Contracts

The central procurement office should identify those commodities and services that other state agencies or nonprofit charities are not likely to be able to supply, or at least, not in the quantities that are needed. Once that is done, the central procurement office should establish indefinite quantity/indefinite delivery term contracts in advance for those items. Here are some examples of what those contracts might cover:

- Transportation services
- Tent rental with climate control option of heat and/or air
- Generator rental with requirement of on-site refueling
- Portable lighting
- Chain saws
- Communication equipment
- Fuel tankers with drivers and with the capability of on-site refueling—tanker to vehicle (diesel and gasoline)
- Fuel contracts
- Portable toilets and service
- Cots, blankets, sheets, pillows, and linens
- Sanitary requirements
- Portable outside lighting
- Body bags
- Meals ready to eat
- Food sources
- Office supplies
- Water (bottle and bulk—for drinking and for general use)
- Earth moving equipment
- Housing, feeding, and sanitation capabilities

For necessary items that are time-sensitive or otherwise in short supply, the central procurement office should develop a short contract form, such as a memorandum of understanding, which it can use to procure these items in the early stages of the emergency recovery. When obtaining pricing for equipment rental, the central procurement office should seek pricing with daily, weekly, and monthly options.

General Services Administration Contracts

The United States General Services Administration (GSA) has programs for state and local governments to assist them in emergency situations. The GSA Disaster Purchasing Program[11] allows purchases from approved GSA Federal Supply Schedule suppliers to prepare for, respond to, and recover from presidentially declared disasters or acts of terrorism.

The GSA National Wildland Fire Program[12] allows for the purchase of United States Forest Service approved wildland fire protection equipment and supplies from GSA's Global Supply Program. GSA also has Federal Supply

Schedules that are accessible to federal grantees during public health emergencies.

Identifying Supplier Resources

As part of emergency preparedness, a central procurement office must determine the resources that are available from suppliers. The office should maintain a current centralized listing of registered prospective suppliers who can supply specific emergency needs to the state. The listing of suppliers should include their emergency contact information for nights, weekends, and holidays.

The best practice is for supplier information to be retained in a searchable electronic format accessible to emergency responders. Internet access may not be available during an emergency, so the procurement office's response team should maintain a file saved on an electronic media storage device with a hard paper copy. The file should include each commodity or service with the name, address, and emergency telephone contact information. The emergency supplier listing should be updated at least annually for current emergency contact information and telephone numbers.

Purchase Orders, Contracts, and Purchase Cards

Developing a standardized simple emergency purchase request form for use by state agencies, local governments, and nonprofit organizations that are a part of the SEOC during emergency operations is critical. The request form and contract templates should be available electronically or through e-mail, but also through a paper process to make it flexible. Expedited procedures for ordering, approving, and tracking requests and verifying receipt of commodities and services must also be in place.

The central procurement office should establish a purchase card for emergency purchases with procedures in place for its use. The card should be the preferred method for ordering from a contract, with the issuance of a purchase order to be used if use of the card is not appropriate for some reason.

Documentation

Documentation is critical during and after the emergency. The central procurement office should maintain detailed logs of all purchases (including purchase orders), competition information including bids obtained, suppliers contacted, activities, messages, approvals (signatures), and any correspondence relating to a purchase request.

Statewide contracts already in place should be utilized for purchases whenever possible. If they cannot meet needs, the central procurement office should document the reasons why those contracts were not used. Documentation should also include any dealings with other entities such as FEMA, the Army Corps of Engineers, local governments, the private sector, and other public entities and nonprofit organizations.

Purchases during emergency situations may be subject to federal reimbursement, so the central procurement office must ensure that it understands FEMA's requirements and complies with them to the best of its ability.[13] State central procurement offices that have had experience with large-scale emergencies indicate that before approving any reimbursement of expenses, FEMA has requested to see documentation that competition was implemented.

Procurement officials must ensure that competition is carried out where possible. If a noncompetitive purchase is contemplated, procurement officials should attempt to seek guidance from FEMA regarding requirements for federal reimbursement of noncompetitive purchases. They also need to ensure that any noncompetitive purchases are well documented and comply with all applicable state and local government requirements.

Post-Disaster Financial Documentation

After the disaster response, the central procurement office will be required to provide complete and timely documentation to support the purchases made during the disaster. Documentation may include electronic spreadsheets showing all detailed information including purchase order numbers by date/time, supplier award, cost information, commodity or service description, user agency requester, and the procurement officer conducting the purchase. Information must demonstrate compliance with the financial and competitive requirements of the federal and state government.

CONCLUSION

Procurement clearly has a significant role to play in any emergency, and that role is to locate and provide needed commodities, services, and construction that are not otherwise available. Planning and preparation are necessary to ensure the central procurement office is ready to provide support in emergency situations. The central procurement office must understand the role it plays within the state or local government emergency operation plans, and have its own emergency plans to ensure it has adequate personnel, equipment, and resources to provide purchasing services to support the emergency response. Finally, procurement officials must ensure that the procurement procedures and documentation for emergency purchases are adequate to satisfy requirements for federal reimbursement and eventual federal, state, or local audits.

ENDNOTES

1. http://www.naspo.org/Publications/ArtMID/8806/ArticleID/2182
2. https://www.dhs.gov/homeland-security-act-2002
3. https://www.dhs.gov/
4. https://www.fema.gov/
5. https://www.fema.gov/robert-t-stafford-disaster-relief-and-emergency-assistance-act-public-law-93-288-amended
6. https://www.dhs.gov/publication/homeland-security-presidential-directive-5
7. https://www.fema.gov/nims-doctrine-supporting-guides-tools
8. FEMA's National Integration Center "provides specialized expertise and services to state, local, tribal, and territorial (SLTT) partners to improve emergency management capabilities based on greatest need, risk, national priorities, and resources available." https://www.fema.gov/fema-technical-assistance-program
9. https://www.fema.gov/media.../final_national_response_framework_20130501.pdf
10. https://training.fema.gov/emi.aspx
11. https://www.gsa.gov/acquisition/purchasing-programs/gsa-schedules/state-and-local-government-customers/state-and-local-disaster-purchasing
12. https://www.gsa.gov/acquisition/purchasing-programs/gsa-schedules/list-of-gsa-schedules/schedule-84security-fire-law-enforcement/wildland-fire-program
13. https://www.in.gov/dhs/files/reimburse.pdf

CHAPTER 19: eProcurement

RECOMMENDED BEST PRACTICES

- eProcurement systems have significantly improved the state and local government procurement process, providing documented savings for both the public entities using them and for suppliers seeking business opportunities.
- eProcurement systems can provide critical information about the specific commodities and services that a public entity purchases, thus allowing for spending patterns to be tracked and analyzed. Those purchasing trends are important for making procurement process improvements, such as accumulating all of the public entity's needs for a commodity or service to achieve volume pricing from suppliers.
- eProcurement systems should permit the public entity to conduct all of its procurements through that system, including formal and informal ones, and reverse auctions.

An eProcurement system is the technology platform that enables state and local governments to systematize their procurement processes. The capability of individual systems varies from simplistic *shop, order, and pay* functionality to more complex systems that allow for full integration with a public entity's financial system, solicitation management, and analytic data reporting.

These systems produce an almost immediate return on investment by reducing costs, improving processes, and providing data to enhance government-to-business electronic trade. Over the past decade, state and local governments have worked at developing and implementing eProcurement programs to accomplish these results and relieve the pressures of austere budgets.

This chapter provides an overview of public eProcurement systems, primarily at the state government level.

THE *BEFORE ePROCUREMENT* EXPERIENCE

The effort of state and local governments to efficiently purchase commodities and services has always been a daunting task, but was even more so prior to the advent of eProcurement solutions.

Public procurement officers in user agencies trying to purchase supplies for those agencies were often faced with a multitude of price lists, returns for errors in product or pricing, and time-consuming, paper-based processes. Additionally, they knew that multiple user agencies needed the same commodities but had no data to assist in identifying those agencies. They realized, however, that combining all user agencies' needs would secure better prices.

Suppliers often had similar frustrations. For example, prior to eProcurement, suppliers who wanted to sell office supplies to a public entity had to first find the procurement offices of each user agency and hope that those offices might be interested in their commodities. Only then could they market their commodities to those public agencies' procurement officers.

Suppliers often had to travel in person to these offices to register and to find available business opportunities. If they were lucky, the state or local government might issue a periodic publication of solicitations, available only with a paid subscription. The publication usually listed only the largest procurement opportunities; and the smaller opportunities that could help suppliers build their business were not readily apparent. The mail delivery of the paper publications often lagged, so that suppliers could even be late in responding to solicitations.

Even after contract award, there were still a large number of inefficiencies in the process. If a supplier was able to win the contract for office supplies, for example, it had to send out a paper catalog to the public procurement officers—an expensive proposition. If prices on a particular commodity dropped, suppliers were obliged to send out price sheet updates to many procurement offices.

Sales representatives of contractors perpetually had to make sure that public procurement officers used the correct price sheets to ensure compliance with contract pricing. Since business was almost entirely conducted on paper, suppliers could not automate their supply chains for delivery. All of this rework and back-and-forth communication had the potential for inefficient delays in supplying state and local governments with what they needed—and in suppliers finally receiving payment for commodities and services.

The inefficiencies and missed opportunities embedded in this old way of doing business clearly cost the public entity and suppliers too much. The situation had to change, and a new way of doing business using electronic procurement was envisioned as the next evolution of procurement.

ePROCUREMENT BENEFITS AND SAVINGS

Contrast that scene with the landscape after eProcurement systems came into use, which the remainder of this chapter discusses. States with eProcurement systems have documented significant benefits including cost savings. Those benefits include:

- **Purchase transparency and government accountability:** Public procurement is just that—public. The public taxpayers want to know that their dollars are being spent wisely; they are interested in what the state or local government is buying and how much it is spending for purchases. They demand that their government be held accountable. Suppliers doing business with the state or local government ask that the procurement process be transparent, so they can be assured that procurements are being conducted in a fair, open, and honest manner with equal access to the business opportunities for all. These electronic procurement systems open the process to public scrutiny in an instant.
- **Leveraged buying power:** Using data from the eProcurement system, senior managers and public procurement officers are able to take an enterprise view of procurement with visibility into expenditures, enabling a state or local government to better leverage buying power when awarding contracts. Thus the data provides the ability to reduce costs and ensure the best value, resulting in better contract awards.
- **Increased administrative efficiency:** As much as a 70% reduction in the time from issuance of a solicitation to contract award has been achieved under some eProcurement systems, including eVA, the Commonwealth of Virginia's award-winning eProcurement system. eProcurement systems now have the capability to integrate seamlessly with financial systems, improving internal controls while increasing efficiencies even further. The Commonwealth of Virginia achieved $20.6 million in savings from increased administrative efficiency through electronic processing of purchase orders in fiscal year 2017.
- **Reduced cost of commodities and services:** The cost of commodities and services is reduced through increased competition, with greater supplier participation and decreased administrative costs. For example, the Commonwealth of Virginia's eVA platform provides electronic supplier self-registration and account maintenance, making it easy for suppliers to transact business with public entities. This resulted in over $22 million in savings for the 2017 fiscal year.
- **Increased opportunities and competition:** Access to business opportunities is improved, enabling more suppliers to participate, which increases competition. With eProcurement, suppliers are able to register one time and make their commodities and services visible to state user agencies and many local government procurement offices that use a state eProcurement system. Suppliers' costs are reduced by a reduction in travel and administrative time spent at numerous procurement offices. Some eProcurement

systems have seen as much as a 200% increase in the number of suppliers registering and significant increases in the number of suppliers submitting bids and proposals. New Jersey has seen more than 13,000 suppliers register for its NJSTART eProcurement system since its implementation in 2016. This increased competition has resulted in reduced prices of commodities and services.

- **Improved access to business opportunities for small, women-owned, and minority-owned businesses:** Small, women-owned and minority-owned businesses often do not have the resources used by larger businesses to identify business possibilities and participate in them. The eProcurement system increases their participation by providing easy access to opportunities, including chances for small purchases, with the use of tools such as streamlined quote capabilities and push notifications for all relevant opportunities regardless of size.
- **Faster delivery time:** State governments with eProcurement systems have reported reduced delivery time—for some suppliers as much as 25%—through the electronic processing of orders. Faster order fulfillment for suppliers can result in faster payment and better cash flow for their businesses.
- **Avoidance of system duplication and unnecessary investment:** Often, state and local government procurement offices and user agencies create their own procurement systems. This can result in non-standard processes that reduce efficiency, amplify complexity, and increase administrative costs. The eProcurement system creates a network allowing multiple offices to use the same system and standardize processes.

The benefits of using an eProcurement system to streamline and modernize a public entity's procurement processes have been clearly quantified and demonstrated by states leading the charge in the eProcurement arena. Virginia, for example, reports savings and value that exceed the annual cost of the program. In fiscal year 2017, eVA delivered $51.16 million in total savings, while costing only $22.7 million to operate, resulting in net savings to the Commonwealth of $28.46 million. Other states have reported significant savings and increased efficiencies across their procurement process as well. Wisconsin recently implemented a full enterprise resource planning (ERP) system including eProcurement capabilities, and is set to realize nearly $100 million in savings over the next decade.

EXISTING ePROCUREMENT SOLUTIONS IN STATE CENTRAL PROCUREMENT OFFICES

According to the National Association of State Procurement Officials' (NASPO's) 2018 Survey of State Procurement Practices: of the 48 responding states, 47 states use an eProcurement or ERP system, as shown in Figure 19.1. Six of those states use a solution that was partially or completely created internally within that state government.[1] The section of this chapter entitled *Enterprise Resource Planning Solutions and eProcurement* discusses the difference between eProcurement and ERP systems and how they are often integrated to maximize efficiencies for the enterprise as a whole.

Additionally, the NASPO research brief entitled *The Value of eProcurement/ERP Solutions: Case Studies* provides important information about how some states have implemented their eProcurement systems.[2]

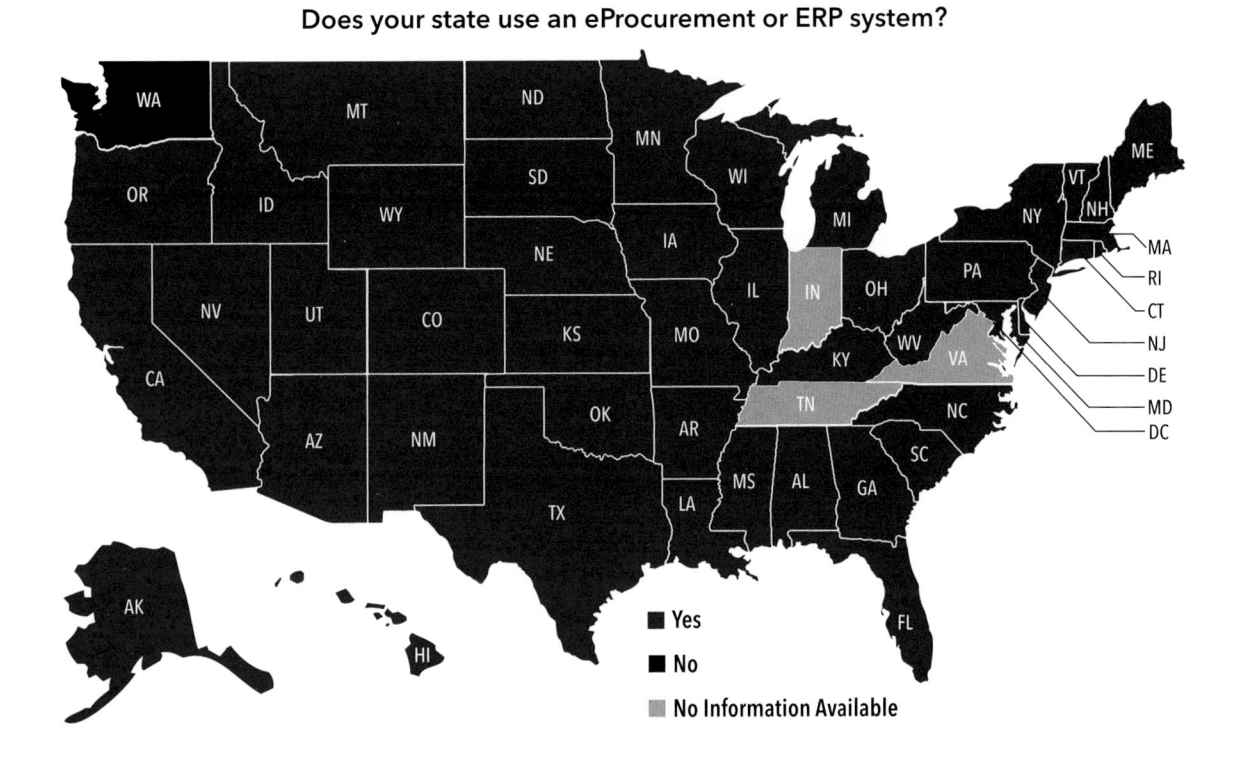

FIGURE 19.1 | E-PROCUREMENT OR ERP SYSTEMS

Does your state use an eProcurement or ERP system?

- Yes
- No
- No Information Available

ESSENTIAL ELEMENTS OF ORDER-TO-PAY ePROCUREMENT SOLUTIONS

To achieve a full order-to-pay function, eProcurement systems need the following essential tools:

- **Single ePortal:** A single gateway should reside on the Internet, through which many different public entities and suppliers conduct business, allowing the state to function as a single enterprise. New Jersey's NJSTART[3] is a recent example; it provides a unique web portal that consolidates all procurement activities into a one-stop shop, making it easier for suppliers to do business with the state.

- **Procurement data warehouse and analytical reporting:** The data warehouse should capture information on all purchases in the eProcurement system and make this information available to public procurement officers for better procurement decisions and to suppliers for business planning and market analysis. This information is also available to the public, either through the procurement system or through alternate open data portals, to promote transparency and visibility of procurement transactions and accountability for the use of taxpayer dollars. Using the information captured in the data warehouse, standard and custom reports are produced for public procurement officers for analysis and use for strategic sourcing and spend management.

- **Supplier self-service registration:** A single site on the Internet should exist for suppliers to register to do business throughout the state and establish their electronic account profile. This saves suppliers' resources by not having to register multiple times with numerous public entities.
- **Electronic bidders list:** An electronic list of bidders should be accessible to send an invitation for bids (IFB) or request for proposals (RFP) and to receive responses from suppliers electronically.
- **Standard coding for commodities/services and electronic catalogs with crosswalk:** The solution should use an industry-friendly coding system for two eProcurement purposes—solicitations and expenditure analysis. Often the NIGP commodity/services code is used as the basis for registering suppliers, notifying them of contracting opportunities and collecting purchase/spend data. It also is often used for inventory maintenance in public entities having significant inventories. The NIGP code is effective for categorizing the types of commodities and services, some of which are unique to government. Industry, on the other hand, uses the United Nations Standard Products and Services Code taxonomy of commodities and services for commercial products for electronic supplier catalogs. A crosswalk can create a list of equivalent categories between the two systems.
- **Push technology:** Suppliers should be able to identify the business opportunities of interest by commodity code, and the system should automatically push an e-mail or other electronic notification to suppliers when a business opportunity (solicitation) becomes available on the website. This saves the public entity and suppliers both time and money. The public entity is no longer obliged to print and mail solicitation documents to suppliers, and suppliers are not compelled to search through volumes of information.
- **Single electronic posting:** A single Internet site should be available on which public entities and user agencies can post procurement solicitations or business opportunities. It allows all suppliers to have greater access to business opportunities throughout the state or local government. Posted solicitation modifications or addenda are shown sequentially in the directory of contracting opportunities. This alleviates the need to mail or otherwise give notice to potential competitors individually, and places the onus on the supplier community to check for solicitation updates prior to a bid or proposal submission.
- **Electronic bid lockbox:** The system should have an electronic lockbox for receiving bids and proposals, and for holding them until the designated time of opening, sending an acknowledgment receipt to the supplier. This lockbox must be totally secure such that even the software service provider does not have access before the designated opening. There should be a confidentiality and nondisclosure agreement in place with that provider to protect the information.
- **Punch-out/electronic catalogs:** The eProcurement solution should be able to access the Internet catalog of suppliers having web-enabled catalog and configuration systems, collect the information on what items a user agency wishes to buy, and place an order into the eProcurement solution using a purchase card or electronic purchase order.
- **Procurement tools:**
  - ◊ **Electronic storefronts:** A tool for shopping statewide contracts and supplier catalogs in an electronic storefront on the Internet using a purchase card or electronic purchase order.
  - ◊ **Simplified quote capability:** eProcurement for small-dollar procurements in a public entity. With this quote capability, a public procurement officer can

request a quote from the electronic bidders list, receive the quote electronically, and make a purchase award electronically.
  ◊ **IFB/RFP advanced procurement:** A tool for conducting formal procurements using electronic sealed bidding or electronic competitive sealed proposals.
- **Reverse/surplus auctions:** Electronic reverse auctions to place a procurement requirement on the Internet for which suppliers bid multiple times within a designated period of time. Electronic surplus auctions allow public entity surplus property to be placed for sale on the Internet allowing the public to bid on buying that property.
- **Post-award contract management and administration:** eProcurement tools to handle the activities of management and administration of contracts post-award.
- **Category procurement for staff augmentation and consultant staffing:** eProcurement tools to procure electronically and efficiently temporary staffing resources to supplement the workforce and execute special consulting needs.
- **Electronic ordering:** Capability for suppliers to receive orders electronically using different delivery methods.
- **Purchase card acceptance:** The ability to use a purchase card to purchase commodities and services. Optimally, it includes the ability for public procurement officers to use a virtual procurement card that resides in the solution, eliminating the need for a physical card.
- **Electronic invoicing:** When commodities are received, production of an electronic invoice to speed up the payment process.
- **Online receiving:** eProcurement tools for receiving commodities at a central receiving location with the receiving event recorded in the system to permit payment.

SOME DEVELOPMENT AND IMPLEMENTATION CHALLENGES

Start-Up and Project Approvals

Executive-level approval may be required to launch or update an eProcurement project, and approvals often require concurrence from various internal government departments, such as finance, technology, and administration. A business case is often required. Chapter 20 (*Procurement of Information Technology*) discusses in detail the steps, including making a business case, that a project such as implementing an eProcurement solution requires.

Historically, little data was available for development of a business case prior to eProcurement implementation. Now, with eProcurement projects implemented by many state and local governments, it is easier to obtain the data to support the business case and develop a return-on-investment strategy using actual state and local government experience.

Typically, a technology procurement request with the business case assessment is submitted to the technology departments within a public entity for their approval. Those departments usually have explicit requirements that must be documented before the request can move forward. The investment of time and resources needed to justify the request can be sizable.

An appropriation for the project often must be approved by the legislative body—a state legislature or city council, for instance—if not funded from within the central procurement office. This step is equally important if the project funding strategy is a fee-based model (discussed later). Under the laws of some states, the fee may be considered an unauthorized tax under the law if the law does not explicitly authorize the fee.

The appropriation language should also stipulate that the funds will be used only to fund

CHAPTER 19: ePROCUREMENT

the eProcurement solution and not for other governmental purposes. This kind of limiting language is especially important where suppliers are asked to finance the system or otherwise assume financial risk associated with the implementation.

As it is in the case of other large information technology (IT) projects, eProcurement system implementation can encounter resistance by those who will have to use it. Continuous communication and efforts to obtain support from senior government executives are critical. Press releases to the public may also be useful for demonstrating the commitment of the government to the project.

Funding Strategies Generally

There are at least three different approaches to the funding of an eProcurement system for the central procurement office: (1) traditional direct government funding, (2) the use and collection of contract transaction and other fees, and (3) the use of a public/private partnership.

According to the 2018 NASPO Survey of State Procurement Practices, most states with eProcurement systems receive some state funding. Some states fund their system through a combination of state funding and either supplier fees or fees charged to user agencies, contract rebates, or both user agency and supplier fees.[4] These percentages can be seen in the pie chart graph in Figure 19.2.

Some of the states that currently utilize a type of fee to pay for their ongoing eProcurement system funded the system initially through a public/private partnership strategy. The public/private partnership approach is a somewhat unique strategy for funding an eProcurement system. These systems are still procured competitively because, although there may be no initial cost

FIGURE 19.2 | TYPES OF FUNDING FOR EXISTING STATE E-PROCUREMENT SYSTEMS

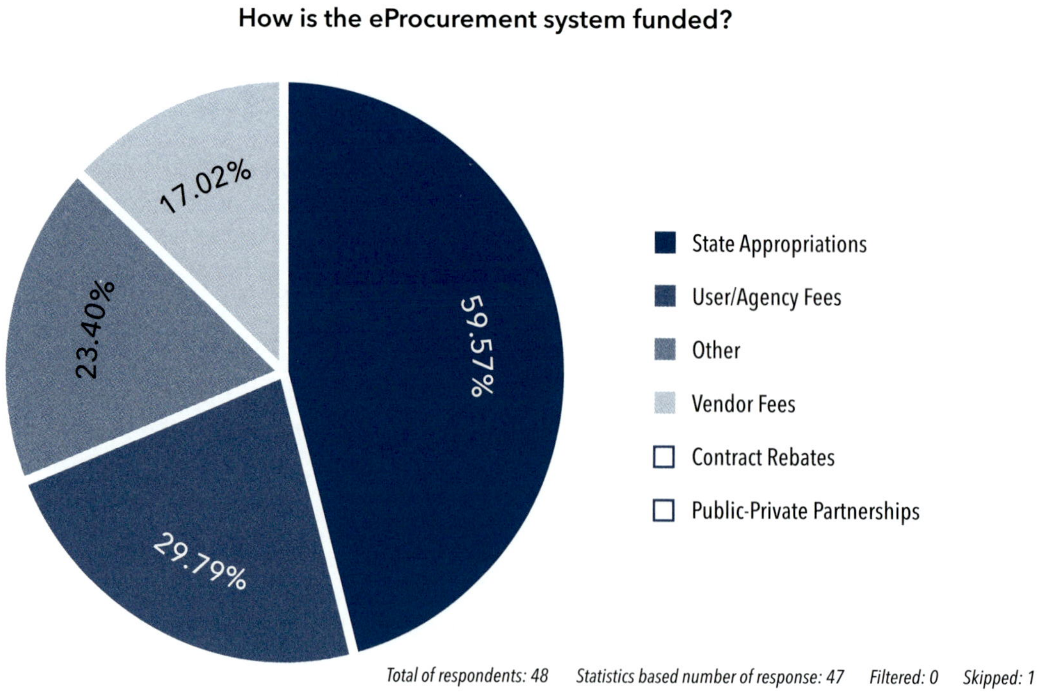

How is the eProcurement system funded?

- State Appropriations: 59.57%
- User/Agency Fees: 29.79%
- Other: 23.40%
- Vendor Fees: 17.02%
- Contract Rebates
- Public-Private Partnerships

Total of respondents: 48   Statistics based number of response: 47   Filtered: 0   Skipped: 1

to the public, there is a significant and ongoing future reimbursement to the private sector contractor.

Under that model, the supplier of the eProcurement platform itself, at no cost to the state, pays the cost to build and implement the state's eProcurement system in exchange for receipt of revenues associated with the use of the system. States using this approach found it necessary to later modify or renegotiate contracts based on actual experiences with the public/private partnership contract. Florida, North Carolina, and Virginia all used versions of this model.[5]

While NASPO does not endorse any single approach to the funding of eProcurement systems, there are a number of options for funding—each with its pros and cons. For example, if the funding model is fee-based, a procurement office may need a treasury loan in order to get started. Otherwise, the procurement office may have to use some of its own funds as an initial start-up investment, develop the required business case, and then obtain approvals.

Project Management Leadership

Implementing or updating an eProcurement system is a classic example of the importance of sound project management. To be successful, the project executive leadership must include representatives from procurement, finance, and technology departments, with emphasis on experienced individuals, including the Chief Procurement Officer. Chapter 20 (*Procurement of Information Technology*) offers guidance on developing teams for these types of complex technology projects.

The team should be led by the central procurement office and the technology department working together as co-project leaders. However, central procurement office representatives, rather than those from the technology department, need to lead the development of the end product's look and feel since a broad range of users and suppliers will be accessing the system. Past history has shown that success depends on this approach. Still, success also depends on all disciplines on the team participating in making decisions. In short, teamwork is critical.

The project executive leadership must adopt a process that allows issues to be quickly analyzed and decisions made. Indecisiveness or unnecessary configuration delays may draw out the implementation process and affect the project's timeline and budget. The leadership must then work closely with the contractor for the system before and after decisions are made, to ensure agreement so that decisions are quickly implemented.

Political and External Forces

Implementation of these systems involves classic change management challenges as well. In the past, eProcurement has not been well understood by some state senior officials, employees, suppliers, and particularly the small business community. As the project is launched, there will be questions until all those affected by the system become better informed.

The central procurement office must institute a strong marketing, training, and information campaign, and maintain communication with all stakeholders[6] concerned. The office should also organize government and supplier user groups to provide feedback as the project proceeds, and to build grassroots support.

Support must be both top-down and bottom-up if the project is to succeed. There must be strong backing from government executives and cabinet officials having direct connections to the governor and the legislature. Advocacy for the project is a key role of senior leadership as they work with others at their level to solve problems and continue to promote the business case for eProcurement.

Contracts for eProcurement Systems

Contracts for eProcurement systems vary widely among the states, due in large part to the initial funding sources and ongoing funding strategies used. For contracts in which the contractor is paid by fees charged to system users, user and supplier adoption is key to driving the volume through the system to achieve the revenue stream needed to finance the system.

Because typical pay-for-service contract provisions may not be adequate, special attention is required to define the method of payment, revenue capture responsibilities and methods of sharing the revenue, and other key underlying assumptions. Contracts may need unique options provisions, milestone reviews and other special provisions that allocate risk fairly.

Further, as is the case with other large-scale IT implementations, change is a natural byproduct of these systems. As the eProcurement project proceeds, new information comes to light that affects the project. The leadership must quickly assimilate this information and apply it. Often, this information was not available at the time of initial contract award. As a result, the contract may be affected in terms of scope, time, and possibly cost. Procurement must be flexible in adjusting the contract scope to take advantage of new information.

If the central procurement office holds rigidly to the original contract without being flexible, the success of the project may be placed at risk. The flexibility required can make eProcurement systems a strong candidate for an agile/modular procurement approach.[7]

Legal Recognition of Electronic or Digital Signatures

An *electronic signature* is an electronic sound, symbol, or process attached to, or logically associated with, a record and executed or adopted by a person with the intent to sign the record. A *digital signature* is a form or subset of electronic signature. It achieves encryption of data/documents through an encryption key and requires that the recipient have a corresponding key in order to decrypt.

Since many eProcurement systems require electronic or digital signatures, procurement laws must be analyzed to ensure that the digital functionality of eProcurement systems can be accommodated. Many states have adopted a proven technical approach that complies with their laws and rules/regulations, provides the security required, and is reasonably familiar to suppliers.

Additionally, blockchain technology[8] is emerging as an effective tool for states to maintain accurate and secure records and ledgers. Blockchain, like a digital signature, ensures encryption throughout the process, and as the transaction moves from step to step (or chain to chain), the encryption is recorded and tracked, ensuring process integrity. Used initially for cryptocurrency, blockchain is being considered for any process that requires security integrity and authentication throughout its transaction life cycle.

Online Reverse Auctions

Holding reverse auctions is one of the tools in the eProcurement portfolio. Chapter 7 (*Competition: Solicitations and Methods*) discusses this source selection method in more detail. When used correctly, the tool can be a strong asset to public procurement officers and suppliers. As in the case of electronic signatures and digital transactions, state and local governments must be sure that their laws allow for this special kind of sourcing.

ENTERPRISE RESOURCE PLANNING SOLUTIONS AND ePROCUREMENT

This chapter has so far emphasized the cost savings and efficiencies arising from the use of eProcurement systems. However, a significant amount of transaction cost can be attributed to the state or local government's accounting steps related to the procurement process. Even greater efficiencies can be achieved through systems that effectively integrate both the procurement and the accounting aspects of transactions.

ERP Systems and eProcurement

Accounting systems typically are at the core of ERP solutions. ERP systems are usually accounting-oriented software systems that identify and help plan the resource needs of an enterprise such as a government.

The NIGP Dictionary notes that an ERP system "may include finance, accounting, human resources, procurement, inventory control, and other activities" and deploying it is "generally an enterprise-wide process, involving analysis, replacement of legacy systems, and the development of new work processes and procedures."[9] Many organizations, including state and local governments, use ERP systems to integrate their activities across their organizations.

ERP system providers often promote eProcurement as a feature of their services. Traditionally, ERP systems have focused on providing basic procurement functionality, such as requisitioning, ordering, receiving, and invoicing, to meet the core accounting requirements. Because of their integrated nature, ERP systems offer a common database of all expenditures to many users at once, allowing a holistic approach to budgeting, accounting, and procurement, and providing for a *single point of truth* (that is, for data integrity and consistency).

However, the challenge of this common database is that the data is stratified from an accounting perspective rather than the procurement commodity or service perspective needed for procurement spend data. ERP systems' functionality generally lags behind that of standalone eProcurement applications that are developed specifically for the purpose of procurement; and that functionality is often delivered under a software-as-a-service (SaaS) model. The ERP systems are typically challenged to meet the public access and openness required of public procurement, such as solicitation publication.

Functionalities that are common in eProcurement tools but are unlikely to be offered in standard ERP packages include supplier self-certification, personalized supplier portals, requisitioning, complex catalog hosting and shopping capabilities, electronic procurement (including reverse auctions), team-based bid and proposal evaluations, and open/unlimited supplier access to catalogs, accounts, and reports.

Other features often missing from ERP packages include support for use by local governments, access by the public to reporting, capability of certifying suppliers eligible for socioeconomic preferences, a central portal for publicly advertising solicitations, integration with social media for posting public notices, and support for mobile access to government data. As a result of these deficiencies, and in order to take advantage of the added capabilities of eProcurement systems, governments appear to be accelerating the adoption of stand-alone or integrated eProcurement solutions with robust procurement capabilities.

ERP System Integration

There are two eProcurement system deployment models—stand-alone or integrated. Stand-alone systems appear attractive because they divorce procurement implementation from the challenges of implementation of the ERP or accounting system. Yet after deployment of a stand-alone eProcurement system, public procurement officers may find that, despite their success in conducting individual transactions, there are significant drawbacks to operating separately from the public entity's primary ERP system.

A key disadvantage of a stand-alone eProcurement system is that it generally serves only the needs of the procurement function and is not used to pay invoices or record to the public entity's accounting ledger. As a result, detailed data related to procurement and contracting is maintained in a separate procurement database from the financial expenditure database.

This separate data is not consolidated into a common database with invoice payment and budget data, or it requires a separate operation to consolidate. The separate databases impair a central procurement office's ability to carry out: full procure-to-pay and budget analysis, trending, or forecasting; identification of opportunities for consolidated spending and strategic sourcing; enforcement of procurement policy to eliminate rogue spending; provision of accurate management reporting on purchase trends or category spending; and responses to public requests for access to procurement information. Further, the separation of these systems requires adoption of manual processes to enter supplier and order data into the ERP system to process invoices, receipts, and payments.

Suppliers of eProcurement systems have attempted to meet this need by offering receiving and invoicing capabilities in their suites. However, eProcurement offerings may not provide the level of capability offered by traditional ERP applications with respect to accounts payable, asset accounting, project accounting, general ledger maintenance, or banking.

More recently, suppliers of eProcurement systems have evolved their offerings to overcome the disadvantages of the stand-alone model by introducing standard technologies to seamlessly integrate their functionality and processes with ERP systems. This integrated model, when successful, provides for the enhanced functionality of eProcurement and further increases transaction efficiencies by simultaneously creating a common database of procurement, payment, and budget data.

ERP suppliers are also updating their solution suites to offer their own, branded, eProcurement functionalities. Central procurement offices should evaluate whether the functionality inherent in their existing ERP solution can meet their needs and weigh the loss of some features/functionality against the costs and impacts of deploying and supporting a separate eProcurement system and the required integration. They should also evaluate the development plans of the ERP system supplier to determine whether they have a strategy and are investing to evolve their system to achieve the same functionality as their eProcurement system competitors.

Central procurement offices looking to integrate an independent eProcurement system within their ERP system will need to understand and weigh the financial and resource costs for periodic system upgrades. This can create a significant impact on staff resources if, for example, the eProcurement supplier goes through three upgrades per year.

Software as a Service eProcurement Solutions

SaaS as a potential delivery mechanism for eProcurement software has emerged as an alternative to the more traditional public entity-hosted model. SaaS, or Cloud-hosted solutions, can offer state and local governments several benefits. Since it is a web-based solution, there is no hardware to purchase or maintain—only implementation costs and a yearly subscription fee. Additionally, SaaS puts the responsibility on the supplier for all software and hardware support, maintenance, and upgrades.

Other efficiencies and benefits of the SaaS delivery mechanism for eProcurement include contract compliance, strategic sourcing, process savings, and purchase card savings. Business processes will likely be streamlined as well. Typically, data is owned by the public entity and, in the case of system failure or contract termination, must be returned to the public entity in an appropriate form for use in a follow-on system. Data security is managed by the supplier, and the service level agreement determines penalties associated with a data breach or data corruption.

One important difference between SaaS and other hosted models is the use of a subscription fee. While public-entity-hosted eProcurement systems historically involved implementation fees, paid-up licenses permitted perpetual use of the system. Annual costs were normally driven by post-implementation maintenance agreements to keep the software updated and the entire system on an upgrade path for future improvements in technology. The system software and data generally resided on public-entity-owned servers.

SaaS solutions, on the other hand, are financed with subscription fees while the system is used. The SaaS supplier does not license the underlying system but maintains responsibility for maintenance and upgrades to its system. The system is located at the supplier's facilities. With the software and data hosted at supplier sites, or specialized cloud service locations, security and ownership of data becomes an especially important consideration.

CONCLUSION

A number of states are now considering (or will soon be faced with) whether to transform their procurement systems, retire their legacy systems, integrate eProcurement functionalities into their state's ERP systems, or deploy a separate eProcurement system. These decisions involve considerations that transcend traditional procurement activities. They involve analysis of business processes, managing the change that comes with implementations of this size, and a reexamination of the relationship between procurement and accounting, as well as between suppliers and the user agencies. At the end of the day, each state and local government is different, and the best eProcurement solution for one public entity will not necessarily be an ideal solution for the next. Information, such as that in this chapter, assists Chief Procurement Officers in their efforts to choose the best solution that effectively addresses their public entity's needs.

ENDNOTES

1. For more information on specific eProcurement systems or funding mechanisms used in each state, refer to the full results of the survey published and kept current on NASPO's website here: https://www.naspo.org/2018Survey
2. http://www.naspo.org/Publications/ArtMID/8806/ArticleID/3312
3. www.NJSTART.gov
4. See Endnote 1.
5. Public/private partnerships in the context of public infrastructure are discussed in Chapter 11, *Procurement of Construction and Related Services.* Some of the same considerations apply to any public/private partnership.
6. Chapter 20 discusses what the term *stakeholder* means in large information technology projects.
7. For more information on agile or modular procurement, check out NASPO's resources on the subject here: https://www.naspo.org/Publications
8. "Blockchain is an open, distributed ledger that can record transactions between two parties efficiently and in a verifiable and permanent way. The ledger itself can also be programmed to trigger transactions automatically . . . With blockchain, we can

imagine a world in which contracts are embedded in digital code and stored in transparent, shared databases, where they are protected from deletion, tampering, and revision. In this world every agreement, every process, every task, and every payment would have a digital record and signature that could be identified, validated, stored, and shared . . ." Marco Iansiti and Karim R. Lakhani. *The Truth about Blockchain*. Harvard Business Review, January-February 2017. https://hbr.org/2017/01/the-truth-about-blockchain

9. Access to the dictionary is available at: http://www.nigp.org/home/find-procurement-resources/dictionary-of-terms

CHAPTER 20: PROCUREMENT OF INFORMATION TECHNOLOGY

RECOMMENDED BEST PRACTICES

- Information technology (IT) procurements should remain focused on the public entity's business requirements and the value to be brought to that business before identifying possible technology solutions.
- Project governance must be effective to enable successful IT procurement. IT project management and procurement must partner throughout the project to ensure effective procurement and contract management.
- Market research should be conducted and IT suppliers should be involved before the public entity develops solicitation documents.
- Solicitation documents for IT projects should not be overly prescriptive and should encourage suppliers to bring innovative, creative solutions to the table.
- Before investing in technology, a public entity should use pilots and demonstration projects to test the technology.
- Contract terms and conditions should not be allowed to reduce competition. A risk-based approach to negotiating terms and conditions should be used, and public procurement officers should understand where flexibility is possible.
- Solid supplier management best practices should be established for contractors under long-term or high-risk contracts to ensure that successfully negotiated terms can be leveraged to ensure the success of large IT implementations.
- A bimodal[1] way of approaching technology procurement must be embraced to ensure the process fits the user agencies' needs as well as the project and its intended outcomes.

Public procurement officers support the needs of the user agencies they serve. Those needs are increasingly reliant on technology. As demands on state and local governments change, public procurement is also expected to reinvent sourcing policies and processes to encourage the innovation, creativity, and flexibility required to purchase effectively in technology markets.

What are sought includes an agile culture and a process that allows user agencies to take advantage of supplier expertise to deliver solutions that propel government services forward. This chapter describes new approaches and processes around which the public procurement community, public chief information officers, and IT suppliers must rally to ensure that the public sector's increasing use of technology is seamlessly and successfully planned, procured, and implemented.

At the outset, it is useful to put IT and the role that it plays in a governmental structure into context. IT is a tool for collecting, analyzing, and processing information. Today, it is also an essential means of providing governmental information to those outside of a government, including the public. Finally, it plays a significant role in managing state contractors for large government programs such as Medicaid and mental health programs.

In this chapter, the term *program* means the specific activity that a law or executive order directs the government to sponsor or provide; for example, Medicaid or highway construction. It also can mean those activities under the authority of a public entity's chief information officer, who is responsible for the public entity's IT infrastructure. While the term *program* also has a specific IT meaning as well, the term is not used in that way in this chapter.

A *project*, as used in this chapter, means all of the activities related to determining the best IT solution for supporting or implementing a governmental program. The steps in a large IT project are addressed in upcoming paragraphs. The purchase of standard, commercial IT commodities, such as laptops, desktop computers, and other commercial hardware and software, are not addressed in this chapter.

Finally, the *project sponsor*, a term that is used regularly in this chapter, means the governmental official responsible for the program for which the IT project is being initiated.

CALLS FOR AND COLLABORATION ON REFORM

Over two decades ago, the State Procurement Administrator for the State of Arizona at the time articulated a basic conflict inherent in the procurement of IT:

> *Today, state government officials are still trying to cope with the immediate need to buy the tools necessary to operate faster, better, and cheaper, while adhering to a procurement process that maintains the traditional safeguards of ensuring both integrity and a fair opportunity for all interested vendors. [. . .] In fact, the traditional role of the procurement official—to ensure that the process is fair and eliminates favoritism—often runs headlong into the role of the state information systems planner—to ensure that the state promptly obtains the most current technology, thus permitting state programs and services to operate effectively.*[2]

That basic conflict still exists today, but efforts have been made and are still in progress to reconcile the two often competing interests in order to create an innovative process that fulfills the goals of both parties.

Currently, there is an abundance of calls for and collaboration on public procurement reform relating to IT. For instance, the National Association of State Chief Information Officers (NASCIO) in collaboration with the National

Association of State Procurement Officials (NASPO) has published a series of briefs that contain forward-looking recommendations for reform in IT procurement aimed at delivering improved results.[3]

Another voice in the call for reforms is Integrated Justice Information Systems. IJIS is a nonprofit organization that brings industry and government together to improve national security and promote effective information sharing and safeguarding. The IJIS Institute's *Procurement Innovation Report* dated December 2013 notes that, "as the costs of [IT] procurement and subsequent contract negotiations within the public sector continue to rise, it becomes critically important to introduce reform and innovation rather than to simply accept the status quo."[4] The report, written by a task force of volunteers representing the public and private sector, provides key recommendations for innovation and reform, while recognizing the need for rigor, repeatability, and appropriate regulation.

Adding to the imperative for change are cost pressures that are driving many public entity IT leaders to consider and implement shared services delivery models where outsourcing replaces services traditionally delivered by public entities.

To meet today's challenges, IT procurement in the public sector must strike the proper balance among transparency, the fairness essential to public procurement, and the agility necessary to meet the requirements and expectations of multiple stakeholders.[5] IT procurement cannot be viewed solely as a project to be managed or a procurement that is completed at award.

Successful large-scale technology procurements require the expertise, knowledge, and active engagement of cross-functional teams that go beyond IT technical and procurement staff. In addition, success also depends on the engagement of executive leadership, risk management officers, project management professionals, subject matter specialists, and financial experts, all using a shared roadmap with clearly articulated government business goals.

FOUNDATIONAL PLANNING

It seems obvious that the groundwork of a successful comprehensive IT procurement begins with planning. Often, however, planning is either deficient or incomplete. Planning is a key to driving successful outcomes, which in IT means optimizing business value for the public entity. Chapter 4 (*Strategies and Plans*) discusses planning in general. The following discussion sets forth the key elements of a well-thought-out planning process for the complexities that many IT procurements pose.

Establishing the Business Case

A *business case* is a "structured proposal that justifies a project for decision makers. [It] includes an analysis of business process performance and requirements, assumptions, and issues. [It] also presents the risk analysis by explaining strengths, weaknesses, opportunities, and threats."[6] It is often used to compare various state or local government business solution alternatives and to provide a basis for selecting the one that delivers the greatest value to that government, the user agency, and other stakeholders. The business case stage of planning can be a simple or more detail-oriented investment analysis, depending upon the scale of the project at hand.

For cutting-edge, innovative projects with lower relative spend and risk, a business case may contain a problem statement that a user agency is trying to solve with an IT procurement and the desired outcome, along with budget estimates. A more comprehensive analysis may identify many more quantitative and qualitative evaluation and risk factors serving as the basis for the selection of a business solution.

It is during the business case planning stage that different service delivery models should be considered. Those models may have differing mixes of operating expenses, such as purchasing IT services contracts versus capital expenditures, or buying IT hardware and software.[7] A well-researched and thorough cost-benefit analysis for each alternative will help support the subsequent procurement process, including drafting a statement of work and other elements of a contract.

Ultimately, use of a business case should help the organization prioritize its technology investments by making smart decisions. It also should provide the basis for evaluation of business outcomes following project closure.

Questions to be answered at this phase may include:

- Why begin the project now?
- What is the impact of not carrying out the project?
- How does the project support user agency goals?
- What business problem does the project solve?
- What is the financial impact?
- When will the project show results?

The Department of Information Resources of the State of Texas is an example of a public entity that has embraced an in-depth planning process. The business justification phase of a process is part of *The Texas Project Delivery Framework*.[8] It includes a template for writing a business case.[9] The State of California's Department of Technology also offers templates for each phase of an IT project.[10]

Using an Integrated Procurement Strategy

An integrated procurement strategy provides a roadmap for the procurement activities associated with an IT project. This strategy document can be a part of the business case analysis. The procurement strategy is refined as the project details emerge and eventually results in a procurement plan.

For complex system procurements, an effective procurement strategy that is aligned with the business case will help the procurement and contractor selection process to answer key questions aimed at attaining the best contract solution possible. It ensures that the sourcing methodology is working with the project rather than against it. The procurement strategy outlines the objectives of the procurement and addresses the following:

- Key elements in the procurement approach
- Constraints impacting the procurement
- User agency goals and requirements, such as replacing an old system or purchasing a new one
- Procurement team roles and responsibilities
- Executive and stakeholder oversight

Conducting Market Research

Market research must be a part of the business case or procurement plan, regardless of the cost or complexity. The results of market research are critical to determining the appropriate procurement methodology.

When planning a technology procurement, market research is typically conducted by technical staff from the office of a public entity's chief information officer. That research must be understood and validated by public procurement officers to ensure that the correct procurement process is selected.

Especially for emerging technologies, there may not yet be a stable market in which there is normal competition, and a traditional competitive sealed proposals process will not yield successful results. This is where researching the market for alternatives such as the use of cooperative contracts (discussed later in this chapter) and reseller distribution contracts—generally contracts under which a distributor provides manufacturers' commodities—is recommended.

The breadth and depth of the market research depends on the urgency, dollar value, and complexity of the procurement. Market research should include the following tasks:

- Analyze the marketplace and identify the usual commercial practices for similar types of projects. This research will ensure that the cost structure of the procurement aligns with the way in which the industry prices its commodities and services.
- Consider all potential business models and service delivery methods that can achieve the desired results. Today's *as a service* cloud-based solutions should be realistically evaluated along with traditional IT commercial off-the-shelf service models. Find out which provides the best fit, considering the public entity's enterprise architecture, business objectives, and overall strategic plan, as well as the total cost of ownership.
- Use the market analysis to create functional requirements for the commodities and services. By doing so, the public entity will be able to ensure that the requirements are not overstated or needlessly limiting, which could eliminate qualified commercial items and supplier products. Consider publishing these functional requirements in the form of a draft solicitation, and invite suppliers to provide comment on them.
- Document the effects of the research on the development of the requirements, such as whether next generation technology is emerging but not quite matured as the market research is being conducted.
- Identify likely suppliers that can meet the business objectives.
- Request price/cost estimates from interested potential service suppliers for the purposes of planning and budgeting. These ballpark figures will help determine if the solution that the public entity is seeking is possible within funding constraints. A change in scope or other requirements may be necessary.
- Issue a request for information (RFI),[11] if necessary. It is important to be realistic about the benefits of the RFI process. It can be time-consuming, so the public entity must clearly define the objectives of the process and construct the RFI document and activities accordingly.
- Research what experience other public entities have had with the type of procurement needed for the IT project.

The State of Wisconsin offers guidance in the form of a 2017 presentation related to this topic entitled *Market Research and Solicitation Development*.[12]

Creating the Project Charter

Since large-scale IT procurement is so complex and involves such a great number of stakeholders, it becomes a *project* rather than a simple, traditional procurement. Once a decision has been made to move forward with an IT project, a project charter is developed that formally authorizes work to begin. As defined by the State of California, a *project charter* is a "document issued by senior management that gives the project manager authority to apply organizational resources to project activities and formally recognizes the existence of a project."[13]

One of the purposes of a project charter is to document decisions regarding technology investments. It authorizes both the project and the project manager through an agreement between the project manager (likely the technology arm of the public entity) and the sponsor requesting the project (the user agency or agencies) before significant resources are committed and expenses incurred.

Too often, limited resources are directed toward efforts based on an informal and passive approach to starting a project. In many cases, projects are initiated without a clear understanding of the critical factors that affect project success, such as scope, use of resources, oversight authority, roles, and responsibilities. A well-crafted project charter can be the remedy for this situation.

Specifically, the charter confirms agreement among stakeholders on the business goals and needs that justify the project. It includes the primary objectives in support of the business goals that will be a measure of the project's success. By formally chartering a project, the project manager and project team have clear guidance on how the project should be planned and managed.

The State of California's Office of Systems Integration offers a template for developing a project charter.[14] It is divided into the following parts:

- Project purpose
- Business problem
- Project background
- System concepts
    ◊ Project goal and objectives statements
    ◊ Project scope
    ◊ System concept
    ◊ Critical success factors
- Project approach
    ◊ Acquisition approach (procurement, development, and implementation to the extent known)
    ◊ Key project work products
    ◊ Project milestones
    ◊ Assumptions and constraints
    ◊ Project impacts
    ◊ Successful completion criteria
- Organization (sample organization chart provided)
    ◊ Project authority and oversight defining the authority and problem resolution mechanisms
        ▪ Project sponsor—the person who makes the business case for the project and generally secures and controls the funding
        ▪ Project manager—the person who is given the authority to plan, execute, monitor, and control the project
        ▪ Project oversight—level of oversight and management rigor
        ▪ Controls—relationship between senior management and the project manager
    ◊ Roles and responsibilities of the project manager, the project sponsor, and the project team along with the roles and responsibilities of key organizations, primarily addressing authority and decision making, to be spelled out further in the governance plan and staff management plan. Identifies procurement oversight stakeholder and fiscal oversight stakeholder as key stakeholders
- Project analysis
    ◊ Project priority in terms of resources, schedule, and scope, and whether those are not flexible, somewhat flexible, or most flexible
    ◊ Preliminary risk assessment
    ◊ Charter acceptance—signatures of the project manager from the Office of Systems Integration, the chief executive of the sponsor organization, and the director of the Office of Systems Integration

The project charter should include the appropriate business case information to ensure that a comprehensive view of the project is communicated. It should be developed in coordination with stakeholders, and activities under it should not be undertaken without the approval of key stakeholders. Because this is a collaborative effort, it is important to establish a solid partnership among the various stakeholders to help improve project management processes and achieve on-time, on-budget delivery of the desired project outcome.

The project charter should clearly spell out the roles and responsibilities of the project team. This enables the project manager and the project sponsor to ensure accountability of performance and timely decision making. The project charter should be referenced throughout the project since it provides an overview of what the project is about, why it is being conducted, who is involved and in what capacity, and the general approach and timeline that exists for the project.

Measures of success are an important part of any successful project. Success factors must be realistic and thoroughly vetted with the user and other stakeholders. The user agency(ies)-sponsor(s) must approve measures of success. These become critical project and contract performance measures and must be included in the project charter. Documented success factors not only provide the foundation for evaluation of supplier proposals and performance after contract award, but also are the yardstick used to measure the overall performance of the project and the project team.

ESTABLISHING A GOVERNANCE PLAN

Effective governance is a key component of any successful IT procurement project implementation. A good governance plan will contribute to project success by optimizing IT project investment and managing risk. One of the primary benefits of a well-crafted governance plan is that it provides a decision-making framework that clearly defines authority and responsibilities for the project team and stakeholders.

The goal of the governance plan is to provide the management framework for project decision making. An effective governance model will provide transparent project oversight and establish a bridge between IT and the users of the technology.

Components of a Governance Plan

The State of California's Office of Systems Integration offers useful information about preparing a governance plan.[15] It also provides insight into what project management means in relationship to the particular program that is the beneficiary of the project.

Early in the life cycle, the program guides and directs the projects on desired goals and benefits. Program leadership also influences the approach for managing the individual projects within it. Later in the life cycle, the projects report to the program on status, risks, changes, costs, issues and other information with program-wide or cross-project implications. [State of California, Office of Systems Integration. Best Practices: Government Framework].[16]

For additional information and resources related to project management visit the Project Management Institute (PMI).[17] That office also provides a template for a governance plan. The template notes that a governance plan is not to be developed during the project initiation phase because there is no project at that point. Thus, the appropriate time to establish the governance plan is during the planning phase of the project.

The template requires the plan to do the following:

- Identify all of the stakeholders and organizations involved in the project, focusing on level of authority and decision making. Avoid names of persons and do not describe roles. Key participants include the project sponsor, the sponsor legal department, affected outside organizations and the public, agencies such as finance, general services (procurement), office of the state chief information officer, project executive steering committee, user agencies, governor's office, legislative offices, federal government stakeholders (if any), prime contractor, and others.
- Identify project governance, that is, who makes the final decisions/approvals for the following:
  ◊ Project approvals
  ◊ Project funding including expenditure tracking

- ◊ Project management including work products (project charter and project plans) including who reviews them and who approves them
- ◊ Supplier contract management
  - Prime contract management
  - Consultant contract management
- Identify issue resolution and escalation process[18]

The following are some other issues that the governance plan may need to address:

- Define what success looks like for both the sponsor-user agency and other stakeholders. The definition may change over the course of the project.
- Specify the frequency of project team reports on progress through the life of the project.
- Define clearly how scope and change decisions, and changes to any contracts, are made so that stakeholders are always aware of consequences such as those to scope, budget, and timeline.
- Identify the methods of conducting reviews at the start of each stage of the project and criteria for making decisions to move forward with the next stage.
- Specify the conditions that justify terminating a project based on a clear set of objective criteria and documented risks.

RACI Chart Analysis

A Responsible, Accountable, Consulted and Informed (RACI) chart can be used to define authority and accountability based on expertise and roles. "A RACI chart (RACI matrix) clarifies roles and responsibilities, making sure that nothing falls through the cracks. RACI charts also prevent confusion by assigning clear ownership for tasks and decisions."[19]

Each role is assigned the corresponding decision rights for each activity or decision point in the IT project. Each role of the RACI chart is defined as:

Responsible—*person or role responsible for ensuring that the item is completed.*

Accountable—*person or role responsible for actually doing or completing the item.*

Consulted—*person or role whose subject matter expertise is required in order to complete the item.*

Informed—*person or role that needs to be kept informed of the status of item completion.*

Variations on the roles and responsibilities chart also include *support* and *quality* (*assurance*) roles that can be added:

Support—*person or role that does not have a direct stake in approving, but has the resources to assist responsible and accountable parties with implementing decisions and changes. The support role also carries a responsibility to assist with the implementation of final changes within the public entity.*

Quality review—*ad hoc subject matter experts serving in an advisory role to ensure quality standards are met for a decision or change.*

The State of Minnesota's Department of Transportation maintains a RACI workbook template online.[20]

Measures of success are an important part of any project. Success factors must be realistic and thoroughly vetted with users and other stakeholders. The user agency-sponsor must approve measures of success. These become critical project and contract performance measures and must be included in the project charter.

PREPARING PROJECT PLANS

Project plans identify how and when the activities, processes, and procedures will be used to manage the IT project. These plans also describe assumptions and constraints, organizational structure and governance, and the management of parameters for cost, quality, staffing, and communications. They should include a description of how the project plans will unfold for both the project deliverables and the corresponding management activities, such as the project kickoff meeting, status meetings, project monitoring, and reporting.

The plural *plans* is used here as the project may be broken down into subject matters. The State of California's *Statewide Information Management Manual* offers helpful templates.[21]

Note that planning will not succeed unless there is an integrated project team made up of all critical positions. Some examples of key stakeholders are the sponsor, project manager, subject matter (business) experts, technical experts, procurement staff, and legal staff.

An essential element of the planning process is the development of a communication plan. This plan describes not only how information will be stored and distributed throughout the project, but how questions that arise will be promptly addressed.

At the beginning of the project, it may be important to assess the communications competency of the project. For a complex IT service project, an effective outside organization whose interest in success is aligned with that of the public entity is critical. Examples are Medicaid providers who submit invoices and receive payments from the state electronically. As in any collaboration, this requires an effective communications process at all stages to ensure that the project team, stakeholders, potential offerors, and the contractor have timely and effective information.

NASPO has recently highlighted the importance of engaged, skillful communications in a 2017 webinar entitled *Best Practices in Agency Relations and Communications*.[22] Also useful is NASPO's white paper entitled *Effective Communication between State Procurement and Industry*.[23] Although NASPO published it in 2012, it is still relevant.

Additional resources on the importance of finding prudent, fair, and flexible methods to maintain communication between state government and industry are published by the United States Office of Management and Budget, *Mythbusting* papers II[24] and III.[25]

Another key aspect of project planning is establishing a requirement to write and retain a set of records that chronicle the development of the technology. Some examples of documents or e-records that may describe and detail project key work products are:

- System requirements specifications
- Detailed design specifications
- Database schema
- Test and evaluation plan
- Data conversion plan
- User reference guides
- Training plan
- Implementation plan

MANAGING RISKS

IT procurement-related risk depends on the circumstances of the individual procurement. Factors affecting risk include the technology's stability, application size, ability to articulate desired solution or outcome, security and privacy, and experience of the procurement team members.

As can be seen from the earlier discussion concerning the development of the project charter, possible risks must be identified at the earliest point in an IT project—as many of the risks as possible. This list may then be used to initially draw up a risk register, a tool used to document project risk in an easy-to-understand format. A skilled team made up of experts in procurement, finance, legal, security, technology, and business ownership is key to collaboratively identifying risk.

Many of the risks that must be taken into account are the risks associated with developing the procurement strategy for an IT project. A public procurement officer, in concert with other project team members, must continuously evaluate risks throughout the procurement process by employing the appropriate tools, methodologies, benchmarks, and other mitigation techniques. Chapter 4 (*Strategies and Plans*) discusses the importance of risk and managing for it in many procurement decisions, and provides some insight on risk assessment tools.

It is important not to overlook risk during the negotiation of effective price and terms and conditions as well as an effective contract management plan in the risk register. Security and privacy are generally critical risks that need to be registered, and the proposed contractor's systems should be thoroughly scrutinized. The chart in Appendix C entitled *Sample Checklist for Contractor Security and Hosting Standards and Practices* is an example of the types of questions that should be asked concerning such risks. Throughout the negotiations, the outstanding items for negotiation should be tracked along with appropriate negotiating positions.

Table 20.1 is an example of a risk matrix from NASCIO's IT Procurement Modernization Series Part III entitled *Procurement: Avoiding Risky Business*.[26]

Table 20.1 Sample risk matrix

Likelihood of Event Occurrence	Event Severity			
	Extreme Level X Event	**Major Level 3 Event**	**Moderate Level 2 Event**	**Minor Level 1 Event**
Remote	• Targeted terrorism • Loss of life (workplace violence)	• Major supply chain disruption • Major natural event (hurricane, tornado, earthquake) • Internal sabotage • Cyberterrorism	• Minor supply chain disruption	• Impact if the risk occurs on normal operations • Failure to document all requirements at the beginning of the procurement/project
Low Probability	• Severe brand damage • Political instability • Level 1 terrorism • Loss of key sponsors	• Transportation infrastructure disruption • Telecom infrastructure disruption	• Kidnap & ransom • Facility fire • Major flooding • Minor natural event	• Feature creep (incorporation of additional features during the project) • Failure to understand and document business processes related to the procurement
High Probability	• Major hazmat incident	• Worksite accident • Loss of life (limited) • Delays associated with subcontractors or third-party stakeholders	• Attrition of key personnel • Knowledge capital loss • Telecom outage	• Attrition of nonessential personnel
Anticipated	• Major natural event (hurricane, tornado, earthquake) • Epidemic		• Power outages	• Minor flooding

Managing the risks should include using periodic reviews by answering questions such as these:

- Is there a regular status review and update of key risks to assure they are under control?
- Is the top risk list reviewed and updated (weekly, monthly, quarterly)?
- Has the top risk list been disseminated to the appropriate people within the organization?
- For each scheduled risk response action, is there progress in addressing the risk as planned?
- For any risk exceeding defined trigger values, has the appropriate level of management approved the implementation of the contingency plan?
- Has any required risk status report been prepared for disseminating information at progress (and any other appropriate) reviews?
- Has the project schedule been updated to reflect the implementation of any approved risk contingency plans?
- Has the project team been reviewing the project for other risks that have appeared?
- Has the process to accept additional risks from project members and outside stakeholders been followed?

SOURCING AND PROCUREMENT ISSUES

Complex IT projects need effective partnerships to succeed. Carrying them out successfully takes the appropriate sourcing vehicle, which is why the sourcing strategy and procurement plan are so important to IT procurements. With a move to more rapid adoption of running IT projects (and procurements) in an agile fashion, it is time for public procurement offices to begin considering that there is more than one way to approach buying different categories of technology solutions.

Bimodal and Modular Sourcing

Bimodal sourcing encompasses a two-pronged approach for acquiring IT: the first type focuses on traditional IT characterized by stability and efficiency; and the second type aims at creating an experimental, agile public entity focused on time-to-market, rapid application evolution, and tight alignment with user agencies.[27] Bimodal sourcing is not a new concept. As it applies to public procurement of IT, it offers an opportunity to *fit* a more traditional procurement process to the projects where it is most suitable, and to account for a more flexible, agile process where it is appropriate (such as new or niche solutions or solutions that require services from multiple suppliers to create one common solution).

For example, in the case of categories that offer the most standardization potential, such as laptops, desktops, and other commodities, a more traditional or *legacy* approach to procurement or sourcing may be effective and still produce value. In fact, as these IT products become standard commodities, the procurement process will likely more closely resemble non-IT commodity purchases. Often, cooperative contracts are a good source to leverage for these types of purchases.

Conversely, for highly complex systems, a more agile process of selection, typically of multiple contractors, may be a more effective method. It focuses on managing the final sourcing solution, like a project where requirements are more fluid and delivery is done in *sprints* such as for Maintenance Management Information Systems[28] and other large software solutions. This approach can also be referred to as an iterative process, that is, a process for reaching a desired result by means of a repeated cycle of operations, with each repetition bringing the project closer to the desired outcome. It is carried out through frequent interaction of a core, cross-functional team to test, accept, and implement large systems under a contract.

Modular procurement also offers effective strategies for breaking up large and complex technology procurements into smaller increments. For more guidance on the importance of adopting a mind-set, skill set, and practical tools for modular procurement, NASPO issued a paper entitled *Modular Procurement: A Primer*[29] that includes a description of the steps used in this process.

Procurement Issues

The Scope of Work

The scope of work is the key component in IT procurement solicitation and contains the important elements of the procurement's objectives. Chapter 5 (*Non-Construction Specifications and Scopes of Work*) and Chapter 10 (*Contracting for Services*) also address the critical nature of a scope of work. A statement of work template and related tools are offered by the Commonwealth of Virginia's Virginia Information Technologies Agency.[30]

For IT procurements, it is best for the scope of work to be developed in consultation with all stakeholder groups in the IT project. One of the biggest drafting mistakes made by public entities is being overly prescriptive in defining the specifications for a solution and how to deliver the solution. Being prescriptive transfers the risk and responsibility for addressing the problem to the public entity and, while the solution delivered may meet the specifications, it may not solve the problem. Overly prescriptive solicitations impede a supplier's ability to propose the most effective technology solution.

A request for proposals (RFP) should contain a statement of what problem the IT project is trying to solve. This provides the supplier community with the information it needs to be innovative and to propose its comprehensive solutions. Suppliers should be encouraged to offer alternatives. An alternative may provide a better solution than that contemplated by the project team. The solicitation should identify the types of information the alternative solutions should, at a minimum, contain.

Discussions/Negotiations During Evaluation

A best practice allows for discussions or negotiations during the evaluation. The law of the public entity should authorize discussions and negotiations as part of the proposal evaluation process when RFPs are issued. The American Bar Association Model Procurement Code for State and Local Governments (Model Procurement Code) permits discussions and negotiations. Chapter 7 (*Competition: Solicitations and Methods*) and Chapter 9 (*Bid and Proposal Evaluation and Award*) discuss the legal authority for discussions and negotiations in more detail, including the Model Procurement Code language.

Through discussions during the evaluation process, including discussions regarding price, the likelihood is increased that both the public entity and the offeror will be satisfied when the award is made to the most optimal solution in response to the RFP. Procurement processes where technical and price proposals are separated, with a contract award being made to the offeror submitting the technically acceptable, lowest-priced offer, will unnaturally disconnect the two critical factors in the selection process and are highly unlikely to yield the best outcome.

Flexibility and Innovation

The procurement process is the place to be innovative. A January 2013 report prepared by NASPO and NASCIO, *Designing for Agility: Advancing IT and Procurement Modernization*, emphasized both the importance of forging true partnerships between state Chief Information Officers and Chief Procurement Officers, and also the value of embracing innovation in the shared goal of improving IT procurement.[31] The report highlights case studies of success in the State of California through their use of agile development techniques in system redesigns,

CHAPTER 20: **PROCUREMENT OF INFORMATION TECHNOLOGY**

IT PROCUREMENT NEGOTIATIONS

Possessing strong negotiation skills as a public procurement professional is important no matter what you're buying. However, the importance of skillful negotiators handling Information Technology (IT) procurement cannot be overstated. Buying tech solutions can be very different from buying other commodities or services.

In early 2016, the National Association of State Chief Information Officers (NASCIO) released, and the National Association of State Procurement Officials (NASPO) endorsed, five recommendations for improved IT procurement, available for review on NASPO's website.[1] NASPO and NASCIO continued to work together on improving IT procurement, and in 2017, formed the Joint Task Force on Negotiations in IT Procurement, pairing up the majority of state Chief Procurement Officers (CPOs) and Chief Information Officers (CIOs) to work together to solve difficult IT negotiation problems. As part of that work, task force members answered survey questions, convened an in-person, two-day workshop, and released 18 recommendations for improving IT procurement.[2]

The task force focused on four areas described below:

Centralization—As with any complicated process in modern government, success only comes with a clear understanding of roles, responsibilities, and organization. Projects can and have failed because teams lacked strong leaders, clear marching orders, and/or a shared vision. Centralized IT procurement allows for controlling costs for the taxpayers and leads to a collective vision for the future of state technology. Having both enterprise-architecture-driven policies and centralized IT procurement reduces confusion and chaos, and helps provide needed direction and vision.

Procurement process—In the survey responses, many CIOs and CPOs stated that meeting early and often was a key component in successful IT procurements; and the survey results revealed that CIOs and CPOs are, generally, meeting and communicating on a regular basis. The survey also asked specific questions about when and how the CIO is involved in the procurement process, with the task force focused on ways to improve the quality of the CIO involvement to benefit everyone and reach better outcomes.

Policy and legislation—In state government, a lack of modern or reformed legislation is often cited as a barrier to innovation and success. Sometimes states may have to embark upon a rigorous legislative change process to improve. However, sometimes legislation isn't required, and policy and cultural changes can have the biggest impact when it comes to IT procurement reform.

Relationship building—Throughout the work conducted by the task force, one common thread seemed to emerge: the health of the CPO and CIO relationship can significantly affect the IT procurement process. Every work environment will have challenging personalities and situations, and those issues are only magnified under the intense microscope of state government. The external challenges and pressures faced by state procurement and IT can be made exponentially worse if there is internal strife as well.

All 18 IT negotiation recommendations are listed in Appendix D and the joint report is available on the NASPO website.[3]

---

[1] https://www.naspo.org/Publications/ArtMID/8806/ArticleID/2269
[2] http://www.naspo.org/Publications/ArtMID/8806/ArticleID/4531
[3] http://www.naspo.org/Publications/ArtMID/8806/ArticleID/4531

and in the State of Ohio through IT optimization and harmonization.

Most important, the report highlights four key dimensions for which it recommends changes:

- Establish a governance and organizational structure through collaboration and creativity, and select the key individuals who will serve on cross-functional technology boards or equivalents to oversee IT procurement projects.
- Encourage more teaming and role clarity through more regular education and communication between procurement and IT as functions.
- Reform the way IT and procurement staff and leadership interact by establishing rules of engagement.
- Improve budgeting and forecasting by acknowledging that close partnerships between, and innovative approaches of, Chief Procurement Officers and chief information officers can reduce waste and enhance efficiencies.

Multiple-Round RFPs

Multiple-round RFPs or multistep RFPs evaluations are used by some states, including the Commonwealth of Massachusetts and the states of California and Oregon.

The details of the procurement plan can vary, but generally the RFP expresses that the selection and award of the contract will be made in multiple stages. The first stage usually describes evaluation criteria for selecting proposals deemed suitable for award.

After the first round of selection, and in some cases after a protest period, the selection process moves into a second round. Second-round selection factors may be included in the initial RFP, or the request may describe selection factors generally, with specific factors developed after the first-round selection.

The second round offers the opportunity to score and evaluate demonstrations, transition plans, or project-specific plans. During second-round evaluations, the evaluation committee is able to assess the differentiators that should help separate the offerors that are best suited to meeting the overall needs of the project. While two evaluation rounds are typical, additional rounds may be warranted if the RFP contemplated more than two rounds and the complexity of the project warrants.

Best Value Evaluation Methodology

Best value is an evaluation method that allows flexibility in the procurement process by evaluating offers on factors other than just technical acceptability and lowest price. Best value as the standard for evaluating proposals and awarding a contract is highlighted in Chapter 7 (*Competition: Solicitations and Methods*) and Chapter 9 (*Bid and Proposal Evaluation and Award*).

Best Value Procurement

Best value procurement, also known as Performance Information Procurement System (PIPS), is also a process where both price and performance are considered in the selection decisions. However, there are few key differences between a best value procurement approach and a more traditional RFP, including those using best value as a standard for evaluation and contract award.

Chapter 7 (*Competition: Solicitations and Methods*) discusses this in more detail. Additionally, an example of the State of Alaska's use of this approach can be found in the next subsection.

Best Value Procurement: Alaska Case Study

In 2015, the State of Alaska conducted a procurement to provide core voice, video, data, and help center services for the entire state. The procurement contemplated a 5-year contract consisting of: 500 access sites, 77 video end points, 1,400 routers, 6,200 phones, 30.4 million annual phone minutes, 175 data centers, and 17,000 government staff members.

CHAPTER 20: PROCUREMENT OF INFORMATION TECHNOLOGY

Through a best value procurement approach focused on suppliers' expertise, the state was able to award contracts to two separate offerors that proposed a 400% increase in network speed along with a 48% reduction in overall contractor fees paid. The time that the procurement consumed was reduced by 45% (two months) in comparison to the previous traditional procurement process.

The state's central procurement office directed the procurement process and used its own procurement staff resources, who were trained in the PIPS/best value procurement approach. That office also employed the PIPS program from Arizona State University.

For this specific project, there were four distinct services being sought, and offerors were allowed to submit proposals to provide any combination of those services. The process described here was repeated for each of the four service offerings. Offerors' proposals were anonymous to the evaluation committee through most of the process and were limited to 15 pages, consisting of fillable forms and prohibiting any marketing material.

The PIPS/best value procurement approach entails evaluating offerors and their proposals through a series of filters or evaluation phases. The following describes the four filters used in this particular procurement.

Filter 1

Filter 1 used a pass/fail grade and addressed the state's administrative requirements for proposals. Offerors were required to acknowledge a series of items including the contents of the RFP, disclosure of any potential conflicts of interest, minimum requirements, and a completed proposal checklist. There was no limit on the number of offerors that could advance to Filter 2 and all three proposals received did advance.

Filter 2

Filter 2 consisted of an evaluation of past performance, cost, project approach, strategic fit, and whether the offeror qualified for the statutory preference that the state's law requires to be given to local suppliers. Several of the items were scored blindly by cleansing the proposal sections of names and identifying information. Here is how the evaluation proceeded during this phase:

- Past performance information was derived from the scores submitted on the state-provided survey forms that offerors asked their customers to complete and return for scoring.
- Cost proposals provided data used to calculate cost score in accordance with state guidelines and were based on the ten-year total cost of the proposal.
- Project approach consisted of a work plan that covered the plan for managing project scope, schedule, and project implementation. It also included a transition plan to migrate from existing systems to the proposed ones (including training) and a plan to monitor performance throughout the contract term. The risk assessment and value-added plan included a prioritized list of major risk items including both the items the offeror could control and those it could not. The value-added plan gave the offerors the opportunity to add options that might benefit the state but were not included in the cost. The state determined in an earlier phase what value-added items would be accepted or rejected.
- Strategic fit considerations included an evaluation of the offeror's personnel and experience, impact to state staff, exceptions to terms and conditions, and software functionality and technical requirements.
- The state's preference law allowed qualified offerors who had local state addresses to receive point preferences.

At the end of Filter 2, all offerors were determined to be within the competitive range and advanced to Filter 3.

Filter 3

During Filter 3, the central procurement office conducted interviews with offerors' key staff. Each of the individuals was interviewed separately and the questions were not disclosed prior to the interviews. All interviews were conducted in person on specified dates. The offeror with the highest score received the maximum number of points.

Offerors then gave demonstrations that were evaluated based on three scenarios: financial, procurement, and human resources/payroll. The demonstrations were awarded scores in the same manner used for the offeror staff interviews.

The final step in this phase was to determine cost reasonableness. If the cost proposal of the offeror with the highest score was within the state's means, and the ten-year-total cost was within 10% of the next highest ranked offeror's ten-year-total cost, the state would invite the highest-ranking offeror to the pre-award phase. If the highest scorer was more than 10% greater than the second highest-ranked offeror's ten-year-total cost, the state reserved the right to invite the next highest offeror to the pre-award phase. If the highest ranked offeror's total cost exceeded the state's means, the state reserved the right to invite the next highest ranked offeror whose total cost fell within the state's means.

As it turned out, the highest ranked offeror was invited to participate in the pre-award phase.

Filter 4

Filter 4 was the pre-award or planning phase in which the single potential best value offeror identified from Filters 1–3 worked with appropriate state officials to develop the following:

- Detailed project plan
- Uncontrolled risk minimization
- Project schedule development
- Performance system implementation

These four items were included in the contract as a risk management plan.

Once the contract was signed, risk minimization began, consisting of the contractor providing weekly risk reports documenting risks affecting cost, schedule, and state's expectations. Through these weekly reports, the state was kept well informed and in a good position to work with the contractor to minimize risks to the project.

Pilot Projects or Demonstrations

Pilot or demonstration projects can provide a wealth of information and improve solutions for public entities. Chapter 7 (*Competition: Solicitations and Methods*) discusses pilot projects.

Pilot projects are appropriate when uncertainty exists as to whether an IT commodity or process will effectively operate as promised.[32] Typically, a supplier who delivers a pilot solution is precluded from responding to any subsequent, related solicitations.

An alternative to pilot projects is to incorporate demonstrations through a phase during the procurement process. Such a demonstration enables the project team to see how a proposed solution addresses the needs of the organization.

One type of trial run is utilized at the federal government level. In an article in the April 6, 2017 issue of *Government Technology*, entitled *How Government Is Reforming IT Procurement and What it Means for Vendors*, the author, Ben Miller, discusses the creation in 2014 of the digital consulting group known as *18F* within the United States General Services Administration.[33] 18F has adopted many private sector ideas and experiences into government procurement and those ideas are now affecting change in other states, such as California and Ohio.

Government Technology describes 18F in an August 8, 2016 article appropriately titled, *What is 18F?*[34]

> *Very much a startup within government, 18F operates as a digital consultancy to help agencies buy, build, and share modern software. The group, composed of about 200 employees, does not choose its projects or customers. Instead, federal agencies contract 18F's various teams to answer specific challenges. These developers, data scientists, designers, researchers, policy analysts, and contracting specialists then go to work applying tech startup operating principles like agile development, human-centered design, open source code, and data-driven decision-making to enable an array of IT solutions.*

More information about 18F is available on its website.[35]

Test driving potential solutions has endless possibilities for helping to address the challenges facing state and local government IT clients. That, in turn, introduces a different model of conducting a competition.

Cooperative Purchasing

Cooperative purchasing offers public entities access to procurement resources beyond what its own resources can deliver. By taking advantage of contracts established and made available by other public entities and cooperatives, the public procurement officer has access to contracts that leverage the buying power of multiple organizations.

In addition, using these contracts reduces the need for repeating the procurement activities already performed by others. This increases access to suppliers and streamlines the procurement process without increasing headcount. Chapter 12 (*Cooperative Purchasing*) provides additional information about cooperative purchasing resources.

Outside Technical Assistance

Outside technical assistance through third parties is a valuable resource available to public entities. Contracting with a firm with expertise in the type of procurement, solution, or technology needed can help educate the IT project team, improve the written solicitation, and enhance the overall procurement process. What is learned during one procurement can often be applied to many more, spreading the benefit of the expenditure over many projects.

The use of outside advisors can provide a knowledge base to a project team that may otherwise lack specific experience with the solution sought. Finding the right advisor can be as easy as consulting colleagues who have implemented similar solutions with third-party assistance.

ALTERNATIVES TO BUYING IT HARDWARE AND SOFTWARE

There are occasions when the IT solution is not to buy hardware or software, but to take a different approach. Some of these are discussed in the following paragraphs.

Lease Versus Purchase

Leasing is an alternative to the outright purchase of technology. A NASPO paper entitled *Tech Next: Leasing vs. Owning Hardware and Software* highlights the issues that arise in each case by comparing the two approaches to acquiring technology.[36]

Leasing and seat management, discussed later in this chapter, have been used as feasible, cost-effective alternatives to purchasing IT hardware, particularly in the areas of desktop and laptop computers. When considering procurement options, public entities need to compare the advantages of purchasing information technologies outright, leasing the hardware (no permanent ownership), or seat management/managed services contracts (a managed-service form of contracting for IT).

It is not always easy to compare leasing, seat management, and outright purchasing, due to the unique costs or services that each option presents. There are risks and benefits with all three procurement options.

A direct purchase can be the simplest way to obtain an IT asset, but additional costs must be considered to determine the total cost of ownership.[37] As part of the evaluation process, the terms and conditions of the purchase must be carefully examined to identify potential additional costs. Some of the questions that should be asked are:

- Are the terms of the hardware warranty clear, especially the length of the warranty and the conditions describing how and where maintenance will be performed and by whom?
- Will additional commodities need to be procured to maintain productivity while a unit of hardware is being serviced?
- Is the user agency responsible for shipping hardware to be repaired?

Public entities should consider the value of expending additional monies for an extended maintenance contract. It is not unusual for the annual cost of maintenance contracts to reach 20% of the original purchase price. The useful life of most IT equipment is currently five-plus years. That equates to spending double the original equipment cost over five years and does not take into consideration any technology refresh due to changes in technology capabilities.

Not all leases are created equal. The public entity should carefully evaluate lease agreements, including a review by its attorneys, and should add language to the agreement to protect the user agency and the public entity. Supplier standard lease agreements typically favor the lessor.

Lease/lease-purchase contracts are another beneficial option if a public entity has a limited budget for purchasing hardware. Spreading technology procurements into consistent annual or monthly payments can improve the public entity's ability to acquire needed technologies. Government executive management and finance personnel can best determine the proper accounting practice based on relevant statutes and the public entity's practices.

As in the case of a purchase, some in-depth research is required to ensure that the public entity is acquiring the correct tool set to satisfy its business needs. The terms and conditions of warranty coverage are just as important for leases as they are for purchases. For example, the lease should allow for financial relief if a warranty repair by the manufacturer takes too long to complete. Also, the public entity should consider the value of the warranties and extended maintenance agreements available within the contract. Chapter 13 (*Quality Assurance*), discusses warranties in more detail.

Leasing usually provides the advantage of allowing for refreshing the technology. Negotiating a three-year lease will generally allow public entities an easier path toward staying current with technology changes. However, long-term planning is required to determine future cycles of lease renegotiation, change management, and training.

Another important point to consider in the case of a lease is what will happen to the equipment at the end of the lease. Technically, the contractor leasing the equipment (lessor) still owns it. Public entities desiring to negotiate a buy-out of the lease at the end of the lease term should be careful to obtain a reduced fair market or residual value. It is important in the original lease agreement to negotiate the expense of returning the equipment to the lessor at the lessor's cost. The proper packing and shipping of retired equipment can add significant cost for one party or the other in a lease. Many of the same considerations that exist when purchasing equipment are still present, such as:

- Who maintains operating system monitoring and patching?
- Is there a budget for hardware upgrades?
- Can those upgrades be included under the lease?
- If no maintenance contract is purchased, who supports these hardware units?
- What is the annual cost for maintenance support?
- Does the public entity have the expertise to provide such support?
- What is the estimated useful life of the hardware units?
- How many backup hardware units should be purchased and stocked to keep affected staff productive?

Seat Management/Managed Services Contracts

Seat management/managed services contracts go beyond the simple leasing of IT assets. They encompass outsourcing the complete management of assets, from inventory to software distribution to enterprise-wide technology updates. Seat management is a managed service form of contracting for IT that is structured around the functional requirements of organizations. This creates an environment where the supplier manages the technology supporting the public entity so that the public entity can concentrate on supporting its constituencies and core mission.

Seat management contracts often require challenging negotiations and reviews. Some seat management agreements are similar to leases with additional hardware support built into the agreement. Others may provide hardware and a whole suite of services including productivity software and help desk support.

These types of agreements also help public entities, particularly small ones that face challenges recruiting, training, and retaining skilled IT staff. These costs should be considered as potential cost avoidance factors when estimating the total cost of ownership of seat management contracts. Transferring these responsibilities to a contractor may be the public entity's best solution for acquiring reliable IT hardware and software to conduct daily business.

Negotiations with a supplier should not only include the specific technology offered, but also the roles and responsibilities of all parties and service levels of support. Service levels are discussed in Chapter 10 (*Contracting for Services*). Significant research on specific public entity requirements must be undertaken in preparing to negotiate an agreement with a contractor.

Similar to lease/lease-purchase agreements, seat management/managed services contracts can offer public entities the capability to divide high-dollar IT purchases into smaller, consistent, annual or monthly amounts. Warranty, maintenance and service level agreements are crucial considerations in developing a seat management contract. Transition planning is also required to address the role of suppliers and public entity staff in the proper handling of equipment at the end of the agreement.

Seat management tends to be the most expensive IT procurement strategy over time due to the wider range of services supplied under the agreement. In evaluating seat management contracts, public entities should consider any savings or cost avoidance that might be achieved through outsourcing. Existing and future costs for employees, training, and maintenance should be part of the analysis when calculating savings and cost avoidance.

Cloud Services

Services provided through the cloud include Software as a Service (SaaS), Platform as a Service (PaaS), and Infrastructure as a Service (IaaS). Public entities can use these services in any of the deployment models cited here:

- **Software as a service**—a software distribution model in which a third-party provider hosts applications and makes them available to customers over the Internet. SaaS delivers applications, such as e-mail, customer relationship management, and collaboration software.
- **Platform as a service**—a cloud computing model in which a third-party provider delivers hardware and software tools—usually those needed for application development—to users over the Internet. It delivers an application framework that supports design and development, testing, deployment, and hosting. PaaS enables public entities to develop custom applications on one platform, which then easily deploy to many hosting environments that support the same platform, based on various pricing and service level agreement (SLA) models.
- **Infrastructure as a service**—delivers computing hardware, storage, networking, and other managed services such as backup, monitoring, and virtual private network.[38]
- **Cloud broker**—a third-party individual or business that acts as an intermediary between the purchaser of a cloud computing service and the sellers of that service. The broker helps to normalize the multiple services available, creating an apples-to-apples comparison in pricing and functionality as much as possible. In addition, the cloud broker can provide a single, unified web interface so that end users can design, procure, provision, monitor, and govern the services.

There are currently four different deployment models for cloud—public cloud, private cloud, hybrid cloud, and community cloud:

- **Public cloud**—the provider delivers common IT capability in a shared environment with great scalability.[39] Demands from multiple customers with similar requirements are pooled together to optimize physical resources. Access is via an on-demand public network capability, such as the Internet.
- **Private cloud**—IT resources are dedicated and customized with the capabilities, resources, and administration required by a specific organization. Access is generally through a secured or managed network. Private clouds require a data center location, IT physical resources, virtualization, and operations team support. A virtual private cloud is characterized by having a specific capacity in a public cloud carved out and dedicated to a particular organization and made available through a secured, managed virtual network.
- **Hybrid cloud**—the provider blends both private and public cloud features together, with combination preferences usually driven by a particular market niche or consumer group based on an application or system that has partial needs for highly secure or nonvirtual resources.
- **Community cloud**—a specific community of consumers from organizations that share the same types of concerns.

It is important to research the types of deployment models available for cloud computing. Knowing the options for deployment will maximize the capabilities of the solution. There are also different types of cloud suppliers—direct service provider, reseller, and cloud broker:

- **Direct service provider (DSP)**—Supplier maintains the supplier-designed, supplier-built data center. There are basic DSPs that offer basic services and boutique DSPs that offer enhanced and flexible services. Boutique DSPs often provide more flexibility in regard to SLA and customer protections. Basic DSPs generally provide access controls (for example, a self-serve portal[40]), but customers are responsible for their own related services such as encryption and backup.
- **Reseller**—Third-party provider that offers access to DSP(s) via an already established

contract with DSP(s). Resellers generally provide enhanced support for the DSP services they offer and typically provide access to a single DSP.
- **Cloud Broker**—Similar to resellers, except they generally offer multiple DSP options in addition to value-added services such as aggregated billing and a service portal to multiple DSPs. Cloud brokers can also offer online tools to facilitate comparisons among suppliers, establish contracts with cloud service suppliers, and provide systems to help agencies manage and operate the cloud services from multiple service suppliers at once. DSPs can also serve as cloud brokers.

Public entities should review their workload and place it in the most appropriate cloud environment. Development and testing records or data with no personal identifying information are good candidates for the public cloud. A hosted private cloud offers physical separation of data, which may be more appropriate for applications that include confidential data. Potential users should consider starting with a pilot project—for instance, putting a single application or public data with no confidential information in the public cloud as a first step.

Comparing cloud pricing models can be difficult due to variables in product and pricing offerings. Some suppliers offer full IT solutions, (hardware and software infrastructure, middleware platforms, and application system components) while others only provide pricing for each service. Various pricing models include on-demand, subscription, and reserved capacity, described as follows:

- **On-demand or pay-as-you-go pricing models**: provide hourly-based pricing for virtual resources based on various combinations of central processing units (CPUs), memory, storage, and network capacity. The resources are billed after they have been provided and allocated for a designated time.
- **Subscription pricing models:** (also known as monthly package pricing or reserved instance pricing) involve a prepayment for some fixed capacity. This may be a monthly or yearly subscription for the fixed capacity, whether it is used or not. The advantage is lower per-hour or per-capacity pricing than the on-demand model, since it is prepaid.
- **Reserved capacity:** (also known as virtual private dedicated capacity or utilized capacity) pricing models define a specific total amount of CPUs, memory, storage, and network capacity that is dedicated and always available to the customer. The advantage is that it provides consistent pricing on a month-to-month basis.

It is best to understand the type of data being used in the application and determine which applications are appropriate for the cloud. Cloud services may be a good fit for some applications within the public entity, but may not be appropriate for others. In general, cloud services should be considered for applications that:

- Require rapid deployment
- Need technology refresh and/or the end of contractual obligations to a legacy environment
- Have variable storage needs
- Need bursting capability that allows cloud services to exceed planned or allocated thresholds when capacity is maximized
- Use virtual services rather than physical servers
- Use federal funding with cloud-first recommendations[41]

The public entity should consider any specific application requirements or compliance regulations they entail. It is essential to identify all applications' compliance requirements, such as security, privacy, or accessibility. The application that is being considered for the cloud will determine the level and type of security that is required. Compliance requirements may exist, depending on the type of data being stored.

Comparing Costs for Various Approaches

There are many different methods for comparing various IT solutions. Hard costs for hardware, software, and maintenance are relatively simple to calculate. Other measures such as cost avoidance are more difficult to quantify. A decision matrix can be a helpful tool for comparing and contrasting IT procurement options. It presents a side-to-side comparison of procurement options and factors for consideration. A decision matrix should be considered only as a starting point for IT procurement deliberations.

CONTRACT TERMS AND CONDITIONS

Terms and conditions define the relationship between the parties and, ideally, allow both parties to understand the risks of the contract and manage them to a point that is known and acceptable to both parties. IT terms and conditions have several key elements that make them more complex than other more mature types of contracting.

Public entities have typically applied a single set of consistent terms and conditions across all contracts to frame the relationship between the state or local government and the supplier, and to protect the public's interests. But these terms and conditions have not kept pace with dynamic IT issues, such as ownership of intellectual property.

Another factor affecting terms and conditions in IT contracts has been the passage by Congress in 2002 of federal legislation known as the Sarbanes-Oxley Act of 2002 (SOX).[42] SOX is aimed at reducing the possibility of fraudulent accounting activities by publicly held corporations.

Publicly held IT contractors not only have a fiduciary duty to shareholders, but also have legal reporting requirements of assets and liabilities, including their contracts. Under Section 302 of SOX, an executive of a publicly held company is required to have systems in place to identify material information that must be disclosed to investors and other third parties who rely on financial statements of publicly traded companies.

Since most IT suppliers with which public entities deal are publicly held, SOX requires them to understand and quantify the risks and potential liability under a public entity's terms and conditions. IT suppliers tend to resist terms that, for instance, require them to accept all costs related to a data security incident.

Sourcing methods that require mandatory compliance with all terms and conditions and prevent discussion or negotiation of terms will typically restrict competition. Contractors with good solutions and strong expertise may be prevented from executing contracts that have terms and conditions they cannot accept. Lack of competition is not healthy, and awards to contractors that cannot meet contractual responsibilities result in marginal outcomes and a false sense of protection of the public entity's interest.

For major IT system procurements, it is unlikely that a standard template of terms and conditions will fit without extensive modification. A complete risk assessment and mitigation framework should be completed before developing the terms and conditions. This will help the state understand the likelihood of risk for the type of work being completed. It also allows the project team to decide how risk will be managed, for example, by asking whether the risk will be accepted, mitigated, or transferred. Any approach to risk management has trade-offs. A thorough understanding of the risks and trade-offs is a prerequisite to establishing or negotiating terms and conditions.

Both California and Oregon have recently reviewed their IT terms and conditions in collaboration with industry. These efforts resulted in more market-reasonable terms and conditions for both parties. The first step in any effort to review how viable and realistic a public entity's terms and conditions are is to identify all the stakeholders within the public entity who have decisional authority over terms and conditions. The next step is to assess how viable the terms and conditions are in the marketplace and whether they affect securing top-notch IT responses, realizing that the public interest must still be protected. If changes are needed, an effective procedure would be to examine what is working well within other public entities or, if undertaking a review and rewrite, to engage industry trade associations and public entity stakeholders to review and revise the terms and conditions with a view toward making them more market-reasonable.

Key IT Terms and Conditions

Intellectual Property

Many public entities believe, or want to believe, that they are legally required to own the intellectual property (IP) of the software and processes used in systems they purchase or cause to be designed and installed at the public entity's cost. Contractors typically use third-party software for which they cannot give IP rights to the public entity because they do not own the IP themselves. Even if they did, they often refuse to give this right away for the life of the system or contract. One best practice for resolving this issue is for the contractor to grant a license for the use of the IP for the purposes intended under the contract. This allows the public entity to obtain the performance it needs under the contract and allows the contractor to retain or pass through the license.

A second element of dealing with IP is that the public entities need to be indemnified against an action or claim by an outside party that the contractor providing the software or process does not have the right to offer it to the public entity because it is the IP of that outside party. A best practice is to require the contractor to indemnify the public entity from those third-party IP claims.

Limitation of Liability

IT project implementations through contracts can be high risk. According to the Project Management Institute's (PMI's) 2017 *Pulse of the Profession*, 2017 was the first year in five years that IT project failure rates dropped over prior years, demonstrating the continued risk involved.[43]

A major IT project failure is always highly visible. As a result, both parties to an IT contract must understand their own and the other parties' responsibilities for the success of the contract. The performance deliverables and measures of successful performance must be clear. If the contractor fails in some fashion, what are their liabilities to the public entity?

There are essentially three types of failures in IT contracts: (1) failure to perform as the contract requires (contract default), (2) failure to take reasonable care in performing the contract (negligence), and (3) failure to protect information or access to information that is confidential by law (data incidents or breaches). Such failures, if the contract is written correctly, will also constitute a failure to perform the contract's material terms. In IT contracts, damages for data incidents or breaches are generally treated separately from other contract defaults or contractor negligence, even if the incident or breach is due to contractor negligence or default. Contract damages, damages for negligent behavior, and damages due to data incidents or breaches are all considered separately.

IT contractors will invariably want to limit their damages for contract default to what are known as direct damages,[44] and to be immune from responsibility for the cascading effects of that default on the public entity—damages such as consequential,[45] incidental, or punitive damages. Additionally, IT contractors will generally not agree to unlimited liability in cases in which their action or inaction causes an authorized access—actual or suspected—to information that is confidential by law. Damages in these situations come in the form of costs to the public entity of forensic services to detect the problem, breach notification to the victims, call center services, credit monitoring, and legal fees.

IT contractors do not generally balk at liability for direct contract damages, but they will want the public entity to waive any entitlement to anything but direct damages. They will also want a cap on liabilities relating to data incidents or breaches, and perhaps even on negligence, that is, cases in which, for instance, one of their employees on site at the public entity injures one of that entity's employees. Given the refusal of the most experienced and seasoned IT contractors to take on unlimited amounts of liability, the public entity will have to assess the likelihood of the risks, and arrive at a reasonable amount to protect the public entity's interest.

For major IT projects, determining the risk and potential costs can be difficult, and in some cases impossible, for either the public entity or the IT contractor to quantify. From the public entity's viewpoint, the simplest solution is to require the contractor to assume unlimited liability.

A good compromise is setting a cap on some types of liabilities. The cap amount must be sufficient to reasonably address the risk of the type of damage on which the cap is placed. This often means that both parties give something up in terms of maximum protection. A commonly used cap is twice the amount of the fees to be paid under the contract. Approaches like this seem to be a fair and reasonable way to apportion risk and mitigate damages in the event of a breach or negligence, and provides a known definite amount on which both parties can agree.

It is important to remember that this protects the state only when a contractor fails to perform or executes below-standard acts, and it does not protect the state from actions or inactions that are attributable to the public entity's obligations under the contract. A public entity must conduct rigorous project management throughout the project to exercise and document its timely decision making and fulfillment of its contractual obligations.

Beyond standard contract terms, IT involves complex challenges in the understanding and negotiation of software licensing agreements and subscription terms and conditions. However, licenses must be negotiated with the same prudent diligence as any other contracts, to mitigate risks, particularly related to issues such as data protection and audit.

Cloud Computing

Cloud computing brings additional challenges when it comes to drafting terms and conditions. NASPO has issued a useful infographic entitled *Has State Government Moved to the Cloud?*[46] It lists some challenges in addition to those already discussed previously in this chapter.

CONTRACT MANAGEMENT

Suppliers must be held accountable for their performance. Contract management goes beyond project management. Contract monitoring, acceptance, change management and dispute resolution all fall within the realm of contract management.

At times, program staff or project managers may not have the incentive to enforce contract terms because of potential negative impacts to the project schedule or the risk of missing project milestones. The risks are too high, however, and contract management must be vigorous as discussed more broadly in Chapter 14 (*Contract Management and Contract Administration*).

The State of California's Office of System Integration website contains a wealth of information about the project management life cycle, including a contract management plan and an array of tools that may be tailored to meet the needs of state and local government.[47]

Automated Tools

Automated tools are extremely useful when managing complex contracts with hundreds or thousands of deliverables to manage. These tools can provide tracking, routing, acceptance, and documentation for contract administration.

The key to effective contract administration is discipline; documentation; and timely, effective communication. Oftentimes, program staff will have considerable contract administration responsibility. Training may be needed so that the contract is clearly understood; and the roles and responsibilities explained so that a systematic, consistent approach to contract management is achieved.

The combination of properly training contract administrators and using automated systems with template management, document storage, and retrieval and approval workflow is the key to effective contract management programs that drive success and contract savings, especially in IT.

Timely Decisions

Timely decisions are important when managing large, complex contracts. Governance also plays a key role in contract management, especially when issues need to be escalated for resolution. Earlier portions of this chapter as well as Chapter 14 (*Contract Management and Contract Administration*) provide helpful information on contract management.

QUALITY ASSURANCE

Quality assurance planning is a key component in any IT project. Chapter 13 (*Quality Assurance*) and Chapter 14 (*Contract Management and Contract Administration*) also discuss this topic.

There are several approaches to quality assurance for procurement. Independent observers may be contracted to provide oversight and assurance that the procurement is being conducted in a way that meets the statutory requirements of the public entity, or an internal quality assurance team may be formed.

Independent verification and validation (IV&V) ensures a project, service, or system meets specifications and requirements and fulfills its intended purpose. The State of Maryland Department of Information Technology publishes an enterprise policy that addresses the rigors of IV&V as well as goals and methods for procuring IV&V services.[48]

An internal quality assurance team can be used effectively to ensure that the procurement is conducted in an ethical manner and in accordance with public procurement laws and rules/regulations, and that all interactions with the potential offerors are conducted in a fair and ethical manner. The use of such a team also sends a clear message to the suppliers, evaluators, and other stakeholders that the state is dedicated to ensuring an ethically conducted procurement.

Responsibilities may include weekly team member meetings throughout the duration of the procurement to address any procurement-related issues such as conflict of interest, procedural concerns, and other issues affecting the handling of the procurement. Team meetings may also include a key member of the IT project team to discuss specific issues. All team actions should be documented and placed in the procurement file to support how and why decisions were made.

Case Study

The State of Wisconsin used quality assurance teams for the procurement, contract management, and implementation of a large enterprise resource planning system in 2015. One responsibility of the team was to appoint a business and functional owner for every major aspect of the project (human resources, procurement, finance) participating in the selection and the implementation of the project with the third-party systems integrator.

The efforts of this team and the governance best practices employed for the project resulted in a successful implementation that received recognition for its efficiency and cost savings potential through centralized data collection, management, and decommissioning of legacy systems. More information about the Wisconsin project can be found on the NASCIO website.[49]

CONCLUSION

IT procurements are a challenge for any large entity, even private ones, because of their complexity and the multiple opportunities they present for something to go wrong. They are even more of a challenge in the public sector because of the fact that historic methods of purchasing commodities and services, as they have been practiced for a long time, do not always work well in the case of large-scale IT procurements. The innovation, groundwork, and teamwork needed to successfully conclude a major IT procurement require public procurement officers to be at the table during the planning stages. As this chapter has shown, they also require those officers to think creatively, using their full legal authority to generate processes within the law that permit full consideration of innovative contractor solutions.

ENDNOTES

1. "In 2014, Gartner [Inc.] introduced a prescriptive organization model for enterprise IT called 'Bimodal IT.' It posits that IT organizations of the future will have two separate flavors, if you will: Type 1 is traditional IT, focused on stability and efficiency, while Type 2 is an experimental, agile organization focused on time-to-market, rapid application evolution, and, in particular, tight alignment with business units." Golden, B. (January 27, 2013). *What Gartner's Bimodal IT Model Means to Enterprise CIOs*. https://www.cio.com/article/2875803/cio-role/what-gartner-s-bimodal-it-model-means-to-enterprise-cios.html

2. McConnell, M. (1996). The Process of Procuring Information Technology. *Public Contract Law Journal, 25*(2), 379–392. Retrieved from: http://www.jstor.org/stable/25754218 . pp. 379, 384.

3. https://www.nascio.org/Content/PublicationsView/PID/652/evl/0/CategoryID/30/CategoryName/Procurement

4. Procurement Innovation Task Force (2013). *Strategies for Procurement Innovation and Reform*. IJIS Institute. Retrieved from: www.ijis.org/docs/procurement_report.pdf

5. *Stakeholders* as used in this chapter means anyone who is involved in or affected by a course of action. Since IT within a public entity affects so many—citizens, user and user agencies, suppliers, media, legislative bodies, government executive leadership such as governors and mayors, public procurement personnel, and public IT personnel, to name some of those affected—this chapter uses the term *stakeholder* to encompass all of who rely on or who are touched by a state or local government's IT system.

6. State of California, Office of Systems Integration. *Best Practices: Government Framework*. http://www.bestpractices.ca.gov/sysacq/governance_framework.shtml

7. "*Capital expenditure*—an amount paid out that creates a long-term benefit (as one lasting beyond the taxable year); especially: costs that are incurred in the acquisition or improvement of property (as capital assets) or that are otherwise chargeable to a capital account." Merriam-Webster Law Dictionary. https://www.merriam-webster.com/legal/capital%20expenditure

8. http://dir.texas.gov/View-Resources/Pages/Content.aspx?id=16

9. http://dir.texas.gov/View-Search/Generic.aspx?keyword=\business%20case%20template
10. http://capmf.cio.ca.gov/Templates.html
11. Chapter 7, *Competition: Solicitations and Methods*, discusses requests for information.
12. https://doa.wi.gov/Documents/DEO/MarketResearchandSolicitationDevelopmentSlides.pdf
13. http://www.bestpractices.ca.gov/sysacq/governance_framework.shtml
14. See Endnote 13.
15. See Endnote 13.
16. See Endnote 13.
17. https://www.pmi.org/
18. Section 1.1 of the Issue and Escalation Process template of the State of California Office of Systems Integration states in part: "The purpose of the [issue and escalation] process is to ensure unanticipated issues and action items are assigned to a specific person for action and are tracked to resolution. However, when a resolution cannot be reached, the item should be escalated to ensure a decision is made before it causes impact to the project. The escalation process documents how to raise an issue to a higher-level of management for resolution, particularly when resolution cannot be reached at the project level." http://www.bestpractices.ca.gov/sysacq/governance_framework.shtml
19. RACI Charts: How-to Guide and Templates. http://racichart.org/
20. https://www.dot.state.mn.us/pm/documents/RACI-table-template.xlsx
21. http://capmf.cio.ca.gov/Templates.html
22. http://www.naspo.org/Publications/PID/8806/CategoryID/202/CategoryName/White-Papers-and-Issue-Briefs
23. http://www.naspo.org/Publications/ArtMID/8806/ArticleID/2088
24. https://obamawhitehouse.archives.gov/sites/default/files/omb/procurement/memo/myth-busting-2-addressing-misconceptions-and-further-improving-communication-during-the-acquisition-process.pdf
25. https://obamawhitehouse.archives.gov/sites/default/files/omb/procurement/memo/myth-busting_3_further_improving_industry_communications_with_effectiv....pdf
26. https://www.nascio.org/Portals/0/Publications/Documents/Risk-Procurement_Sept2013.pdf
27. See Endnote 1.
28. A Maintenance Management Information Systems is a mechanized claims processing and information retrieval system for Medicaid that is required by the federal government.
29. http://www.naspo.org/Publications/PID/8806/ev/1/CategoryID/219/CategoryName/Procurement-Processes
30. https://www.vita.virginia.gov/supply-chain/scm-policies-forms/
31. https://www.nascio.org/Portals/0/Publications/Documents/2017/2016_NASCIO-NASPO_Topical_Roundtable.pdf
32. http://kaipartners.com/difference-pilot-project-trial-implementation/
33. http://www.govtech.com/biz/How-Government-Is-Reforming-IT-Procurement-and-What-it-Means-for-Vendors.html
34. What Is 18F? Government Technology (August 8, 2016). http://www.govtech.com/civic/What-is-18F.html
35. https://18f.gsa.gov/
36. http://www.naspo.org/Publications/ArtMID/8806/ArticleID/4558
37. Total cost of ownership analysis is defined in Chapter 7, *Competition: Solicitations and Methods.*
38. "A virtual private network (VPN) is a technology that creates a safe and encrypted connection over a less secure network, such as the internet." https://searchnetworking.techtarget.com/definition/virtual-private-network
39. *Scalability* "is the ability of a computer application or product (hardware or software) to continue to function well when it (or its context) is changed in size or volume in order to meet a user need. Typically, the rescaling is to a larger size or volume." https://searchdatacenter.techtarget.com/definition/scalability

40. "A self-serve access portal gives end users access to a particular system, along with other features and services as a part of a digital login and authentication process." https://www.techopedia.com/definition/32204/self-serve-access-portal
41. For information about the federal government's *Cloud First Policy*, go to: https://obamawhitehouse.archives.gov/sites/default/files/omb/assets/egov_docs/federal-cloud-computing-strategy.pdf
42. https://www.congress.gov/bill/107th-congress/house-bill/3763
43. https://www.pmi.org/-/media/pmi/documents/public/pdf/learning/thought-leadership/pulse/pulse-of-the-profession-2017.pdf
44. Direct damages are those that a reasonable, ordinary, and prudent person would expect the nonbreaching party to suffer from a contractor failure. "Assume a build-to-suit, owner occupied restaurant. This restaurant's roof suffers from a defect . . . [T]wo years after completion, that wind blows through, peeling the roof off of our restaurant like the top off a can of chocolate pudding. Little controversy would exist that the building's designer or builder needs no specialized or intimate knowledge to expect that the damage from the under-strength connectors will include the costs to retrofit the connectors and restore the roof. So, those costs qualify as direct damages." https://www.americanbar.org/publications/under_construction/2013/april_2013/direct_vs_consequential_damages.html
45. "But suppose a week before the roof blows off, our restaurateur contracts to sell the restaurant at a handsome profit, and the purchase and sale contract allows the buyer to withdraw if the restaurant building suffers serious damage before closing. The buyer and the buyer's lender examine the debris and decide that despite the promise of rapid restoration, and seller insurance to pay for it initially, the risk is too great and the buyer exercises its right to withdraw. It's fair to posit that when contracting to design or build the restaurant, our reasonable, ordinary, prudent and comparable stranger designer or builder wouldn't have expected the owner to contract to sell the restaurant only two years after completion, unless, of course, the stranger is clairvoyant or our restaurateur shared a business plan projecting a sale in 18 to 36 months after opening. And so, the restaurateur's lost profit on the sale of the restaurant likely will qualify as consequential damages." See Endnote 46.
46. http://www.naspo.org/Publications/ArtMID/8806/ArticleID/2158
47. http://www.bestpractices.cahwnet.gov/
48. https://doit.maryland.gov/epmo/Documents/DoIT-IVV-Policy.pdf
49. https://www.nascio.org/portals/0/awards/nominations2017/2017/NASCIO2017WisconsinSTAR.PDF

CHAPTER 21: PROFESSIONAL DEVELOPMENT

RECOMMENDED BEST PRACTICES

- State and local government officials and the central procurement office should support professional certification and encourage public procurement officers to qualify for it.
- State and local government officials and the central procurement office should encourage and support public procurement officer participation in training programs and in membership or affiliation in one or more procurement professional associations.
- The central procurement office should maintain a current library of and subscriptions to procurement materials such as those addressing technology, contract law, management theories, and procurement theory.
- The central procurement office should provide career paths within the public procurement profession by offering continuing management and administrative experience for public procurement officers.

CHAPTER 21: PROFESSIONAL DEVELOPMENT

Procurement laws, policies, and organizational structure must provide the framework for a coherent public procurement process that is transparent and responsive to the public's highest expectations of integrity. But the process will succeed only through the efforts of the public procurement professional—the public procurement officer.

This chapter discusses the nationally recognized standards for assessing the readiness of an individual to serve as a public procurement professional. The role of state training and certification programs is also explored. Finally, the chapter addresses professional development trends, emerging technology, and available resources.

THE CASE FOR PUBLIC PROCUREMENT AS A PROFESSION

The Oxford English Dictionary defines *profession* as follows:

> *An occupation in which a professed knowledge of some subject, field, or science is applied; a vocation or career, especially one that involves prolonged training and a formal qualification.*[1]

Publications like this 3rd Edition of *State & Local Government: A Practical Guide* (*Practical Guide*), the development of academic degrees in public procurement, and the increasing recognition of the importance of public procurement certifications have moved public procurement careers closer to meeting that traditional standard. And, most proudly, it is the practitioners of this career, rather than legal or other outside mandates, who are the driving force in advocating for and creating structures to establish public procurement as a profession.

Professions are built around bodies of knowledge like those maintained by the Universal Public Procurement Certification Council (UPPCC). The UPPCC has developed two bodies of knowledge: one applicable to the certified public procurement officer certification;[2] and another that applies to the certified public procurement buyer certification.[3] These are discussed in more detail later in this chapter.[4]

Uniformity of criteria is especially important if the practitioner's work is to be recognized as a unique discipline, and the UPPCC bodies of knowledge are accepted standards in state and local government public procurement. All who practice the profession, regardless of the place in which they may be practicing, should uphold those principles and standards consistently.

Principles of public procurement differ in significant ways from those that apply to the procurement process within commercial entities. Public procurement involves spending taxpayer dollars. Thus, there is a broader and higher level of stewardship that public procurement officers must exercise.

PROFESSIONAL CERTIFICATION

The establishment of a certification program is a voluntary action by a professional group to institute a system for granting recognition to professionals who have met a stated level of training and work experience. Certified individuals have demonstrated that they have met the standards of the credentialing organization. Those who are certified are entitled to make the public aware of their credentialed status through the use of the certification initials after their name and in all forms of address.

Certification—national and state specific—can have many benefits for the procurement office, its staff, and the profession itself. For the procurement office, encouraging or in some cases requiring certification demonstrates a knowledgeable and capable procurement staff.

Developing a program for professional certification has been an ongoing joint effort of the National Association of State Procurement Officials (NASPO) and the National Institute of Governmental Purchasing (NIGP). In 1978, NIGP and NASPO joined in chartering the UPPCC, an independent entity formed to govern and administer the Certified Public Procurement Officer (CPPO) and Certified Professional Public Buyer (CPPB) certification programs.

The UPPCC is composed of a Governing Board as well as a Board of Examiners whose primary responsibility is to develop and administer exams. It is accredited by the International Federation of Purchasing and Supply Management.[5]

Benefits of Certification

Table 21.1 shows potential benefits of certification to both the public procurement officer and the public procurement office.

Certification by the Universal Public Procurement Certification Council

UPPCC Certifications

The UPPCC certifications signify that the certified person demonstrates a standard of competency in public procurement. They also indicate to the public that, having mastered a body of knowledge, the certified person should be able to make sound decisions that reflect maximum value for the taxpayer's dollar.

With over 10,000 professionals certified in the United States, Canada, and other countries, the CPPO and CPPB programs are highly respected among procurement professionals and employers involved in public procurement. It is not unusual today to see a CPPB or CPPO certification as a required, or at least desired, qualification in job announcements for public procurement officers at a state, county, or municipal government level.

When the individual meets the UPPCC eligibility requirements and successfully passes the exam,

Table 21.1

Benefits to the Public Procurement Officer	Benefits to the Public Procurement Office
Professional recognition	Increases the professionalism, skills, and accountability of procurement staff
Personal satisfaction	
Increased knowledge and skills	Helps foster ethical behavior of staff
Continued professional development opportunities and a defined path for growth	Produces better purchasing and contracting outcomes in the state central procurement office and agencies by improving competencies of employees with purchasing and contracting responsibilities
Increased credibility with suppliers	
Demonstrated commitment to the profession	Promotes responsible expenditure of public funds that complies with state purchasing laws and rules
Portability of professional certifications, which are earned by the individual and go with them wherever their professional path may take them	Ensures the skills and competencies of employees
	Promotes recognition of staff as purchasing professionals
Prominence of professional certifications on resumes—often a factor in hiring and salary decisions	Provides professional development opportunities to staff and a defined path for continuous growth
	Provides objective benchmarks for evaluating skills

the UPPCC issues a credential to the newly certified person that is valid for a period of five years. After that term, the certified person must renew the credential for an additional five-year period through the UPPCC recertification process.

The UPPCC programs are designed specifically for state and local government public procurement officers. Only those individuals who have government-specific procurement experience are eligible. There are three essential components for eligibility:

- Formal education and degree from a certified institution[6]
- Public procurement experience[7]
- Coursework/training in procurement[8]

Unlike most procurement certification programs, the UPPCC requires substantial work experience within the public sector. This work experience must be complemented by coursework/training specifically within the field of procurement.

Eligibility Requirements

The minimum eligibility requirements for UPPCC certification are listed below in Table 21.2.[9]

Testing and Bodies of Knowledge

UPPCC exams measure professional competence and the understanding of the bodies of knowledge surrounding public procurement. Each exam consists of 190 multiple-choice questions (175 scored questions and 15 pretest or unscored questions). The exams are administered in a network of professional testing centers in a computer-based format. Candidates are allotted a maximum of 3.5 hours in which to complete the examination.

The UPPCC website provides a wealth of helpful information about the examination process, including a list of books and other reading materials that will assist the applicant in preparing for the appropriate exam.[10]

Updating the Bodies of Knowledge

The UPPCC describes the process of updating the bodies of knowledge as follows:

> *Every 5 years, the UPPCC commissions a new Job Analysis study to ensure that the certification exams maintain alignment with the critical skills and knowledge needed for competent performance in the ever-evolving public procurement*

Table 21.2

Certified Public Procurement Officer (CPPO)	Certified Professional Public Buyer (CPPB)

• Bachelor's Degree
• Coursework/Training can be satisfied through the completion of 1 of the following 3 options:
  ◊ 3 credit hours of public procurement coursework and 72 contact hours of *instructor-led* procurement training/education
  ◊ 6 credit hours of procurement-related coursework and 72 contact hours of instructor-led procurement training/education
  ◊ 174 contact hours of instructor-led procurement training/education
• 5 years of public procurement experience completed within the previous 10 years, of which a minimum of 3 years is in a management or supervisory position
	• Associate's Degree
	• Coursework/Training can be satisfied through the completion of 1 of the following 3 options:
	  ◊ 3 credit hours of public procurement coursework and 56 contact hours of *instructor-led* procurement training/education
	  ◊ 6 credit hours of procurement-related coursework and 56 contact hours of *instructor-led* procurement training/education
	  ◊ 158 contact hours of *instructor-led* procurement training/education
	• 3 years of public procurement experience completed within the previous 10 years

profession. This study, which consists of several activities designed to cull information about the profession from the profession, includes the development of a survey tool, dissemination of the survey, the compilation of survey results, and finally, the development of the Body of Knowledge. The Job Analysis process provides assurance to stakeholders that individuals designated by a UPPCC certification possess an essential common body of public procurement knowledge that is objectively assessed and validated by the profession. It provides defendable evidence to support the content that is tested as well as the consistent standard employed to award CPPO and/or CPPB certification(s).

Other National Certifications

Although the UPPCC certifications are the most valuable for preparing for the profession of public procurement, and although public procurement offices will give them the most weight in hiring, there are others that have value, as well, although they are not specifically oriented toward state and local procurement. The Institute for Supply Management (ISM) and the National Contract Management Association (NCMA) offer well-regarded professional certification programs.

Institute for Supply Management

ISM was founded in 1915, and its mission is to lead the supply management profession through its standards of excellence, research, promotional activities, and education.[11] Its primary focus is on commercial procurement and supply management. ISM offers two certifications, the Certified Professional in Supply Management (CPSM®) and the Certified Professional in Supplier Diversity (CPSD™).

The CPSM is intended for professionals with supply management experience. Applicants must pass three exams and meet the eligibility requirements set forth by ISM. The certification exam focuses on critical concepts in procurement and sourcing, negotiating, contracts, and leadership.

The CPSD is more specialized than CPSM and is focused upon the growing area of supplier diversity, which is also an important topic in public procurement. ISM describes *supplier diversity* as follows:[12]

An organization's efforts to include different categories of suppliers in its sourcing process and active supply base and to address the opportunities and challenges that arise from differences and similarities.

It adds that *supplier diversity* is a "proactive business process that seeks to provide diverse suppliers equal access to purchasing opportunities," and that diversity "promotes supplier participation reflective of a company's diverse customer base and the diverse business community."

Eligibility requirements for both certificates, along with exam descriptions, may be found on the ISM website (see Endnotes).

National Contract Management Association

The National Contract Management Association (NCMA) was founded in 1959 and is dedicated to the professional growth and educational advancement of procurement and acquisition personnel worldwide.[13] Much of what the NCMA concentrates on revolves around federal government procurement and contract management, and its members include federal contractors, federal acquisition officials, and federal contract managers. NCMA offers three certifications: the Certified Professional Contract Manager (CPCM), the Certified Federal Contract Manager (CFCM), and the Certified Commercial Contract Manager (CCCM).

State Certification Programs

The UPPCC bodies of knowledge provide foundational elements in which all public procurement officers should be competent. Achieving the CPPB or CPPO designation demonstrates a mastery of this knowledge and is a nationally recognized achievement.

Many states, however, have also identified the need for their own internal certification programs that incorporate elements specific to practicing procurement in that state. State procurement officials, legislators, educators, and others are recognizing the need both to train the procurement workforce and then to assess their abilities. A well-developed training program in conjunction with certification through assessment allows for this.

Although state certification has been in existence for several years, it is still a growing trend in state procurement offices. These programs are tailored toward the role and expectations of a public procurement officer in that state. Certification in conjunction with ongoing training programs allows states to develop public procurement officers with specific knowledge about the laws and policies of a particular state.

The body of knowledge being taught and assessed within most state certification programs is heavily influenced by the laws, rules/regulations, and policies of that particular state. However, UPPCC bodies of knowledge can be utilized as the foundation from which to build a state training and certification program that incorporates national best practices as well as state-specific elements.

State certification programs can be established through several different means, including legislation or internal office policy. As governors and state legislatures recognize the need for qualified public procurement officers, legislation mandating training and certification programs becomes a popular course of action.

There may also be mandates within the legislation or executive order that govern the creation of the program. The development and implementation of the actual program then typically becomes the responsibility of the central procurement office.

State of Florida

There are states with well-established certification programs, and still more in the process of developing or improving their programs. One model of a state-specific program is the Florida Certified Contract Manger (FCCM) curriculum.[14] In 2012, the Florida Legislature implemented a statutory requirement for the Florida Department of Management Services (DMS) to develop a certification program for contract managers. The law mandated that state contract or grant managers responsible for managing contracts or grants in excess of $100,000 annually become certified within 24 months of the establishment of the criteria for certification.

A needs assessment revealed that as of June 2014, 2,400 state employees required this certification, and as of July 2015, this number had increased to almost 3,500 based on user agencies' self-reporting. To meet this task, the Department of Management Services, Division of State Purchasing, created a Professional Development Team (PDT) to develop and administer the new program.

To achieve their goal; the PDT utilized a blended training approach, including online modules, live instruction, and a final assessment. Certification now requires the successful completion of eight online training modules, a two-day instructor-led training, and a final assessment—with a minimum score of 80%. The result of the PDT's efforts was the creation of a new FCCM designation and the ability to certify up to 1,200 state user agency employees a year.

Commonwealth of Virginia

Another model program is the Commonwealth of Virginia's Virginia Institute of Procurement (VIP).[15] It is an educational program for public procurement officers that offers three certification levels: Virginia Contracting Associate Officer, Virginia Contracting Officer, and Virginia

Contracting Master Officer. Participation in the program is voluntary and open to employees of the Commonwealth of Virginia and employees of other public entities that meet the eligibility criteria of the certification level they wish to pursue. The VIP is sponsored by the Virginia Department of General Services, Division of Purchases and Supply.

SOURCES OF PROCUREMENT EDUCATION

Formal curricula to prepare individuals to be public procurement officers are becoming more readily available as the importance of professionalism in public procurement is increasingly recognized. There is a rapidly emerging trend for institutions of higher education to offer public procurement certificate programs and even degrees.[16] NASPO is partnering with several nationally recognized supply chain management[17] programs at academic institutions to further support the development of these programs and degrees.

In many cases, public procurement officers have come to their careers inadvertently and accidentally, with little or no prior training or education. The absence of an explicit discipline leading to a college degree in public procurement, however, does not mean there is no opportunity to obtain an education in public procurement.

Sources for Procurement Training

There is no question that the experience of day-to-day operations contributes substantially to the growth of knowledge and expertise of a state or local government procurement officer. As valuable as this experience is, it represents at best an unstructured form of education. It needs to be accompanied by formal training and instruction programs.

In recent years states have revised and strengthened their internal training programs. These training programs are often tied to state certification programs. State central procurement offices with their own certification and training programs are frequently responsible for providing training to their own staff and to user agencies as well. To meet these demands and provide effective curricula, states provide training on a variety of topics in multiple formats. Many states are increasingly implementing online elements for their training.

In addition to training provided in the central procurement office, professional procurement organizations are an excellent source for public procurement training and education. In early 2014, the NASPO Board of Directors undertook a strategic planning initiative. As a result, it recognized the need to create innovative strategies in education and professional development specifically for state public procurement officers.

To achieve this goal and deliver these needed resources to its membership, NASPO initiated Procurement U.[18] Today, Procurement U includes multiple initiatives focusing on the promotion of certification, development of higher education degrees/programs, educational publications, and the delivery of public procurement courses.

Utilizing a learning management system, Procurement U offers online courses open to all public procurement officers. Procurement U courses cover many foundational topics as well as timely and emerging topics. The intent of these courses is to provide quality training in a flexible and accessible format. UPPCC certification exam preparation courses are also available through Procurement U.[19]

There are several other national associations that provide procurement training as well. NIGP provides online and live public procurement courses on a variety of topics.[20] ISM focuses on commercial procurement issues and training, some of which may be useful for public procurement officers.[21]

CHAPTER 21: PROFESSIONAL DEVELOPMENT

EFFECTIVE NEGOTIATION TEAMS

Selecting the right people for a negotiation team is not always easy, particularly for large, complicated procurements. The goal should be to identify members that have the personalities, skills, and expertise that are needed in order to achieve the targeted negotiation outcome, and if those skills aren't available on staff, then use professional development and training to grow those skills in the office. An earlier call-out in Chapter 9 suggested the acronym *TEAM* to help remember some of the basic roles needed for almost any type of negotiation. Additionally, the various roles that are often called upon for negotiations can be expanded and defined as follows:

- **The procurement official**—This role is the decision maker, speaks with authority for the team, and can accept or decline changes.
- **Project manager**—This person will be responsible for the goods/services use and monitoring for the end user. A good project manager will decrease the time it takes to create contracts, help to keep all parties accountable to well-written statements of work during an implementation, and assist in documenting performance of the state and suppliers when it counts.
- **Subject matter expert (SME)**—The SME provides review of technical specifications or requirements and may have industry-specific knowledge of the market, vendors, and best practices that can be invaluable at the negotiation table.
- **Financial analyst**—This person understands the financial impact of the market as well as the buying entity's budget. They also support the negotiation for cost elements as well as terms and conditions related to government finances.
- **Legal expert**—Typically a lawyer with expertise or experience in procurement, the legal expert role understands the legal considerations for the product market, such as laws concerning hazardous waste disposal, and supports the team in all legal matters and negotiation of terms and conditions.
- **Buyer**—The buyer role is critical, and provides an understanding of the specifications, solicitation, process, bid/proposal evaluation, and contract needs. The buyer should always be present during negotiations, as the negotiation team lead.

This list of roles provides just a snapshot of the core roles that should be considered for any negotiation team. However, the available employees on staff may not always have the skills and experience needed to fill all of these roles. Therefore, developing a wide range of skills and expertise among staff through professional development is critical for any procurement office.

Professional organizations like NASPO can be an excellent source for public procurement training and education to ensure staff are prepared for any type of negotiation that may come up. For example, online courses or trainings through professional organizations can provide the basics of negotiations to new buyers, while an introductory course covering the full procurement process can help those in legal, finance, or subject matter roles to understand how the full procurement process works and the role negotiation plays in the overall process.

Whether it's on topics like negotiation, technical writing, facilitation, or project management, investing in professional development, and more important, encouraging staff to occasionally put training ahead of the day-to-day work of the office, will pay dividends when it matters most.

Check out what NASPO has to offer through its professional development and education arm, Procurement U: www.naspo.org/procurementu

Finally, NCMA also provides training primarily focused on federal-level public procurement.[22]

Technology and Learning Effectiveness

Public procurement officers must make decisions about how to go about professional development. These decisions require an understanding of the essential principles of adult learning as discussed in the subsequent paragraphs.

Technology has an important role in the training. The use of media and online training, however, does not eliminate the need to use other accepted approaches to effective teaching. A good public procurement training program—and an individual's decisions about the format for his or her training—must take these considerations into account.

Benefits and Limitations in Using E-training Tools

There are benefits and disadvantages to using e-training tools for teaching public procurement officers. As may be seen from the following discussion, they should not be the exclusive means for training delivery.

In their helpful guide for developing training—*Telling Ain't Training, 2d Ed.* (ASTD Press, 2011)[23]—Harold D. Stolovitch and Erica J. Keeps emphasize that technology helps extend the reach of training and improves efficiency. However, it is not a substitute for application of other sound training approaches.

Telling Ain't Training underlines the importance of providing immediate, practical skills and resources. While e-learning platforms can be interactive, other training approaches may better foster practical, active learning. For example, small group activities or peer-to-peer training can be designed for students, giving them tasks such as developing practical checklists (like procurement planning checklists) or action plans relevant to the students' needs.

E-learning platforms offer particular advantages in sequencing and dividing up formal courses, particularly for novice learners. They can be on-demand learning resources that permit students to engage the content at their own speed. Further, these systems can be used after completion of training to refresh learning about specific topics.

Effective training also takes into account the experience of adult learners who want some autonomy in learning and expect tailored training that recognizes their past experience and knowledge. An e-learning platform that helps assess initial knowledge and supports adaptation of content to account for existing expertise is beneficial.

One approach is to use *micro-learning*. This consists of typically short, (5–10 minute) videos or modules focused on one or two key learning objectives. They are meant to provide quick, easily accessible learning on key topics.

E-learning systems are superior platforms for managing testing as an assessment tool. Ideally, they are also configurable, so a public entity's unique laws, rules/regulations, and practices are part of the test. They permit a combination of types of test questions from simple recall to application-based answers and are configurable to support assessment of different levels of learners.

The use of e-learning platforms should be dependent on their ability to support the essential elements of learning: readiness and motivation, autonomy, a variety of action-oriented learning activities, and feedback and assessment. Effective training is a pillar of any professional development program.

Non-Technology-Based Procurement Education

As noted before, learning is more effective when a variety of methods of engagement with topics are used. This is called *blended learning*.

E-learning platforms can provide part of the training experience for a public procurement officer, but they should not be the exclusive delivery method. There is still room for other creative approaches that can constitute training—such as peer-to-peer training, co-presentations with experienced public procurement officers, organized panel discussions, negotiation simulations, organized lunch-and-learn sessions, and small group training that better utilizes inquiry-based learning models.

Feedback and assessment are critical to effective training as well. Feedback conversations with other public procurement officers can be a useful part of any training plan. For example, when a procurement officer invites a trainee to a pre-bid meeting or supplier debriefing, it can be an especially rich training opportunity. Or peers can participate in an after-the-fact review of a procurement—a discussion of what worked and what might have been improved. These kinds of activities can be recorded on individual professional development plans and may prove to be useful supplements to the online testing that computer-based training typically supports.

CONCLUSION

The highly complex service, management, policy development, and consulting roles that are responsibilities of a public procurement officer today have nearly relegated that person's routine buying function to history. The essential need for continuing professional development in the field of public procurement is increasing along with these growing responsibilities. It is imperative that each professional not only increase their own knowledge and skills, but also support the professional development of others.

ENDNOTES

1. http://www.oed.com/viewdictionaryentry/Entry/152052
2. https://www.uppcc.org/Portals/0/Documents/CPPO-BOK-2013.pdf
3. See Endnote 2.
4. As this *Practical Guide* goes to press, the current bodies of knowledge, issued in 2013, will be replaced by new ones. Access to them will be available on the UPPCC website.
5. http://www.ifpsm.org/
6. https://www.uppcc.org/certified/Formal-Education
7. https://www.uppcc.org/certified/Experience
8. https://www.uppcc.org/certified/Coursework
9. https://www.uppcc.org/certified/Eligibility
10. https://www.uppcc.org/certified/Preparation
11. https://www.instituteforsupplymanagement.org/index.cfm?SSO=1
12. https://www.instituteforsupplymanagement.org/resources/content.cfm?ItemNumber=23515&SSO=1
13. https://www.ncmahq.org/
14. https://www.dms.myflorida.com/business_operations/state_purchasing/public_procurement_professional_development/florida_certified_contract_manager
15. https://dgs.virginia.gov/procurement/VIP_Home/home/
16. A list of bachelor's degree programs in public procurement or in certain elements of public procurement can be found on the NIGP website: http://www.nigp.org/grow-professionally/education/higher-education-procurement
17. "Supply chain management encompasses the planning and management of all activities involved in sourcing and procurement, conversion, and all logistics management activities. Importantly, it also includes coordination and collaboration with channel

partners, which can be suppliers, intermediaries, third party service providers, and customers. In essence, supply chain management integrates supply and demand management within and across companies." Council of Supply Chain Management Professionals. https://cscmp.org/CSCMP/Educate/SCM_Definitions_and_Glossary_of_Terms/CSCMP/Educate/SCM_Definitions_and_Glossary_of_Terms.aspx?hkey=60879588-f65f-4ab5-8c4b-6878815ef921

18. https://www.naspo.org/Procurement-U/About-Procurement-U
19. See Endnote 18.
20. http://www.nigp.org/grow-professionally/education/take-a-course
21. https://store.instituteforsupplymanagement.org/StoreMeetingApp/MeetingCalendar
22. http://learning.ncmahq.org/
23. Stolovitch, H. D., Keeps, E. J., & Rosenberg, M. J. (2011). *Telling Ain't Training*. Alexandria, VA: ASTD Press.

CHAPTER 22: EMERGING ISSUES IN STATE AND LOCAL PROCUREMENT

RECOMMENDED BEST PRACTICES

- Public procurement officers do not have a crystal ball from which they may predict the next societal influences or political strategies affecting their governments that may affect the procurement process. Placing the Chief Procurement Officer at an executive level within a government offers the best opportunity for emerging public policy directives to be well-served by the procurement process. It alerts those who are part of the procurement process in advance of that direction and avoids the need to play catch up.
- Collaboration with associations of state officials in non-procurement positions such as chief information officers and chief administrative officers is another way of keeping abreast of issues on the horizon.

CHAPTER 22: EMERGING ISSUES IN STATE AND LOCAL PROCUREMENT

The discussion in this chapter is aimed at arming public procurement officers with the knowledge to more readily anticipate public policy issues that affect the procurement process. It also offers some advice on where to turn for help in addressing those issues.

Procurement as a profession is constantly evolving, and state and local government procurement is no exception. The evolution is often spurred by new sourcing methods and technologies that are tested either within existing environments or in new, innovative frameworks.

At other times, the evolution is driven by forces outside the public procurement communities' control, for better or for worse. The challenge for public procurement officers is to use their ingenuity and limited resources to keep pace with change.

RECOGNIZING EMERGING ISSUES

No attempt will be made here to identify possible specific emerging issues. That is because any emerging issue has a rapid life cycle that brings it from being identified as *on the horizon* to becoming a priority that needs to be dealt with promptly (or to *fading from view*). Predictions are too unreliable.

Additionally, many emerging issues tend to have a temporary effect on public procurement offices and are simply noted in passing. Some, however, grow into larger issues that demand attention, change, and resources.

Public procurement officers can learn much about the characteristics of emerging issues by looking at past examples, including how they came onto the procurement scene, their impact, and whether they survived and became part of a public procurement officer's day-to-day work. Some of these are discussed in upcoming paragraphs, along with Figure 22.1, which demonstrates the emerging issue life cycle.

FIGURE 22.1 | EMERGING ISSUE LIFE CYCLE

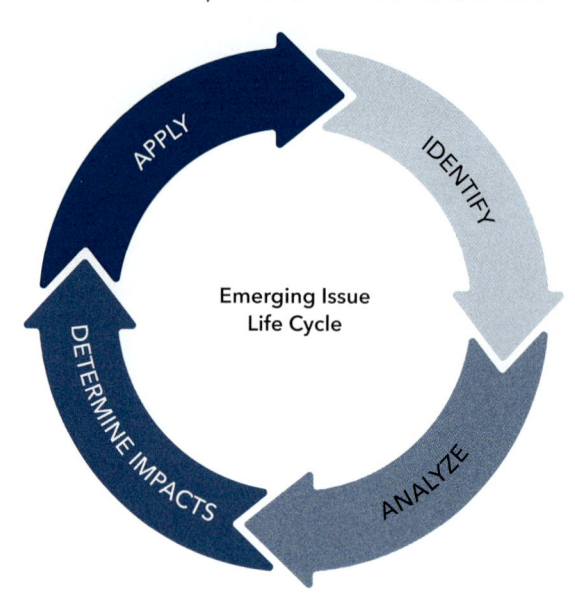

Emerging Issue to Everyday Concern: Sustainable Purchasing

Green and sustainable purchasing appeared on the state and local government public procurement horizon around 2007. It reflected societal concerns about the environment and demonstrated how social concerns and policies can directly affect the procurement process.

Socially driven concerns such as sustainable purchasing are a challenge for a public procurement officer, given the level of scrutiny involved in public spending and the strong belief among some of the public that social concerns have no place in the purchasing process. It can be very difficult to strike a balance between the additional procurement requirements related to social concerns with the expectation that the procurement process be efficient and favor the lowest price.

Once a social policy or concern gains momentum and attains critical mass, it becomes firmly embedded in the *culture* of public procurement across all levels of government. Green and sustainable purchasing is a notable example of this, starting with just a handful of states developing any sort of green purchasing program in the early 2000s and growing to 30 states by 2015, according to a NASPO survey. Signs show that this expansion will continue.

As sustainable purchasing matured and gained acceptance, more resources and information became available to assist public procurement officers in learning about and conducting green purchasing. There is a wealth of resources to support green and sustainable purchasing, as noted in Chapter 6 (*Sustainable Procurement Considerations and Strategies*). Green and sustainable purchasing is now a common term in public procurement circles, with recognition by procurement offices at all levels of government.

Changing Priorities: Trans-Pacific Partnership

The Trans-Pacific Partnership (TPP)[1] was not commonly known to the public at first, but became a rallying point for some after the United States withdrew its signature to the agreement in 2017. It is an excellent example of an emerging issue that can be on fire one minute and dying the next.

The TPP is a trade agreement among twelve nations in the Pacific that evolved from an initial 2005 agreement among a subset of these nations. The TPP was signed in early 2016, but still needed to be ratified in order to take effect.

In the interim, the TPP was examined to determine the impacts it could have on public procurement in the United States. The federal government contacted various states' governors. Federal officials met with those states' procurement offices and work began to highlight the portions of the TPP relevant to state government procurement. An analysis ensued to estimate and prioritize potential impacts on state procurement processes and to serve as a basis for recommending changes to the agreement's terms.

The TPP was an emerging issue, but it was politically driven as opposed to societal, in contrast to green purchasing. As such, the TPP was subject to a different set of influences.

With the change in the United States presidency in 2017, the United States withdrew its signature, meaning the TPP could not be ratified. The remaining eleven countries that were parties to the original TPP agreed to a new trade pact called the Comprehensive and Progressive Agreement for Trans-Pacific Partnership, which was signed in 2018. Since the United States was not a party to the pact, the possible effect on public procurement was no longer an issue, at least for the present time.

Emerging issues that do not make it into the mainstream sometimes fade away completely. Others simply lie dormant for some period of time. The TPP is a good example of the latter. While effectively on hold as an emerging issue, its political nature means that it may be revisited in the future.

The National Association of State Procurement Officials (NASPO) *Guide to International Trade Agreements* is a useful resource on this issue.[2]

Changing at the Speed of Technology: IT Procurement

The purchase of information technology (IT) has long been an issue for public procurement offices. IT-related topics have been noted as a priority on the NASPO *Top 10 Priorities for State Procurement*, published annually since 2015.[3] With IT supporting every governmental function and encompassing a vast array of services and commodities, the sudden and drastic changes in available technologies that occur at a moment's notice mean that IT procurement issues will remain a priority far into the future in some form or another.

CHAPTER 22: EMERGING ISSUES IN STATE AND LOCAL PROCUREMENT

While best practices concerning IT procurement have been developed and provide some stability as to how to approach these challenging procurements, the underlying technologies being acquired are constantly developing and changing. For example, it was merely an expectation just a few years ago that government services for citizens would be available 24 hours a day, seven days a week. That is now a reality for most state and local governments. This creates a new set of weighty expectations. Although one portion of this emerging issue may have matured, there are always new sub-issues arising, and sometimes fading. Some of those sub-issues themselves may become emerging issues.

To this end, in 2018 NASPO published a *Top Three Horizon Issues* list to accompany its annual *Top 10 Priorities for State Procurement*. The intent of this companion list was to focus strictly on emerging issues that have just started to enter the vision of state procurement offices. It is no surprise that all three are related to IT:

1. Leveraging data management and advanced analytics in state procurement
2. Automation and emerging technologies for immersive experiences
3. Blockchain technology—procurement applications and benefits to the enterprise

It will be interesting to watch as these issues go through their life cycle to see how they affect state and local government procurement offices of the future. Chapter 20 (*Procurement of Information Technology*) offers a good look at the challenges relating to many IT procurements.

Along with consideration of what is being acquired, IT purchasing focuses attention on the how. The idea of applying Agile[4] software development concepts, along with continuous improvement philosophies such as Lean[5] and Kaizen[6] to procurement became a hot topic in 2017 and continues to be so today.

RESOURCES FOR STATE AND LOCAL PROCUREMENT OFFICES

Trying to keep up with what is coming along can be a daunting task for any public procurement officer. There is an abundance of information available, and discerning what is important can be complicated. Fortunately, there are a number of organizations, publications, and tools available that can help determine what the priorities are and where to focus resources.

NASPO Research and Innovation Team

The Research and Innovation Team within NASPO works to keep track of issues that may affect state and local government procurement. This team develops work products that aim to anticipate any impacts those issues may present and to update publications and toolkits continuously to keep pace with changes.

This team is responsible for compiling the *Top 10 Priorities for State Procurement* mentioned earlier. This annual publication uses a variety of sources to determine the most important areas upon which state procurement offices should focus. Those topics are then compiled and ranked by state procurement leaders across the nation. The *Top 10 Priorities* help to set the agenda for leadership and conference programming for state Chief Procurement Officers and their staff. In 2018, this list was accompanied by the *Top Three Horizon Issues*, which has a focus strictly on emerging issues.

Along with white papers, webinars, and primers on a multitude of issues, the NASPO Research and Innovation Team also publishes the *Procurement Pulse* blog,[7] which is intended to serve as a current, topical resource for emerging issues. The blog will keep pace with real-world issues affecting government procurement offices.

Other State Associations

NASPO is one of many associations of state officials. Those associations are each focused on a particular area of state government, such as central procurement offices. Given the importance of IT, NASPO has a close partnership with the National Association of Chief Information Officers (NASCIO).[8] These two organizations have worked jointly on a number of publications and other work products related to IT purchasing, such as *State IT Procurement Negotiations: Working Together to Reform and Transform*, created by the NASPO-NASCIO Joint Task Force on Negotiation in IT Procurement.[9] Given the ever-changing nature of IT, this partnership will be very important in the years to come.

Similarly, NASPO has partnered with the National Association of State Chief Administrators,[10] who typically oversee the state procurement office as part of their scope of duties. This partnership allows procurement offices to learn more about priorities coming their way and proactively prepare for them.

Other state associations that may be good sources of information regarding upcoming issues are the National Association of State Facilities Administrators,[11] the National Association of State Budget Officers,[12] and the National Governors Association.[13]

Other Procurement-Related Organizations

There are a number of organizations in the United States and abroad that deal with issues surrounding procurement, both directly and indirectly. NIGP is one such organization.[14] These types of organizations can be found through sources such as online searches and procurement-related discussion forums.

CONCLUSION

The challenges that the future will bring to public procurement constitute a tough agenda under the best of circumstances. Such circumstances, however, are not likely to exist any time soon, due to ongoing state and local government budget challenges, reductions in workforce, and other topics covered in this 3rd Edition of *State & Local Government: A Practical Guide*.

One key to a successful future and a strengthened capability in the procurement office is the vital role of a single procurement leader who reports to the state or local government, an issue that is discussed in detail in Chapter 2 (*Procurement Leadership, Organization, and Value*). Without that level of visibility, authority, and support, procurement offices will not be as well-equipped to meet future challenges as they must be. Being at the executive table, which is also described in Chapter 2, permits a thoughtful, reasoned procurement response rather than a reactionary, rushed one.

Whether or not this organizational structure change is made—or if this structure already exists—the procurement profession will continue to be an exciting environment in which professional and motivated people can work to see real changes in the important programs implemented by state and local governments.

ENDNOTES

1. https://ustr.gov/trade-agreements/free-trade-agreements/trans-pacific-partnership/tpp-full-text
2. http://www.naspo.org/ita/
3. For the 2018 priorities, go to: https://www.naspo.org/Publications/PID/8806/CategoryID/215/CategoryName/Yearly-Top-Ten-Priorities

4. https://www.agilealliance.org/agile101/ NASPO has a webinar available on using Agile concepts in procurement at: https://www.naspo.org/News/ArtMID/6856/ArticleID/4486
5. https://www.lean.org/WhatsLean/
6. https://in.kaizen.com/about-us/definition-of-kaizen.html
7. https://pulse.naspo.org/
8. https://www.nascio.org/
9. https://www.nascio.org/Publications/ArtMID/485/ArticleID/549/State-IT-Procurement-Negotiations-Working-Together-to-Reform-and-Transform
10. https://www.nasca.org/
11. https://www.nasfa.net/
12. https://www.nasbo.org/home
13. https://www.nga.org/
14. http://www.nigp.org/

APPENDIX A: RESOURCES

ORGANIZATIONS

1. National Association of State Procurement Officials (NASPO)

https://www.naspo.org
110 West Vine Street, Suite 600
Lexington, KY 40507
859-514-9159

NASPO is a nonprofit association dedicated to advancing public procurement through leadership, excellence, and integrity. It is made up of the directors of the central purchasing offices in each of the 50 states, the District of Columbia, and the territories of the United States. NASPO is an organization that helps its members achieve success as public procurement leaders through promotion of best practices, education, professional development, research, and innovative procurement strategies.

Procurement University

Procurement U is a multi-faceted education platform provided to members of NASPO and other state government procurement professionals. Procurement U provides professional development opportunities, training, resources, publications, and more that are specifically tailored to meet the needs of state procurement officials and staff, although other public procurement professionals (including federal, city, and county government employees) may also benefit from courses.

Research and Publications

NASPO's library of research and publications is available as a resource to all public procurement professionals online at https://www.naspo.org/Publications. Several of these publications are used or referenced throughout this guide.

Survey of State Procurement Practices

The Survey of State Procurement Practices, referenced throughout this guide, is a comprehensive research effort conducted by NASPO and frequently updated. It explores statutory, regulatory, and policy requirements in state procurement, as well as existing practices in member states and territories. A summary of the latest results can be found at: http://www.naspo.org/survey

Procurement Pulse Blog

In 2018, NASPO's Research and Innovation Team launched Procurement Pulse—a blog that monitors state issues in procurement, and offers a go-to source for the latest news, best practices, and emerging issues in state procurement. It can be accessed at: https://pulse.naspo.org

State and Local Government Procurement: A Practical Guide, 3rd Edition

APPENDIX A: **RESOURCES**

2. National Institute of Governmental Purchasing (NIGP)
http://www.nigp.org
2411 Dulles Corner Park, Suite 350
Herndon, VA 20170
1-800-FOR-NIGP

NIGP, Inc. is a national, membership-based nonprofit organization providing support to professionals in the public sector purchasing profession. NIGP focuses on developing, supporting, and promoting the public procurement profession through premier educational and research programs, professional support, technical services, and advocacy initiatives that have benefited members and constituents since 1944.

3. Universal Public Purchasing Certification Council (UPPCC)
http://www.uppcc.org/
201 East Main Street Suite 1405
Lexington, KY 40507
636-449-5071

Co-founded by NASPO and NIGP, the UPPCC's mission is to govern and administer the professional standards required for success in the public purchasing profession. It offers a professional certification program to become a Certified Public Purchasing Officer (CPPO) or a Certified Professional Public Buyer (CPPB).

4. National Association of State Chief Information Officers (NASCIO)
https://www.nascio.org/
201 East Main Street, Suite 1405
Lexington, KY 40507
859-514-9153

Founded in 1969, NASCIO represents state chief information officers (CIOs) and information technology (IT) executives and managers from the U.S. states, territories, and the District of Columbia. NASCIO provides state CIOs and state members with products and services designed to support the challenging role of the state CIO, stimulate the exchange of information and promote the adoption of IT best practices and innovations. From national conferences, peer networking, research and publications, and briefings and government affairs, NASCIO is the premier network and resource for state CIOs.

5. Institute for Supply Management (ISM)
https://www.instituteforsupplymanagement.org/
309 W Elliot Rd, Suite 113, Tempe, AZ 85284
480-752-6276

Founded in 1915, ISM is the largest supply management association in the world. ISM's mission is to enhance the value and performance of procurement and supply chain management practitioners and their organizations worldwide. ISM fulfills its mission through education, research, information dissemination, and maintaining standards of excellence. ISM offers certification programs for the Certified Professional in Supply Management (CPSM) and Certified Professional in Supplier Diversity (CPSD).

APPENDIX A: **RESOURCES**

6. National Contract Management Association (NCMA)
https://www.ncmahq.org
21740 Beaumeade Circle, Suite 125
Ashburn, Virginia 20147
1-800-344-8096

NCMA, founded in 1959, is a leading professional resource for those in the field of contract management. The organization, which has over 20,000 members, is dedicated to the professional growth and educational advancement of procurement and acquisition personnel worldwide.

7. National Association of Educational Procurement (NAEP)
https://www.naepnet.org/
8840 Stanford Boulevard, Suite 2000
Columbia, MD 21045
443-543-5540

NAEP's mission is to facilitate the development, exchange, and practice of effective and ethical procurement principles and techniques within higher education and associated communities, through continuing education, networking, public information, and advocacy. NAEP provides professional development and networking opportunities regionally and nationally. These meetings, workshops, and seminars provide knowledge transfer in procurement ranging from beginning to advanced professionals and are conducted throughout the year and across the nation.

8. National Association of State Chief Administrators (NASCA)
https://www.nasca.org
201 East Main Street, Suite 1405
Lexington, KY 40507
859-514-9156

Founded in 1976, NASCA is a nonprofit, 501(c)3 association representing state chief administrators—public officials in charge of departments that provide support services to other state agencies. NASCA provides a forum to exchange information and learn new ideas from each other and private partners. NASCA's mission is to help state chief administrators and their teams strategically transform state government operations through the power of shared knowledge and thought leadership.

9. Canadian Public Procurement Council (CPPC)
https://www.cppc-ccmp.ca
P.O. Box 44534
Lévis, Québec G7A 4X5
1-418-619-1951

The CPPC is a nonprofit corporation dedicated to providing appropriate leadership and promoting dialogue in public procurement. Additionally, CPPC seeks to help add value to the supply chain management function of member organizations and exchange ideas, information, and experiences on procurement-related activities. CPPC's objective is also to consider operational impacts of emerging policies and practices in public procurement, including the trade agreements, the electronic marketplace, and public-private partnerships.

APPENDIX A: **RESOURCES**

10. The American Bar Association (ABA)

https://www.americanbar.org/aba.html

Chicago Headquarters
321 North Clark Street
Chicago, IL 60654
312-988-5000

Washington, DC Office
1050 Connecticut Ave. N.W., Suite 400
Washington, DC 20036
202-662-1000

Founded in 1878, the ABA is committed to supporting the legal profession with practical resources for legal professionals while improving the administration of justice, accrediting law schools, establishing model ethical codes, and more. Membership is open to lawyers, law students, and others interested in the law and the legal profession.

Two sections of the ABA that concern public procurement are its section on State and Local Government Law and its section on Public Contract Law. Both sections sponsored the project to develop the Model Procurement Code for State and Local Governments referenced throughout this guide. The Section of Public Contract Law offers memberships to procurement professionals. The ABA's website provides information on the sections concerning procurement, as well as news resources and publications.

11. National Governors Association (NGA)

https://www.nga.org
444 North Capitol, Suite 267
Washington, D.C. 20001
202-624-5300

NGA is the bipartisan organization of the nation's governors. Through the NGA, governors share best practices, speak with a collective voice on national policy, and develop innovative solutions that improve state government and support the principles of federalism.

APPENDIX B: CHECKLIST FOR ESSENTIAL STATUTORY OR ORDINANCE COVERAGE

The procurement statute/ordinance should:

- [ ] Address in one place all elements of a comprehensive procurement system, including organization and leadership, contractor selection methods, contract administration, dispute resolution, and property management and disposal, based on the American Bar Association Model Procurement Code for State and Local Governments.
- [ ] Establish as the lead procurement authority a centrally located procurement office headed by a Chief Procurement Officer (CPO) whose sole and full-time responsibility is the public entity's procurement system.
- [ ] Establish the central procurement office and the CPO at a high management level to ensure leadership, sufficient authority, and independence to implement the goals and objectives of the procurement program.
- [ ] Clearly and concisely announce the legislative intent of the public entity's procurement law while authorizing administrative discretion for the CPO. The statute or ordinance should not be so detailed and definite as to be unduly restrictive.
- [ ] Define the applicability of the law over all of the public entity's procurements. Exclude blanket exemption for any executive agency or department, and transfer any prior rights and powers relating to procurement and supply management from departments and agencies to a CPO. If exclusions are considered necessary, define them narrowly by the types of commodities or services sought, and not so broadly as to exclude all the procurements of certain agencies or departments.
- [ ] Establish requirements of professional qualification and prior experience for the position of the CPO and provide for performance-based tenure.
- [ ] Enumerate in a broad, nonrestrictive fashion the responsibilities and authority of the CPO and the central procurement office.
- [ ] Authorize the CPO to establish rules or regulations and high-level procurement policies.
- [ ] Authorize the CPO at his or her discretion to delegate, and monitor the delegation of, authority to conduct procurements and related functions under the law.
- [ ] Define key words and phrases and any words having special meaning.
- [ ] Provide for increased public confidence in the procurement process by requiring the publication of all procurement laws, rules, and administrative procedures.
- [ ] Grant discretion to the CPO to determine the types, formats, and distribution of manuals addressing the procurement process.
- [ ] Address all elements of a comprehensive procurement system including: leadership, organization, contractor selection methods, contract administration, dispute resolution, property management, and disposal.
- [ ] Leave operational details to separate implementing rules or regulations and guidelines.
- [ ] Allow for flexibility in the procurement system to be agile and responsible, and for the public entity to respond to ever-changing needs.

APPENDIX B: **CHECKLIST FOR ESSENTIAL STATUTORY OR ORDINANCE COVERAGE**

- ☐ Authorize the CPO to promulgate rules or regulations to:
  - Prescribe the conditions, manner, and documentation by which the CPO may delegate procurement authority to other departments or agencies.
  - Define additional key terms not defined in a statute or ordinance.
- ☐ Authorize the CPO to have sole authority to establish procurement procedures and manuals, forms, and documents such as solicitations and contracts, including specifications and contractual terms and conditions.
- ☐ Require that all agencies, institutions, and departments with delegated or limited procurement authority publish their internal procurement procedures consistent with the central procurement office's procurement manuals and, after review and approval by the CPO, ensure that a current copy is on file with the central procurement office.

APPENDIX C: SAMPLE CHECKLIST FOR CONTRACTOR SECURITY AND HOSTING STANDARDS AND PRACTICES

No.	Control Requirements	Yes/No?	Comments/ Compensating Controls
1.	Are the following teams and individuals involved in information security at contractor and are their roles and responsibilities clearly defined? a) Executive-level oversight committee b) Corporate information c) All lines of business (LoBs) d) Individual information security managers who are assigned by each LoB		[Confirm the existence of written documentation.]
2.	Do contractor's information security policies and practices include sufficient detail guiding principles for: a) Development? b) Executive approval? c) Implementation? d) Maintenance?		[Confirm the existence of written documentation.]
3.	Do contractor's information security policies promote the practice of: a) Compartmentalization of information? b) Least privilege? c) Need-to-know? d) Segregation of duties?		[Confirm the existence of written documentation, including periodic testing.]
4.	Are the following individuals subject to contractor organizational security policies? a) All full-time and part-time employees? b) Temporary employees? c) Independent contractors[1] and subcontractors[2]?		[Confirm the existence of written documentation.]
Additional Comments:			

[1] The term *independent contractor(s)* means independent contractors retained by a contractor and its subsidiaries that provide services for the benefit of the contractor and its subsidiaries.
[2] The term *subcontractor(s)* means subcontractors retained by a contractor and its subsidiaries that assist in performing all or any part of the services that the contractor has undertaken to perform.

APPENDIX C: SAMPLE CHECKLIST FOR CONTRACTOR SECURITY AND HOSTING STANDARDS AND PRACTICES

No.	Control Requirements	Yes/No?	Comments/ Compensating Controls
5.	Does contractor policy define the following information assets as protected data and promote adherence to minimum handling requirements by all contractor personnel? a) Personally Identifiable Financial Information (PIFI/ePIFI)—Covered under Gramm-Leach-Bliley Act (GLBA aka Financial Services Modernization Act of 1999) b) Payment Card Information (PCI/ePCI)—Covered under Payment Card Industry Data Security Standard (PCI DSS) c) Protected Health Information (PHI/ePHI)—Covered under the Health Insurance Portability and Accountability Act of 1996 (HIPAA) d) Personally Identifiable Information protected by law (PII/ePII)		[Confirm the existence of written documentation.]
6.	Does contractor policy require implementation of antivirus and personal firewall software?		[Confirm the existence of written documentation, including software specifications.]
7.	Does contractor use a computer program to manage the distribution of updates and hotfixes to computers?		[Confirm the existence of written documentation, including periodic testing.]
8.	Do contractor asset classification and control security policies apply to the following individuals? a) All full-time and part-time employees? b) Temporary employees? c) Independent contractors and subcontractors?		[Confirm the existence of written documentation.]
9.	Do contractor policies establish requirements for acceptable nonpersonal business-related use of contractor's: a) Corporate network? b) Computer systems? c) Telephony systems? d) Messaging technologies? e) Internet access? f) Reprographic systems? g) Other company resources?		[Confirm the existence of written documentation.]
Additional Comments:			

APPENDIX C: **SAMPLE CHECKLIST FOR CONTRACTOR SECURITY AND HOSTING STANDARDS AND PRACTICES**

No.	Control Requirements	Yes/No?	Comments/ Compensating Controls

10.	Does contractor have a code of ethical conduct that:
	a) Establishes high standards for ethics and business conduct?
	b) Applies to every level of the company?
	c) Applies to every location where contractor does business throughout the world?
	d) Applies to all full-time and part-time employees?
	e) Applies to temporary employees?
	f) Applies to independent contractors and subcontractors?
	g) Covers the topic of legal and regulatory compliance?
	h) Covers the topic of business conduct and relationships?
	i) Requires compliance-tracked training that occurs biennially (i.e., once every 2 years) in:
	  a. Ethics?
	  b. Business conduct?
	  c. Sensitive information handling?
			[Confirm the existence of written documentation.]

Additional Comments:			

APPENDIX C: **SAMPLE CHECKLIST FOR CONTRACTOR SECURITY AND HOSTING STANDARDS AND PRACTICES**

No.	Control Requirements	Yes/No?	Comments/ Compensating Controls
11.	Does contractor policy establish corporate-level mandates for complying with the U.S.-European Union Safe Harbor Program's EU Data Protection Directive of 1998 on maintaining the privacy and integrity of personal data?		[Confirm the existence of written documentation.]
12.	Does contractor policy establish mandates for frequently undergoing the second of three AICPAs (American Institute of CPAs) Service Organization Controls audits (i.e., the "SOC 2" audit) to measure the following controls related to contractor's provision of IT and data center services: a) Security? b) Availability? c) Processing integrity (ensuring system accuracy, completion, and authorization)? d) Confidentiality? e) Privacy?		[Confirm the existence of written documentation.]
13.	Does contractor policy provide high-level mandates for log retention, review, and analysis covering: a) Minimum log requirements? b) Responsibilities for the configuration and implementation of logging? c) Alert review? d) Problem management? e) Retention? f) Security and protection of logs? g) Compliance review?		[Confirm the existence of written documentation.]
14.	Does contractor policy establish information erasure guidelines that cover: a) Data erasure from all types of electronic media? b) Cost-benefit analysis of physical destruction vs. post-sanitization recycling?		[Confirm the existence of written documentation.]
Additional Comments:			

APPENDIX C: **SAMPLE CHECKLIST FOR CONTRACTOR SECURITY AND HOSTING STANDARDS AND PRACTICES**

No.	Control Requirements	Yes/No?	Comments/ Compensating Controls
15.	Does contractor policy describe access control requirements for all contractor systems, including: a) Authentication? b) Authorization? c) Access approval? d) Provisioning? e) Revocation for employees and other contractor-defined *users* with access to contractor systems that are neither internet-facing nor publicly accessible?		[Confirm the existence of written documentation.]
16.	Does contractor policy require use of strong password controls by contractor employees,[3] independent contractors, subcontractors, and temporary employees that include instructions on how to: a) Choose effective passwords? b) Protect passwords? c) Change and store passwords and PINs?		[Confirm the existence of written documentation.]
Additional Comments:			

[3] The term *contractor employees* means full-time and part-time employees of contractor.

No.	Control Requirements	Yes/No?	Comments/ Compensating Controls
17.	Does contractor policy establish requirements for the development, maintenance, and testing of the following: a) Emergency response? b) Disaster recovery? c) Business continuity practices?		[Confirm the existence of written documentation.]
Additional Comments:			

State and Local Government Procurement: A Practical Guide, 3rd Edition

APPENDIX C: **SAMPLE CHECKLIST FOR CONTRACTOR SECURITY AND HOSTING STANDARDS AND PRACTICES**

No.	Control Requirements	Yes/No?	Comments/ Compensating Controls
18.	Does contractor policy require its appropriate treatment of the following information assets that reside on contractor, customer, and/or third-party systems to which contractor may be provided access in connection with the provision of the services: a) PIFI/ePIFI? b) PCI/ePCI? c) PHI/ePHI? d) PII/ePII?		[Confirm the existence of written documentation.]
19.	Does contractor policy require timely and efficient reporting of and response to information security incidents?		[Confirm the existence of written documentation.]

20.	Does contractor maintain a detailed incident response plan that:
	a) Defines roles and responsibilities?
	b) Establishes procedures detailing actions taken during the incident based on:
	   a. Incident type (e.g., virus, hacker intrusion, data theft, system destruction)?
	   b. Severity of threat to system or data?
	   c. Status of incident (e.g., active, contained)?
			[Confirm the existence of written documentation.]

No.	Control Requirements	Yes/No?	Comments/ Compensating Controls
21.	Does contractor policy provide requirements for contractor employees, independent contractors, subcontractors, and temporary employees to notify identified contacts internally in the event of suspected unauthorized access to: a) Customer data? b) PII/ePII? c) PIFI/ePIFI? d) PCI/ePCI? e) PHI/ePHI?		[Confirm the existence of written documentation.]
Additional Comments:			

APPENDIX C: **SAMPLE CHECKLIST FOR CONTRACTOR SECURITY AND HOSTING STANDARDS AND PRACTICES**

No.	Control Requirements	Yes/No?	Comments/ Compensating Controls
22.	Do contractor physical security standards restrict access to service locations to only the following: a) Contractor employees? b) Independent contractors and subcontractors? c) Temporary employees? d) Authorized visitors?		[Confirm the existence of written documentation.]
23.	Do contractor standards require that identification cards be issued to and worn or require biometric access only while on the premises by the following individuals: a) Contractor employees? b) Independent contractors and subcontractors? c) Temporary employees? d) Authorized visitors?		[Confirm the existence of written documentation.]
24.	Do contractor standards require authorized visitors to adhere to the following guidelines when on the premises: a) Sign a visitor's register? b) Be escorted and/or observed? c) Enter into a written confidentiality agreement with contractor? d) Return contractor-issued identification cards upon departure?		[Confirm the existence of written documentation.]
25.	Do contractor standards require contractor security to monitor: a) Possession of keys/access cards? b) Ability to access service locations?		[Confirm the existence of written documentation.]
26.	Do contractor standards require: a) Keys/cards to be returned by staff leaving contractor's employment? b) Keys/cards to be deactivated upon termination? c) After-hours access to service locations to be monitored and controlled by contractor security? d) All repairs and modifications to the physical security barriers and/or entry controls at service locations to be authorized by contractor security?		[Confirm the existence of written documentation.]
Additional Comments:			

APPENDIX C: **SAMPLE CHECKLIST FOR CONTRACTOR SECURITY AND HOSTING STANDARDS AND PRACTICES**

No.	Control Requirements	Yes/No?	Comments/ Compensating Controls
27.	Does contractor policy employ intrusion prevention and detection systems within the contractor network to provide continuous surveillance: a) For intercepting and responding to security events? b) In real time as security events are identified? c) By using a network-based monitoring approach to detect attacks on open ports? d) By using signature detection to match patterns of environment settings and user activities against a database of known attacks? e) By updating the signature database as new releases become available for commercial distribution? f) For dispatching alerts to contractor's personnel who will review and respond to potential threats?		[Confirm the existence of written documentation.]
28.	Does contractor policy require use on the contractor network of: a) Access control lists? b) Segmentation to separate customer data?		[Confirm the existence of written documentation.]
29.	Do contractor standards require: a) Management and monitoring by contractor's IT department of all routers and firewall logs? b) Safeguarding of network devices via centralized authentication? c) Auditing of network usage?		[Confirm the existence of written documentation.]
30.	Do contractor standards require contractor to access the environments residing on customer's system over the Internet by using either of the following technologies: a) Encrypted network traffic via an industry standard VPN or equivalent technology, as specified in the order? b) Technology permitted by customer's network administrator?		[Confirm the existence of written documentation.]
Additional Comments:			

APPENDIX C: SAMPLE CHECKLIST FOR CONTRACTOR SECURITY AND HOSTING STANDARDS AND PRACTICES

No.	Control Requirements	Yes/No?	Comments/ Compensating Controls
31.	Does contractor policy require that upon termination of services or at customer's request, contractor will: a) Delete the environments located on contractor computers in a manner designed to ensure that they cannot reasonably be accessed or read, unless there is a legal obligation imposed on contractor preventing it from deleting all or part of the environments? b) Archive environments on tape for six months following termination of the services, unless otherwise specified in writing by customer or by judicial or regulatory order?		[Confirm the existence of written documentation.]
Additional Comments:			

No.	Control Requirements	Yes/No?	Comments/ Compensating Controls
32.	Does contractor policy require that, in a production environment, contractor will take the following additional measures: a) Frequently evaluate and respond to incidents that create suspicions of unauthorized misappropriation of customer's data, inform contractor security of such incidents, and depending upon the nature of the activity, define escalation paths and response teams to address the incidents? b) If contractor determines that data in customer's environments may be or has been subject to a legal determination that a security incident has occurred (including by a contractor employee) or any other circumstance in which customer is required to provide a notification under applicable law, report within 24 hours such misappropriation in writing to customer's privacy officer?		[Confirm the existence of written documentation.]
33.	Does contractor policy require that contractor personnel be instructed in addressing incidents where handling of data has been misappropriated, including prompt and reasonable reporting and escalation procedures?		[Confirm the existence of written documentation.]
Additional Comments:			

APPENDIX C: **SAMPLE CHECKLIST FOR CONTRACTOR SECURITY AND HOSTING STANDARDS AND PRACTICES**

No.	Control Requirements	Yes/No?	Comments/ Compensating Controls
34.	Does contractor policy prohibit contractor from disclosing data located on contractor systems, including text and images, except in accordance with customer's contract, customer's written instructions, or to the extent required by law?		[Confirm the existence of written documentation.]
35.	Does contractor policy require that contractor use diligent efforts to inform customer, to the extent permitted by law, of any request for such disclosure before disclosure is made?		[Confirm the existence of written documentation.]
Additional Comments:			

No.	Control Requirements	Yes/No?	Comments/ Compensating Controls

36.	Does contractor policy require contractor to maintain the following standards for provisioning access to and creating passwords for the environments that are in the control of contractor:
	a) Access is provisioned on a need-to-know basis?
	b) Passwords conform to strong password guidelines that include:
	  a. Complexity?
	  b. Expiration?
	  c. Non-redundancy?
	  d. Length?
	c) Passwords are neither written down nor stored online unencrypted in a reversible format?
	d) Passwords are treated as contractor confidential information?
	e) At customer's request, contractor will agree with customer on a schedule for periodic password changes?
	f) User IDs and passwords to customer's systems are not communicated to any other person without customer's prior written authorization?
			[Confirm the existence of written documentation.]

Additional Comments:			

APPENDIX C: **SAMPLE CHECKLIST FOR CONTRACTOR SECURITY AND HOSTING STANDARDS AND PRACTICES**

No.	Control Requirements	Yes/No?	Comments/ Compensating Controls
37.	Does contractor policy require in the event of employee terminations, deaths or resignations, contractor will take actions to terminate network, telephone, and physical access for such former employees?		[Confirm the existence of written documentation.]
38.	Does contractor policy require that contractor security frequently review accounts of terminated employees to verify that access has been terminated and that stale accounts have been removed from contractor's network?		[Confirm the existence of written documentation.]
Additional Comments:			

No.	Control Requirements	Yes/No?	Comments/ Compensating Controls
39.	Does contractor policy require contractor to maintain mechanisms for computers that were issued to contractor employees, independent contractors, subcontractors, and temporary employees and that have the following capabilities: a) Scans e-mail sent both to and from any contractor recipient/sender for malicious code? b) Deletes e-mail attachments that are infected with known malicious code prior to delivery?		[Confirm the existence of written documentation.]
40.	Does contractor policy require all contractor employee, independent contractor, subcontractor, and temporary employee laptops to be equipped with virus protection software?		[Confirm the existence of written documentation.]
41.	Does contractor policy require contractor to maintain mechanisms that ensure: a) Virus definitions are regularly updated? b) Updated definitions are published and communicated to contractor employees, independent contractors, subcontractors, and temporary employees? c) Contractor employees, independent contractors, subcontractors, and temporary employees are able to automatically download new definitions and update virus protection software? d) Compliance reviews are frequently conducted by contractor?		[Confirm the existence of written documentation.]
42.	Does contractor require that all customer data stored by contractor on laptops or removable media be encrypted?		[Confirm the existence of written documentation.]
Additional Comments:			

APPENDIX C: **SAMPLE CHECKLIST FOR CONTRACTOR SECURITY AND HOSTING STANDARDS AND PRACTICES**

No.	Control Requirements	Yes/No?	Comments/ Compensating Controls
43.	Does contractor policy establish an *Information Security Manager* role under which an advocate within contractor has the following responsibilities: a) Communicate information security awareness to contractor employees, independent contractors, subcontractors, temporary employees, and management? b) Work effectively with contractor employees, independent contractors, subcontractors, temporary employees, and management to help implement and comply with contractor's corporate security practices, policies, and initiatives?		[Confirm the existence of written documentation.]
Additional Comments:			

No.	Control Requirements	Yes/No?	Comments/ Compensating Controls
44.	Does contractor code of ethical conduct require compliance with and acknowledgment of it by the following: a) Contractor employees? b) Independent contractors? c) Subcontractors? d) Temporary employees?		[Confirm the existence of written documentation.]
45.	Does contractor code of ethical conduct stress reduction of the following risks: a) Human error? b) Theft? c) Fraud? d) Misuse of facilities?		[Confirm the existence of written documentation.]
46.	Do contractor's efforts include: a) Personnel screening? b) Making personnel aware of security policies? c) Training employees to implement security policies?		[Confirm the existence of written documentation.]
Additional Comments:			

APPENDIX C: **SAMPLE CHECKLIST FOR CONTRACTOR SECURITY AND HOSTING STANDARDS AND PRACTICES**

No.	Control Requirements	Yes/No?	Comments/ Compensating Controls
47.	Does contractor policy require contractor employees, independent contractors, subcontractors, and temporary employees to take the following measures to protect the security of the environments: a) Adhere to written confidentiality agreements? b) Comply with company policies concerning protection of confidential information? c) Store materials containing data securely and share those materials internally only for the purposes of providing the services? d) Dispose of paper copies of confidential materials and materials containing data in shredding bins designated for confidential information, and not in non-secure recycling bins or trash cans (if shredders are available at client site)?		[Confirm the existence of written documentation.]
Additional Comments:			

No.	Control Requirements	Yes/No?	Comments/ Compensating Controls
48.	Does contractor policy require that contractor enter into the following written agreements with each independent contractor and subcontractor: a) Confidentiality agreement? b) Services provider agreement that includes the contractor standards which require implementation of physical, technical, and administrative safeguards consistent with contractor's obligations under the order and the MCCCD Contractor Security and Hosting Standards document? c) Network access agreement?		[Confirm the existence of written documentation.]
49.	Does contractor policy establish that contractor is responsible for assuring that the independent contractors and subcontractors access, use, and protect the security of the environments in a manner consistent with: a) The terms of customer contract? b) Customer security standards?		[Confirm the existence of written documentation.]
Additional Comments:			

APPENDIX C: **SAMPLE CHECKLIST FOR CONTRACTOR SECURITY AND HOSTING STANDARDS AND PRACTICES**

No.	Control Requirements	Yes/No?	Comments/ Compensating Controls

50.	Does contractor policy establish that all contractor employees, independent contractors, subcontractors, and temporary employees complete online information protection awareness training that satisfies the following requirements:
	a) Conducted upon hiring and at least every two years thereafter?
	b) Instructs participants on their obligations under the various central contractor privacy and security policies?
	c) Instructs participants on data privacy principles and data handling practices that may apply to their jobs at contractor and are required by company policy, including those related to:
	  a. Notice?
	  b. Consent?
	  c. Use?
	  d. Access?
	  e. Integrity
	  f. Sharing?
	  g. Retention?
	  h. Security?
	  i. Disposal?
			[Confirm the existence of written documentation.]

51.	Does contractor policy require that contractor: a) Perform periodic compliance reviews to determine if contractor employees, independent contractors, subcontractors, and temporary employees have completed training? b) Promptly notify and instruct contractor employees, independent contractors, subcontractors, and temporary employees to complete training if contractor determines they have not done so? c) Prepare and distribute written materials to promote awareness about security-related issues?		[Confirm the existence of written documentation.]
Additional Comments:			

APPENDIX C: **SAMPLE CHECKLIST FOR CONTRACTOR SECURITY AND HOSTING STANDARDS AND PRACTICES**

No.	Control Requirements	Yes/No?	Comments/ Compensating Controls
52.	Does contractor policy require that: a) Contractor conduct security reviews, assessments, and audits periodically to confirm compliance with contractor information security policies, procedures, and practices? b) Contractor employees, independent contractors, subcontractors, and temporary employees who fail to comply may be subject to disciplinary action, up to and including termination?		[Confirm the existence of written documentation.]
53.	Is contractor willing to provide the general results of audit reports with customer and particularly that information that is material to contractor's ability to comply with customer contract and security standards?		
54.	If contractor is selected as the awardee, is it willing to provide a controlled-environment electronic review of the policies identified in this checklist to select representatives of customer?		
Additional Comments:			

APPENDIX D: NASPO-NASCIO RECOMMENDATIONS FOR IT PROCUREMENT

NASPO-NASCIO JOINT TASK FORCE ON NEGOTIATIONS

Joint report available for download at: http://www.naspo.org/Publications/ArtMID/8806/ArticleID/4531

RECOMMENDATIONS FOR IT PROCUREMENT

Relationships Matter

- Base communication and interaction on the assumption that the other party has the best intentions and is working in the best interest of the state. Ensure that there is clear communication among all staffing levels.
- Cross-educate and train to ensure that everyone involved in the IT procurement process is aware of the expertise and value brought to the table by all parties.
- Clearly define roles and responsibilities, identify and address key challenges in the IT procurement process, and collaborate to proactively plan and streamline each IT procurement.

Centralization of IT Procurement

- Centralize the IT procurement management process under one umbrella to increase and leverage the state's buying power; save the state time and money; and ensure clarity in roles, responsibilities, and best practices.
- Don't focus on who *owns* IT procurement; rather, focus on having the tools needed for successful IT procurements.
- Use centralization of IT procurement to increase awareness and visibility and to maintain and strengthen subject matter expertise in the state's enterprise architecture.
- Remain or become aligned with the state's enterprise standards and architecture-driven technology plan.
- Use centralized IT procurement for better vendor management, metrics, and performance—all of which contribute to improved negotiations, streamlined terms and conditions, and cost savings for the state.

Procurement Process Partnerships

- Cross-educate CIO and CPO teams and appreciate the perspectives of both teams to ensure an understanding of priorities and objectives, defined roles, and shared terminology.
- Establish a central point of contact in both CPO and CIO offices to promote better communication and workflow.
- At the beginning of the procurement process, determine if it is permissible to negotiate and, if so, when and what to negotiate.

APPENDIX D: NASPO-NASCIO RECOMMENDATIONS FOR IT PROCUREMENT

- Work with all parties—including those from the private sector—to establish a process that increases flexibility and communication.
- Craft requests for information and requests for proposals in a manner that encourages solutions from the private sector rather than focusing on overly prescriptive specifications.
- Use iterative/non-waterfall procurement methodologies when appropriate to improve procurement cycles, add flexibility, and reduce risk.

Strategies for Policy and Legislation

- Work together to achieve executive action and legislative authority to allow negotiations to benefit the state and provide best-value for all IT procurements.
- Leverage cooperative purchasing, master service agreements, and pre-qualified vendor pools, when appropriate, to achieve the best value for state IT procurements.
- Be flexible, but maintain consistency when interpreting internal policy and procurement code to promote a culture of innovation while balancing risk.
- Explore small-scale IT procurement negotiations to build the case for widespread adoption.

INDEX

Accountability, 18
Adequate competition, 23
Affirmative responsibility criteria, 124
Alternative dispute resolution (ADR), 243–244
American Bar Association, 5
    Model Procurement Code for State and Local Governments, 5, 8, 13, 14, 18–19, 22, 75, 107, 108, 125, 130, 147, 155–156, 168, 170, 175, 182, 200, 226, 232, 244, 282
Antitrust laws, 22. *See also* Competition
    federal, 32–39
    state. *See* State antitrust laws
    violations, detecting, 30–31
Architects, 175
Article 2 of the UCC, 203–204
Assessment, 308
Authority
    and central oversight, 128
    delegation of, 13
Automated tools, 295
Awards, 138–139. *See also* Evaluations
    contract, 144, 149
    multiple source, 150–151

Ballistic Resistance of Body Armor NIJ Standard-0101.06, 199
Benefits calculation, 101
Best value procurement, 284–286
    minimal specifications, 79
Best value procurements
    competitive sealed proposals, 117–118
    contracting for services, 158
Bid(s)
    competitive sealed bidding, 107, 108–112
    evaluations of, 139, 140, 141–144
Bid bond, 177
Bidder
    conferences, 121–122
    defined, 107
Bid protests, 238
    administrative procedures, 239–240
    avoiding, tips for, 241–242
    avoiding contract claims, 243
    debriefings, 245
    decision, 244–245
    handling, tips, 242–243
    judicial remedies, 245
    requirements, 244
    risks and disadvantages, 240
    timelines, 244
    value/benefit, 239–240
Bimodal sourcing, 281
Blended learning, 307–308
Bonding requirements, 177
Bribes, 229
Brooks Architect-Engineer Act (Brooks Act), 175
Business case, 273–274

Cannibalization to surplus property, 233
Central procurement office
    ethical standards, 222–224
    responsibilities of, 16–17
Certification/certification programs, 300–305
    benefits, 301
    national, 301–303
    state, 303–305
    UPPCC, 301–303
Certified Professional in Supplier Diversity (CPSD), 303
Certified Professional in Supply Management (CPSM), 303
Certified Professional Public Buyer (CPPB), 301, 302
Certified Public Procurement Officer (CPPO), 301, 302
Chief Procurement Officer, 165
Clayton Act, 34, 35–37, 39–40
Cloud broker, 290, 291
Cloud computing, 294
Cloud services, 289–291
    deployment models, 290
    pricing models, 291
    suppliers, 290–291
Commodities and services (sustainable), 89, 90
    purchasing through cooperative agreements, 98
    selecting targeted, 95–96
Commonwealth of Virginia, 304–305
Community cloud, 290
Competition, 21–45. *See also* Antitrust laws; Source selection methods
    adequate, 23
    combating anticompetitive practices, 28–30
    formal. *See* Formal competition
    importance, 22–23
    informal, 106
    overview, 22
    practices and laws restraining, 25–28
    practices encouraging, 23–25

INDEX

Competitive sealed bidding, 107, 108–112
    basis/standard for contract award, 109–110
    bidder request to modify/withdraw bid, 111
    competitive sealed proposals *vs.*, 112–113
    invitation for bids, 109
    late bids, 111–112
    mistakes, 112
    public opening and confidentiality, 111
    receipt and control of bids, 110–111
    responsive bid, 108–109
Competitive sealed proposals, 107, 112–118
    basis/standard for contract award, 115
    best value procurements, 117–118
    competitive sealed bidding *vs.*, 112–113
    conducting discussions, 116–117
    evaluation committees, 116
    evaluation criteria, 115–116
    request for proposals, 113–115
Conferences
    pre-award, 121–122
    pre-solicitation, 121
Conflicts of interest
    laws, 228–229
    organizational, 228
Construction
    bonding requirements, 177
    contract administration, 177–178
    defined, 168
    environmentally friendly, 178
    procurements, authority to conduct, 168–169
    project delivery method, 169–175
Construction manager (CM), 171, 176
Contingency plan, 253
Contract(s)
    eProcurement, 266
    leveraged state, 18
    types of, 177
Contract administration, 177–178
    closeout activities, 218
    compliance reports, 216–217
    construction, 177–178
    defined, 210
    focus of, 212
    issue and dispute resolution, 217–218
    kickoff conference, 215
    maintaining contract file, 215
    plans, 214
    progress meeting, 216
    steps in, 214–218
    team, use of, 214–215
    tools, 216
Contract administrator, role of, 212–213
Contract claims, avoiding, 243
Contract forms, sources of, 176–177

Contracting for services, 153–166
    best value procurements, 158
    governmental services, 161–165
    human services, 165–166
    performance measurements, 158–161
    preparing service description, 156–158
Contract management
    defined, 210
    general levels of, 211–212
    IT procurement, 294–295
    overview, 211–213
Contractors, selection of, 97–98
Cooperation with enforcement authorities, 31–32
Cooperative agreements, 98
Cooperative purchasing, 181–194
    administration costs, 190
    alliances and trends, 185–187
    benefits, 190–191
    challenges, 191–192
    cooperative agreements and, 98
    defined, 182
    federal government issues, 192–194
    initiating, best practices for, 188–190
    legal authority for, 183–184
    overview, 182–183
    types, 183
Cooperative purchasing, IT procurement, 287
Cost analysis, 150
Costs, IT procurement, 292

Dallas Area Rapid Transit (DART), 171
Demonstration projects, 134–135, 286–287. *See also* Pilot projects
Department of Homeland Security, 250
Deployment models, cloud services, 290
Design-bid-build method, 170
Design-build method, 171–172
Design-build-operate-maintain (DBOM), 174
Direct service provider (DSP), 290
Disposition process, of state and local surplus property, 232–235
Disputes and claims, 238–239, 246
Documentation, 255–256
    post-disaster financial, 256

Ecolabels, 99–100
Education, 305–308
    blended learning, 307–308
    technology, 307
    training, 305–307
E-learning platforms/systems, 307, 308
Electronics Environmental Benefits Calculator, 101
Electronic signature, 266

INDEX

Emergency management process, procurement in, 252–256
    contingency plan, 253
    documentation, 255–256
    GSA contracts, 254–255
    identifying supplier resources, 255
    pre-establishment of statewide contracts, 254
    training, 254
Emergency preparedness, 249–256
    federal law and directives, 250–252
Emergency procurements, 131–132
Emerging issues, 312–314
Energy Star, 101
Enforcement authorities, cooperation with, 31–32
Engineers, 175
Enterprise resource planning (ERP), 260
    eProcurement and, 267–269
Environmentally friendly construction, 178
Environmental Protection Agency (EPA), 95, 99–100
    Electronics Environmental Benefits Calculator, 101
    Waste Reduction Model (WARM), 101
eProcurement, 18, 107
    benefits and savings, 259–260
    best practices, 257
    challenges, 263–266
    defined, 258
    ERP solutions and, 267–269
    essential elements, 261–263
    evaluations using, 151
    funding, 264–265
    software as a service solutions, 268–269
    solutions in state central procurement offices, 260
ERP system integration, 267–268
Ethical standards, 222–224
Evaluations, 137–151. *See also* Awards
    bids, 139, 140, 141–144
    eProcurement, 151
    proposals, 139–140, 144–149

Federal antitrust laws, 32–39
    business practices and, 38–39
    Clayton Act, 34, 35–37, 39–40
    Federal Trade Commission (FTC) Act, 37
    guidelines, 38
    Robinson-Patman Price Discrimination Act, 37–38
    Sherman Act, 33, 34, 35, 36, 37, 39–40, 42, 43, 44, 45
    summary of, 33, 34
Federal Emergency Management Agency (FEMA), 250
Federal funds, 128–129
Federal surplus property, 235–236
Federal Trade Commission (FTC) Act, 37
Federal Transit Administration (FTA), 192–193
Feedback, 308

Flexibility, IT procurement, 282, 284
Florida Certified Contract Manger (FCCM), 304
Florida Department of Management Services (DMS), 304
Formal competition, 106
    source selection methods, 107–108
Funding, eProcurement, 264–265

General Services Administration (GSA), 193–194, 254–255
Governance plan, IT procurement, 277–278
    components, 277–278
    RACI chart, 278
Governmental services, 161–165
Government-produced services or commodities, 132
Greenwashing, 99

Harvard Business Review, 8
Homeland Security Act, 250
Homeland Security Presidential Directive 5 (HSPD-5), 251
Horizontal restraints, 38–39
Human services contracting, 165–166
Hybrid cloud, 290

Informal competition, 106
Infrastructure as a service, 290
Innovation, IT procurement, 282, 284
Institute for Supply Management (ISM), 303
Integrated Justice Information Systems, 273
Integrated procurement strategy, 274
Integrated project delivery (IPD), 172
Integrity, 222–227
    government, 222–226
    suppliers, 226–227
Intellectual property (IP), 293
Investigation and preserving record, 129
Invitation for bids (IFB), 107, 109
IT procurement
    best practices, 271
    calls for and collaboration on reform, 272–273
    contract management, 294–295
    emerging issues, 313–314
    foundational planning, 273–277
    governance plan, 277–278
    hardware and software, alternatives to buying, 287–292
    issues, 282–287
    overview, 272
    project plans, 278–279
    quality assurance, 295–296
    risk management, 279–281
    sourcing, 281–282
    terms and conditions, 292–294

INDEX

Job order contracting, 170–171

Kickbacks, 229

Law, 11–13
  addressing unethical behavior, 228–230
  approach to reducing exemptions, 13
  case, 41–42
  consistent, importance of, 18–19
  delegation of authority, 13
  exemptions from, 12–13
Leadership in Energy and Environmental Design (LEED) Green Building Rating System, 178
Leasing *vs.* purchasing, 287–289
Limitation of liability, 293–294
Little-Sherman Act, 39–40

Manuals, 14–16
  operations or procedures, 15–16
  supplier, 16
Manufacturer and dealer warranties, 205
Market research, 274–275
Micro-learning, 307
Mini-Clayton Act, 39–40
Model Procurement Code for State and Local Governments (ABA), 5, 8, 13, 14, 18–19, 22, 75, 107, 108, 125, 130, 147, 155–156, 168, 170, 175, 182, 200, 226, 232, 244, 282
Modular Procurement: A Primer (NASPO), 282
Modular sourcing, 282
Multiple awards, 150–151
Multiple-round RFPs, IT procurement, 284
Multi-step bidding, 118–119

National Association of Chief Information Officers (NASCIO), 272–273, 315
National Association of State Agencies for Surplus Property (NASASP), 236
National Association of State Chief Administrators, 315
National Association of State Procurement Officials (NASPO), 1–2
National Contract Management Association (NCMA), 303
National Incident Management System (NIMS), 251
National Institute of Governmental Purchasing (NIGP), 8, 304
National Institute of Justice (NIJ), 199
National Response Framework (NRF), 251–252
Negotiations
  IT procurement, 282, 283
  strategies, 62, 63
  teams, 306
Noncompetitive/limited competition procurements, types of, 129–135

Offeror
  conferences, 121–122
  defined, 107
On-demand or pay-as-you-go pricing models, 291
Online reverse auctions, 266
Operations/procedures manuals, 15–16
Organizational conflicts of interest, 228
Outside technical assistance, IT procurement, 287
Outsourcing, 161–165. *See also* Sourcing
Owner controlled insurance program (OCIP), 178

Performance metrics, 17
Personal Body Armor Consumer Product List (CPL), 199
Piggybacking, 182–183
  defined, 182
  restrictions, 192–193
Pilot projects, 124–125, 134–135, 286–287
Planning
  data/information sources, 50–52
  for negotiations, 63
  procurement office, 49–50
  with user and user agencies, 48–49
Platform as a service, 290
Pre-award conferences, 121–122
Pre-solicitation conferences, 121
  information, 121
Price analysis, 150
Pricing models, cloud services, 291
Private cloud, 290
Procurement
  codes, 40
  education, sources, 305–308
  of government-produced services or commodities, 132
  guiding principles of, 2–3
  law, 11–13
  leadership, 4, 8–10
  with or from other governments' contracts, 132–133
  of other governments' property, 132
  as profession, 4
  rules/regulations, 13–14
  training, sources, 305–307
  value of, 4–5, 17–19
Procurement Innovation Report (IJIS Institute), 273
Procurement Pulse, 314
Procurement Technical Assistance Center (PTAC), 18
Profession
  bodies of knowledge, 300
  defined, 300
Professional certification. *See* Certification/certification programs
Professional Development Team (PDT), 304
Project charter, for IT procurement, 275–277

INDEX

Project delivery methods
    selection methods for, 176
    short-term, 169–175
Project Management Institute (PMI), 277
Project management leadership, eProcurement, 265
Project plans, IT procurement, 278–279
Proposals
    competitive sealed, 107, 112–118
    evaluations of, 139–140, 144–149
Public cloud, 290
Public-private partnerships, 174–175
Purchasing *vs.* leasing, 287–289

Quality assurance, 197–207
    Article 2 of the UCC, 203–204
    best practices, 197
    definitions and overview, 197–199
    non-UCC warranties, 205
    planning, for IT projects, 295–296
    programs, 200–202
    supporting, 205–207

RACI chart, 278
Recommendations of Standards and Ecolabels for Use in Federal Procurement, 100
Records, openness and maintenance of, 222
Reporting suspicious behavior, 225–226
Request for proposals (RFP), 107, 113–115. *See also* Competitive sealed proposals
Research and Innovation Team (NASPO), 314
Reseller, 290–291
Reserved capacity, 291
Responsive bid, 108–109
Restraint of trade, 22
Reverse auctions, 119–120
Risk analysis, 66–67
Risk management, 66–68
    IT procurement, 279–281
    suppliers identifying risks, 67–68
Robert T. Stafford Disaster Relief and Emergency Assistance Act. *See* Stafford Act
Robinson-Patman Price Discrimination Act, 37–38

Sarbanes-Oxley Act (SOX), 292
Scope of work, IT procurement, 282
Seat management/managed services contracts, 289
Service contract warranties, 205
Service level agreement (SLA), 159
Service levels, developing, 160
Sherman Act, 33, 34, 35, 36, 37, 39–40, 42, 43, 44, 45
Single procurement administrator, 8–10
Small purchases, 120–121
Software as a service, 290
    eProcurement solutions, 268–269

Sole source procurement, 130–131
Solicitations, 106. *See also* Source selection methods
Source selection methods
    affirmative responsibility criteria, 124
    competitive sealed bidding, 107, 108–112
    competitive sealed proposals, 107, 112–118
    conferences, 121–122
    key terms defined, 106–107
    multi-step bidding, 118–119
    notifying suppliers, 122–123
    overview, 107–108
    pilot projects, 124–125
    reverse auctions, 119–120
    small purchases, 120–121
    special procurement methods, 125–126
Sourcing. *See also* Outsourcing
    bimodal, 281
    IT procurement, 281–282
    modular, 282
    strategic, 53–54
Special procurement methods, 125–126
Specifications
    brand name, 75–76
    brand-name-or-equal, 76
    design, 78
    management, 74–75
    minimal, under best value approach, 79
    objectives, 73–74
    overview, 73
    performance, 78–79
    procedures for developing, 81–84
    qualified products list (QPL), 76–77
    requirements using federal funds, 84–85
    standardization, 80–81
    types, 75–79
Staff development, 17
Staffing for strategic procurement services, 10–11
Stafford Act, 250
Stakeholders, sustainable procurement
    building, 91–92
    participation of, 90–91
State Agencies for Surplus Property (SASP), 235–236
State and local public procurement, 3–4
State antitrust laws, 32–33, 39–41
    conflict of interest statutes, 41
    first amendment antitrust immunity, 44–45
    immunities related to partnering, 44
    lack of knowledge or intent, 43
    Little-Sherman and Mini-Clayton Acts, 39–40
    regulated industries, 45
    state action antitrust immunity, 43–44
    state and local procurement codes, 40
    state competition statutes, 41
    state constitutions, 39

INDEX

statutory exemptions and exceptions, 45
statutory protections, 43
unilateral action, 42
vertical buy-sell transactions, 42–43
State associations, 315
State IT Procurement Negotiations: Working Together to Reform and Transform, 315
Strategic sourcing, 53–54
Strategies
    complex information technology procurements plan, 61
    construction project delivery methods, 62
    contract administration plan, 61
    contract pricing and terms, 60–61
    contract types, 56–60
    cost savings, 52–53
    length of contracts, 54–56
    negotiation, 62, 63
    network security and cyber risks, 62
    obtaining supplier diversity, 64–65
    socioeconomic programs, 62, 63–66
    source selection methods, 54
    strategic sourcing, 53–54
Subscription pricing models, 291
Suppliers
    cloud services, 290–291
    identifying risks, 67–68
    integrity, 226–227
    manuals, 16
    notifying, 122–123
    registering, 123
    sustainable procurement program, 97
Surplus property, 231–236
    allocation of sales proceeds, 235
    authority over, 232
    disposition process, 232–235
    federal, 235–236
Suspicious behavior, reporting, 225–226
Sustainable procurement, 87–102
    commodities and services. *See* Commodities and services (sustainable)
    defined, 88–89
    social considerations, 89
Sustainable procurement program
    benefits calculation, 101
    building stakeholder and executive buy-in, 91–92
    creating, 90–92
    drafting policy for, 92–94
    ecolabels, 99–100
    educating *vs.* mandating, 92
    effectiveness, measuring and marketing, 100–101
    implementation, 94–98
    maintaining, 101–102
    standards, 98–99
Sustainable purchasing, 312–313

Technology, 4
Telling Ain't Training, 2d Ed. (ASTD Press), 307
Terms and conditions, IT contracts, 292–294
Timely decisions, 295
Top 10 Priorities for State Procurement (NASPO), 314
Top Three Horizon Issues (NASPO), 314
Training, 17, 305–307. *See also* Education
    feedback and assessment, 308
    technology, 307
Trans-Pacific Partnership (TPP), 313
Transparency, 18

Unethical behavior, laws addressing, 228–230
Uniform Commercial Code (UCC), 161
    Article 2 of, 203–204
    certifications. *See* UPPCC certifications
    supplier warranties, 205
Universal Public Procurement Certification Council (UPPCC), 300. *See also* UPPCC certifications
Unsolicited offers, 133–134
UPPCC certifications, 301–303
    bodies of knowledge, 302–303, 304
    eligibility requirements, 302
U.S. Green Building Council, 178

Value
    bid protests, 239–240
    procurement, 4–5, 17–19
Vertical buy-sell transactions, 42–43
Vertical restraints, 39
Virginia Institute of Procurement (VIP), 304–305

Warranties for services, 161
Waste Reduction Model (WARM), 101